MW00768204

Daily Lives, Miracles, and Wisdom of the Saints

& Fasting Calendar

2023

ORTHODOX CALENDAR COMPANY ✢ PITTSBURGH, PENNSYLVANIA

This calendar follows the Revised Julian Calendar (New Calendar). All listed commemorations and Scripture readings are according to the Greek Orthodox Church liturgical calendar.

The fasting guidelines are those prescribed by the Church. Fasting is a spiritual discipline, and it is recommended that each Orthodox Christian consult with their spiritual father.

Fast-free — All foods allowed.

Strict Fast — Abstain from meat products, dairy products, fish, oil, and wine.

Copyright © 2022 Orthodox Calendar Company
All rights reserved.

Orthodox Calendar Company
Tel: 412-736-7840
Email: OrthodoxCalendarCompany@gmail.com
Facebook.com/OrthodoxCalendarCompany

ISBN-13: 978-0-9980817-8-6

Printed in the United States of America.

Front Cover:
THE MIRACULOUS ICON OF THE TAXIARCHIS MICHAEL
(*Taxiarchis* is the Greek name given to the Archangels Michael and Gabriel)

Icon of Archangel Michael where the monastery bell was heard

This icon of the Archangel Michael is housed in a shrine built in 1941 in Tarpon Springs, Florida, at 113 Hope Street. It was built by the command of Archangel Michael by Mary Tsalichis to honor the Archangel for the miraculous cure of her son. Archangel Michael is said to be a healing saint. Many visitors have been cured, including the crippled and those suffering from cancer, wounds, blindness, deafness, and barrenness. Those who are cured leave offerings, which are seen hanging at the bottom of the Icon. These include votives in the shape of the healed limb, or jewelry, either in gratitude or to strengthen their request to the Archangel Michael.

In 1937 Mary visited the Taxiarchis Michael of Panormitis Monastery on the island of Symi, Greece, to fulfill a promise made by her husband when he was in danger on a voyage as a seaman. She gave the gift to the abbot, who thanked her with the small silver icon of the Archangel Michael (on left), which she took home. A year later, on November 6, 1938, she and other visiting relatives heard a church bell ringing that sounded like the bell at the monastery. The sound was coming from the icon and lasted from 9 p.m. until 3 a.m. The next day, which was the feast day of Archangel Michael, Mary took the icon to the priest at St. Nicholas Church in Tarpon Springs. Later, she took the icon home, and the same bell was heard the next year and the following.

In 1939, Mary's son, Steve, became extremely ill and was hospitalized, but fifteen doctors and professors were unable to diagnose him. Steve soon looked like a skeleton, as he did not eat, speak, or recognize anyone. After three months, they just waited for Steve to die, as he was in a coma. Suddenly, Steve said to his mother, "Mama, I want you to bring me the Icon of Taxiarchis." Then he said, "Mama, the Taxiarchis came." They put the icon on his breast, and Steve started to ramble. They heard him say, "Yes, but my mother has no money." And then, "Mama, Taxiarchis wants you to build his shrine." To appease Steve, Mary agreed, as she thought he was in a state of delirium. Then Steve said, "Mama, say yes with your heart, for he says tomorrow at 10 a.m. I will be cured." The following day, Steve was cured, and the attending doctor was astonished. Steve later became a mathematics teacher at the high school in Tarpon Springs.

After many discouraging roadblocks to begin building, Mary dreamt that Archangel Michael caught her by the arm and took her to where the shrine should be built. It was a lot that Mary owned. He said to her, "You must start it, and I will help you finish it." Mary had marks on her arm where the Archangel had grabbed her. She poured Holy Water on the lot as Archangel Michael had instructed, and the erection of the chapel began. In a short time, it was completed, and services are held there.

Photo from personal collection
May 2022

SUNDAY

**Circumcision of Christ
Sunday before Epiphany
Fast-free**

JANUARY 1

Colossians 2:8-12; Luke 2:20-21, 40-52

God keeps us not that we are worthy, but because He is very merciful.

† *Elder Arsenie Papaciac of Romania*

NEW HIEROMARTYR ALEXANDER TRAPITSYN, ARCHBISHOP OF SAMARA. Alexander was from the mid-nineteenth-century farming village of Volma, Russia, and his father was a deacon. His parents had eight sons, and three became priests. Alexander graduated from theological school, married, was ordained to the priesthood, and taught at a women's diocesan school. In 1891 when famine broke out in Russia due to crop failures, Alexander called upon the wealthy to help the unfortunate with money, clothes, and food. In the years before the Russian Revolution, the Russian people had become lukewarm in their faith. Alexander preached that forgetfulness of God, unbelief, the pursuit of gain and pleasures, and self-love and interest had brought the people down to the level of pagans. When Alexander's wife died, he became a monk. This made a great impression on the young seminarians, as he was a zealous Church figure when people were demanding freedom of conscience in religious matters. Alexander said that they should place their hope in God on all difficult paths. He was made a bishop in the Vologda diocese and made rounds of all the monasteries and parishes. He found an absence of spiritual connection between members of those parishes. After the revolution, persecutions of the Orthodox Church began. Alexander exclaimed to the Soviets that to repudiate proper veneration of saints' relics is to reject what God Himself had glorified. In 1923 Alexander was arrested and accused of connections with monasticism and agitation. He was sent to a concentration camp along with 23 priests, and they were martyred.

COMMEMORATIONS: Basil the Great; Gregory of Nazianzus; Theodosius of Tryglia; Fulgentius of Ruspe; Basil of Ancyra; Peter of the Peloponnesus; Platon of Revel, with Michael, Nicholas, and Alexander; Theodotos and Telemachus; Athanasius of Poltava; Hieromartyr Jeremiah; Clarus of Vienne; Fanchea of Killeany; Eugendus of Condat; Emilia, mother of St. Basil the Great (Slavonic Calendar).

January 2

A possession ought to belong to the possessor not the possessor to the possession. Whosoever, therefore, does not use his patrimony as a possession, who does not know how to give and distribute to the poor, he is the servant of his wealth, not its master; because like a servant he watches over the wealth of another and not like a master does he use it of his own. Hence, in a disposition of this kind, we say that the man belongs to his riches, not the riches to the man.

St. Ambrose of Milan

MARTYR BASIL OF ANCYRA. Basil lived in fifth-century Ancyra during the reign of Julian the Apostate. Because he was a Christian, he was arrested and brought before the governor. When he boldly confessed his faith, he suffered a series of inhuman tortures. He was suspended, and his skin was scraped and carved. He was stretched on a rack, where his shoulders and hands were dislocated. His skin was pierced with iron instruments. With God's help, Basil bore it all resolutely. He was thrown into a fiery furnace, but prayer preserved him unharmed. Finally, he was taken to Caesarea and thrown into the arena to fight wild animals. It was there that Basil prayed that his struggles would end, and he finally won his martyr's crown. His relatives and others carefully gathered his relics, wrapped them in a linen cloth with myrrh, and honorably buried him. Later a church was built and dedicated to St. Basil.

COMMEMORATIONS: Cosmas I, Patriarch of Constantinople; Sylvester, Pope of Rome; Theogenes, Bishop of Parium; Gerasimus II, Patriarch of Alexandria; Theodota, mother of the first Cosmas and Damian; Sergios of Caesarea; Ammon of Tabennisi; Mark the Deaf; Righteous Theopemptos; Sylvester of the Kiev Caves; Juliana of Lazarevo; Martyr Theopistos; George (Zorzes) the Georgian; Nilus the Sanctified; Basil of Ancyra; Gennadios of Kerkyra; Smaragda, abbess of Nezhinsk (Ukraine); Schotin, hermit of Ireland; 1,000 Martyrs of Lichfield; Repose and second finding of the relics of St. Seraphim of Sarov.

JANUARY 3

Romans 6:18-23; Matthew 8:5-13

In a society where each one sees himself as the first no one makes any progress. If, however, one always considers oneself to be the last, meeting someone else becomes each time the opportunity for spiritual profit and progress. So it is best to be the last. If I am the first, life is infernally tiresome. If I am the last, life is a continual joy, because I am always learning something useful.

St. Sophrony of Essex

ST. PETER OF ATROA. At the age of eighteen, Peter became a monk in late eighth-century Phrygia, following a vision of the Mother of God. He became a disciple of St. Paul the Hesychast. On the day of his ordination to the priesthood, Peter healed a man possessed by an unclean spirit. This was the beginning of his numerous miracles. As a confessor, he was able to perceive the souls of his parishioners. While on a pilgrimage to Jerusalem with his teacher St. Paul, he had a vision from God that directed them instead to Mount Olympus in Bithynia, where Paul founded the Monastery of Zacharias. Peter succeeded him as abbot in 805, and the monastery flourished for ten years until the iconoclast persecutions. The monastery disbanded, and Peter escaped imperial troops by miraculously becoming invisible. He moved to several places because of his reputation as a healer. He was accused of practicing magic and evoking devils, but St. Theodore the Studite came to his defense, clearing Peter of the charges. He returned to the Monastery of St. Zacharias, which he renovated and helped reorganize two other monasteries that he had founded. But iconoclasm increased in the area, which the local bishop supported. So, Peter sent his monks into hiding, and he went to a monastery in Hellespont. Later, he returned to the Monastery of St. Zacharias, and shortly after that, he reposed.

COMMEMORATIONS: Prophet Malachi; Genevieve of Paris; Peter of Atroa; Gordius at Caesarea; Euthymius, the 'Man of God' of Tbilisi; Titus, Bishop of Tomis; Thomais of Lesvos; Findlugan of Islay; Three Martyrs, a mother and her two children slain by fire; Finding of the relics of New Monk-Martyr St. Ephraim of Nea Makri.

*I*f you would be simple hearted like the Apostles, would not conceal your human shortcomings, would not pretend to be especially pious, if you would walk free from hypocrisy, then that is the path. While it is easy, not everyone can find it or understand it. This path is the shortest way to salvation and attracts the grace of God. Unpretentiousness, guilelessness, frankness of soul—this is what is pleasing to the Lord, who is lowly of heart. *Except ye become like children, ye shall not enter the Kingdom of God* (Mt. 18:13).

St. Leonid of Optina

ST. GREGORY, BISHOP OF LANGRES. Gregory was from a distinguished sixth-century family. He governed the area of Autun for forty years, dispensing justice fairly but sternly. Late in life, after the death of his wife, Gregory turned from the world and gave himself to God. He was soon elevated to Bishop of Langres by the vote of the people and clergy. He showed great devotion to his pastoral duties, and he concealed his strict fasting from the knowledge of others. He often spent his nights in prayer. His epitaph read that any severity he had displayed as a secular ruler was counterbalanced by the tender charity he showed to all in his last years. The miracles recorded after his death showed that he gave preference to those who were prisoners of human justice.

COMMEMORATIONS: Synaxis of the 70 Apostles; Eustathios I of Serbia; 13 Syrian Fathers of Georgia; Gregory, Bishop of Langres; Theoctistus of Cucomo; Euthymios the New of Thessalonica; Zosimas the Hermit and Athanasios the Commentarius; Aquila of the Kiev Caves; Euthymios and 12 monks of Vatopedi; Dafrosa of Rome; Symeon of Smolensk; Holy 6 Martyrs; Apollinaria of Egypt; Chrysanthos and Euphemia in Constantinople; Timothy the Stylite of Kakhshata; Nikephoros the Leper; Onuphrius of Gabrovo; Mark of Sergievsk; Ethiopian Eunuch of Queen Candace.

JANUARY 5

*L*ook, my child! Our God, in His desire to educate His children who believe, trust, love Him and worship Him, resorts to various ways, methods and plans. Among the plans of our God is also the imposition of rules, which of course always aspire to the salvation of our souls… We cannot change or delete God's plans. What is more, we cannot impose any on Him. But we can however ask of Him and beseech Him, and He, being the philanthropist that He is, can hearken to our prayers and shorten time—or even dispense with it. Either way, it is up to Him. We ask for something, and He is the one who will approve.

St. Porphyrios of Kavsokalyvia

ST. TALIDA, ABBESS OF ANTINOE, AND HER DISCIPLE TAOR. In the Egyptian town of Antinoe, founded by the Roman emperor Hadrian, was a monastery of twelve women. Amma Talida lived there for eighty years, and everyone held great respect for her. Talida's disciple, Amma Taor, had known Talida for thirty years. Taor would never wear new clothes or a cloak and shoes, saying that she didn't need them; therefore, no one could compel her to go out. When the others went to church, she would stay home dressed in rags and hard at work. She was dazzlingly and attractive, but she had such a gift of self-denial that she could turn lustful eyes into reverence and respect.

COMMEMORATIONS: Syncletike of Alexandria; Phosterios and Menas of Sinai; Gregory at Akrita; Martyr Sais; Theopemptos of Nicomedia and Theonas; Martyr Theoeidos; Righteous Domnina; Righteous Tatiana; Romanos of Carpenision; Talida of Antinoe, and Taora; Theophan of the Rykhlovsk; Symeon of the Pskov Caves; Niphon, Bishop of Cyprus; Cera (Kiara) of Ireland; Andrew Zimin, his wife Lydia, their three daughters, and Domnica, of Russia.

The sign of sincere love is to forgive wrongs done to us. It was with such love that the Lord loved the world.

St. Mark the Ascetic

VENERABLE LAURENCE OF CHERNIGOV. Laurence was a good student, gifted in music, and a choir director at the age of fourteen. He became a monk and went to the Chernigov-Trinity Monastery at the archbishop's request. He foresaw that Laurence would become a great man of prayer. He was made the abbot at the age of 27. Laurence was always joyful and radiated love with everyone, which was the fruit of his prayer. When he visited his village, he had the spiritual insight to see which girls were inclined to monasticism, and he would pray for them and nurture their love for prayer. Once while building a monastery during bad weather, the stucco froze until Laurence made the sign of the cross, and it became pliable. During wartime, the enemy would not allow the monks to harvest the monastery wheat, but Laurence prayed, and it was permitted. He said, "When a person is wicked he has a demon within, but when you pray, the demon scampers away." He also said, "It's so difficult for a Christian to live in this world. The devil doesn't give him any peace." He once told a girl not to enter a convent but to marry. When she objected, he said, "then who will give birth to priests and bishops." She married and had a son who became an archpriest. Laurence talked much about the end times and how the Antichrist will become the single world leader after a terrible war. "In the last times they will banish the true Christians," and the mark of the beast will be necessary to buy and sell, but "the Lord will not abandon His children. One mustn't fear!" He said the rivers and lakes would dry up, and grain would not grow, but those "under the powerful influence of the Jesus Prayer" will not see those false signs. After a few months of a short illness, Laurence died on the Feast of Theophany in 1950.

COMMEMORATIONS: Holy Theophany of Our Lord Jesus Christ; Romanus of Lacedemonia; Laurence of Chernigov; Melanius of Remes; Repose of St. Theophan the Recluse.

Synaxis of St. John the Baptist
Fast-free

Acts 19:1-8; John 1:29-34

The first step of humility…is that a man keeps the *fear of God* always *before his eyes* (Ps. 35 [36]:2) and never forgets it. He must constantly remember everything God has commanded, keeping in mind that all who despise God will burn in hell for their sins, and all who fear God have everlasting life awaiting them. While he guards himself at every moment from sins and vices of thought or tongue, of hand or foot, of self-will or bodily desire, let him recall that he is always seen by God in heaven, that his actions everywhere are in God's sight and are reported by angels at every hour.

St. Benedict of Nursia

THE MIRACLE OF THE HOLY FORERUNNER JOHN IN CHIOS IN 1740. St. Athanasios of Paros wrote the following narrative. There was a church dedicated to St. John the Baptist outside the city, in the vicinity of Atzike, and beyond it in the countryside were mosques. The Ottomans would travel there to say their prayers, and in winter, this was a hardship. Therefore, seven men discussed seizing the church by imperial decree, and they sent letters with a trusted person by ship to prominent members in Chios. However, two men in that group disagreed with this plot and refused to sign those letters. One night the five members of the group met at the tower where they conducted their meetings. Suddenly an earthquake caused the collapse of their part of the building, killing all five men. Miraculously, the other side housing innocent women and children did not collapse, thus sparing their lives. The letters were lost at sea when the entire ship sank to the bottom.

COMMEMORATIONS: Synaxis of St. John the Forerunner; Miracle of St. John the Baptist in Chios; Translation of the right hand of St. John the Baptist; Athanasios of Attaleia and Smyrna; Cedd, Bishop of Lastingham; Brannock (Brynach) of Braunton (England); Kentigerna of Loch Lomond; Paphnutius (Kostin) of Optina Monastery; Nicholas (Parfenov), Bishop of Atkarsk; Julian and Julius of Aegina; Repose of St. Ieronymos of Simonopetra.

JANUARY 8

*H*oliness is entrance into Paradise, a foretaste of the ineffable joy of the eternal Kingdom of Heaven.

† *Elder Moses the Athonite*

ST. JOSEPH THE NEW OF CAPPADOCIA. Joseph lived in the mid-1800s in Cappadocia. He was a peddler and a great man of prayer, and he shared the word of God wherever he went. At the age of thirty, during a journey, he suddenly died, and after his burial, a light often appeared above his grave. Later his relatives dug up his relics and once exposed, the bones suddenly joined together of their own accord, making them easy to gather. Later, when the tired relatives were returning to Caesarea, they fell asleep on the road, and they said, "If you are a saint, show us a sign!" The five relatives were awakened by a slap on the face and before them lay five loaves of fresh bread. They divided the saint's relics among themselves and honored them. One relative returned home and could not open her door. Inside she heard the sound of a censor, like that in church. When she entered her home, a wonderful fragrance filled the room where the holy relics were kept. Another time, Joseph appeared to her, saying, "I am the patron saint of your house! I have come to tell you that such and such a neighbor vowed to bring me a container of oil but did not bring it." Then he vanished. The neighbor later confessed to this. Joseph also healed the infirmities of many faithful who went to the house to venerate his relics. Once, a relative removed one of the saint's fingers, and immediately her hand broke out in sores. When Joseph appeared to her in a dream, she returned it and became well. Many were healed with water blessed by St. Joseph's relics during an epidemic in Cappadocia.

COMMEMORATIONS: Carterios of Caesarea; Dominica of Carthage; Atticus and Cyrus of Constantinople; George the Chozevite; Agathon of Egypt; Abo the Perfumer; Elias of Egypt; Julian, Basilissa, Marcionilla, Celsus, Anthony, Anastasius, 7 children, and 20 soldiers; Theophilus and Helladius; Gregory of Orchid; Gregory of the Kiev Caves; Gregory of the Kiev Caves, recluse; Paisius of Uglich; Macarius of Vatopedi; Isidore and 72 companions; Severinus, apostle of Austria; Theodore of Constantinople.

JANUARY 9

2 Timothy 2:1-10; Mark 1:9-15

*S*o, brothers, since we have been given no small opportunity to repent, let us take the occasion to turn to God who has called us, while we still have One to accept us. For if we renounce "earthly pleasures" and master our soul by avoiding their evil lust, we shall share in Jesus' mercy. Understand that "the day" of judgment is already "on its way like a furnace ablaze" (Mal. 4:1), and the powers of heaven will dissolve (Isa. 34:4) and the whole earth will be like lead melting in fire. Then men's secret and overt actions will be made clear. Let us then, repent with our whole heart, so that none of us will be lost.

St. Clement of Alexandria

VENERABLE EUSTRATIOS THE WONDERWORKER. Eustratios became a monk when he was twenty years old and remained one for seventy-five years. He was known as a man of prayer and a great ascetic. He repeated the prayer, "Lord have mercy," throughout each church service. As an act of self-discipline, he never slept on his left side, only on his right. He died peacefully at the age of ninety-five.

COMMEMORATIONS: Peter, Bishop of Sebaste, brother of Basil the Great and Gregory of Nyssa; Polyeuktos of Melitene in Armenia; Eustratios of Tarsus; Philip II, Metropolitan of Moscow; Jonah, founder of Holy Trinity Monastery in Kiev; Adrian of Canterbury; Parthena of Edessa; Finian, Bishop of Lindisfarne; Prophet Shemaiah (Sameas); Berhtwald, Archbishop of Canterbury; Fillan, abbot of Strathfillan; Translation of the relics of St. Judoc, hermit of Ponthie

*R*emember that while you pray, God expects from you a positive answer to His question: "Do you believe that I can fulfill your prayer?" You must be able to answer from the bottom of your heart: "Yes, I believe, O God," and then you will be answered according to your faith.

St. John of Kronstadt

ST. SMARAGDA ONISHCHENKO OF NIZHYN. Smaragda was from the mid-1800s Chernigov province. As a young child, she was often so ill that her mother did not have hope that she would live, so a coffin was made. At the age of five, Smaragda was taken to a school for orphan girls at the Vvedensky Monastery in Nizhyn. When she graduated college, she reentered that monastery, became a nun, and was later unanimously elected their abbess. And yet she continued to show deep humility and would not move to the chambers of the abbess, preferring to work on an equal footing with all the sisters. In 1922 Smaragda was arrested by the communists, interrogated, tortured, and left for dead. The nuns were allowed to take her body but later found her still alive. Again, they arrested and imprisoned Smaragda for three years. She returned to her monastery, but it was finally closed and turned into an artillery warehouse. In 1930 she was jailed for anti-Soviet agitation, which ruined her health. She endured another cycle of arrest and release. Foreseeing her death, she asked to be buried in a shallow grave, knowing that she would later be moved twice, which came to pass. Later, the casket was opened, and her body was found incorrupt. The Ukrainian Church canonized St. Smaragda in 2014.

COMMEMORATIONS: Gregory, Bishop of Nyssa; Theophan the Recluse; Theosebia the Deaconess; Marcian of Constantinople; Dometian, Bishop of Melitene; Ammon of Nitria; Paul of Obnora; Ephraim and 6 incorrupt monks of Obnora; Macarius of Pisemsk; Peter Uspensky of Radushino; Antipas of Calapodesti, Romania; Macarius of Pisma Monastery; Miltiades, Pope of Rome; Antipas of Valaam; Anatole of Odessa; Arsenia, abbess in Shuisk; Smaragda of Nizhyn.

*L*et's say, for example, someone has a particular passion. He acknowledges the fact, he struggles to cast it off, he repents and he becomes humble. His inner disposition and struggle to break the bad habit are known to God, Who provides assistance. On the other hand, how can God give His Grace to one who does not make any effort to change; but—instead—continues to sin? God's Grace does not come to someone who is in a false spiritual state, because this would not be helpful to that person. If it were helpful, then God would have given His Grace to the devil himself.

St. Paisios the Athonite

MARTYR MAIROS. Mairos was a Roman soldier during the Christian persecutions under emperors Diocletian and Maximian in the late third and early fourth centuries. While in the city of Gaza, Mairos was accused of being a Christian. He stood before the tribunal and confessed his faith. With intensity, he was continuously beaten for seven days by thirty-six soldiers, one after the other, and the ground was made red with his flowing blood. St. Mairos bravely endured this until he gave up his soul.

COMMEMORATIONS: Theodosios the Great; Theodosios of Trebizond; Theodosios of Antioch; Stephen of Placidian; Agapius of Apamea; Romilos the Hermit of Veddin; Vitalis of Abba Serid; Michael of Klops; Nikephoros of Crete; Martyr Mairos; Hyginus, Pope of Rome; Vladimir the Confessor of Minsk; New Martyrs Nicholas, Theodore, and Vladimir; Synaxis of the Myriad of Angels; *Chernigov-Eletskaya* Icon of the Mother of God.

JANUARY 12

Acts 18:22-28; John 10:39-42

*I*f you want the Lord to hide your sins, then don't talk to people about what kind of virtues you have. For as we relate to our virtues, so God relates to our sins.

St. Mark the Ascetic

SYNAXIS OF PANAGIA OF THE AKATHIST: THREE MIRACULOUS ATHONITE AKATHIST ICONS OF THE MOTHER OF GOD.

The "Panagia of the Salutations the Myrrhgusher" icon is housed at the Dionysiou Monastery on Mount Athos. It was given to St. Dionysius by Emperor Komnenos. According to tradition, this icon was carried around the walls of Constantinople when the Persians and Scythians attacked in the year 626. A sudden hurricane dispersed the enemy fleet, tossing the ships onto the shore near the Church of the Theotokos at Blachernae. In 1592 pirates stole the icon, but after a frightening dream, a fierce storm, and a miracle, they returned it to the monastery. The story relates that they had hidden the icon in a chest, but the icon shattered it, and it was found drenched in myrrh. Some of those pirates became monastics. In 1769 thieves stole this small icon, but shepherds retrieved it and took it to the Greek island of Skopelos. The monks of Dionysiou Monastery requested its return, but they were denied. Three months later, a plague struck Skopelos with great tragedy. The officials repented and returned the icon. The "Panagia of the Akathist" Icon is located on the iconostasis at the Hilander Monastery on Mount Athos. In 1837 a fire broke out and caused great destruction around the icon, but it remained untouched. The "Panagia of the Akathist Proangellomeni (the Notifier)" is located at Zographou Monastery and is celebrated on October 10.

COMMEMORATIONS: Tatiana of Rome; Peter Absalom in Palestine; 8 Martyrs of Nicaea; Philotheus of Antioch; Mertius of Mauretania; Theodora of Alexandria; Eupraxia of Tabenna; Elias of *The Paradise*; John of Tula; Galacteon and Martinian of White Lake; Martyr Euthasia; Benedict of Wearmouth; Eulogia, mother of St. Theodosius; *The Milk-giver, Of the Akathist* (Hilander), *Popska*, and *Mesopanditissa* Icons of the Mother of God.

JANUARY 13

*W*e mustn't despair when we struggle and continuously see nothing but the slightest progress. We all do nearly nothing, some a little more, some a little less. When Christ sees our little effort He gives us an analogous token, and so our nearly nothing becomes valuable, and we can see a little progress. For this reason, we mustn't despair, but hope in God.

St. Paisios the Athonite

VENERABLE ELEAZAR OF ANZERSK. Eleazar was born into a merchant family in the late sixteenth-century city of Kozelsk. With his parent's blessing, he went to live the monastic life at the Solovki Monastery under the guidance of St. Irenarchus. Eleazar became a talented woodcarver and was chosen to help beautify the Transfiguration cathedral. Later, with the permission of his elder, he went to Anzersk Island and became a hermit, living a life of meditation and continuous prayer. Eleazar carved wooden cups to earn a living. He would leave them at a nearby dock, and the fishermen would leave him food and supplies in return, and for this, they were blessed with great catches. In time, others settled near Eleazar to learn from him. He created a strict monastic rule for them based on the monasteries of old. The monks lived far from one another and only congregated for weekend services. The future Patriarch Nikon was a disciple of Eleazar's. Hearing of Eleazar, Tsar Michael brought him to Moscow and gave him funds to build a monastery and a stone church on Anzersk Island. Eleazar also wrote books about monastic life and wisdom. He received foreknowledge of his death, which happened in great old age.

COMMEMORATIONS: James, Bishop of Nisibis; Hermilos and Stratonikos at Belgrade; Hilary, Bishop of Poitiers; Maximos of Kavsokalyvia, Mt. Athos; Peter of Anium; Irenarchus of Rostov; Martyr Athanasios; Martyrs Pachomius and Papyrinos in Greece; Remigius of Rheims; Eleazar of Anzersk Island at Solovki.

JANUARY 14

Ephesians 6:10-17; Matthew 4:1-11

If you pray from all your heart for salvation—even a little—you will be saved.

St. Moses of Optina

ST. FELIX OF NOLA. In the third century, Felix's father left him and his brother an estate near Naples, Italy. He feared that this wealth might entangle his soul, so he gave most of it to the poor and was ordained a reader and later a priest by Bishop Maximus of Nola, who was grooming Felix to replace him. When Emperor Decius began his persecutions, Maximus fled to the desert, and Felix was arrested. He was scourged, and heavy chains were laid about his neck, hands, and legs. Then he was cast into a dungeon, where the floor was covered with shards of broken pots. He could not even find a comfortable place to stand. One night an angel of God appeared to him and instructed him to go to Maximus, who was in distress. Felix's chains fell off, and the prison doors opened of their own accord. He followed the angel to Maximus, who was senseless, dying of cold and hunger, and filled with anxiety for his flock. Felix prayed for some food, and a bunch of grapes appeared that revitalized Maximus. Then Felix carried him back to his house, where an old woman cared for him. Felix hid until the emperor died, but the pagans tried to arrest him when he emerged. But he crawled through a crevice in an old wall, and spiders quickly covered the opening with their web. He hid in an old well for six months and was brought food by a Christian woman until peace was restored. When Maximus died, Felix was the unanimous choice for bishop, but he deferred the honor to another priest, Quintus, who nonetheless carefully followed Felix's advice. Towards the end of his life, St. Felix rented a small piece of land that he tilled. It fed him, and he also gave his crop to the poor.

COMMEMORATIONS: Sava I, first Archbishop of Serbia; Nina (Nino), Enlightener of Georgia; Holy Fathers slain at Sinai and Raithu; Theodoulos of Sinai; Acacius of Tver; Macrina, grandmother of St. Basil the Great; John of Verkhoturye; Martyr Agnes; Meletius of Ryazan; Stephen of Chenolak-kos; Joseph of Raithu; Felix of Nola; Kentigern of Glasgow.

Twelfth Sunday of Luke
Fast-free

JANUARY 15

Galatians 5:22-6:2; Luke 12:32-40

*T*here is nothing colder than a Christian who does not seek to save others.

St. John Chrysostom

VENERABLE PROCHORUS OF PSHINA. Prochorus was from eleventh-century Bulgaria. His parents were barren for many years, but their prayers were answered and Prochorus was born. When he became an adult, they began to encourage him to marry. Confused, Prochorus went to church to pray for guidance and salvation. When he heard the Gospel reading, "Assuredly, I say to you, there is no one who has left house or parents or brothers or wife or children, for the sake of the kingdom of God, who shall not receive many times more in this present time, and in the age to come eternal life," he burst into tears, left the church, and fled to the desert. He found a small cave with a spring of water and happily settled there, eating fruits, grasses, and roots, just once a week. He labored, shed tears, and slept on a stone during bitter winters and hot summers. He was an earthly angel, replete with virtues. For thirty-two years, he saw no one. One day a deer raced breathlessly to Prochorus and lay at his feet. Soon a hunter named Diogenes approached, and Prochorus called him by name and told him that he would one day be a king in Constantinople. After this, Prochorus found another cave nearby and lived there another thirty years until angels came for his soul. Soon after, Prochorus appeared in a dream to Diogenes, who was now the king, and he sent soldiers to return with the body of Prochorus, but they were unable to lift the beautiful coffin they had laid him in. St. Prochorus informed the king that he wished to remain there. The king had a monastery built there, where many monastics came to live, and the myrrh that flowed from the saint's relics healed many.

COMMEMORATIONS: Paul of Thebes; John Calabytes of Constantinople; Pansophios of Alexandria; Prochorus of Pshina; Maurus, disciple of St. Benedict; Maximus of Nola; Salome and Perozhavra of Sivnia; Ita of Killeedy; Maura and Britta of Touraine; Gabriel of Lesnov; Gerasimos of Alexandria; Benjamin of Romanov; Nectarius of Tobolsk; Ceolwulf of Northumbria.

Through prayer we flee to God.

St. Nektarios of Pentapolis

ST. ROMILOS THE SINAITE, OF RAVANICA MONASTERY. As a child in fourteenth-century Bulgaria, Romilos was very mature and disliked childish games. He longed to become a monk, and when his parents encouraged him to marry, he fled to the Hodigitria Monastery, where he became known for his virtues and humility. His monastic goal was to live a quiet life of prayer, and to this end, Romilos moved many times. He went to the wilderness to be in obedience to St. Gregory of Sinai. He carried wood and water to the monastery, helped in the kitchen, and tended the sick. When St. Gregory died, Romilos resettled several more times. Finally, he traveled to Mount Athos, but the other monks would seek him for spiritual guidance, and the elders would send their disciples to him for correction. Romilos would admonish them to never contradict or question their spiritual father, but only to obey him because those who do not are easily led astray by the adversary. Yet again, he fled for solitude to the northern part of Athos, but the more he fled glory, the more it found him. When enemies attacked Mount Athos, Romilos fled to Albania. Again, laymen and monks alike found him there since they were filled with ignorance and the passions and had no other shepherd. With his disciples, Romilos finally moved to a monastery dedicated to the Mother of God in Ravanica, Serbia. There he died peacefully, and a wonderful fragrance emanated from his grave. The saint's prayers expelled demons and healed disease and suffering even after his death.

COMMEMORATIONS: Veneration of the Precious Chains of Apostle Peter; Speusippos, Eleusippos, and Meleusippos, with Neon, Turbo, Leonilla, and Jonilla in Cappadocia; Honoratus, Archbishop of Arles; Danax the Reader; Damascene of Bulgaria; Maximus of Totma; Nicholas of Mytilene; Romilos of Mt. Athos, with Nestor, Martinius, Daniel, Sisoes, Zosimas, and Gregory; Sigebert, King of the East Angles; Fursey of Burgh Castle; James of Tarentaise.

St. Anthony the Great
Fast-free

Hebrews 13:17-21; Luke 6:17-23

*S*t. Anthony the Great affirms: *'If a person places the burden on himself, he finds rest. The moment he casts it on someone else, he will feel troubled internally.'* Try it when the opportunity arises. If, during a temptation, you blame the other person, internally you will feel troubled, distressed—a mess! On the other hand, as soon as you think: *'The other person is not at fault, I am to blame. Why am I speaking about another person? Have I forgotten who I am? I have made so many mistakes and sins … hence, I should not be speaking at all,'* you will feel as if you are landing on solid ground and are no longer in danger of falling. Whereas previously, when you were soaring high, you were fearful and uneasy: *'I am about to fall at any moment.'* Once you descend low, and set foot on solid ground, you no longer have anything to fear.

† *Elder Ephraim of Arizona*

VENERABLE ANTHONY OF METEORA, FOUNDER OF THE MONASTERY OF ST. STEPHEN. Monastic life began at Meteora on the rock of St. Stephen in the twelfth century. But in the first half of the early fifteenth century, Anthony Kantakouzenos founded the first monastery there and became the abbot. The Monastery of St. Stephen was rebuilt in the mid-sixteenth century by St. Philotheos. It may have been that Anthony was the son of Nikephoros II, the ruler of Epirus. We do not know much more about his life. Later the monastery was abandoned, and in 1961 it was converted into a convent for nuns.

COMMEMORATIONS: Anthony the Great; Theodosios the Great; George of Ioannina; Anthony the Roman of Novgorod; Macarius (Kalogeras) of Patmos; Achilles of Egypt; Anthony the New of Verea in Macedonia; Anthony of Dymsk Monastery (Novgorod); Anthony of Chermoezersk Monastery; Anthony of Krasnokholmsk Monastery (Tver); Severus the Pious, Bishop of Bourges; Mildgyth of Minster; Sulpitius II, Bishop of Bourges.

St. Athanasios and St. Cyril
Abstain from meat and
dairy products, and fish.
Hebrews 13:7-16; Matthew 5:14-19

The fasting of a diet is so easy when one wants to slim. And so difficult is the Wednesday and Friday fast when the Church wants it.
† *Gerontissa Gavrilia of Leros*

ST. ATHANASIOS THE GREAT OF ALEXANDRIA. Athanasios was a young deacon to the archbishop of Alexandria in Egypt. When Arius, an elderly priest from Alexandria, was spreading his heresy that the Holy Trinity was separate and not one Godhead, Athanasios wrote brilliant sermons entitled *Against the Arians* and spoke well against them at the Council of Nicaea in 325. When the patriarch died, Athanasios assumed the post at only thirty years of age. Arius was excommunicated for his heresy, but when Arius deceived the emperor into believing that he had accepted the Nicene Creed, Athanasios correctly understood that Arius was not to be believed and would not reinstate him, and for this, Athanasios was exiled. The Arians would not be defeated for another two hundred years. Because of his enemies, a few years later, Athanasios was banished by a synod in Antioch. Instead of imprisonment, he escaped and did not return until the year 345, and this is what is commemorated today. All three emperors, as well as Bishop Eusebius, Arius, and others, persecuted Athanasios. He hid in places like a well, a grave, the desert, and private homes, seeking solace and spiritual counsel from his elder St. Anthony the Great.

COMMEMORATIONS: Cyril and Athanasios, Archbishops of Alexandria; Joachim, Patriarch of Turnovo; Maximus, Archbishop of Wallachia; Cyril and Maria, parents of Sergius of Radonezh; Martyr Xenia; Theodula, Helladius, Evagrius, Macarius, and Boethos of Anazarbus; Marcian of Cyrrhus in Syria; Silvanus of Palestine; Ephraim, Bishop of Mylasa in Caria (Asia Minor); Ephraim the Lesser of Georgia; Leobardus of Gaul; Athanasius of Novolotsk Monastery (Karelia); Alexis of Teklati, Georgia; Athanasius of Syadem and Vologda; Ninnidh of Inismacsaint; Vladimir Zubkovich of Smolevichi (Belorussia).

St. Macarius the Great of Egypt
Fast-free

JANUARY 19

Galatians 5:22-6:2; Matthew 19:16-26

*T*he Lord, indeed, is the Lover of mankind, so full of tender compassion whenever we turn completely toward Him and are freed from all things contrary. Even though we, in our supreme ignorance, childishness, and tendency toward evil, turn away from true life and place many impediments along our path because we really do not like to repent, nevertheless, He has great mercy on us. He patiently waits for us until we will be converted and return to Him and be enlightened in our inner selves that our faces may not be ashamed in the day of judgment.

St. Macarius the Great

VENERABLE MACARIUS THE DEACON OF THE KIEV CAVES. Macarius lived during the thirteenth and fourteenth centuries. He continuously read the Holy Scriptures, labored in fasting, and was known for his lack of covetousness. As a child, he was frequently sick, and his parents vowed to offer their son to the Kiev Caves Monastery if he was restored to health, which came to pass. Because of his humility and mildness, Macarius earned the love of his fellow brethren, and they taught him to read and write. St. Macarius was ordained a deacon, and God granted him the gift of wonderworking.

COMMEMORATIONS: Macarius the Great; Mark Eugenikos of Ephesus; Arsenius of Corfu; Euphrasia of Nicomedia; Macarius of Alexandria; Meletios of Mt. Galesios; Anton the Stylite; Theodore of Novgorod; Macarius the Faster; Macarius of the Kiev Caves; Macarius the Roman of Novgorod, and Chariton; Anthony Rawah the Qoraisite; Branwalader of Cornwall; Peter of Petrograd; Translation of the relics of St. Gregory the Theologian and St. Peter the Wonderworker from Rome to Argos; Uncovering of the relics of St. Sabbas of Zvenigorod.

**St. Euthymios the Great
Abstain from meat and
dairy products, and fish.**
2 Corinthians 4:6-15; Luke 6:17-23

A poor man when he reaches out to you does not beg, but offers you the kingdom of God.

† *Elder Arsenie Papacioc of Romania*

ST. EUTHYMIUS, PATRIARCH OF TURNOVO. Euthymius was from fourteenth-century Bulgarian nobility, but he became a monk for the future blessings of heaven. He would stand in all-night vigil and sleep sitting in a chair. His elder once foretold that the Ottomans would conquer that country and that Euthymius would suffer an apostle's persecution. When the invasions began, these two went to Constantinople, and the people flocked to them to feed their hungry souls. Euthymius then moved to Mount Athos and later returned to Turnovo in Hungary to live in a cave. Disciples soon gathered around him, and he translated divine books from the Greek into Bulgarian. When Patriarch Theodosius died, Euthymius was unanimously chosen to replace him. He taught with his sermons and by his gentle and humble example. He also drove off those who would corrupt his people. One time when a drought threatened a famine, Euthymius fell on his knees, lifted his arms in prayer, and a penetrating rain began that would help yield plentiful crops. When the Ottomans attacked and conquered Turnovo, Euthymius tried to appease the king, but his appointees still slaughtered Christians, even in church. Euthymius was taken to the execution site, and without fear, he encouraged the executioner to follow orders. But the executioner's arms became paralyzed, so they released Euthymius. Finally, he was sent into exile to a mountainous region, where he helped the people until his death.

COMMEMORATIONS: Euthymios the Great; Leo I, Emperor of Byzantium; Inna, Pinna, and Rimma in Scythia; Euthymius Kereselidze of Georgia; Bassos, Eusebius, Eutychios, and Basilides at Nicomedia; Martyrs Thyrsos and Agnes; Peter the Publican of Constantinople; Anna at Rome; Euthymius, Patriarch of Turnovo, Bulgaria; Euthymius the Silent of the Kiev Caves; Laurence the Recluse of the Kiev Caves; New Martyr Zacharias of Patras; Theodore Kuzmich of Tomsk; Euthymius of Syanzhemsk; Euthymius of Archangelsk; Paul Dobromyslov of Ryazan.

St. Maximos the Confessor
Fast-free

Philippians 1:12-20; Luke 12:8-12

*J*ust as ignorance divides those who are deluded, so the presence of spiritual light draws together and unites those whom it enlightens.

St. Maximos the Confessor

MARTYR NEOPHYTOS OF NICAEA. Neophytos was the son of Christian parents in late third-century Nicaea, Bithynia, during the persecutions of Emperors Diocletian and Decius. From the beginning of his life, he was filled with the Grace of God. At the age of nine, he prayed and miraculously fed his fellow students one day when they were thirsty and hungry. One night as his mother was praying, she saw a dove come down from heaven and perch on her son's bed. In a human voice, it said, "The Holy Spirit sent me to hover over the bed of Neophytos so that I should cast out every assault of the enemy and preserve his bedding pure and blameless." She died from fright when she heard the voice, but Neophytos raised her from the dead with prayer. Guided by the dove, ten-year-old Neophytos soon left to live in a cave on Mount Olympus. He had to send away the wild animals living there, and an angel of God fed him. A year later, he left the cave to see his parents, who were now at the end of their lives, and after giving away their possessions, he returned to his cave. At fifteen, a divine angel guided him to Governor Maximus to proclaim Christ as true God. The governor ordered him beaten and thrown into a fiery furnace, but he remained unharmed. Even the wild beasts would not harm him. Finally, the enraged Maximus took a spear and pierced St. Neophytos in the heart.

COMMEMORATIONS: Maximos the Confessor; Neophytos of Nicaea; Zosimas, Bishop of Syracuse; Agnes of Rome; Maximus the Greek of Russia; Eugene, Candidus, Valerian, and Aquila at Trebizond; Anastasius, disciple of St. Maximos the Confessor; Neophytos of Vatopedi; 4 Martyrs of Tyre; Timon, monk of Kostroma; Fructuosis of Tarragona, Spain; Synaxis of the Church of Holy Peace by the Sea, Constantinople; *Consolation* (Paramythia) and *The Stabbed* Icons of the Mother of God.

Fifteenth Sunday of Luke
Fast-free

January 22

1 Timothy 4:9-15; Luke 19:1-10

*I*f we seek the things that are perfect, the secondary things will follow. The Lord says, "Seek first the kingdom of God and His righteousness, and all these things shall be added to you." What sort of person do you think the children of such parents will be? What kind of persons are all the others who associate with them? Will they not eventually be the recipients of countless blessings as well? For generally the children acquire the character of their parents, are formed in the mold of their parents' temperament, love the same things their parents love, talk in the same fashion and work for the same ends. If we order our lives in this way and diligently study the Scriptures, we will find lessons to guide us in everything we need.

St. John Chrysostom

APOSTLE TIMOTHY OF THE SEVENTY. Timothy was one of the Seventy Apostles, and his teachers were the Apostle Paul and later St. John the Evangelist. He witnessed St. Paul healing the man lame from birth. He also traveled to many cities with Apostle Paul, spreading the faith. Timothy later served as bishop of Ephesus. During the idol-worshipping festival called Katagogium, pagans killed Timothy. His relics were later translated to Constantinople and buried in the Church of the Twelve Apostles next to the graves of St. Luke the Evangelist and St. Andrew the First-called.

COMMEMORATIONS: Apostle Timothy of the Seventy; Joseph Samakos the Sanctified of Crete; Anastasius the Persian; Manuel, Bishop of Adrianople; Anastasius of the Kiev Caves; Macarius of Zhabynsk; Martyrs Manuel, George, Peter, Leontius, bishops, and Sionius, Gabriel, John, Leontus, and Parodus, presbyters, and 377 companions in Bulgaria; Brithwald of Wilton; Wendreda of March; New Martyr Gregory of Pec.

St. Clement of Ancyra
Fast-free

JANUARY 23

Philippians 3:20-4:3; Mark 2:23-3:5

*T*he soul which has found the Lord, the true treasure, by seeking of the Spirit through faith and much patience, works out the fruits of the spirits with much ease.

St. Macarius the Great

VENERABLE GENNADIUS OF KOSTROMA. Gennadius was from a wealthy family in the sixteenth-century city of Mogilev. He loved the Church and often visited monasteries, which displeased his parents. One day he secretly left home in old clothes, saw the holy places in Russia, then set out for Novgorod, where he met St. Alexander of Svir. Alexander advised Gennadius to go to St. Cornelius of Komel in the Vologda Forest. Cornelius became his spiritual father and tonsured him a monk. These two moved to the shores of Lake Sura and began a monastery that became known as the Gannadiev Monastery, with Gennadius as the abbot. He worked daily with the other monks cutting and carrying firewood and making candles and prosphora. As an ascetic discipline, Gennadius also wore heavy chains. He loved writing icons, which were displayed throughout the monastery. Because of all his labors, God granted him the gift of wonderworking and clairvoyance. He once told a nobleman named Zakharin that his daughter Anastasia would one day be the Tsaritsa of Russia, and she later married Tsar Ivan the Terrible. St. Gennadius would advise his monks to toil constantly, be at peace with everyone, strive towards the light, and shun the darkness.

COMMEMORATIONS: Clement, Bishop of Ancyra, and Agathangelos; Salamanes the Silent of the Euphrates; Dionysios of Olympus and Mt. Athos; 2 Martyrs of Parion; Gennadius of Kostroma; Eusebius of Mt. Coryphe; Mausimas the Syrian; Ascholios of Thessalonica; Seraphim (Bulashov), abbot, and Virgin Martyrs Eudokia, Ecaterine, and Militsa, of Moscow; Barlaam of Siberia; Commemoration of the Sixth Ecumenical Council; Translation of the relics of St. Theoctistus of Novgorod; Synaxis of All Saints of Kostroma.

JANUARY 24

Galatians 5:22-6:2; Mark 6:1-7

I often hear some people saying that the tempter, the devil, is the cause of their spiritual tribulations, when, in fact, it is their own fault for not confronting the situation appropriately. After all, the tempter tempts us. Can it avert us from doing evil? It's just doing its job. Let's not blame everything on the devil.

St. Paisios the Athonite

VENERABLE CADOC, ABBOT OF LLANCARFAN IN WALES. Cadoc was the oldest son of King Gundleus, the warrior, and Queen Gwladys, who later became hermits and were venerated as saints. Cadoc refused to take the throne and decided to serve God as well. He is considered one of the founding fathers of monasticism in south Wales. He founded the monastery of Llancarfan, which housed 1,000 monks, and it was a great center of learning. It also had a seminary and a hospital, and they served the needy. Cadoc was known for his outstanding intellect and was called "Cadoc the Wise." Today at least fifteen churches in Wales are dedicated to St. Cadoc, and he is invoked against deafness. The Norman Conquest dissolved the Llancarfan monastery in 1086.

COMMEMORATIONS: Babylas, Timothy, and Agapius of Sicily; Philo, Bishop of Carpasia; Zosimas of Cilicia; Gerasimus, Bishop of Perm; John of Kazan; Xenia, deaconess of Rome, and 2 female slaves; Xenia of St. Petersburg; Martyrs Hermogenes and Mamas; Neophytos the Recluse of Cyprus; Philip the presbyter and Barsimus of Syria and his two brothers; Paul, Pausirios, and Theodotion of Egypt; Macedonius of Mt. Silpius, near Antioch; Lupicinus of Gaul; Felician, Bishop of Foligno in Italy; Sophia of Shamordino Convent; Cadoc of Llancarfan; Translation of the relics of St. Anastasius the Persian.

WEDNESDAY

St. Gregory the Theologian
Abstain from meat and
dairy products, and fish.

JANUARY 25

Hebrews 7:26-8:2; John 10:9-16

*F*irmly control anger and desire, and you will speedily rid yourself
of evil thoughts.

St. Thalassios of Libya

VENERABLE APOLLO OF THE THEBAID. Apollo was a fourth-century monk who lived many years in a monastic community. At the age of eighty, he founded and became the abbot of a monastery of many monks near Hermopolis. They dressed in coarse white robes, and every day they confessed their sins and received Holy Communion. Apollo was known for his joy, and he believed that melancholy and sadness were evil. He inspired cheerfulness to encourage the spirit of zeal, mixed with tears of penance, and said that these were the fruits of charity. Apollo always prayed not to be deceived by illusions of pride. Once when he drove out an evil spirit from a possessed person, the demon cried out that he could not withstand Apollo's humility. Of the miracles accredited to Apollo, the most remarkable was the continuous multiplication of bread over four months during a famine, not only for the brethren but for the entire surrounding population.

COMMEMORATIONS: Gregory the Theologian, Archbishop of Constantinople; Moses, Archbishop of Novgorod; Gabriel, Bishop of Imereti; Castinus, Bishop of Byzantium; Apollo of Thebes; Mares the Singer of Syria; Felicitas of Rome and her 7 sons; Publius of Syria; Medula and companions; Bretanion of Romania; Demetrios Skevophylax of Constantinople; Anatole I of Optina; Gregory of Golutvin; Vladimir of Kiev; Auxentios of Constantinople; Praejectus, Bishop of Clermont; Dwyn of Llandwyn; Athanasia (Lepeshkin) of Zosima Hermitage; Basil, Bishop of Priluksk; Peter, Archbishop of Voronezh; Margaret (Gunaronulo) of Menzelino; *Assuage My Sorrow* and *Unexpected Joy* Icons of the Mother of God.

JANUARY 26

Ephesians 4:14-17; Mark 6:30-45

*A*ccept humbly what God has revealed to us. Don't try to probe what God has kept hidden.

St. John Chrysostom

VENERABLE AMMONAS OF EGYPT. It was said that St. Anthony the Great once showed Ammonas a rock and told him to hit it and rebuke it. After Ammonas did this, Anthony foretold that Ammonas would reach such a high state of spiritual perfection that, like the rock, he would not be affected by people's insults. And it came to pass that Ammonas would never judge anyone, and he seemed to be unaware of all evil. He said that at one point in his life, he prayed to God night and day for fourteen years to be freed from the passion of anger. Once, a certain monk scandalized the local people by having an affair with a woman. When Ammonas visited that place, they asked him to go to the monk's cell, where the woman now was, so that they could scorn him. Knowing the plan, the monk hid the woman in an earthen jar. When the group arrived, Ammonas perceived where the woman was hiding and went and sat on the vessel. He told the people to search the cell. Having found nothing, they left, and Ammonas admonished them for the false accusations. Then he said to the monk, "Brother, be on your guard." Then he left. When Ammonas was bishop, a young pregnant girl was brought to him to receive a punishment. Making the sign of the cross on her womb, he asked for sheets to be given to her, saying that if she or the baby died in childbirth, they would need them since he could see that she was close to death. From that time, no one dared to accuse anyone anymore. St. Ammonas died peacefully.

COMMEMORATIONS: Xenophon, Maria, John and Arcadius of Constantinople; Symeon the Ancient of Mt. Sinai; Ammonas of Egypt; Ananias the presbyter, Peter, and 7 soldiers in Phoenicia; Joseph, Bishop of Thessalonica; Clement and Germanos of Mt. Sagmata; David IV the Restorer of Georgia; Gabriel, abbot at Jerusalem; Paula of Rome; 2 Martyrs of Phrygia; Xenophon of Novgorod; Joseph Naniescu of Romania; Cyril, Metropolitan of Kazan; Maria of Gatchina; Conon, bishop on the Isle of Man.

FRIDAY

JANUARY 27

**Translation of the Relics of
St. John Chrysostom
Abstain from meat and
dairy products, and fish.**
Hebrews 7:26-8:2; John 10:9-16

*W*hat we need is a little labor! Let us endure this labor that we may obtain mercy.

St. Dorotheos of Gaza

NEW HIEROMARTYR PETER, ARCHBISHOP OF VORONEZH.

Peter was from late-nineteenth-century Moscow, the son of a protopriest, and he zealously attended services with his father. He had a vision of Jesus during his childhood, and after that, he never got angry, did anything bad, and restrained himself in everything. Peter later became a monk and was ordained to the priesthood. He taught at the seminary, became an inspector at the Novgorod Theological Academy, and became a rector of several men's monasteries. But during the Communist regime, Peter was repeatedly arrested starting in 1917. During this time, Patriarch St. Tikhon consecrated him bishop of Balakhin. Peter introduced courses in the law of God for children, and he was popular and loved by the people. Because of this, the renovationist Archbishop Eudocimus, who was a tool of the Communists, hated Peter and continually persecuted him for 'arousing religious fanaticism.' Peter's health severely declined during his many imprisonments. He even lost all his teeth from scurvy. During times of freedom, a group of parishioners would form a guard around him, and one time the whole congregation followed him to the police station. The last time he was arrested, he was charged with spreading counter-revolutionary rumors. During a typhus outbreak in a prison camp, Peter fell ill and refused to eat for 14 days, saying, "I do not want to live any longer. The Lord is calling me to Himself." Some prisoners paid to have a coffin made, and Peter was buried in new vestments, and a column of light suddenly appeared over his grave.

COMMEMORATIONS: Peter of Egypt; Marciana (Euphemia) the Empress; Venerable Claudinus; Peter, Archbishop of Voronezh; Leonty of Ivanovo; Demetrius at Constantinople; Demetrius Klepinine of Paris; Translation of the relics of St. John Chrysostom.

St. Ephraim the Syrian
Fast-free

JANUARY 28

Galatians 5:22-6:2; Luke 6:17-23

*I*nstead of an avenger, be a deliverer. Instead of a fault-finder, be a soother. Instead of a betrayer, be a martyr. Instead of a chider, be a defender. Beseech God on behalf of sinners that they receive mercy, and pray to Him for the righteous, that they be preserved.
St. Isaac the Syrian

VENERABLE EPHRAIM THE SYRIAN. Ephraim was born in early fourth-century Nisibus, Syria, during the reign of Constantine the Great. He studied theology and hymnology and left his mark on Orthodox literature and music written in the Syrian language. He was taught by Bishop Iakovos, who tonsured him a monk, and he was a friend of St. Basil the Great. After he was ordained a deacon, he taught and directed a Syrian theological school, excelling as a teacher of the Bible. He also wrote insightful commentaries on the Old and New Testaments. Because of the persecutions, he spent the last ten years of his life in Edessa, near the Euphrates River. He is credited with writing some of the most beautiful hymns and prayers of the Orthodox Church. Preferring to remain a monk, Ephraim once feigned madness and ran through the streets holding his clothes rather than to be made a bishop.

COMMEMORATIONS: Ephraim the Syrian; Isaac the Syrian, Bishop of Nineveh; Ephraim, Bishop of Pereyaslavl (Kiev Caves); Palladios the Hermit of Antioch; James (Jacob) the Ascetic of Porphyreon in Palestine; John of Reomans (Gaul); Theodosius, founder of Totma Monastery (Vologda); Martyr Charitos; Ephraim, founder of Boris and Gleb Monastery (Novotorzhsky); Ignatius, Bishop of Skopin, with Vladimir, Bartholomew, and Olga; Leontius (Stasevich) of Jablechna (Poland); Arsenius (Stadnitsky), Metropolitan of Tashkent and Turkestan; *Sumorin Totma* Icon of the Mother of God.

Sunday of the Canaanite Woman
Fast-free

JANUARY 29

2 Corinthians 6:16-7:1
Matthew 15:21-28

*T*he Lord is loving unto man, and swift to pardon, but slow to punish. Let no man, therefore, despair of his own salvation.

St. Cyril of Jerusalem

VENERABLE APHRAHATES THE PERSIAN. Aphrahates was a fourth-century Persian who settled in Edessa and was baptized a Christian. He became a hut-dwelling hermit outside the city walls. Though he was uneducated, he knew just enough Greek to destroy the arguments of the heretics. He accepted nothing from those who came to see him and would only take bread from one friend. Later he labored for his soul at a monastery near Antioch. Upon hearing that the Arian Emperor Valens exiled hierarchs and bishops, Aphrahates left his solitude to strengthen and teach Christians the correct doctrine. One day when he happened to meet Valens, Valens asked Aphrahates why he had abandoned his silence. He replied that if he saw his father's house on fire, he would need to put out the fire and that the Lord's house was now ablaze. Valens' eunuch threatened to kill Aphrahates for this remark, but soon after, the eunuch fell into a vat of hot water and died. This frightened Valens, and he dared not punish or exile Aphrahates. On another occasion, a favorite pedigreed horse of Valens developed a disease. When it was taken to Aphrahates for healing, he anointed it with oil and gave it water blessed by the cross, and it became well. Still, Valens fought against Jesus Christ. Later, Valens died by fire in a battle lost against the Goths. St. Aphrahates died peacefully.

COMMEMORATIONS: Silvanus of Emesa, Luke the Deacon, and Mocius the Reader; Sarbelos and his sister Bebaia; Barsimaeus the Confessor; Gerasim, Pitirim, and Jonah of Perm; 7 Martyrs of Samosata; Aphrahates of Persia; Laurence of the Kiev Caves; Ignatius of Smolensk; Demetrios of Chios; Ashot Kuropalates of Tao-Klardjeti; Righteous Acepsimas; Gildas the Wise; Severus of Gaul; John, Leontius, Constantine, and 5 Martyrs; Translation of the relics of St. Ignatius the God-bearer; Synaxis of All Saints of Yekaterinburg; (Last Sunday of January: Synaxis of the Holy New Martyrs and Confessors of Russia; St. Peter, Metropolitan of Krutitsa).

Synaxis of the Three Great Hierarchs
Fast-free

Hebrews 13:7-16; Matthew 5:14-19

*L*ike the sun's rays passing through a crack and lighting up the house, show up even the finest dust, the fear of the Lord on entering the heart of a man show up all his sins.

St. John Climacus

MARTYR THEOPHILUS THE NEW. Theophilus was born and raised in eighth-century Constantinople during the reign of King Constantine. He became a general, and he was sent with the Roman fleet to an area known as Kivyrraea to fight against Arab pirates known as the Saracens. He was assisted by two admirals who were envious of him. When the enemy drew closer, Theophilus maneuvered into the middle of their fleet and overpowered them. However, the two admirals deserted him and sailed away. Because the enemy had more ships, they surrounded Theophilus, taking him prisoner to their country for four years. They released him and alternately flattered and threatened him to sacrifice to their idols. When he firmly refused, St. Theophilus was beheaded.

COMMEMORATIONS: Synaxis of the Three Hierarchs: Basil the Great, Gregory the Theologian, and John Chrysostom; Hippolytus of Rome, with Censorinus, Sabinus, Ares, Chryse, Felix, Maximus, Herculianus, Venerius, Styracius, Mennas, Commodus, Hermes, Maurus, Eusebius, Rusticus, Monagrius, Amandinus, Olympius, Cyprus, Theodore, Maximus, Archelaus, and Cyriacus; Zeno of Antioch; Zeno the Faster of the Kiev Caves; Grand Dukes Paul Alexandrovic and Dimitri Konstantinovich, and Eugene Poselianin; Adelgonda of Maubeuge; Demetrius of Sliven; Peter, King of Bulgaria; Hadji Theodore of Mytilene; Theophilus the New in Cyprus; Theophil, Fool-for-Christ; Pelagia of Diveyevo; Bathild of France; *Panagia Evangelistria* Icon of the Mother of God in Tinos; Commemoration of the Great Martyr St. George in Zakynthos.

JANUARY 31

The farmer plows the earth, cleans, sows seed, and awaits the mercy of God. If God doesn't send rains and helpful winds when they are necessary, the farmer's toils are in vain. It's the same with us. If God doesn't send the purifying waters of His grace, we remain devoid of fruit and our works become the fodder of demons. For our passions drown them and we don't harvest anything. We mustn't forget that virtuous deeds that are not done for the right reason become evil deeds.

St. Joseph the Hesychast

MARTYR TRYPHAINA OF CYZICUS. Tryphaina was the daughter of a nobleman and a Christian mother during the persecutions of Emperor Diocletian. When the idol-worshippers reported that Tryphaina was a Christian, she came forward of her own accord, ridiculed the idols, and denounced the shameful acts of the pagans who honored them. She taught them to forsake the false gods instead and turn to faith in Christ. Governor Caesarius had her thrown into a fiery furnace, but she emerged unharmed by the grace of Christ. Undeterred, they suspended her from a high post over iron nails. When the ropes were cut, her body was pierced, then she was thrown to wild beasts to be devoured. At first, they did not harm her, but an angry bull gored her, and she gave up her spirit. It is said that a spring of clear water gushed forth from the site where St. Tryphaina was martyred. After childbirth, women who could not give milk drank this water, and their milk flowed.

COMMEMORATIONS: Cyrus and John the Unmercenaries, and with them Martyrs Athanasia and her daughters Theoctiste, Theodota, and Eudoxia, at Canopus in Egypt; Tryphaina of Cyzicus; Victorinus, Victor, Nicephorus, Claudius, Diodorus, Serapion, and Papias of Egypt; Nicetas of the Kiev Caves; Marcella of Rome; Pachomius of Keno Lake; Athanasius, Bishop of Methone; Arsenius the New of Paros; Elias Ardunis of Mt. Athos and Kalamata; Julius and Julian of Aegina.

A certain Philosopher asked St. Anthony:
Father, how can you be so happy when you are
deprived of the consolation of books?

Anthony replied:
My book, O Philosopher, is the nature of created
things, and any time I want to read the words of
God, the book is before me.

The Wisdom of the Desert
*Sayings from the Desert Fathers
of the Fourth Century*

Forefeast of the Presentation
Strict Fast

Romans 8:28-39; Luke 10:19-21

*C*onverse with God as a son with his Father.

St. Isaac the Syrian

VENERABLE BENDIMIANOS OF MOUNT ST. AUXENTIUS. From his youth, Bendimianos wanted to serve God and live a life of poverty. Throughout his life, he wore one garment and never wore shoes. He longed to find a quiet place to live where he could pray. Finally, he found the ascetic Auxentius living on a nearby mountain with harsh terrain, steep precipices, and a dense forest. Bendimianos implored Auxentius to tonsure him a monk, and he progressed quickly in obedience and virtues. Auxentius soon died, and without a mentor, Bendimianos wore himself out with excessive fasting and labor. Jesus appeared to Bendimianos and commanded him to move into his elder's hut and told him not to struggle more than his elder had. Disciples came to learn from Bendimianos, and on one occasion, they became highly disgruntled due to a lack of food. The clairvoyant Bendimianos told them to descend the mountain, and there they would meet a man who was on his way to supply them with bread. Another time they had no oil for their lamps, so the monks stopped cleaning them. Bendimianos told them to mind their duties and that oil would arrive. Soon after, a man and his family came, bringing with them oil. After a brief illness, as Bendimianos was dying, he reminded his disciples to love one another, be charitable, and help the poor. Then he went into his cell, boarded up the window, and died kneeling in prayer. He had lived there in his elder's cell for forty-two years.

COMMEMORATIONS: Perpetua, Felicitas, Saturus, Revocatus, Saturninus, and Secundulus of Carthage; Basil, Archbishop of Thessalonica; Peter of Galatia; Tryphon of Campsada; Brigid of Kildare; Tryphon of Pechenga; Bendimianos of Bithynia; Martyr Carion; Theion with 2 children at Kariona; Elias the New of Damascus; Timothy the Confessor; David, Symeon, and George of Mytilene; Seiriol of Penmon; Tryphon, Bishop of Rostov; Anastasios at Nauplion; *Socola* Icon of the Mother of God.

FEBRUARY 2

Presentation of Our Lord and Savior
Fast-free

Hebrews 7:7-17; Luke 2:22-40

*L*et us watch our hearts; let us evaluate what goes from within us and from our mouths, not what enters them. Let us live according to the commandments of holy love, for the entire Law of Christ can be summed up in one statement: Love your neighbor as yourself (Mt. 22:39; Mk. 12:31; Lk. 10:27). Let us remember this, and God will bless us and forgive all our sins.

St. Luke the Physician of Simferopol

MARTYR AGATHODOROS OF TYANA IN CAPPADOCIA. Agathodoros was from the Cappadocian city of Tyana, present-day Nidra. When he confessed Jesus Christ to be the true God, he was taken to the head of that city. They cruelly inflicted on him one inhumane torture after another. They tore his skin, put him on a hot grid, cut out his tongue, pulled his teeth, skinned him with a razor, broke his legs, pierced his side with a spear, and poured hot metal on his temples. He died from these tortures and received a martyr's crown from heaven.

COMMEMORATIONS: Presentation of Our Lord and Savior Jesus Christ; Anthimos of Chios; Agathodoros of Tyana in Cappadocia; Gabriel at Constantinople; Jordan of Trebizond, at Constantinople; Synaxis of Panagia *Koutsouriotissa* in Erateini of Phocis; Synaxis of Panagia *Ypapanti* in Kalamata; Synaxis of Panagia *Sergena* of Santorini; Synaxis of Panagia *Chrysaliniotissa* in Nicosia of Cyprus; Synaxis of Panagia *Goumenissa* of Kilkis; Synaxis of Panagia *Marouliani* in Oia of Santorini; Synaxis of Panagia *Thalassitra* in Kastro of Milos; Synaxis of Panagia of *Holy Obedience* in Kostos of Paros; Synaxis of Panagia of the *Wicked Bees* in Levadi of Kythera.

Synaxis of St. Symeon the God-Receiver and Holy Prophetess Anna
Strict Fast
Hebrews 9:11-14; Luke 2:25-38

*N*either should we tire ourselves of trying to persuade people with egoism and ill will to come to the knowledge of the truth (despite the fact that they say they are Christians), for within them the truth does not fit.

St. Paisios the Athonite

VIRGIN MARTYR IA OF ST. IVES. Ia was born in the late fifth century and was the sister of St. Erc of Slane and St. Euny of Lelant. Although she was not born a Christian, Ia received baptism from St. Padrig. She wanted to become an anchoress and preach the Gospel in Cornwall, so she made plans to travel there by ship with St. Fingar and St. Piala. However, they left without her. According to St. Ia's hagiographer, she prayed to God for help while on the shore and a leaf floated by her. She poked at it with a stick, but it failed to sink, and instead, it grew, became firmer, and the sides curled up. She climbed atop the leaf, and it carried her across the Irish Sea, arriving before the ship carrying her friends. With the permission of the local prince, Ia set up an anchorage at what is now St. Ives. The prince later sponsored a church nearby. Ia lived in solitude and lived a prayerful life. Through her prayers, a holy well sprang up there for her to draw water. She evangelized the countryside. In the middle of the sixth century, St. Ia and Sts. Fingar and Piala were all beheaded by the wicked Breton Prince Tewdwr.

COMMEMORATIONS: Symeon the God-receiver and Anna the Prophetess; Prophet Azarias; James, Archbishop of Serbia; Nicholas, Enlightener of Japan; Symeon, Bishop of Polotsk and Tver; Ansgar, Bishop of Hamburg; Blaise of Caesarea; Papias, Diodorus, and Claudianus at Perga; Adrian and Eubulus at Caesarea; Savvas of Ioannina; Paul the Syrian; Sviatoslav-Gabriel and Dimitry of Yuriev; Nicholas, Stamatios, and John of Chios; Romanus, Prince of Uglich; New Martyr Alexander, in Russia; Ignatius of Mariupol in Crimea; Ia of St. Ives; Werburga of Chester; Laurence of Canterbury; Vladimir (Zagreba) of Borisoglebsk Monastery.

FEBRUARY 4

2 Timothy 2:11-19; Luke 18:2-8

*M*ay we never risk the life of our souls by being resentful or by bearing grudges.

St. Gregory of Nyssa

NEW VENERABLE MARTYR ANTHONY OF KARYES. Anthony was from an Orthodox family in fifteenth-century western Ukraine. Despite his upbringing, he became an arrogant man, and circumstances led him to commit murder. However, deep feelings of guilt made him realize the seriousness of his crime, and Anthony prayed for repentance. Still, this crime weighed heavily upon his soul, so he entered the Surprasl Monastery in Poland under the obedience of abbot Paphnutios. Anthony exceeded his obligations, yet he felt a greater need to atone for the crime and desired a martyric death. Elder Paphnutios opposed this and sent him to Mount Athos to receive guidance from the holy fathers there, and they also opposed Anthony's wishes. They sent Anthony to live in the cell of St. Sava of Serbia to practice humility and repentance, even directing that he be locked in a tower in hopes he would abandon his desire for martyrdom. But later, news spread throughout Mount Athos of the death of a New Martyr George, which again inflamed Anthony towards martyrdom. He left Mount Athos and went to Thessalonica, to the Church of the Panagia that had been converted to a mosque. Anthony intended to provoke them to murder him. Upon entering the mosque, he fell to his knees and made the sign of the cross. He was arrested, tortured, and imprisoned for ten days without food. The judge tried to persuade Anthony to renounce his Orthodox faith, but he refused. Finding him not guilty, the judge returned him to the commander. After one more opportunity to save himself, St. Anthony was burned to dust in flames.

COMMEMORATIONS: Isidore of Pelusium; Nicholas the Confessor; Abramios of Arbela; Lucius, in Africa; Martyrs Jadorus and Isidore; John of Irenopolis; Martyr Theoktistos; Iasimos, Wonderworker; George of Vladimir; Joseph of Aleppo; Abraham and Coprius of Pechenga; Phileas of Thmuis and Philoromus; Evagrius of Tsikhedidi; Cyril of New Lake; Modan of Stirling; Aldate of Gloucester; Anthony of Karyes.

FEBRUARY 5

*Y*ou do not know what a gift of God is silence and the fact that you do not need any word.

St. John Chrysostom

VENERABLE THEODOSIOS OF SCOPELUS IN CILICIA. When Theodosios heard the gospel reading about the merchant who sold all that he had to buy that one precious pearl, he decided to forego his aristocratic future in search of the Kingdom of Heaven. He found a forest next to the sea, built a shelter, and began his ascetic pursuits. He fasted strictly, slept on the ground, wore a hair shirt, and prayed. He also severely burdened himself by wearing heavy chains and iron about his body to fight his passions and pride. He plowed and planted his crops and fed anybody that passed by. He also wove baskets and mats to sell. Many visited Theodosios to learn about his way of life and to live near him. They made handicrafts to sell, and they grew crops. A dock was built so merchants could sell these products abroad. Theodosios believed that monastics should provide for themselves. When the seawaters were rough, sailors would pray to the God of Theodosios, which would calm the waters. At one time, the Isaurians began ravaging the cities and taking prisoners. However, when they encountered the holy Theodosios, they asked only for his prayers and some food. Once, there was no water in another monastic community that was built below a huge stone. He struck the rock with his staff, and immediately water gushed forth and flowed like a river to the monastery. When St. Theodosios died, the faithful in Antioch discovered the chains with which he had burdened himself.

COMMEMORATIONS: Polyeuctus, Patriarch of Constantinople; Theodosius, Archbishop of Chernigov; Agatha of Palermo; Savvas the New of Sicily; Anthony of Athens; Theodosios of Skopelos; Matushka Agatha, Eugene, and Paramon of Belorussia; Gregory Rosca of Romania; Valeriu Gafencu of Romania; Avitus of Vienne; Martyrs Alexandra and Michael; *In Search of the Perishing, Eletsk-Chernigov,* and *Divnogorsk-Sicilian* Icons of the Mother of God.

St. Photios the Great
Fast-free

FEBRUARY 6

Hebrews 7:26-8:2; John 10:9-16

*T*here is a lot of bitterness in life: failure, illness, poverty, and so on. But if a person believes in God, then the Lord can sweeten a bitter life.

St. Barsanuphius of Optina

ST. VEDAST, BISHOP OF ARRAS. Vedast left his home in the west of France and went to live a holy life hidden from the world in the diocese of Toul. The bishop noticed Vedast and ordained him to the priesthood. While returning from a military victory, Clovis, the King of France, stopped at Toul and asked for a priest to instruct him in Christianity. Vedast was assigned to accompany the king on his way home. They encountered a blind beggar on the road who asked for Vedast's assistance. Vedast prayed and blessed the beggar, and he immediately recovered his sight. This miracle convinced the king to accept his wife's religion, and Vedast became the king's advisor. One day when a nobleman attempted to give Vedast a glass of wine, he found the cask empty. Vedast asked the servant to go back and bring him what little he could coax out of the cask, and the servant saw the barrel overflowing with excellent wine. Vedast was named the first bishop of Arras, France. On the day of Vedast's peaceful death in 539, the locals saw a luminous cloud ascend from his house. Later an abbey was founded in his honor in Arras. St. Vedast was also honored in Belgium and England, and three churches in England were dedicated to him.

COMMEMORATIONS: Barsanuphius the Great and John the Prophet of Palestine; Bucolos, Bishop of Smyrna; Photios the Great, Patriarch of Constantinople; Dorothea of Caesarea, and with her Christina, Callista, and Theophilus; James of Cyrus; Julian of Emesa; Fausta, Evilasius, and Maximus at Cyzicus; Dorothea of Kashin; John of Thebes; Arsenios of Ikaltoi, Georgia; Amand, apostle of Maastricht; Vedast, Bishop of Arras; Mael, Bishop of Ardagh; Basil Nadezhnin of Moscow; Valentina of Minsk.

FEBRUARY 7

*𝒟*o not read rebellious books or pamphlets that mention Church matters if you wish to be calm, since you are not responsible for such serious affairs. You have need of book that will assist you in repentance.

St. Paisios the Athonite

NEW MARTYR GEORGE OF CRETE. George was from nineteenth-century Crete. His father and grandfather were both priests, and although George was not well educated, he learned how to read. While his job was to plant vineyards, his greatest joy was to read the Lives of the Saints, especially the martyrs from the Synaxarion. Every evening he would read until midnight. His prayer was that he might be counted worthy one day to become a martyr. In the year 1866, a revolt occurred in Crete. George took a job as a letter carrier for the revolutionary leaders. One day the Turks surrounded a village of revolutionaries, and George was taken into custody with two others. The two others were cut to pieces, but the military leader knew and had cared about George from their youth and told him to accept their religion to be set free. George responded with the words of Jesus from the Gospel, "Therefore whoever confesses Me before men, him I will also confess before My Father who is in heaven" (Mt. 10:32). George was relentless in his conviction and would not be swayed. He even thanked the executioners, saying that they would be helping him to gain abundant glory and joy. St. George was cut to pieces and finally beheaded. His relics, along with the other two, were never recovered.

COMMEMORATIONS: Parthenios, Bishop of Lampsacus on the Hellespont; Aprionus, Bishop of Cyprus; Augulius, Bishop of Brittany; 1,003 Martyrs of Nicomedia; 6 Martyrs of Phrygia; Mastridia of Jerusalem, woman ascetic of the desert; Luke of Mt. Steirion; Theopemptus and his brotherhood; Peter of Monovatia; Euthymius of Glinsk; George of Crete; Richard, King of Wessex; Ronan, Bishop of Kilmaronen; Barlaam Ryashentsev, Archbishop of Perm; Boniface of Feofania (Kiev).

St. Theodore the Commander
Fast-free

FEBRUARY 8

Ephesians 2:4-10; Matthew 10:16-22

*F*or the Father loves the Son and gives everything into His hand (cp. Jn. 3:35). If only we ourselves loved Him, our heavenly Father, in a truly filial way! The Lord listens equally to the Monk and the simple Christian layman provided that both are Orthodox believers, and both love God from the depth of their souls, and both have faith in Him, if only as a grain of mustard seed; and they both shall move mountains.

St. Seraphim of Sarov

MARTYR COINTHA OF ALEXANDRIA. St. Dionysius, Bishop of Alexandria, wrote a letter to Bishop Fabio of Antioch about the bloodshed of several martyrs in Alexandria, Egypt, under the emperor Decius. He noted that the Christian woman, Cointha, was led into a pagan temple and was forced to worship their god, but she was horrified and resisted. She was tied by the feet to a horse and dragged through the city on rough pavement. Then they slammed her on large stones, scourged her, and returned her to the temple, where she was stoned to death. This account was cited by the ecclesiastical historian Eusebius of Caesarea.

COMMEMORATIONS: Theodore Stratelates the Commander, of Heraclea; Prophet Zechariah of the Twelve Minor Prophets; Sabbas II, Archbishop of Serbia; Cointha of Alexandria; Martha and Mary the sisters, and Lycarion the child Martyr of Egypt; Martyrs Nikephoros and Stephen; Martyrs Philadelphus and Polycarp; Martyr Pergetus; Macarios, Bishop of Paphos; John and Basil of the Kiev Caves; Lyubov of Ryazan, Fool-for-Christ; Cuthman, hermit of Steyning; Kew, virgin of Cornwall; Agathangelus, Bishop of Damascus.

Fast-free

FEBRUARY 9

1 John 1:8-2:6; Mark 13:31-14:2

*T*here is no greater blessing for man than when God calls him to the monastic dwelling. And let the monk never for a second forget that God Himself called him.

† *Elder Joseph of Vatopedi*

VENERABLE ROMANOS THE WONDERWORKER OF CILICIA. Romanos was from Cilicia in Asia Minor. He lived in a small cell at the foot of a mountain outside the city walls of Antioch, where he found silence and solitude. His ascetic struggles were both to purify his soul and to mortify his flesh. To this end, his sustenance was bread and salt, and a little water. He even lived without fire or a lamp for light. Romanos wore a rough hair-shirt, and his hair grew down to his feet. He wore chains wrapped around his body. Through all of these struggles, Romanos received the gift to heal the sick and barren women. He modeled himself after Moses and King David, who were known for their humility, and Jacob, a simple, unaffected man. Pilgrims would go to the sweet and gentle-mannered Romanos for spiritual guidance and to be cured of their illnesses. His emaciated appearance alone would inspire veneration. St. Romanos died peacefully.

COMMEMORATIONS: Nicephoros of Antioch; Peter, Bishop of Damascus; Marcellus, Philagrius, and Pancratius, disciples of Apostle Peter; Aemilianus and Bracchio of Tours; Romanos the Wonderworker of Cilicia; Apollonia of Alexandria; Pancratius of the Kiev Caves; Gennadius and Nicephorus of Vazhe Lake (Vologda); Teilo, Bishop in Wales; Alexander and Ammon at Soli of Cyprus; Uncovering of the relics of St. Innocent of Irkutsk; Uncovering of the relics of St. Tikhon, Patriarch of Moscow and All Russia.

St. Haralambos the Hieromartyr
Fast-free

2 Timothy 2:1-10; John 15:17-16:2

There is no one, nor has there ever been, nor will there ever be anyone on the earth who is blameless, without fault, and without stain. No one can boast that he has preserved his heart clean and unblemished. Nonetheless, God's compassion is so effective, this medication is so powerful and potent that it wipes out everything. It makes wondrous interventions, performs unbelievable operations, and saves man's soul from certain death.

† *Elder Ephraim of Arizona*

ST. LONGINUS OF KORYAZHEMSK. Longinus at first lived in several monasteries until he settled with his fellow ascetic Simon. Deep in the countryside near Vychegda in northwestern Russia, they built cells and a chapel. When the fame of Longinus began to spread, brethren gathered around him. They built a church dedicated to St. Nicholas, and this became known as the Koryazhemsk Monastery, and Longinus was their abbot. Nearby the saint dug out a well himself. St. Longinus died peacefully in the year 1540 and was buried near the entrance to the church. Sixteen years later, he was moved inside the church.

COMMEMORATIONS: Haralambos, Bishop of Magnesia, and Porphyrios and Baptos; Anastasius II, Archbishop of Jerusalem; Anatole, Metropolitan of Odessa; Zeno of Caesarea; Prochoros the Orach-eater of the Kiev Caves; Ennatha, Valentina, and Paula of Palestine; John Chimchimeli of Bachkovo; Scholastica of Italy, sister of St. Benedict; Anna of Novgorod, wife of Yaroslav I; Longinus of Vologda; Raphael and Ioannicius of Svatogorsk; Merwinna, abbess of Romsey; Synaxis of Novgorod Hierarchs: Joachim, Luke the Jew, Germanus, Arcadius, Gregory, Martyrius, Anthony, Basil, Moses, Symeon, Gennadius, Pimen, and Athonius; Commemoration of the Deliverance of Zakynthos from the Plague by St. Haralambos; *Areovindus* Icon of the Mother of God.

St. Blaise of Sebaste
Fast-free

Hebrews 4:14-5:6
Matthew 10:1, 5-8

The spiritually advanced person is the one who arrives at a place of
no identity and who has understood in his depths that whatever
happens is the will of God or by the permission of God.

† *Gerontissa Gavrilia of Leros*

NEW MARTYR GEORGE OF KRATOVO. George was an eighteen-
year-old goldsmith in sixteenth-century Kratovo, Serbia. He moved to the
town of Sophia to escape the envy of Turkish jewelers. His craft flourished
there, and George caught the eye of a Turkish magistrate's daughter. He was
offered her hand in marriage, but George would not renounce his Orthodox
faith. Therefore, he was tried for treason and condemned. He was offered
the court's mercy if he would deny Christ, but when Romanos refused, he
was thrown into a burning fire and gave up his soul. However, the flames
did not burn his body. The mob that was gathered there wanted the fire to
totally consume the martyr's body, so the magistrate had an enormous fire
built. They threw in animal carcasses to make it difficult for the Christians
to distinguish whether the bones belonged to Romanos or the animals.
Finally, when they saw George's body still intact and sound, they decided to
let him burn for a whole day. By night, a Christian secretly took the body
of St. Romanos to a church, and the priest buried him.

COMMEMORATIONS: Blaise, Bishop of Sebaste; Theodora the
Empress, protectress of Orthodoxy; Lucius of Adrianople in Thrace; George
of Kratovo, at Sofia; Demetrius of Priluki Monastery; Vsevolod (Gabriel),
Prince of Pskov; Gobnait of Ireland; Caedmon of Whitby; Benedict of
Aniane; Gregory of Sinai; Finding of the relics of Prophet Zacharias, father
of St. John the Baptist; *Corfu* Icon of the Mother of God.

Sunday of the Prodigal Son
Fast-free

FEBRUARY 12

1 Corinthians 6:12-20
Luke 15:11-32

There is no possession more precious than prayer in the whole of human life. Never be parted from it; never abandon it. But, as our Lord said, let us pray that our toil may not be for nothing, 'When you stand in prayer, forgive if you have anything against anyone, that your heavenly Father may forgive you your faults.'

St. Ephraim the Syrian

ST. BASSIAN OF UGLICH. Bassian was descended from the lineage of prince St. Theodore of Smolensk. In 1473 he became a monk at the Protection Monastery as a disciple of St. Paisius of Uglich, when he was thirty-three years old. Bassian became known for his great abstinence and willing obedience. After twenty years, he asked Paisius for a blessing to go into the wilderness to live as a hermit. Paisius blessed him to go and said that he would soon form his own monastery. He moved to a solitary place thirty versts south of Uglich, but pilgrims soon learned about him and came to him for spiritual counsels. Bassian built a wooden church, and those who desired to live the monastic life went there to be guided by him. After seventeen years, Bassian died peacefully. Shortly afterward, miracles of healing began to occur at his gravesite. Thirty-nine years after his death, in 1548, the incorrupt relics of St. Bassian were unearthed, and a stone crypt was built over them.

COMMEMORATIONS: Meletios of Antioch; Anthony II Kauleas of Constantinople; Anthony III the Studite; Alexis, Metropolitan of Moscow; Meletius, Archbishop of Kharkov; Mary, called Marinos, and her father Eugene; Alexius, Bishop of Voronezh; Martyrs Plotinus and Saturninus; Bassian of Uglich; Nikoloz Dvali, Prochorus the Georgian, Luke of Jerusalem, and the Holy Fathers of the Georgian monasteries in Jerusalem; Chrestos at Constantinople; Meletios of Ypseni, Rhodes; Urbanus of Rome; Ethilwald of Lindisfarne; Gertrude of Nijvel; Callia of Serbia; Appearance of the *Iveron* Icon of the Mother of God (Mt. Athos); (2nd Sunday of February: 383 God-bearing Fathers of the Eighth Ecumenical Synod in 879–880).

February 13

Try to know yourself and your wickedness. Do not think about the sin of your brother, but about what in him is better than yourself.

St. Tikhon of Zadonsk

ST. GEORGE, ARCHBISHOP OF MOGILEV. Throughout his life, George was prolific in his achievements for Orthodoxy. In early eighteenth-century Ukraine, he attended the Kiev Theological Academy, where he perfectly mastered Latin, Polish, Greek, Hebrew, and German. George became a monk at the Kiev Caves Lavra and a teacher at the Kiev Theological Seminary. He wrote an instruction "On the Order of Teaching Subjects in All Classes" and became a professor of theology. George was made the Archbishop of Mogilev, which marked the revival of ecclesiastical life there. A printing house was established, and many Orthodox works were published. He defended the right to education for all, opening schools in many areas. He replenished the clergy and constructed a cathedral, seminary, and several churches. He was a proponent of social equality and openly denounced many other religions and nefarious organizations that he believed opposed Orthodoxy. George also became a member of the mixed court for the resolution of religious disputes. He compiled a manual on many Orthodox subjects, including the duties of parish presbyters. He advocated for the mass return of the Uniates, and over 112,000 people returned to the Orthodox Church. George also collected a rich library and opened hospitals, hospices, and almshouses. He distributed money every Saturday to paupers, widows, and orphans. St. George died peacefully and was buried in the Transfiguration Cathedral in Mogilev. Eighty years later, his relics were uncovered and found preserved.

COMMEMORATIONS: Eulogios I, Patriarch of Alexandria; Martinian of Caesarea; Aquila and Priscilla, of the Seventy; Symeon the Myrrhgusher; Zoe of Bethlehem and Photina; Joseph of Volokolamsk; father and son, crucified; Timothy of Alexandria; George of Mogilev; Modomnoc of Ossory; Castor of Karden; Huna of Huneya; Ermenhilda of Ely; Seraphim of Bogucharsk; Silvester of Omsk; Translation of the relics of St. Edward, King of England.

FEBRUARY 14

1 John 3:9-22; Mark 14:10-42

*J*oy, radiant joy, streams from the face of him who gives and kindles joy in the heart of him who receives.

St. Seraphim of Sarov

ST. CYRIL, EQUAL-TO-THE-APOSTLES, TEACHER OF THE SLAVS. Cyril was a Slav from ninth-century Thessalonica, and from the age of fourteen, he was raised together with the emperor's son. He was very well educated and became a priest and a professor of philosophy in Constantinople. He would successfully debate with the iconoclasts and with Moslems. Cyril and his brother Methodios, a monk of Mount Olympos, were sent by Emperor Michael to preach Christianity to the Khozars. The prince of the Khozars was persuaded by their preaching, and all his people accepted Christianity. The prince wanted to reward the brothers with rich presents, but they refused and instead asked for the release of all the Greek captives. Cyril and Methodios returned to Constantinople with 200 prisoners that had been set free. Then prince Rostislav sent Cyril and Methodios to Moravia to preach Christianity in the Slavic language. They compiled a Slavonic alphabet, then translated to Slavonic the Gospels, Epistles, the Psalter, and many Divine service books. Finally, the brothers were invited to Rome by the pope, and with them, they brought the relics of St. Clement, which they had discovered in Cherson. Cyril soon became ill. Shortly before his death at the age of forty-two, he received the rank of schemamonk. St. Cyril's relics were buried in the Roman church of St. Clement, which also houses the relics of St. Clement.

COMMEMORATIONS: Auxentios of Bithynia; Cyril, Equal-to-the-Apostles and teacher of the Slavs; Peter, Patriarch of Alexandria; Abraham, Bishop of Charres; Philemon, Bishop of Gaza; Theodore of Chernigov; Maron of Cyrus, Syria; George Paizan the Tailor of Mytilene; Nicholas of Corinth; Hilarion the Georgian; Isaac of the Kiev Caves; Damian the New of Philotheou and Kissavos, at Larissa; Onisimus, Bishop of Tula; 12 Greek Master-builders of the Dormition Cathedral in the Kiev Caves.

FEBRUARY 15

Philemon 1:1-25; Mark 14:43-15:1

*E*xpect Satan's attack when you pray.

St. John Chrysostom

REPOSE OF MONK MARCU DUMITRESCU OF SIHASTRIA, ROMANIA. Marcu endured imprisonment, torture, and continuous hardship as a political prisoner beginning in 1939 in Romania. The soles of his feet were struck with iron bars, his hands and legs were bound, and he had been stabbed all over with knives. Yet, he endured everything without a sound or denouncing anyone, and this astonished his persecutors. During his time in prison, Marcu had a vision that he was holding on to a barbed-wire fence, about to lose his grip, when someone dressed as a monk grabbed his hand and pulled him out towards the light, and the monk was Christ Himself. Marcu spent his time in hesychastic prayer and practicing the virtues in the Gospel. He was nicknamed the "Man of God." He was finally released in 1956, and when he decided to become a monk, he received guidance at the Slatina Monastery. He was arrested again in 1960, and then in 1964, he joined the Sihastria Monastery, where he received monastic tonsure. Father Cleopa, his instructor in monasticism, said about Marcu, "Whenever something miraculous occurred, it was probably the result of his prayers!" Late in life, Marcu would tell his disciples that he could not have made it through twenty years of torture if not for God's grace helping him. He said only God's mercy kept him alive, and he did not fear anyone but himself.

COMMEMORATIONS: Apostle Onesimos of the Seventy; Anthimos of Chios; Major of Gaza; Oswy, King of Northumbria; Eusebios of Syria; Paphnutius of the Kiev Caves; Dalmatus, abbot in Siberia; New Hieromartyrs Michael Piataev and John Kumin, priests; Priests Nicholas, Alexis, Alexis, and Simeon the deacon; Paul (Kozlov) of St. Nilus Hermitage (Tver) and Virgin Martyr Sophia; Theognius, Bishop of Bethelia; Sigfrid of Sweden; Repose of Marcu Dumitrescu of Sihastria, Romania; Synaxis of St. John the Theologian at Diaconissa; *Vilensk* and *Dalmatian* Icons of the Mother of God.

FEBRUARY 16

1 John 4:20-5:21; Mark 15:1-15

Every time that we sin, we are born of the devil. But every time that we do good, we are born of God.

St. John Chrysostom

SYNAXIS OF PANAGIA PLIKATIOTISSA. The miraculous icon "Panagia Plikatiotissa" was found near Epirus, Greece, in 1770. Every night shepherds saw a bright light in a nearby forest. They searched the place carefully until they were exhausted, but the forest was dense. Finally, they found the icon under a tree. The shepherds venerated the Panagia and took the icon to their camp. From there, they let the Panagia decide where she wanted to go. They placed her icon on a lame horse and set it free. When the horse arrived in the village of Plikati, it no longer was limping. The priest and all the villagers greeted the icon and, in procession, took it to the village church. But the priest observed that the icon would move by itself from its shrine to the church entrance. One Sunday after Divine Liturgy, the miraculous icon rose from the shrine and rested on the priest's shoulder. Led by the icon, the priest reached the middle of the village, by the ruins of an old church, and the icon came down from his shoulder. A church was later built there in the name of the Dormition of the Theotokos. After showing the place for her church, the icon rose again onto the priest's shoulder and again guided the procession far outside the village, and it came down again and stood on a rock, where a chapel was built in honor of the Nativity of the Theotokos. Then the icon was taken back to the church where it has since been housed. Other times during the procession of the icon, the people without sins found it light, and those who had sins felt the icon very heavy. The icon has also solved many droughts.

COMMEMORATIONS: Pamphilus, Paul, Valens, Seleucus, Porphyrius, Julian, Theodoulos, Elias, Jeremiah, Isaiah, Samuel, and Daniel, at Caesarea; Flavian of Constantinople; Maruthas of Martyropolis; Macarius (Nevsky) of Moscow; Flavian the Hermit; Romanus of Karpenesion; Basil of Pavlovo-Posadsky; Mary the New of Byzia; Persian Martyrs under Shapur; Synaxis of the *Panagia Plikatiotissa* Icon of the Mother of God.

FEBRUARY 17

St. Theodore the Tyro
Abstain from meat and
dairy products, and fish.
2 Timothy 2:1-10
Luke 20:46-21:4

If you cannot labour with your body, at least make efforts in your mind. If you cannot fast for two days, fast at least till evening. If you cannot fast till evening, be careful not to overeat. If you are not a peacemaker, at least do not be addicted to strife. If you cannot close the mouth of a man who is judging his brother, at least refrain from joining him in this.

† *St. Isaac the Syrian*

GREAT MARTYR THEODORE THE TYRO. Theodore was a Roman soldier in the city of Alasium, in Asia Minor. He became a Christian at twenty-three years of age. He fought with an elite group under Emperor Maximian known as the Terian Legion. Following a victory in battle, his legion was to be honored at the pagan temple. They commanded Theodore to offer sacrifice to idols, but he firmly confessed his faith in Christ. Then he set fire to the temple and was taken to prison to starve to death. Jesus appeared to him there, comforting and encouraging him. He fearlessly confessed his faith again when he was brought before the governor. They subjected him to more torments and condemned him to perish in fire. Theodore climbed onto the bonfire, and with prayer, he gave up his spirit. But his body was unharmed by the flames. St. Theodore was buried in the city of Eukhaitakheia about the year 306.

COMMEMORATIONS: Theodore the Tyro; Mariamne, sister of Apostle Philip; Hermogenes, Patriarch of Moscow; Emperor Marcian and Pulcheria; Auxibios, Bishop of Soli; Theodosius the Bulgarian, and Romanus of Turnovo; Theodore the Silent of the Kiev Caves; Righteous Theosterictus; Theodore of Byzantium; Barnabas of Gethsemane Skete; Theodore of Atjara; Finan of Lindisfarne; Uncovering of the relics of St. Menas the Melodius; Panagia *Dakrirooussa* of the Prophet Elias Skete at Mount Athos; Weeping *Tikhvin* Icon of the Mother of God.

FEBRUARY 18

*T*he Fathers tell us, the souls of the dead remember everything that happened here—thoughts, words, desires—and nothing can be forgotten... If a man helped someone or was helped by someone else, this is remembered as is the persons concerned, or if he injured someone, or was injured by someone, all this is remembered. In fact, the soul loses nothing that it did in this world but remembers everything at its exit from this body more clearly and distinctly once freed from the earthliness of the body ... Whatever is in a man here is going to leave the earth with him, and is going to be with him there.

St. Dorotheos of Gaza

COMMEMORATION OF THE EVENT "GOOD FRIDAY OF RUSSIAN MONASTICISM." One night in 1932, from February 17-18, hundreds of monks and nuns were arrested, imprisoned, and sent into exile. These were from monasteries in the northwestern region of Russia. The arrests continued, and on April 17 and 18, 200 more were arrested. A Russian writer wrote that unnoticed by anyone and now almost unknown to anyone, all of Russian monasticism disappeared to the camps overnight. These were all sent to the Kazakh Territory, which today is officially the Republic of Kazakhstan.

COMMEMORATIONS: Leo the Great, Pope of Rome; Leo and Parigorius of Patara; Nicholas the Catholicos of Georgia; Agapitus, Bishop of Synnada, and Martyrs Victor, Dorotheus, Theodulus, and Agrippa; Blaise of Mt. Athos; Martyr Piulius; Agapetus, Archbishop of Ekaterinoslav; Kosmas of Yakhrom; Colman, Bishop of Lindisfarne; Commemoration of the New Martyrs who suffered during the "Holy Night" in St. Petersburg.

FEBRUARY 19

The root of almsgiving is found in the heart. It starts from the heart and ends in our hand!

† *Elder Ephraim of Arizona*

VENERABLE THEODORE OF SANAXAR MONASTERY. Theodore was persecuted his entire life. As a young man, he enlisted in the Guard Regiment in eighteenth-century St. Petersburg, attaining the rank of sergeant. One day his friend collapsed and died at a drinking party, and Theodore left that city and the guard without permission to live a life dedicated to God in the wilderness. He labored there for three years in great hardship, but the government did not allow monks to live in the wilderness, so he was found and beaten by the villagers. He then sought out a monastery near Kiev but was sent again by the abbot to live in the wilderness. He was found again and sent to Empress Elizabeth in St. Petersburg, charged with desertion. When Theodore explained that he left to save his soul, she pardoned him under the condition that he stay in that city and be tonsured at St. Alexander Nevsky Lavra. Many people went to Theodore for spiritual counsel, but the other monks became jealous and attempted unsuccessfully to stop him. After ten years, Theodore and his disciples moved to the Sanaxar Hermitage, where he was ordained to the priesthood and named the abbot. Because of false accusations of being a troublemaker, he was sent into exile for nine years by a royal edict. Upon his return, he was accused of being a heretic and an atheist, but his accuser was found to be at fault. Yet again, because of jealousy, Theodore was not permitted to receive visitors, so his disciples could only seek advice through letters. St. Theodore died peacefully after a short illness.

COMMEMORATIONS: Philemon and Archippus of the Seventy and Apphia; Theodore of Sanaxar; Eugene and Macarius, at Antioch; Philothea the Athenian; Maximos, Theodotos, Hesychios, and Asklepiodota of Adrianopolis; Nicetas of Epirus; Dositheus of Gaza; Rabulas of Samosata; Conon in Palestine; Mesrop the Translator; Vladimir of Zosima; (3rd Sunday of February: Corinthian co-workers of the Apostle Paul–Titius, Justus, Chloe, and Crispus).

FEBRUARY 20

3 John 1:1-15
Luke 19:29-40, 22:7-39

*N*othing external can influence the blessed state found within the virtuous Christian. This is why they who are barren of virtue and deprived of God's grace, they who do not sense this blessedness within their hearts, but seek it outside of themselves, resemble people who chase after their own shadows.

St. Nektarios of Pentapolis

ST. ELEUTHERIUS, BISHOP OF TOURNAI. Eleutherius was consecrated Bishop of Tournai in 486. The early years of his episcopate were difficult. Rome had fallen and the pagan barbarian invasions had begun, and they established their own capital in Tournai, which forced the bishop to move. But Eleutherius' mission was to convert the pagan Franks and defend the faith against heretics who had wormed their way into Christian communities. Finally, after ten years, Eleutherius baptized King Clovis, and then many pagans were baptized. Once, a young girl fell in love with the bishop, but he would not have anything to do with her. She fell ill and then passed into a coma. Eleutherius told her father, the governor, that he would heal her if he promised to become a Christian. When she was cured, her father reneged, and it is said that the bishop brought a plague upon the land, which soon caused the father to repent and believe. In 520, Eleutherius assembled a synod to condemn the heresies of Arianism and Pelagianism. The Arians claimed that Jesus was not God, and they opposed the Holy Trinity. Pelagianism stressed the goodness of human nature and the freedom of human will and denied original sin and the importance of infant baptism. St. Eleutherius was beaten to death by a group of Arians in 531.

COMMEMORATIONS: Bessarion the Great of Egypt; Agatho of Rome; Sadoc of Persia, and 128 Martyrs; Eleutherius, in Byzantium; Leo of Catania; Cindeus of Pisidia; Cornelius of Pskov Caves, and Bassian of Murom; Righteous Plotinus; Agatho of the Kiev Caves; Yaroslav the Wise, Great Prince of Kiev; Macarius and 34 monks and novices of Valaam Monastery; Eucherius, Bishop of Orleans; Eleutherius, Bishop of Tournai; Bolcan, Bishop of Derkan.

FEBRUARY 21

Jude 1:1-10
Luke 22:39-42, 45-71 23:1

*W*hen you desire to pursue some beautiful work for the love of
God, put death as the limit of your desire.

St. Isaac the Syrian

VENERABLE GEORGE, BISHOP OF AMASTRIS. George was born
to illustrious and pious parents near the city of Amastris, close to the Black
Sea. For the longest time, his parents were childless, but with fasting and
prayers, God gave them George. His goodness amazed everyone who knew
him, and his reputation spread. Later he studied for the priesthood, and a
great crowd attended his ordination. He then decided to leave the world
and withdrew to a mountain in Syria, where he met an old hermit who
trained him. As the hermit approached death, he told George to go live at
the monastery in Bonissa, where he was warmly received and soon became
distinguished. After the death of the bishop of Amastris, George was chosen
by the clergy and the people. When he refused to go, he was taken by force
to Patriarch Tarasius, who had high regard for George because of a prior
charitable act. George was a defender of widows and orphans, fed the poor,
and instructed his flock. He was an example of a God-pleasing life. On one
occasion, when Amastridea was under threat of attack by the Saracens, the
people outside the city walls refused to come inside. But George persuaded
each family to enter the city walls, and when the attacks came, they proved
fruitless by the power of St. George's prayers.

COMMEMORATIONS: Timothy of Symbola on Mt. Olympus in
Bithynia; John the Scholastic, Patriarch of Constantinople; Eustathius,
Archbishop of Antioch; Zacharias, Patriarch of Jerusalem; George, Bishop
of Amastris; Severian, Bishop of Scythopolis; Macarius of Glinsk Hermitage; *Cucuzelis* and *Kozelshchansk* Icons of the Mother of God.

FEBRUARY 22

You must nourish the soul with the word of God, for the word of God is the 'bread of angels'. The soul must be fed who passionately love God.

St. Seraphim of Sarov

VENERABLE ATHANASIUS THE CONFESSOR OF CONSTANTINOPLE. Athanasius was from an affluent and pious family in ninth-century Constantinople. From his youth, he desired a monastic life. He went to Nicomedia of Bithynia, where the bishop had built a poorhouse and a monastery named after Saints Peter and Paul, and here he received monastic tonsure. Athanasius became an exemplary monk in his practice of the virtues, and his fame spread. In the early ninth century, Leo the Armenian propagated Iconoclasm, which forbade the veneration of icons. Athanasius would suffer much because of his steadfast defense of the holy icons. Leo had Athanasius arrested and flogged several times, and he suffered many deprivations. He was also jailed and exiled, but he faced every retribution manfully. Together with Theodore the Studite and John of Kathara Monastery, Athanasius never stopped writing letters defending the veneration of the icons. When Emperor Michael II succeeded Leo, he stopped this persecution, but he still prohibited public discussion of the issue. Yet, St. Athanasius never abated his public and private efforts in their defense. He died peacefully.

COMMEMORATIONS: Thallasios, Limnaios, and Baradates of Syria; Telesphorus, Pope of Rome; Athanasius the Confessor of Constantinople; Titus, Bishop of Bostra in Arabia; Maurice and his son Photinos, and Martyrs Theodore, Philip, and 70 soldiers; Anthusa and 12 handmaidens; Holy Nine Children of Kola; Maximianus of Ravenna; Martyr Synetus; Theoktista of Voronezh; Peter the Stylite of Mt. Athos; Babylas and Comnita of Nicosa; Leontius of Lycia; Abilius, Patriarch of Alexandria; Papius of Hieropolis; Michael Lisitsyn of Ust-Labinskaya; Herman of Stolobny Monastery; Blaise, bishop; Finding of the relics of the Holy Martyrs of Eugenios at Constantinople.

FEBRUARY 23

1 Jude 1:11-25
Luke 23:1-31, 33, 44-56

*T*ry to fill your soul with Christ so as not to have it empty. Your soul is like a cistern full of water. If you channel the water to the flowers, that is, the virtues, you will experience true joy and all the thorns of evil will wither away. But if you channel the water to the weeds, these will grow and choke you and all the flowers will wither.

St. Porphyrios of Kavsokalyvia

NEW MARTYR PAUL KUSHNIKOV. Paul was born in Russia in 1880 and was ordained to the priesthood at the age of thirty-three. He served in the Novgorod Governorate for five years. During the First World War and revolution, he cared for the people, organizing a parish shop to distribute food to the parishioners. In 1917 some of his parishioners denounced him to the authorities. He was charged with advocating disobedience to the new government but was released. The following year he was arrested again and accused of concealing weapons for the white guards. Though they found nothing, he was taken to a local swamp and shot to death. Paul was added to the Synaxis of New Martyrs and Confessors and is commemorated on the day of his martyrdom.

COMMEMORATIONS: Polycarp, Bishop of Smyrna; Gorgonia, sister of Gregory the Theologian; John, Antioch, Antoninos, Zevinos, and Polychronios, Moses, and Damian of Syria; Alexander, founder of the Monastery of the Unsleeping Ones; John Theristes (the Harvester) of Stylos in Calabria; Damian of Esphigmenou, Mt. Athos; Polycarp of Briansk; Moses of White Lake; Michael Edlinsky of Kiev; Lazarus of the Peloponnese; Seraphim (Zenobius) of Tetritskaro; Milburga of Much Wenlock; Nazarius of Valaam Monastery; Martyr Clement; Martyr Thea; Sergius Bukashkin of Novo-Alexandrovka; Antipas Kyrillov of Tatarintsevo; Philaret Pryakhin of Trubino; New Martyr Paul Kushnikov.

First & Second Finding of the Precious Head of St. John the Baptist

Abstain from meat products.

FEBRUARY 24

2 Corinthians 4:6-15
Matthew 6:14-21

*H*umility, even without works, gains forgiveness for many offences; but without her works are of no profit to us, and rather prepare for us great evils.

St. Isaac the Syrian

UNCOVERING OF THE RELICS OF ST. ROMANUS, PRINCE OF UGLICH. Romanus was the son of Prince Vladimir in thirteenth-century Uglich. He was twenty-three years old when the Mongol hordes swept into Russia. Together with his father and brother, Romanus left for Novgorod. After three years, the Tatars left Russia, and the family returned to Uglich. Upon the death of his father and brother, Romanus assumed leadership. He used a large portion of his inheritance to build charity and reception houses for strangers. He built fifteen places of worship in various parts of his kingdom. Romanus listened to the services every day, often talked with the God-fearing monks, and read the works of the Church Fathers. After the death of his wife, Romanus devoted himself wholly to fasting, prayer, and charity. When he died in 1285, he was buried in the Church of the Transfiguration in Uglich. Two hundred years later, his relics were uncovered and found incorrupt. In 1605, the relics of St. Romanus began to work wonders. Only four years after this, the Poles burned the relics and the church where they were housed. His ashes were hidden in the Cathedral Temple of the Transfiguration, in the chapel named after him.

COMMEMORATIONS: First and Second findings of the Venerable Head of St. John the Baptist; Erasmus of the Kiev Caves; Montanus, Lucias, Julian, Victoricus, Flavian, and companions at Carthage; Cummain Ailbe, abbot of Iona; Uncovering of the relics of St. Romanus, Prince of Uglich.

FEBRUARY 25

Galatians 5:22-6:2
Matthew 6:1-13

*T*he mercy of God is limitless. It is immeasurably greater than an infinite ocean. It is in this divine mercy that one can easily drown all his mortal sins if he repents with all his heart.

St. Luke the Physician of Simferopol

ST. THEODORE, THE FOOL-FOR-CHRIST. A biography of St. Theodore's life was found in his hand upon his death. Once, Theodore went to church and heard the Gospel reading to "take up one's cross." He immediately went and cut down two trees and tied them together in the form of a cross. Taking the cross on his shoulders, he set out to find the kingdom of heaven. Theodore met a monk along the way who "noticed that this man was insane and crazy" and sent him to Mount Athos. When Theodore arrived there, at the Hilander Monastery, he asked if it was far to heaven. The abbot told him it was not far and gave him work sweeping the church. While sweeping, he marveled at the person on the cross and asked the abbot why he was nailed to wood? The story continues that Christ descended to the holy fool who shared his meal with Him, and Christ promised to take Theodore to His Father. When the abbot repeatedly asks Theodore about the voices he heard at night coming from the locked church, Theodore eventually confessed that he feeds the One on the cross. The abbot asked Theodore to put in a good word for him to Christ, and when he did, Jesus told him that the abbot was not worthy. However, Theodore implored Christ, and He agreed to take the abbot with him. The story ends with Theodore and the abbot dying at the same time.

COMMEMORATIONS: Tarasios, Archbishop of Constantinople; Reginos, Bishop of Skopelos; Alexander at Drizipara of Thrace; Theodore, Fool-for-Christ; Erasmus and Paphnutius of Kephala; Marcellus, Bishop of Apamea in Syria; Martyr Anthony; Martyrs Alexander and Hypatius at Marcianopolis; Walburga, abbess of Heidenheim; Ethelbert, King of Kent; Venerable Polycarp; Leo Korobczuk of Laskov.

SUNDAY

FEBRUARY 26

Forgiveness Sunday
Cheesefare Sunday
Abstain from meat products.
Romans 13:11-14:4
Matthew 6:14-21

*I*f you have anything against any man, forgive it: you come here
to receive forgiveness of sins, and thou also must forgive him that
has sinned against you.

St. Cyril of Jerusalem

VENERABLE PORPHYRIOS, BISHOP OF GAZA. At twelve years of
age, Porphyrios set off for Egypt, where he pursued asceticism under the
guidance of St. Macarius the Great. When Blessed Jerome was visiting the
Egyptian monasteries, Porphyrios decided to go with him to Jerusalem to
visit the holy places. He then settled in the Jordanian wilderness but soon
became ill. He returned to Jerusalem for healing, and lying at the foot of
Golgotha, Porphyrios beheld a vision of Jesus Christ with the words, "Take
this Wood and preserve it." The Patriarch of Jerusalem soon ordained Porphyrios to the priesthood and appointed him the curator of the Venerable
Wood of the Cross of the Lord. Later, Porphyrios was elevated to the seat
of Bishop of Gaza. Through his prayers, he worked many miracles and
brought more unbelievers to the knowledge of God. When he saw the
injustice those in his diocese suffered at the hands of idol-worshippers and
heretics, he went for help from the patriarch, St. John Chrysostom. John
led Porphyrios to Empress Eudoxia, and she approached the king. The king
anticipated difficulties in unseating the heretic masters of Gaza, but the
queen convinced him that it would be harder to turn down the request of
this bishop. The king agreed, and he ordered the pagan temples in Gaza to
be destroyed and returned privileges to the Christians. He gave a large sum
of money to Porphyrios to build a church where the main pagan temple
had stood. St. Porphyrios worked in this capacity for almost twenty-five
years. He reposed in old age.

COMMEMORATIONS: Porphyrios of Gaza; Photini the Samaritan
Woman, and Anatola, Phota, Photis and others; John Calphas at Con-
stantinople; Martyr Theoclitas, with St. Photina; Sebastian of Poshekhonye;
John of Rylsk; Synaxis of the Venerable Fathers of the Kiev Caves Lavra;
Mezhetsk Icon of the Mother of God.

Clean Monday—Great Lent Begins
Strict Fast

FEBRUARY 27

Isaiah 1:20-20; Genesis 1:1-13
Proverbs 1:1-10

*L*et us now strive more, my children, and the benefits will be great. No one finds Grace without toil… When our fasting coexists, is strengthened and is encompassed with prayer, with contemplation, with watchfulness, with church attendance, with Confession, with Holy Communion, with good works and charity giving, then is fulfilled the beauty of the soul's preparation for the reception of Holy Week. Then we will feel the Holy and Honorable Passion of Christ more profoundly, because our hearts will soften, and they will alter and recognize how boundless the love of God is for man. Then the Holy Resurrection will be alive within us with great strength, we will feast in a divinely-fitting manner and celebrate together with the angels the Holy Pascha.

† *Elder Ephraim of Arizona*

VENERABLE ASCLEPIUS AND JAMES, HERMITS OF SYRIA. The ascetics Ascelpius and James lived separately in the wilds of fourth-century Syria. Asclepius showed kindness, love, and hospitality to everyone. He ate and dressed modestly, lived in extreme poverty, and refused to own anything. He was known to communicate with God regardless of whether he was alone or with a crowd. James lived utterly alone in a cell and saw no one. When pilgrims came to him for spiritual advice, he would talk to them through a hole in the dirt floor that he dug out at the edge of his cell. He never used fire or lamplight in his cell, and he lived in this manner until well over ninety years of age. James allowed his biographer Theodoretos to visit him twice, having dug the hole in his floor larger to allow him entry.

COMMEMORATIONS: Prokopios the Confessor; Julian, Chroniun and Besas at Alexandria; Asclepius and James of Syria; Gelasius the Actor; Stephen of Constantinople; Thalaleos of Syria; Timothy of Caesarea; Pitirim of Tambov; Martyr Nesius; Titus of the Kiev Caves; Elias of Trebizond; Ephraim of Katounakia; Titus of the Kiev Caves, presbyter; Raphael, Bishop of Brooklyn; Macarius, Bishop of Jerusalem; Herefrith, Bishop of Lincolnshire; Leander of Seville.

FEBRUARY 28

Isaiah 1:19-2:3; Genesis 1:14-23
Proverbs 1:20-33

*Ou*r profit from scriptural reading in no way equals the damage we cause ourselves by showing contempt for a brother. We must practice fasting, vigils, withdrawal, and the meditation of Scripture as activities which are subordinate to our main objective, purity of heart, that is to say, love, and we must never disturb this principal virtue for the sake of those others. If this virtue remains whole and unharmed within us nothing can injure us, not even if we are forced to omit any of those other subordinate virtues. Nor will it be of any use to have practiced all these latter if there is missing in us that principal objective for the sake of which all else is undertaken.

St. John Cassian

VENERABLE JOHN CASSIAN THE ROMAN. John was born in Rome to wealthy parents during the fifth century. After a secular education, he studied only the Gospel. He left home in pursuit of better teachers and found them in the desert of Nitria, Egypt, and later in Constantinople in the person of St. John Chrysostom. St. John ordained him a deacon. He returned to Marseilles and established a convent and monastery. John wrote many books for the direction of monks, including "Remedies for the Eight Principal Faults." He noted that those who are given to anger are also easily given to lust. At the request of Pope Leo, St. John also wrote his final work, "Against Nestorius."

COMMEMORATIONS: Proterios, Patriarch of Alexandria, and six companions; Apostles Nymphas and Eubulus; Nestor in Pamphylia; Barsus, Bishop of Damascus; Basil the Confessor; Marana, Kyra, and Domnica of Syria; Kyranna of Thessalonica; Sergius, priest; Martyr Avrikios; Romanus of Condat in Gaul; Arsenius of Rostov; Nicholas of Pskov; (Commemorated February 29 on leap years: John Cassian the Roman; John (Barsanuphius) of Nitria in Egypt; Cassian of the Kiev Caves; Martyr Theocteristos of Pelekete Monastery; Germanus of Dacia Pontica; Cassian of Mu-lake Hermitage; Leo, Cappadocian monastic; Oswald, Archbishop of York; Meletius, Archbishop of Kharkov; *Devpeteruv* Icon of the Mother of God).

MARCH 1

Isaiah 2:3-11; Genesis 1:24-2:3
Proverbs 2:1-22

$\mathcal{R}$emember, O my soul, the terrible and frightful wonder: that your Creator for your sake became Man, and deigned to suffer for the sake of your salvation. His angels tremble, the Cherubim are terrified, the Seraphim are in fear, and all the heavenly powers ceaselessly give praise; and you, unfortunate soul, remain in laziness. At least from this time forth arise and do not put off, my beloved soul, holy repentance, contrition of heart and penance for your sins.

St. Paisius Velichkovsky

NEW MARTYR PARASKEVAS OF TREBIZOND. Paraskevas was from Trebizond in Asia Minor. As he stood before Muslim accusers who wanted to convert him to their faith, he refused and confessed his faith in Christ. He was hanged on March 1, 1659. His relics were taken by Orthodox Christians and buried in the Church of St. Gregory of Nyssa. Years later, his sacred relics were transferred to the Holy Monastery of Panagia Theoskepastos in Trebizond. A divine service was composed in his honor on Mount Athos by the hymnographer Athanasios of Simonopetra.

COMMEMORATIONS: Eudocia of Heliopolis; Antonina of Nicaea; Martyrs Charisius, Nikephoros, and Agapius; Agapios of Kolitsou Skete of Vatopedi, and his 4 companions; Domnina, ascetic of Syria; Martyrs Sylvester and Sophronius; Antonina of Kizliar; Anastasia Andreyevna, Fool-for-Christ; Anthony (Korzh) of Kiziltash Monastery (Crimea); Martyrius, founder of Zelenets Monastery; David of Wales; Paraskevas of Trebizond; Leo-Luke of Corleone, Sicily; Albinus, Bishop of Angers; Swidbert (Suitbert), bishop in southern Westphalia and monastic founder on the Rhine River; Synesios of Lysi in Cyprus: Paraskevas of Trebizond.

MARCH 2

*T*here is an electric generator and in the room there is a lamp. If, however, we don't flip the switch, we will remain in darkness. Similarly, there is Christ and there is our soul. If, however, we don't flip the switch of prayer, our soul will not see the light of Christ and will remain in the darkness of the devil.

St. Porphyrios of Kavsokalyvia

HIEROMARTYR THEODOTOS, BISHOP OF CYRENIA IN CYPRUS. Theodotos lived in fourth-century Cyrenia, Cyprus. He was known for his seriousness and devotion to the Church from his youth. Later, he became a highly respected priest known for his quiet dedication. He was one of the youngest bishops elevated to the throne in Cyprus. He called on the pagans to abandon idol worship and turn to the True God. The Christian-hating Roman emperor Licinius sent his most callous official, Savinus, to be the governor of the island. He quickly ordered the arrest of Theodotos and that he be brought to trial. However, Theodotos did not wait for the soldiers to arrive but went to the governor on his own accord. He told the governor that he was there to preach Christ. Theodotos was suspended, severely beaten, slashed with knives, and left to languish in prison. After the death of Licinius, a more benevolent governor was assigned to Cyprus, and Theodotos was released. He returned to Cyrenia, and after serving two more years as bishop, he peacefully gave up his spirit.

COMMEMORATIONS: Hesychius the Senator of Antioch; Quintus of Phrygia; Euthalia of Sicily; Theodotos of Cyrenia on Cyprus; Arsenius of Tver; Hesychius the Palatine, of Antioch; Troadios of Neo-Caesarea; Joachim (Papoulakis) of Vatopedi; Nestor, Tribimius, Marcellus, and Anthony of Perga; Martyrs Andronicus and Athanasia; Nicholas Planas of Athens; Sabbatius of Tver, and his disciple Euphrosynus; 440 Martyrs slain by the Lombards in Italy; Barsanuphius and Sabbas of Tver; Theodore Sladich of Komogovina; Chad, Bishop of Lichfield; Appearance of the Kolomenskoye *Reigning* Icon of the Mother of God.

*A*s our Lord approached a city called Nain, '*a man who had died was being carried out, the only son of his mother*' (Lk. 7:12). …He 'touched the bier' and said, '*Young man, I say to you, arise*' (Lk. 7:14). He does not simply leave it to the word to effect the raising of the dead, but in order to show that His own body was life-giving… He touches the corpse, and by this act puts life into him who had already decayed. And if by the touch alone of His holy flesh He gives life to that which has decayed, how shall we not profit more richly from the life-giving Eucharist when we taste it? For it will certainly transform those who partake of it and endow them with its own proper good, that is, immortality.

St. Cyril of Alexandria

ST. JOHN CHRYSOSTOM IV, CATHOLICOS OF GEORGIA. The God-fearing parents of John lived in the tenth-century country of Georgia. They were childless for many years and prayed at length to St. Shio of Mgvime for a child. When John was born, his parents sent him to the Shio-Mgvime Monastery to be raised. He acquired wisdom and sanctity, for which he was later called "Chrysostom," meaning "golden mouth" in Greek. He was known by this name throughout the history of the Georgian Church.

COMMEMORATIONS: Eutropius and Cleonicus of Amasea, and Basiliscus of Comana; Alexandra of Alexandria; Righteous Zeno and Zoilos; Hemetherius of Spain; Virgin Piama of Egypt; Theodoretus of Antioch; Caluppan of Auvergne (Gaul); John IV (Chrysostom), Catholicos of Georgia; Nonnita (Non), mother of David of Wales; Winwaloe, abbot of Landevennec, Brittany; Unknown Maiden; *Volokolamsk* Icon of the Mother of God.

SATURDAY

MARCH 4

Commemoration of the Departed
Commemoration of the Miracle
by St. Theodore the Tyro
Abstain from meat and
dairy products, and fish.

2 Timothy 2:1-10; Mark 2:23-3:5

*W*hen we give names to the church for the priests to read, first of
all we should mention the name of our spiritual father.

† *Elder Ioannis Kalaidis of Serres*

BLESSED BASIL, PRINCE OF ROSTOV. At the age of eight, Basil
became the prince of Rostov in thirteenth-century Russia. His closest friend
was Prince Yuri, who ruled Vladimir. Basil was called a vibrantly handsome
figure, intelligent, and good-natured. Beginning at age eleven, Basil participated in many military campaigns, principally against the fierce Mongols
who proved unstoppable. The khan offered Yuri peace, but the conditions
of peace included servitude to the khan. Yuri replied, "A glorious fight
is better than a shameful peace." Moscow was captured and burned, but
Yuri and Basil were determined to battle for the Orthodox Christian faith.
Their last line of defense was the Vladimir Dormition Cathedral, where
the wonderworking Vladimir Icon of the Mother of God was housed. The
Mongols stacked wood around the cathedral and built a tremendous fire that
killed a thousand women and children. The enemy surrounded the Russian
army, and very few Russians survived. Yuri died in the battle, and Basil was
wounded and taken prisoner to the khan. He was ordered to follow their evil
beliefs and fight for them, to which Basil said, "You cannot take the Christian faith from me." They tortured Basil and killed him. The relics of St. Yuri
and St. Basil were found and buried in Rostov at the Dormition cathedral.

COMMEMORATIONS: Gregory of Constantia; Gerasimus of the Jordan; Julian of Alexandria; Gregory of Assos; Paul, Juliana, Quadratus, Acacius, and Stratonicus, at Ptolemais; John of al-Sindiyana; James the Faster;
Saints of Pskov martyred by the Latins: Joasaph of Snetogorsk and Basil
of Mirozh; Dimitry Ivanov of Kiev; Vyacheslav of Nizhegorod; Daniel of
Moscow; Gerasimus of Vologda; Basil of Rostov; (1st Saturday of Great
Lent: St. Theodore of Tyro).

Sunday of Orthodoxy
Abstain from meat and
dairy products, and fish.

MARCH 5

Hebrews 11:24-26, 32-40; John 1:43-51

*W*hen thoughts are choking me like so many thorns, I enter the church, the hospital of souls. The beauty of the icons delight my vision like a verdant meadow, and without my noticing it stirs my soul to praise God.

St. John of Damascus

NURTURING ICON OF THE MOTHER OF GOD. In the Kazan Cathedral on Red Square, there is a list of wonderworking icons glorified throughout Russia. The Nurturing Icon of the Mother of God resided there, but after the destruction of that church in 1936 the original icon was lost. When the church was rebuilt in 1993, a copy of this wonderworking icon was housed there. The icon depicts the Mother of God with the young Christ sitting on her left arm. Christ's right hand is extended up to the Panagia's face. A brief prayer has been associated with this image: "O All-Holy Lady, Virgin Theotokos, save and keep under your protection my children (names), all boys and girls and infants, both those who are baptized and those who are nameless and those being carried in their mother's womb. Cover them with your own maternal mantle. Preserve them in the fear of God and in obedience to their parents. Implore your Son and our Lord to grant them what is needful for their salvation. I entrust them to your maternal providence, for you are the divine protection of your servants. Amen."

COMMEMORATIONS: Mark the Faster; Mark of Athens; Conon of Isauria; Conon the Gardener; Onisius of Isauria; Eulampius of Palestine; Rhais of Antinoe, with Archelaus and 152 Martyrs; Eulogius of Palestine; Theophilus of Caesarea; Basil and Constantine of Yaroslavl; George of Rapsana; Hesychius the Faster; Nikolai Velimirovich of Ochrid; John the Bulgarian; Adrian and Leonid of Poshekhonye; Theodore of Smolensk, with Yaroslav, David, and Constantine; Kieran of Munster; Virgil of Arles; Parthenios of Didymoteichon; *Nurturing* Icon of the Mother of God.

MARCH 6

*T*he Holy Spirit, without Whom "everything we do constitutes a trespass," will not approach unless He finds obedience and humility.

† *Elder Joseph of Vatopedi*

MONK-MARTYRS CONON AND HIS SON CONON, OF ICO-NIUM. Conon lived in third-century Iconium during the reign of Emperor Aurelian. When his wife died, Conon and his son went to live in a monastery. Conon led an extremely pious life, and his prayers cast out demons, healed the sick and the blind, and converted many pagans. Conon and his seventeen-year-old son, Deacon Conon, were arrested by the governor Dometian, who ordered them to sacrifice to pagan idols. When they refused, they were cruelly tortured. They were laid bare on a red-hot metal bed, drenched in hot oil, thrown into a cauldron of boiling tin, sulfur, and tar, hanged upside down, and scorched with a gagging smoke. Through all this, God kept them unharmed. The enraged pagans announced that they would cut the two in half with a wooden saw. The saints were granted time to pray. They thanked God for their suffering, prayed for the Church, that their persecutors be put to shame, for God to strengthen the faithful, and for Him to receive their souls. They heard the voice of God from heaven calling them. Having made the Sign of the Cross, they gave up their souls. Suddenly, an earthquake happened, and all the pagan temples in the city collapsed. Monks secretly buried the martyrs' bodies. Their relics were later transferred to the city of Acerno in Italy.

COMMEMORATIONS: Uncovering of the Precious Cross and the Precious Nails by Empress St. Helen; 42 Martyrs of Ammorium in Phrygia; Hesychios of Galatia; Conon and his son Conon of Iconium; Fridolin, Enlightener of the Upper Rhine; Arcadios of Cyprus, with Julian and Euboulos; Job (Joshua) of Anzersk Island; Martyrs Maximus and Euphrosynus; Cyriacus and 12 companions, in Augsburg; Miraculous Icon of Jesus Christ at Agia Moni; *Chenstokhov* and *Blessed Heaven* Icons of the Mother of God.

MARCH 7

*T*he work of prayer is the first work in Christian life. If in everyday affairs the saying: "live and learn" is true, then so much more it applies to prayer, which never stops and which has no limit.

St. Theophan the Recluse

VENERABLE PAUL THE SIMPLE OF EGYPT. When Paul was fifty years old, he decided to become an ascetic in the Egyptian desert. He was a farmer, and he married a much younger girl who later abandoned him for another. When he arrived at the cave of St. Anthony the Great, he told the saint of his desire to become a monk. St. Anthony said, "You must be at least sixty. You can't become a monk. Live in the town, work for your living, trusting in the grace of God. You would not be able to cope with all the trials of solitude." When Paul remained outside the cave for three days and nights, Anthony saw the depth of his intention and welcomed him. Paul was obedient to Anthony and did everything as he was told. When Anthony realized that Paul now led a disciplined life, he built a cell for him about three or four miles away. Paul was given divine grace to cast out demons and heal the sick. Soon he was visited by the faithful seeking his blessing. He lived in his cave for forty years and died peacefully at 90 years of age.

COMMEMORATIONS: Ephraim, Patriarch of Antioch; Hieromartyrs of Kherson: Basil, Ephraim, Eugene, Capiton, Elpidius, Agathorodus, and Aetherius; Emilian of Italy; Paul the Simple of Egypt; Laurence of Phaneromenh Monastery on Salamis; Nestor and Arcadius of Tremithus; Dandus and All Saints of Thrace; Nilus of St. Joseph of Volokolamsk; Eosterwine of Wearmount; Johannes of Ilomantsi; Ephraim, Bishop of Tomis; Synaxis of All Saints of the Dodecanese; *Surety of Sinners* and *Of Czestochowa* Icons of the Mother of God.

MARCH 8

Isaiah 5:16-25; Genesis 4:16-26
Proverbs 5:15-6:3

*D*o not wrack your brain. Pray to God.

St. Ambrose of Optina

COMMEMORATION OF THE MIRACLE OF THE KURSK ROOT ICON OF THE SIGN OF THE MOST HOLY THEOTOKOS IN 1898.
On March 8, 1898, three young men who were atheists hoped to shake the people's faith in the wonderworking power of the Kursk Root Icon of the Sign. They placed a time bomb next to the icon during a vigil in honor of the Holy Cross, but the bomb did not explode during the service as intended. Instead, it exploded at two o'clock in the morning while the church was empty. Newspaper reports recorded the devastation. The blast shattered the gilded canopy above the icon. The massive marble steps below the icon had split into several pieces and were thrown far away. A huge metal candlestick was blown to the other side of the cathedral, a cast iron door was torn from its hinges and smashed against a wall, and all the windows in the cathedral, including those in the dome, were shattered. However, the wonderworking icon remained in one piece, and its glorification increased. Over 60,000 pilgrims flocked to Kursk to take the icon out on the ninth Friday after Easter. This miracle is commemorated annually on this date.

COMMEMORATIONS: Apostle Hermas of the Seventy; Theophylactos, Bishop of Nicomedia; Paul the Confessor, Bishop of Plousias in Bithynia; Martyr Dion; Venerable Dometius, monk; Quintilian and Capatolinus at Nicomedia; Athanasius and Lazarus of Murom Island; Felix of Burgundy, Enlightener of East Anglia; Andronicus (Lukash), of Tbilisi, Georgia; Senan of Scattery Island (Inis Cathaigh); Julian of Toledo; Pontius of Carthage; *Kursk Root* Icon of the Sign of the Mother of God.

THURSDAY

**Holy 40 Martyrs of Sebaste
Abstain from meat and
dairy products, and fish.**

MARCH 9

Hebrews 12:1-10; Matthew 20:1-16

*I*n our prayer books, there are prayers of the Holy Fathers—
Ephraim the Syrian, Macarios the Egyptian, Basilios the Great,
John Chrysostomos, and other great men of prayer. Being filled
with the spirit of prayer, they were able to up that living spirit
into words, and handed it down to us. When one enters into
these prayers with attention and effort, then that great and prayerful spirit will in turn enter into him. He will taste the power of
prayer. We must pray so that our mind and heart receive the content of the prayers that we read. In this way the act of praying
becomes a font of true prayer in us.

St. Theophan the Recluse

MARTYR URPASIANUS OF NICOMEDIA. Emperor Maximian began
persecuting Christians in his military and his court in the early fourth century. Some abandoned Christianity, while others were steadfast. Urpasianus
went before the emperor and threw his cloak and military belt at his feet,
telling Maximian that he was a warrior of the heavenly king, the Lord Jesus
Christ. Maximian ordered that Urpasianus be tied to a tree and beaten with
thongs. Then he was tied to an iron grate and burned alive. Urpasianus
prayed throughout this agonizing ordeal. The ashes of St. Urpasianus were
thrown into the sea.

COMMEMORATIONS: Holy 40 Martyrs of Sebaste; Caesarius, brother of
St. Gregory the Theologian; Philoromus of Galatia; Urpasianus of Nicomedia; Tarasius of Lycaonia; Jonah of Novgorod; Theodosius of Balta; Bosa of
York; Pacianus of Barcelona; Mitrophan of Voronezh, and Joasaph; Dimitra
of Vvedensk; 2 priests and 40 students of Momisici; Christos and Panagos.

FRIDAY

MARCH 10

Salutations to the Virgin Mary
Strict Fast
Isaiah 7:1-14; Genesis 5:32-6:8
Proverbs 6:20-7:1

*W*herever Orthodox monasticism is absent, the Church does not exist, just as there cannot be a government without an army and a well-governed state without a national guard. The monastics guard the boundaries of our Church and protect Her from her enemies, who, in our contemporary materialistic age, rush to mangle Her like wolves.

St. Amphilochios Makris of Patmos

VENERABLE ANASTASIA THE PATRICIAN OF ALEXANDRIA. Anastasia lived the last twenty-eight years of her life in a cave, in solitude, and disguised as a monk. As a wealthy woman in sixth-century Constantinople, she was given the title of patrician in the court of Emperor Justinian because of her philanthropic deeds and closeness to God. When she saw that Empress Theodora was jealous of her, she hid in the Egyptian desert. She founded a monastery there and made sacred garments for the clergy. When Empress Theodora died, Justinian sent his men throughout the empire to find her, as he had admired her greatly and wished to marry her. When Anastasia heard this, she fled to a remote skete and sought the help of Abba Daniel. He dressed and tonsured her monk Anastasios and sent her to live in a cave. He told her never to leave the cave and that a monk would bring her water and provisions. She followed the monastic rule she was given for twenty-eight years. The Lord revealed to her the day of her death, and she informed Daniel, who had already received a vision of what would happen. Daniel and the disciple who was taking provisions to Anastasia took burial tools and went hurriedly to the cave for her blessing. At the moment of her death, her face became radiant. She saw angels coming for her, and she said, "Let us be off!" St. Anastasia's relics were later taken to Constantinople.

COMMEMORATIONS: Kodratos of Corinth, with Cyprian, Dionysios, Anektos, Paul, Crescens, and Dionysius; Victorinus, Victor, Nicephoros, Claudius, Diodoros, Serapion, Papias, at Corinth; Anastasia the Patrician; Martyr Marcian; Attalus of Bobbio; John of Khakhuli; Michael of Adrianople; Paul of Taganrog; Kessog of Loch Lomond; Alexander of Vologda.

**Abstain from meat and
dairy products, and fish.**

Hebrews 3:12-16; Mark 1:35-44

MARCH 11

If we exclaim, "All saints, pray to God for us!" then the whole
Heaven will immediately pray, "O Lord, help them!"

St. Barsanuphius of Optina

ST. SOPHRONIUS, BISHOP OF VRATSA, BULGARIA. Sophronius
was orphaned at eleven years of age. He grew up in poverty and in failing
health, but he mastered the Greek language and the Psalter with only two
years of education. His life in eighteenth-century Kotel, Hungary, was filled
with trials. At the age of eighteen, his relatives forced him to marry a haughty
wife, proving constant turmoil. Because of his piousness and diligence,
Sophronius was ordained to the priesthood. He proved to be a good teacher
and the most competent of priests. He also transcribed Bulgarian books. An
Athonite monk once gave him a book to translate entitled 'Slavonic-Bulgar-
ian History,' which had a profound impression on Sophronius. Henceforth
he felt called to be a spiritual overseer of the Bulgarians. He was later held
hostage by a pasha, and during this time, his wife died. Finally, Sophronius
moved to a neighboring diocese of twelve villages and was given a parish.
Everyone loved him, but again, a Tatar sultan nearly hanged him. Sophronius was made the bishop of Vratsa. During a severe and bitter winter, he
traveled to Vratsa only to find that a great war had devastated his diocese,
and the inhabitants had fled. Still, he tirelessly labored there for ten years in
dower conditions, sometimes without food and in life-threatening circumstances. Toward the end of his life, St. Sophronius asked to be released from
his diocese. He died following a two-month illness. About 150 years later,
in 1964, he was canonized by the Bulgarian Orthodox Church.

COMMEMORATIONS: Trophimos and Thallus at Laodicea; George
of Sinai; Sophronios of Jerusalem; Sophronius of Vratsa; Euthymius of
Novgorod; George Arselaites; Pionios of Smyrna, with others; John Mos-
chos; Sophronius of the Kiev Caves; Theodora of Arta; George the New;
Eulogius of Cordoba; Alexis of Kiev; Patrick of Valaam; Michael of Svyatogorsk; Angus the Culdee; Translation of the relics of St. Epimachos;
Panagia Tsambika Icon of the Mother of God in Rhodes.

Sunday of St. Gregory Palamas
Abstain from meat and
dairy products, and fish.
Hebrews 1:10-2:3; Mark 2:1-12

*F*asting must be accompanied by self-control. Why? Because eating our fill, even of humble foods, is a hindrance to the purifying mourning, godly sorrow and contrition in our souls, which bring about unswerving repentance leading to salvation. For without a contrite heart we cannot really lay hold of repentance. It is the restriction of self-indulgence, sleep and the senses according to God's will that crushes our hearts and makes us mourn for our sins.

St. Gregory Palamas

VENERABLE SYMEON THE DEVOUT, SPIRITUAL FATHER OF ST. SYMEON THE NEW THEOLOGIAN. Symeon became a monk in the year 942 at the Monastery of Stoudios in Constantinople. He lived there for about 44 years until his repose. Symeon the New Theologian first met his future elder, Symeon the Devout, when he was just fourteen years old and entered the Stoudios monastery at twenty-seven. Symeon the Devout assigned his young disciple the writings of St. Mark the Ascetic and other spiritual writers. Young Symeon's prayers grew longer, and he would pray until midnight. Once, a brilliant radiance descended upon him and filled the room. Then his mind rose to the heavens where he saw a second brighter light, and on the edge, he seemed to see his elder. Young Symeon revered Symeon the Devout like a saint, and he wrote a service in his honor though ecclesiastical officials of the time considered him less than saintly.

COMMEMORATIONS: Gregory the Dialogist, Pope of Rome; Symeon the New Theologian, and his elder Symeon the Reverent; Theophanes the Confessor; Aaron the High Priest, brother of Prophet Moses; Phineas, grandson of Aaron; Demetrius the Devoted, King of Georgia; Cyrus of Alexandria; 9 martyred by fire; Dragutin of Serbia; Paul of Leon in Brittany; Nicodemus of Mammola; Alphege of Winchester; Vladimir of Islavskoe; *Not-Made-by-Hands* (on the pillar) Icon of the Mother of God at Lydda.

MARCH 13

Isaiah 8:13-9:7; Genesis 6:9-22
Proverbs 8:1-21

*B*e more afraid of interior criticism, criticism in thought—and this, because it does not come to light through the spoken word, where is it likely to be corrected by those who hear it. Be careful, I say, about criticism from within, which imperceptibly makes us fatally guilty and deprives us of the life of divine grace and offers, as a most bitter drink, the death of the soul.

St. Justin Popovich

ST. MARIOS, BISHOP OF SEBASTE. Marios is a relatively unknown saint referenced in the *Small Euchologion*. It is believed that he was the Bishop of Sebaste, and he attended the First Ecumenical Synod of Nicaea in the year 325. There are two recent churches dedicated to him on the island of Cyprus. One was consecrated in 2015 and the other in 2017. The recent veneration of St. Marios came about when a young boy named Marios, who suffered from a severe illness, had a vision of St. Marios. He asked his parents for an icon of St. Marios, Bishop of Sebaste. When young Marios was near death at the age of five, he asked his parents to build him a house when he married, and he indicated the exact spot. His father agreed, but soon after, Marios died. Then the parents understood that their son was delivering a divine message to build a church dedicated to St. Marios, Bishop of Sebaste. The church was built through donations given at their son's funeral.

COMMEMORATIONS: Publius, Bishop of Athens; Habib (Abibus) of Hermopolis; Alexander of Thessalonica; Africanus, Pompeius, Maximus, and Terence at Carthage, and 36 with them; Christina of Persia; Leander, Bishop of Seville; Stephen (Bekh), Bishop of Izhevsk; Ypomoni of Serbia; Marios, Bishop of Sebaste; Translation of the relics of St. Nikephoros the Confessor, Patriarch of Constantinople; *Devpeteruv* Icon of the Mother of God.

MARCH 14

Isaiah 9:9-10:4; Genesis 7:1-5
Proverbs 8:32-9:11

*T*he brilliance of the Christian faith is witnessed by the love that
develops within a Christian for the content of his faith. The faithful
person feels his heart burning with the love of Christ. From where
has such love originated? How can someone love the unknown?
....How then has the faithful Christian come to love Christ, Who
is the content of his faith, if he has not come into contact with
Him? How has his heart been wounded by the love of Christ if he
has no knowledge of Him, if he has not heard His voice, if he has
not been enchanted by His beauty and grace? ...Therefore, the love
for Christ indicates that knowledge of Christ exists. Knowledge, in
turn, indicates that a revelation exists. Hence, Christ has revealed
Himself to the person who believes in Him, and, as the God of
love, He has filled this person's heart with love.

St. Nektarios of Pentapolis

**MARTYR EUSTATHIUS AND COMPANIONS, AT CARRHAE,
MESOPOTAMIA.** During the reign of Byzantine Emperor Leo III, those
who venerated icons were persecuted. The Eastern Catholics were also in
danger from Moslem forces pressing into Byzantine territories of the eastern
Mediterranean. Eustathius was one of many captured and imprisoned by
the invaders. After a series of battlefield losses, the Moslems ordered the
mass executions of Christian prisoners from city to city. Even after torture,
Eustathius would not deny his faith and was martyred. Afterward, those
venerating his holy relics received "healing of every kind," according to
St. Theophanes. Later, St. Theophanes was also tortured, imprisoned, and
exiled for opposing the iconoclasts.

COMMEMORATIONS: Euschymon, Bishop of Lampsacus; Benedict
of Nursia; Eustathius and his company at Carrhae, Mesopotamia; Theognostus, Metropolitan of Kiev and Moscow; Alexander of Pidne; Andrew
of Holy Trinity Monastery in Rafailovo, Siberia; Rostislav-Michael, Great
Prince of Kiev; Talmach of Lough Erc; Zosima of Ennatsky; Kostroma
Feodorovskaya Icon of the Mother of God.

MARCH 15

*W*hen you think to do something and you see disturbances in the mind, and after you call on the Name of God they still remain, even if hair-thin, know from this that what you want to do is instilled in you by the evil one, and do not do it. And when after you think of doing something, disturbance attacks you and seizes the mind, then also you should not do what you are thinking of, for nothing done with disturbance is pleasing to God. But when someone opposes (the deed to be done) with a disturbance, one need not at all regard the matter as harmful, but one should look at it to see whether it be good or not. If it is not good, it should be abandoned, and if good, you should do it, disdaining the disturbance by the help of God.

St. Barsanuphius the Great and St. John the Prophet

HIEROMARTYR ALEXANDER OF SIDON IN PAMPHYLIA. In the third century, during the Christian persecutions of the emperor Aurelian, Alexander was interrogated by the governor Antoninus and given over to fierce tortures. But Alexander was miraculously preserved by the Lord. He endured all the torments with surprising courage and finally was beheaded. As the governor was about to leave the judgment place, demons possessed him, and he died in frenzied convulsions.

COMMEMORATIONS: Apostle Aristobulus of the Seventy, Bishop of Britain; Agapios, Pauplius, Timolaus, Romulus, two named Dionysios, and two named Alexander, at Caesarea in Palestine; Alexander of Sidon in Pamphylia; Zachariah, Pope of Rome; Nicander of Egypt; St. Habarestes; Nicander, founder of Gorodnoezersk Monastery (Novgorod); Manuel of Crete; Leocritia of Cordoba.

MARCH 16

Isaiah 11:10-12:2; Genesis 7:11-8:3
Proverbs 10:1-22

If you are tempted, seal your foreheads reverently. For this is the
Sign of the Passion, displayed and made manifest against the devil,
provided that you do it with faith, not to be seen by men, but by
presenting it with skill like a shield. Because the Adversary, when
he sees the strength of the heart and when he sees the inner man
which is animated by the Word show, formed on the exterior, the
interior image of the Word, he is made to flee by the Spirit which
is in you. … By sealing the forehead and eyes with the hand, we
turn aside the one who is seeking to destroy us.

St. Hippolytus of Rome

**ST. PIMEN, ENLIGHTENER OF DAGESTAN, AND HIS COMPAN-
ION ANTHONY MESKHI.** In thirteenth-century Georgia, the Georgian
Church and its people suffered constant invasions by the Mongols. They
lived in a state of oppression, with many people martyred for refusing to
deny their Christian faith. The monk Pimen, the Fool-for-Christ, lived in
the Davit-Gareji Wilderness. He often condemned the unjust and immoral
acts of the nobility and their kings because the Georgian people were following the poor example of their leaders. Therefore, Pimen and the monk
Anthony Meskhi, who labored with him, worked for the salvation of the
Georgian people, correcting and preaching Christianity to the Dagestani
who lived in northern Georgia.

COMMEMORATIONS: Alexander I, Pope of Rome; Julian of Anazarbus;
Ananias of Mesopotamia; Sabinas of Hermopolis; John of Rufinianae; 10
Martyrs in Phoenicia; Serapion of Novgorod; Christodoulos of Patmos;
Papas of Lycaonia; Pimen, Fool-for-Christ of Dagestan, and Anthony of
Meskhi, Georgia; Romanus at Parium on the Hellespont; Ambrose (Khe-
laia) the Confessor of Georgia; Eutropia of Kherson; Abban of Kilabban
(Ireland); Malachi of Rhodes.

FRIDAY

Salutations to the Virgin Mary
Strict Fast

MARCH 17

Isaiah 13:2-13; Genesis 8:4-21
Proverbs 10:31-11:12

*D*o not be led away by gluttonous feasting.

St. Theodoros the Ascetic

VENERABLE THEOSTERICTUS THE CONFESSOR. Theosterictus was pious and cared deeply about monasticism from a young age. After finishing his schooling, he became a monk at the Pelekete Monastery in Triglia of Asia Minor. Because of his virtues, he was selected to be the abbot. During the iconoclast period, Emperor Constantine V succeeded in swaying a majority of bishops to turn against the veneration of icons. He also began attacking monastics and was hostile toward the sacred relics. One of his generals attacked the Pelekete Monastery during Holy Thursday liturgy and set it on fire. Abbot Theosterictus and thirty-eight of his monks endured horrible tortures; their noses were cut off, and their beards burned. Then they were locked in a bathhouse and left to starve. Theosterictus was chained and taken to Constantinople. He was imprisoned there with 342 other confessors of the icons. Monastery properties were stolen and sold, and they used the money to fund their campaigns. Many monks fled to the south of Italy. Finally, Constantine died, and later his son Leo IV died, leaving ten-year-old Leo V and his mother Irene to rule. Irene restored the icons and released the exiles and the prisoners, including Theosterictus. He finally returned to his destroyed monastery and rebuilt it about fifteen years later. St. Theosterictus also composed a canon to the Theotokos that is chanted in times of tribulation. He died peacefully in extreme old age.

COMMEMORATIONS: Alexios the Man of God, in Rome; Patrick, Enlightener of Ireland; Theosterictus the Confessor of Pelekete; Marinos the Soldier, at Caesarea; Ambrose of Alexandria; Paul of Crete; Gertrude of Nivelles; Gabriel the Lesser of Gareji, Georgia; Gurias, Archbishop of Tauria and Simferopol; Beccan of Rhum; Withburga, solitary at Holkham; Macarius of Kalyazin Monastery; Parthenius of the Kiev Caves; Commemoration of the Earthquake of AD 790.

**Abstain from meat and
dairy products, and fish.**

Hebrews 10:32-38; Mark 2:14-17

*F*or [the demons] are cowards, and utterly dread the sign of our
Lord's Cross, since it was on the Cross that the Savior despoiled
them and exposed them.

St. Anthony the Great

ST. CYRIL, ARCHBISHOP OF JERUSALEM. Cyril fought great battles
for Orthodoxy in the fourth century. Raised by pious parents in Jerusalem,
he became a monk, a priest, and then Patriarch. The heretic Arius caused a
division within the Church, swaying many bishops and Emperor Constantius. In the year 351, on the feastday of Pentecost at the third hour, a bright
and shining cross appeared in the sky over Jerusalem. It stretched from
Golgotha over the Mount of Olives, and many people witnessed it. Cyril
reported this miracle to Constantius and all the bishops, urging them to
forgo the path of Arius. During a famine, Cyril used his own wealth to feed
the hungry. When the famine did not abate, he began to sell the church's
gold, silver, and vestments to feed the hungry. His enemies, especially the
heretic metropolitan Akakios, slandered Cyril and had him imprisoned.
When emperor Julian the Apostate took the throne, he had Cyril restored as
Patriarch, seemingly out of piety. A little later, Julian renounced Christ and
gave the Jews permission and the means to rebuild the Temple of Solomon.
Cyril prayed to Christ to destroy this work and predicted it would happen.
An earthquake destroyed the new construction and unearthed the buried
foundation blocks. When the Jews attempted to rebuild it, fire came down
from the heavens and destroyed the tools and equipment. Great fear came
upon all the people. The following night, the Sign of the Cross appeared
on the clothes of the Jewish people, which they could not remove.

COMMEMORATIONS: Cyril, Archbishop of Jerusalem; Trophimos,
Eukarpios, and those with them in Nicomedia; Tetricus, Bishop of Langres
in Gaul; Daniel, monk of Egypt; Cyril of Astrakhan; 10,000 Martyrs of
Nicomedia; Aninas of the Euphrates; Edward, King of England; Maria
(Skobtsova), at Ravensbruck.

Sunday of the Holy Cross
Abstain from meat and
dairy products, and fish.
Hebrews 4:14-5:6; Mark 8:34-9:1

MARCH 19

*𝒟*o not worship only the Christ of the Lord, but also the image of His Cross, because it is a sign of the victory of Christ over the devil and over the whole force of the forces, that's why they tremble and flee when they see Him portrayed.

St. Gregory Palamas

ST. SOPHIA OF SLUTSK AND MINSK. Sophia was the first descendant of a famous family of princes from late sixteenth-century Slutsk and Kopyl. They ruled areas such as Kiev and Novgorod. She was orphaned at the age of one, and her relatives, who were governors, assumed guardianship of the vastly wealthy Sophia. A future marriage was arranged to the prince Janusz Radzivil so that his family could share in this wealth. As the marriage date approached, Prince Janusz, a Calvinist, petitioned the pope for permission to marry the devoutly Orthodox Sophia. She was adamant that she remains Orthodox and that their children be raised in the Orthodox faith. After the marriage, Sophia's sole joy and consolation was her Orthodox faith. She had a significant moral influence on the Orthodox people, protecting them from Uniate violence and supporting them spiritually and financially. Sophia had a law passed by the king prohibiting the Uniates from forcing the Orthodox people of her ancestral land (present-day Belarus) to convert to Catholicism. She was generous in her donations to monasteries, churches, and the clergy. Through her efforts, the city of Slutsk became a religious center for Orthodoxy. St. Sophia died during the birth of her first child at the age of twenty-six. Her incorrupt relics now rest in the Holy Spirit Cathedral in Minsk.

COMMEMORATIONS: Chrysanthus, Daria, Claudius, Hilaria, Jason, Maurus, Diodorus, and Marianus; Maria, wife of Vsevelod III; Innocent of Komel; Bassa of Pskov Caves; Pancharios at Nicomedia; Sophia of Slutsk; Nicholas of Smyrna; Demetrius at Constantinople; Alcmund of Northumbria; Commemoration of the Miracle of Kollyva wrought by St. Theodore the Tyro; Smolensk *Umileniye* (Tender Feeling) Icon of the Mother of God; (Sunday before 3/25: Synaxis of All Saints of Fthiotidos; St. Gregory, Metropolitan of New Patras).

March 20

As sight is the best of all senses, so prayer is the most divine of all virtues.

St. Nilus of Sinai

ST. CUTHBERT THE WONDERWORKER, BISHOP OF LINDIS-FARNE. Cuthbert was from seventh-century Britain. He was a very athletic child, and at the age of eight, while standing on his head, he was admonished by a three-year-old to be sensible, and he foretold that Cuthbert would become a priest and a bishop. Another time, Cuthbert suffered from a swollen knee, and a handsome stranger dressed in white told him which remedy would help his knee, and it healed quickly. Later, Cuthbert revealed that he always received help from the angels of God. When he was still a young boy, he had a vision of angels taking the soul of their bishop, and he later learned that the bishop had died that same hour. Cuthbert became an exemplary monk, and he was chosen to be abbot. He traveled abroad preaching the Gospel, healing the sick, and freeing the demon-possessed. Cuthbert was patient and gentle and corrected their sins. For nine years, he lived a life of solitude. When he was reluctantly made bishop, he remained humble and continued his old habit of traveling to the people and healing their diseases. In his early fifties, Cuthbert sensed his imminent death. During this time, he was assailed by demons more than ever before. He gave instructions to be buried in a stone coffin in a hidden place. When his tomb was opened eleven years later, his relics were found incorrupt. It was reopened over 400 years later, and the relics of St. Cuthbert were both incorrupt and fragrant.

COMMEMORATIONS: 7 Virgin Martyrs of Amisus: Alexandra, Claudia, Euphrasia, Matrona, Juliana, Euphemia, and Theodosia; Nicetas the Confessor; Holy Fathers martyred at the Monastery of St. Sabbas: John, Sergius, Patrick, and others; Martyrs Rodion, Aquila, Longinus, and Emanuel; Euphrosynus of Blue-Jay Lake; Tadros of Edessa; Martin of Braga; Austreigiselis of Bourges; Wulfram, missionary; Cuthbert of Lindisfarne; Archil II, King of Georgia; Myron of Mega Castro; Herbert of Derwentwater; Michael the Sabbaite; Nicholas of Novosiolki.

MARCH 21

Isaiah 25:1-9; Genesis 9:8-17
Proverbs 12:8-22

*N*owhere in the *Sayings of the Desert Fathers* is a certain ascetic praised and projected as an example because he broke the fast for reasons of hospitality! That which is mentioned is that those holy hermits and ascetics broke their own personal ascetic fasting, which was much stricter than what the Church ordained. They ate, for example, a few unboiled, soaked beans or raw greens or a little, soaked biscuit—and this not every day, but every two or three days or even more sparsely. So, if they happened to offer hospitality to someone, then they would boil the beans or the greens and, if it were a day when wine and oil could be eaten, they would throw in a little oil or also drink a little wine. ...As soon as the reasons of hospitality were gone, they would return to their strict fasting or to even more strict fasting to regain the lost ground, lest their own self fool them and they find in hospitality an excuse to slacken their fasting.

† *Elder Epiphanios Theodoropoulos of Athens*

VENERABLE JAMES THE CONFESSOR, BISHOP. James was inclined toward the ascetical life from a young age and became a monk at the Studite monastery. He led a strict life of prayer, fasting, and labor. Due to his great virtue, he was elevated to bishop of the Church in Catania (Sicily). During a ninth-century iconoclast uprising, he championed the cause of icons together with St. Theodore the Studite as far as the royal house in Constantinople. He was repeatedly urged to renunciate the holy icons, but he refused. He was starved and beaten in prison, but he bravely endured the suffering. St. James died in exile.

COMMEMORATIONS: Thomas, Patriarch of Constantinople; Philemon and Domninos of Rome; Cyril, Bishop of Catania; Lupicinus of the Jura Mountains (Gaul); James the Confessor, Bishop of the Studion; Michael of Agrapha; Seraphim of Vyritsa; Serapion the Sindonite of Egypt; Enda of Aran (Ireland); Pachomius of Nerekhta; Sophronius, abbot of St. Theodosius Monastery in Palestine; Serapion, Bishop of Thmuis, Egypt.

MARCH 22

Isaiah 26:21-27:9; Genesis 9:18-10:1
Proverbs 12:23-13:9

The demons are afraid of the Psalms because they are burned as with
a sword of fire by whomever is praying with the Psalms. Great is
the power of the Psalter over the evil spirits. With it, the fathers
of old performed miracles and cast out evil spirits.

† *Elder Paisius of Sihla*

THE IZBORSK ICON OF THE MOTHER OF GOD. During the German siege of Izborsk, Russia, in 1657, the Izborsk Icon of the Mother of
God was brought to the city by a pious widow named Evdokia on the sixth
week of Great Lent. The icon began an overflow of tears from the eyes of
the Mother of God, and it then was transferred to the cathedral dedicated
to St. Nicholas the Wonderworker. Prayers were performed before the icon
for forty days, and Izborsk was delivered from the German invasion. Before
this icon, the faithful pray for healing from the passions that torment body
and soul, for deliverance from enemy invaders, and for the prevention and
cessation of any other evil. The icon portrays the Infant Jesus embracing
His Mother's neck with his right hand and extending His left hand to Her
shoulder.

COMMEMORATIONS: Drosis of Antioch, and 5 Virgin Martyrs; Kal-
liniki and Vasilissa of Rome; Lea of Rome; Basil of Ancyra; Schema-abbess
Sophia (Grineva) of Kiev; Euthymius of Demitsana and Mt. Athos; Paul,
Bishop of Narbonne, Brittany; Basil (Zelentsov), Bishop of Priluk; The
Izborsk Icon of the Mother of God.

MARCH 23

Isaiah 28:14-22; Genesis 10:32-11:9
Proverbs 13:19-14:6

*S*ometimes people find themselves brightly illuminated and refreshed by God's grace for a while, but then this grace may be taken away, and they can fall into depression and start grumbling and even give up dispiritedly instead of energetically renewing their prayers to call down again that assurance of salvation. Such behavior is like an ungrateful beggar taking alms at the palace door and then walking off indignantly because he was not invited in to dine with the king himself.

St. John of Karpathos

MARTYRS VICTORIAN, FRUMENTIUS, AND COMPANIONS. Victorian was proconsul of Carthage on the north coast of Africa. It was the most powerful city in the region because of its proximity to trade routes. He was one of the wealthiest men there and held several important offices under King Hunneric. However, Hunneric resolved to trample out true Christianity and establish the Arian heresy, which regarded Christ as a creature. Victorian said that nothing could separate him from the faith and love of Christ and the Church in which he was baptized and that he was ready to suffer all sorts of torments. He was subjected to the worst and most protracted tortures and was martyred. Many others suffered under the same persecution and were martyred, including Frumentius, Liberatus, and his family.

COMMEMORATIONS: Nikon and 199 disciples in Sicily; Victorian, Frumentius, and companions, in Africa; Bassian, Archbishop of Rostov; Dometius the Persian; Nicon, abbot of the Kiev Caves; Ephraim and Theodosios of Vologda; Pachomius of Nerekhta; Basil of Mangazea in Siberia; Luke of Adrianople and Mt. Athos; Helen of Florovsk Ascension Convent in Kiev; Gwinear of Cornwall; Sergius (Serebriansky) of Tver; Elijan (Vyatlin) of Vladimir; Macarius Kvitkin of Orenburg; Ethilwald of Farne.

Salutations to the Virgin Mary
Strict Fast
Isaiah 29:13-23; Genesis 12:1-7
Proverbs 14:15-26

*W*hat salt is for food, humility is for every virtue.
St. Isaac the Syrian

NEW HIEROMARTYR PARTHENIOS III, PATRIARCH OF CON-STANTINOPLE. Parthenios came from a pious Orthodox Christian family that provided him with a good education. He became a cleric, and in the year 1639, he was elected Metropolitan of Chios, where he was distinguished for his piety and good works. Seventeen years later, he became the Ecumenical Patriarch. Parthenios sided with the Russians in the dispute for the control of the Church in Ukraine. This was also a time when the Greeks were under the four-century rule of the Ottoman Empire. Because Parthenios found the Church in great financial difficulties, he turned to the Russians for assistance by sending letters to the Metropolitan of Nicaea, who was living among the Orthodox Cossacks in Russia. At this time, the Russians were political enemies of the Ottomans. The Ottoman Sultan's officer intercepted Parthenios' correspondence, and they decided that Parthenios should stand trial for treason. They interpreted his letters to say that the Russians should attack the Ottomans. These accusations were proven false. But the sultan ordered his hanging anyway to set an example for those who might try to overthrow them in the future. However, they offered Parthenios a pardon if he would convert to their religion, but he refused, saying he would die 1,000 deaths for Christ; and do it with gladness. Parthenios was beaten, and they inflicted great pain, but he received all this with great courage. St. Parthenios was hanged and left there for three days, and then he was thrown into the sea. His body was found and buried at a monastery on the island of Halki.

COMMEMORATIONS: Artemon of Seleucia; Artemon of Laodicea; Parthenios III, of Constantinople; Zachariah the Recluse; Zachariah the Faster; Zachariah the Hospitable; James of Catania; Martin of Thebes; 8 Martyrs of Caesarea; Stephen and Peter of Kazan; Caimin of Holy Island; Thomas of St. Euthymius Monastery; Dunchad of Iona; Severus of Catania; *The Beclouded Mount* Icon of the Mother of God.

Annunciation of the Theotokos
Abstain from meat and dairy products.

MARCH 25

Hebrews 2:11-18; Luke 1:24-38

*W*hen you want to say something to your children, tell it to the Panagia and She will bring it to pass.

St. Porphyrios of Kavsokalyvia

PANAGIA EVANGELISTRIA OR MEGALOHARI ICON OF THE MOTHER OF GOD. This icon is located on the island of Tinos, Greece, in the Cathedral of the Megalohari. The icon depicting the Annunciation of the Theotokos dates to the beginning of Christianity. It was lost and not found again until the 1800s. In 1821 Michael Polyzois had a vision of the Panagia, directing him to a specific farm to find her icon and to build a church there, where one had once stood in the tenth century. Pirates had burned it down. Michael and other islanders began digging where he had been instructed, but finding nothing, they stopped. Two years later, a young nun named Pelagia had a vision of the Panagia telling her to find Her icon. She needed three visions to convince her. The local Metropolitan and many people enthusiastically began digging and again found nothing. As soon as the digging stopped, a cholera epidemic spread over the island. Out of fear, the digging started again, and finally, a worker found half of the icon and soon the other half. The epidemic stopped. The Metropolitan sent a boy to get water to bless the icon from a nearby well that had dried up and had very little water. But the boy found the well overflowing with water. A church was built where they found the icon, and the water from the well continues to stream today. It has healing properties, and thousands of people have been healed. The icon of the Panagia has worked many miracles. Because multitudes of pilgrims come from around the world to venerate the icon, a larger church was built that houses the icon. The nun Pelagia was canonized as a saint by the Orthodox Church.

COMMEMORATIONS: Annunciation of the Theotokos; Pelagia, Theodosia, and Dula of Nicomedia; Tikhon, Patriarch of Moscow; Nicander of Pskov; Justin of Celije; Sabbas the New; Sennuphios of Latomos; Restoration of Autocephaly of the Georgian Orthodox Church; *Trikeriotissa* in Trikeri and *Evangelistria* of Tinos Icons of the Mother of God.

Sunday of St. John Climacus
Abstain from meat and
dairy products, and fish.
Hebrews 6:13-20; Mark 9:17-31

*L*et us eagerly run our course as men called by out God and King, lest, since our time is short, we be found on the day of our death without fruit and perish of hunger. Let us please the Lord as soldiers please their king; because we are required to give an exact account of our service after the campaign.

St. John Climacus

HOLY TWENTY-SIX MARTYRS OF GOTHIA, IN THE CRIMEA. Christianity took root with the Gothic people, who were a massive German tribe after the time of Constantine the Great in the early fourth century. A Gothic bishop was also present at the Nicaean Council of 325. Their Christian faith and association with the Romans contributed to raising their civilization above the other Germanic tribes. Around 375, the Huns poured out of Asia and invaded Europe. They came to dominate the Goths, as did the Romans, who incorporated the Gothic army into their own. King Ungerich gave orders to burn down a church during the Divine Liturgy. Three hundred eight people perished, of whom only the names of twenty-one are known, and the five children of the two presbyters. Even the man bringing the offering bread for the Eucharist was captured and became a burnt offering. The twenty-six martyrs included the two priests, Vercus and Bathusius, their wives, and their two sons and three daughters.

COMMEMORATIONS: Synaxis of the Archangel Gabriel; Quadratus (Codratus), Theodosius, Manuel, and 40 other Martyrs; Stephen the Confessor and Wonderworker, abbot of Tryglia; 26 Martyrs of Gothia in Crimea, including presbyters Bathusius and Bercus; Basil the Younger; Eusebius, Bishop of Kival, and Pullius the Reader; Irenaeus, Bishop of Sirmium; Malchus of Chalcis in Syria; Montanus the presbyter of Singidunum, and his wife Maxima; George of Sofia, at Adrianople; Eutychios of Alexandria; Braulio of Saragossa in Iberia; Ludger, Bishop of Munster.

MARCH 27

Isaiah 37:33-38:6; Genesis 13:12-18
Proverbs 14:27-15:4

*M*ost people today, foolish and ignorant, not knowing the value of children, are sad when God gives them many children, and murderers, more criminal than all other criminals, slaughter them.

† *Elder Philotheos Zervakos of Aegina*

GLYKOPHYLOUSA (SWEET-KISSING) ICON OF THE MOTHER OF GOD ON MOUNT ATHOS. The Glykophylousa Icon at Philotheou Monastery and the Portaitissa Icon at Iveron Monastery were both saved during the Iconoclast period in the eighth and ninth centuries. Both icons are located on Mount Athos. The Glykophylousa Icon originally belonged to Victoria, the devout wife of a senator who found the veneration of icons distasteful. He intended to burn the icon, so Victoria threw it into the sea to save it, and it floated away standing upright. After a few years, it appeared on the shores of Mount Athos. The abbot and fathers of Philotheou Monastery awaited its arrival after being informed through a revelation of the Theotokos. A holy spring sprouted forth when they placed the icon on the shore. Many miracles are credited to the Glykophylousa icon, including the following: One time, a pilgrim visiting Philotheou stole the valuable offerings left before the holy icon. He escaped to the port of Iveron Monastery and boarded a boat to leave. As the ship began to sail, it mysteriously could not move despite the excellent weather. The monks from Philotheou were sent in all directions when at last two monks saw the immobile ship and realized what had happened. The thief asked for forgiveness, and the monks magnanimously left him unpunished.

COMMEMORATIONS: Paul, Bishop of Corinth; Matrona of Thessalonica; John the Clairvoyant of Lycopolis, Egypt; Prophet Ananias; Cyricus of Thrace; Eutychius, monk; Ephraim, Archbishop of Rostov; Paphnutius, disciple of St. Anthony the Great; Philetos, Lydia, Macedonos, Theoprepios, Cronides, and Amphilochios in Illyria; Alexander of Voche; Anthony, Metropolitan of Tobolsk; Rupert, Bishop of Salzburg; Martyrs Baruch and John; *Sweet Kissing* (Glykophilousa) and *Of the Akathist* Icons of the Mother of God.

MARCH 28

Isaiah 40:18-31; Genesis 15:1-15
Proverbs 15:7-19

*L*et your demeanor, your dress, your walking, your sitting down, the nature of your food, the quality of your being, your house and what it contains, aim at simplicity. And let your speech, your singing, your manner with your neighbor, let these things also be in accord with humility rather than with vanity. In your words let there be no empty pretense, in your singing no excess sweetness, in conversation be not ponderous or overbearing. In everything refrain from seeking to appear important. Be a help to your friends, kind to the ones with whom you live, gentle to your servant, patient with those who are troublesome, loving towards the lowly, comforting those in trouble, visiting those in affliction, never despising anyone, gracious in friendship, cheerful in answering others, courteous, approachable to everyone, never speaking your own praises, nor getting others to speak of them, never taking part in unbecoming conversations, and concealing where you may whatever gifts you possess.

St. Basil the Great

HOLY APOSTLE HERODIAN OF THE SEVENTY. Herodian lived during the time of Christ. He was one of the Seventy disciples and helped spread the Gospel. He worked and traveled with Apostles Peter and Paul and was consecrated Bishop of New Patras. Herodian suffered greatly at the hands of the pagans and Jews. He was beaten, stoned, stabbed, and left for dead. But he arose and continued to serve the Apostles. While serving Apostle Peter on the day of Peter's crucifixion in Rome, in the year 54, St. Herodian was beheaded, along with Apostle Olympas.

COMMEMORATIONS: Apostle Herodion of the Seventy; Priscus, Malchus, and Alexander of Caesarea; Hesychius the Theologian; Hilarion the New; Dionysius the Merciful; John of Manglisi; George of Zagora, Parodus and Peter, and Prince Enravota-Boyan; Eustratius the Faster of the Kiev Caves; Hilarion of Pskov; Jonah of Klimets Monastery; Peter of Chartoviec; The miraculous occurrence of Taxiotis; *Of the Sign* Icon of the Mother of God.

MARCH 29

Isaiah 41:4-14; Genesis 17:1-9
Proverbs 15:20-16:9

*L*et us do all in our power to expel demons that have entered us through our negligence by the prayer of Jesus. It has the property of reviving those deadened by sin, and it has the property of driving out devils.

St. Ignatius Brianchaninov

VENERABLE NIKETAS OF THE ROSLAVL FORESTS. Niketas was from seventeenth/eighteenth-century Orel in western Russia. As a child, he loved to go on pilgrimages to holy places. He left home as a young man to live about a mile from the White Bluff Hermitage. When he was 85 years old, he built a cell on a small hill and dug a well. Those who passed by would leave bread for him, and often animals were seen by his cell. But mosquitoes would bite him mercilessly until he was covered in blood. Yet, he bore everything with patience, and he always shed tears for his sins and for those of others. One time, Father Niketas became very sick, and he lay down without moving. The day before the Feast of the Annunciation, he was so weak that he could not attend the services and was heartbroken. Suddenly, his cell filled with light, and he saw the Panagia surrounded by angels, and he joined them in singing the Troparion of the Feast. Niketas moved around to various places for some time but later returned to his hermitage in the Roslavl Forest. He died there a short time later and was buried next to his cell. Seven years later, his incorrupt relics and clothing were moved to higher ground because of groundwater. On the feastday of St. Niketas, more than 5,000 people gather at his revered grave, where many healings have been witnessed.

COMMEMORATIONS: Mark the Confessor, Bishop of Arethusa, with Cyril the Deacon of Heliopolis and others; Diadochos of Photiki; Jonah and Barachisius in Persia, with: Zanithas, Lazarus, Maruthas, Narses, Elias, Mares, Habib, Sivsithina, and Sabbas; Paul Voinarsky, and Paul and Alexis Kiryan, of Crimea; Eustathius of Kios; Jonah, Mark, and Vassa of the Pskov Caves; Niketas of the Roslavl Forest; Eustasius of Luxeuil; Gundleus and Gwladys, parents of St. Cadoc.

THURSDAY

The Great Canon of St. Andrew of Crete
Abstain from meat and
dairy products, and fish.

MARCH 30

Isaiah 42:5-16; Genesis 18:20-33
Proverbs 16:17-17:17

*A*mong many of the methods which the devil—the enemy and destroyer of our souls—uses to deceive those who correctly practice Orthodox Christianity, particularly youth, is to present another trap, by which he has been able to deceive many young men and completely lead them to perdition. The evil one first presents this trap under a guise which appears to be good and sympathetic, making it appear as an enticement to you, and urging them to freedom, laughter, joking and gesticulations, outspokenness, and finally to the use and misuse of alcohol, all of which appear disastrous to the world, but which are characterized as a means of "freedom," … Thus, getting used to bad habits, youth become filled with passions and are then mocked by demons and men alike. The trap is covered with a heavy shadow…making it appear that all these are very small sins.

St. Daniel of Katounakia

MARTYR VICTOR AND ELEVEN MARTYRS WITH HIM. In the late third and early fourth centuries, during the Christian persecutions, Emperor Diocletian established a Tetrarchy of the Roman Empire, a four-part division to solve the military and political problems. Emperor Maximianus governed Thessalonica. Not much is written to describe these martyrdoms, but the *Roman Martyrology* states that St. Domninos was martyred with St. Victor and others in Thessalonica on the same day. Also, in the *Hieronymian Martyrology*, twelve names of martyrs are commemorated, including St. Victor.

COMMEMORATIONS: John Climacus of Sinai, author of *The Ladder*; John the Hermit of Cilicia; Prophet Joel (Joad), who dwelled in Bethel; Zacharias, Bishop of Corinth; Euboula, mother of St. Panteleimon; John II, Patriarch of Jerusalem; Sophronius, Bishop of Irkutsk; Osburga of Coventry; Victor of Thessalonica and 11 Martyrs with him; Translation of the relics of Martyr-King St. Edmund of East Anglia.

MARCH 31

*L*ocusts, wars, droughts, and disease, they are all scourges. This is not God's way of educating human beings; it is, rather, the result of our moving away from Him. Scourges happen when we stray from God. His wrath then comes to make us remember Him and ask for His help. It's not that He arranges and orders, so to speak, these calamities. Rather, God allows them to happen because He sees how far human evil can go, and how unwilling we are to change our ways. This is His way of bringing us to our senses. But it is not something that He has arranged; rather, it is the natural result of our own self-will, of our own actions.

St. Paisios the Athonite

VENERABLE HYPATIUS THE HEALER OF THE KIEV CAVES. The Kiev Caves Lavra, a type of monastery consisting of a cluster of cells or caves for hermits, was attacked in the thirteenth century by the Golden Horde of Batu Khan. They left it desolate. Even so, some monks still lived there. At this time, Hypatius became a vessel of divine grace through his rigorous fasting of eating only bread and water and his prayerful vigilance. At night he stood in prayer and slept very little. Most importantly, he devoted himself entirely to the service of the sick and received from God the gift of healing. His incorrupt relics rest in the Far Caves, and to this day, those who approach with faith receive healing.

COMMEMORATIONS: Blaise of Amorion and Mt. Athos; Akakios the Confessor, Bishop of Melitene; Hypatios the Wonderworker, Bishop of Gangra; Innocent, Metropolitan of Moscow and Enlightener of Alaska and Siberia; Jonah, Metropolitan of Kiev, Moscow, and All Russia; Joseph the Fair, son of Jacob; Abdas, Bishop of Hormizd-Ardashir, the deacon Benjamin, of Persia, and Ormisdes the Confessor; Martyr Menander; Stephen the Wonderworker; Hypatios of Rufinianus in Chalcedon; Philaret of Glinsk Hermitage; Hypatius the Healer of the Kiev Caves; Apollo, ascetic of the Thebaid; Appearance of the *Iveron* Icon of the Mother of God (Mt. Athos).

To one of the brethren appeared a devil, transformed into an angel of light, who said to him:

I am the Angel Gabriel, and I have been sent to thee. But the brother said:

Think again—you must have been sent to somebody else.

I haven't done anything to deserve an angel. Immediately the devil ceased to appear.

The Wisdom of the Desert
Sayings from the Desert Fathers
of the Fourth Century

*G*od is not unjust. He will not slam the door against the man who
humbly knocks.

St. John Climacus

VENERABLE MARY OF EGYPT. While walking in the desert, monk
Zosimos saw in the distance a very old naked person. The person fled,
attempting to hide from him. Out of curiosity, he gave chase, but as he
approached Mary, she called Zosimos by name, saying that she could not
face him as she was a woman. He gave her his cloak for covering, and she
then told him about her life. She had been a prostitute in Alexandria for
seventeen years until a profound experience changed her life. An invisible
force prevented her from venerating the True Cross in a Jerusalem church.
In fear, she confessed her sins before an icon of the Theotokos and promised to go wherever she was told. Then an invisible force opened the way
for her to pass through the crowd and venerate the Holy Cross. She went
back to the icon to give thanks, and a voice told her that she would find
peace across the Jordan River. She went that evening and spent the next 46
years in asceticism and solitude in the wilderness. She ate plants while she
battled the elements and her passions. When she began to pray, he saw her
miraculously elevated in midair. She asked him to come back in one year
to give her communion on the bank of the Jordan River. The following
year he arrived there. He saw her make the Sign of the Cross and walk on
water towards him. She asked Zosimos to meet her again on April 1, of the
following year, at the place where they initially met, which was a twenty-
day walk from where they stood. When Zosimos arrived on that date, he
found St. Mary's body. A message in the sand read that she had died on the
day he had given her communion one year earlier and asked to be buried.

COMMEMORATIONS: Mary of Egypt; Macarius of Pelekete; Meliton
of Sardis; Achaz of Judah; Abraham of Bulgaria; Gerontius and Basilides;
Gerontius and Pachomius of the Kiev Caves; Euthymius the Wonderworker; Barsanuphius of Optina; Macarius at Pskov; John of Shavta, and
Eulogius; Joachim of Novgorod; Tewdrig of Tintern; Symeon of Dajbabe.

Sunday of St. Mary of Egypt
Abstain from meat and
dairy products, and fish.
Hebrews 9:11-14; Mark 10:32-45

*L*ove does not know how to be angry, or provoked, or passionately to reproach anyone. The proof of love and knowledge is profound humility, which is born of a good conscience in Jesus Christ our Lord.

St. Isaac the Syrian

MARTYR EBBA THE YOUNGER, AND THOSE WITH HER. The Monastery of Coldingham in the ancient kingdom of Northumbria was governed in the ninth century by St. Ebba. About the year 867, several thousand pagan Danish Viking warriors desolated the whole north country of East Anglia. They wreaked vengeance on monks, nuns, and ecclesiastics. When Abbess Ebba got word that the Vikings were near and approaching, she summoned her nuns and exhorted them to preserve their chastity at any cost. Then Ebba seized a razor and mutilated her face by cutting off her nose and upper lip. She called upon her nuns to do the same, and they courageously followed her example. When the barbarians broke into the monastery, they were horrified and fled in panic. The Viking leaders sent back some warriors to burn down the monastery, and the nuns perished on April 2, 870.

COMMEMORATIONS: Gregory of Nicomedia; Titus the Wonder-worker; Theodora (Theodosia) of Tyre; Polycarp of Alexandria; George of Matskveri; Amphianos and Aedesios of Patara, Lycia; Nicetius of Lyons; Sabbas, Archbishop of Sourozh; Ebba the Younger of Coldingham, and those with her; (5th Sunday of Great Lent: St. Savvas the New of Kalymnos).

APRIL 3

Isaiah 48:17-49:4; Genesis 27:1-41
Proverbs 19:16-25

*Y*ou must never be afraid, if you are troubled by a flood of thoughts, that the enemy is too strong against you, that his attacks are never ending, that the war will last for your lifetime, and that you cannot avoid incessant downfalls of all kinds. Know that our enemies, with all their wiles, are in the hands of our divine Commander, our Lord Jesus Christ, for Whose honour and glory you are waging war. Since He himself leads you into battle, He will certainly not suffer your enemies to use violence against you and overcome you, if you do not yourself cross over to their side with your will. He will Himself fight for you and will deliver your enemies into your hands, when He wills and as He wills.

St. Theophan the Recluse and St. Nicodemus of Mt. Athos

MARTYR ULPHIANUS OF TYRE. During the fourth-century Christian persecutions under Diocletian and Galerius, Ulphianus was a young and zealous Christian from Tyre. He was encouraged by the example of St. Apian and other martyrs in Caesarea and boldly confessed Christ before Urbanus, a cruel judge. The enraged Urbanus had Ulphianus horribly scourged, his bones broken, and his joints dislocated on the rack. The martyr was sewn up into a leather sack with a dog and an aspic, then carried in a cart and thrown into the sea.

COMMEMORATIONS: Joseph the Hymnographer; Nicetas the Confessor; Cassius, Philip, and Eutychius of Thessalonica; Paul the Russian; Evagrius, Benignus, Christos, Arestus, Kinnudius, Rufus, Patricius, and Zosima; Illyrios of Mt. Myrsinonos; Elpidephoros, Dius, Bithonios, and Galykos; Nectarius of Bezhetsk; Ulphianus of Tyre; Fara of Faremoutiers.

APRIL 4

*I*t is best to live simply. …The Lord will arrange everything, just
live more simply. Do not agonize over how and what to do; let
things take their course. That is what it means to live simply.

St. Ambrose of Optina

VENERABLE ZOSIMAS OF VORBOZOMSK. Zosimas was a disciple
of St. Cornelius of Komel, the founder of the fifteenth-century monastery
dedicated to the Annunciation of the Theotokos on an island in Lake Ver-
bozoma, near White Lake in northern Russia. We know little of St. Zosimas
except that he built a wooden church there and was responsible for building up the monastery. According to tradition, as an ascetic feat, Zosimas
would carry around an animal bone that he had found. It was the size of a
man, and even after the saint's death around 1550, people would go to see
it. His relics were hidden near the Cathedral Church at the Annunciation
Monastery. The monastery was captured, plundered, and desecrated about
sixty years later. In the nineteenth century, the monastery had declined to
the point where hardly one liturgy was performed. Yet pilgrims would go to
pray to St. Zosimas for his intercessions to heal diseases, as he had become
known as a wonderworker.

COMMEMORATIONS: Publius of Egypt; Theodulus and Agathopous
of Thessalonica; Plato the Studite; Isidore of Seville; Theonas of Thessalonica; Ferfoutha of Persia, with her sister and servants; George of Mt.
Maleon; Zosimas of Palestine; Joseph the Much-ailing of the Kiev Caves;
James of Old Torzhok; Basil of Mangazea; Zosimas, founder of Annunciation Monastery at Vorbozomsk; Nicetas the Albanian; Theonas, Symeon,
and Ferbinus of Egypt; Benjamin and Nichephorus of Solovki; Elias of
Makeyevka; Nicholas, Bishop of Velsk; Nun-Martyr Maria of Gatchina.

APRIL 5

Isaiah 58:1-11; Genesis 43:26-31, 45:1-16
Proverbs 21:23-22:4

I, my child, am here today, and tomorrow I will be gone. But remember what I am about to tell you: A lot of suffering will come to humanity. The cause of the sufferings that exist, and of those sufferings that are coming, and especially the blood that flows at different wars… the cause is abortion. The embryos, that many doctors do not consider to be fully human beings, take revenge. For this sin there is no mercy. Pictured or not pictured, even if it is only one hour from conception, this child on the day of judgement will resurrect as all human beings, as one 33 years of age, but blind because it was not baptised, and he will ask his mother for the reason why she sent him in that way unenlightened. Who had given her this right? I would prefer to embrace you at your funeral dead as harlots, than as mothers with abortions.

† *Elder Gervasios Paraskevopoulos of Patras*

TRANSLATION OF THE RELICS OF ST. JOB, PATRIARCH OF MOSCOW. After his death in 1607, Patriarch Job was buried in the Dormition church of the monastery in Staritsa. Many miracles took place at his grave. Forty-five years later, Tsar Alexei ordered that the relics be uncovered. Under the direction of the Metropolitan Barlaam of Rostov, the relics of St. Job were uncovered and found fragrant and incorrupt. They healed many people from mental and physical illness. Then they were taken in procession to the Kremlin and buried at the Dormition Cathedral, where they remain today. The Alter Crosses in the churches of the monastery of Staritsa and the Tver cathedral contain parts of St. Job's miracle-working relics. He was canonized by the Russian Orthodox Church in 1989.

COMMEMORATIONS: Mark the Anchorite; Mark the Ascetic; Theodora and Didymus; Philip I of Moscow; Theodora of Thessalonica; Publius of Egypt; Maximos and Terence; Theonas, Symeon, and Phorbinus of Egypt; Thermus, Zenon, and Pompey; George of New Ephesus; Translation of the relics of St. Job, Patriarch of Moscow.

APRIL 6

*S*ometimes, in our predicaments, we become excessive and thought-
less. The things we ourselves did not achieve, we expect our children to accomplish. Because we did not manage to become doctors,
we expect our children to do so—without regard to whether or not
they have the capacity to do so. We do not let them study what
they like, but we will bring them more money. We even try to tell
them what to wear, where to go, and which person they should
marry. And yet God Himself, Who rules over us, is not so overly
authoritative with us.

† *Elder Moses the Athonite*

VENERABLE PLATONIDA OF NISIBIS IN SYRIA. Platonida was a
third-century deaconess, but she withdrew into the desert of Nisibis, where
she founded a women's monastery. She established a rule of strict monastic
asceticism. The nuns ate only once a day, and when they were not praying,
they performed various jobs and obediences. On Fridays, all work stopped
in remembrance of Christ's suffering on the Cross. They would spend
the entire day in church with services and readings. St. Platonida was an
example of meekness and love for one's neighbor. She died peacefully in
great old age in the year 308.

COMMEMORATIONS: Eutychios, Patriarch of Constantinople; Metho-
dius, Equal-to-the-Apostles; Platonida of Nisibis; 120 Martyrs of Persia;
Jeremiah and Archilias, of Rome; Gregory the Sinaite; Gregory of the Great
Lavra; Manuel, Theodore, George, Michael, and George of Samothrace;
Gennadios of Dionysiou; Martyrius of Glinsk; 2 Martyrs from Ascalon;
Sebastian of Optina; Alexander Kosmich Fleginsky; Brychan of Brecknock;
Irenaeus of Syrmium.

APRIL 7

Isaiah 66:10-25; Genesis 49:33-50:26
Proverbs 31:8-31

You need to gain three things before all others: The first is freedom from the anxieties of life; the second is a clear conscience; the third is complete detachment, such that your thoughts no longer buzz around materialities. When you have acquired these things, then sit down by yourself in a quiet place, out of the way of everyone, and close the door and withdraw your intellect from all worthless and transient things. And pray in this way: Rest your head down upon your chest and focus your physical sight along with the eye of your intellect upon the center of your stomach, at your navel. Restrain a little the rhythm of drawing in breath through your nostrils so as to allow your intellect to search inside your inner self for the place where the heart is, where all the powers of the spiritual intellect have their dwelling. In the beginning you will find only darkness, dryness, and obscurity. But if you still persist, practicing this task attentively night and day, you will find—and how marvelous it is—the dawning of unceasing joy.

St. Symeon the New Theologian

MARTYR RUFINUS THE DEACON, AQUILINA, AND 200 SOLDIERS OF SINOPE. During the reign of Emperor Maximian, Rufinus was imprisoned in the city of Sinope for confessing Christ. Aquilina attended to him in prison, where she was also arrested. In prison, they converted two hundred soldiers to Christ by their miracles. Rufinus was slaughtered with a knife, St. Aquilina was burned to death, and all 200 soldiers were beheaded. They were martyred in the year 310.

COMMEMORATIONS: George the Confessor, Bishop of Mytilene; Rufinus, Aquilina, and 200 soldiers at Sinope; Daniel of Pereyaslavl; Gerasimus of Byzantium; George, Patriarch of Jerusalem; Hegesippus the Chronicler of Palestine; Gabriel, Archbishop of Ryazan and Zaraisk; Calliopios at Pompeiopolis; Sabbas the New of Kalymnos; George of Rabrichka, Fool-for-Christ; Govan of Cornwall; Uncovering of the relics of St. Serapion, Archbishop of Novgorod.

SATURDAY

APRIL 8

Lazarus Saturday
Abstain from meat and
dairy products, and fish.
Hebrews 12:28-29, 13:1-8; John 11:1-45

The Lord will preserve, as the apple of His eye, His people, that is, Orthodox Christians who love Him and serve Him with all their heart and with all their mind, both in word and deed, day and night. And such are they who preserve entirely all the rules, dogmas, and traditions of our Eastern Orthodox Church, and who with their lips confess the piety which has been handed down by the Church, and who act in very deed in all circumstances of life according to the holy commandments of our Lord Jesus Christ.

St. Seraphim of Sarov

NEW MARTYR JOHN KOULIKAS OF AEGINA. John was known for his wisdom and zeal. One day in the year 1654, out of curiosity, John became interested in the religion of the Hagarenes. However, the Turks misconstrued his intention, beat him, and took him to the judge, where they falsely testified that John had insulted their faith. The judge demanded that he renounce Christ, but he answered, "May God never permit that I should deny my Lord Jesus Christ, even if you subject me to ten thousand deaths." The judge gave orders to imprison St. John, and then he was impaled on iron spikes.

COMMEMORATIONS: Apostles Hermes, Herodion, Agabus, Rufus, Asyncritus, and Phlegon, of the Seventy, and those with them; Celestine, Pope of Rome; Niphon, Bishop of Novgorod; Pausilipus of Thrace; Rufus the Obedient, recluse of the Kiev Caves; John Koulikas of Aegina; John Naukliros the Navigator, on Kos; Philaret of Seminara, Calabria; Josiah and Joseph of Mt. Kharasam, Persia; Perpetuus, Bishop of Tours; *Spanish* Icon of the Mother of God; (Lazarus Saturday: Feast of the Georgian Language).

SUNDAY

Palm Sunday
Abstain from meat and dairy products.
Philippians 4:4-9; John 12:1-18

APRIL 9

The earth is a country of weeping, Heaven is a country of joy. Heavenly joy grows from seeds sown on earth. These seeds are prayer and tears.

St. Ignatius Brianchaninov

MARTYRS HELIODOROS, DESAN, MARIABUS, ABDISEUS, AND 270 OTHERS IN PERSIA. During the fourth-century reign of Persian King Sapor II, his conquests and acquisitions included the lands of Mesopotamia and Armenia. Persecution of Christians began because he wanted them to become Zoroastrians, who worshiped the sun and moon. When Sapor captured the fortress of Bet-Zabde, he imprisoned Bishop Heliodoros, the priests Desan and Mariabus, and four hundred of the clergy. When he heard they had blasphemed his religion, Sapor decreed that anyone who would not worship his gods would be beheaded. Five clergymen paid homage, yet they still suffered premature death. Sapor's men waded through the Christians, killing them with the sword. Abdiesus was wounded but recovered and began preaching again. However, he was found later and stabbed to death. The murderer, his family, and the entire village suffered a twenty-year drought that forced them to leave the area. When the martyrdoms ended, one of the sons of the gravediggers built his house by the tombs. He would venerate the martyrs' relics, and miracles soon occurred, so a church was built there.

COMMEMORATIONS: Heliodoros, Desan, Mariabus, Abdiesus, and 270 others in Persia; Newly Revealed Martyrs Raphael, Nicholas, Irene, and Eleni of Lesvos; Eupsychios of Caesarea; Bademus (Vadim) of Persia; Acacius, Bishop of Amida in Mesopotamia; Woutruide, monastic foundress at Bergen (Netherlands); Martyr Patience; Fortunatus, Donatus, 12 virgins, and 6 laymen at Sirmium; Casilda of Toledo, Spain.

APRIL 10

Matthew 21:18-43; Matthew 24:3-35

*T*he Sacrament of Reconciliation, or Confession, tears up the promissory notes. It destroys the record of our sins. The Communion of the true Body and Blood of Christ gives us the power to be born again spiritually. Although this does not occur immediately, and is perhaps imperceptible to us: the kingdom of God cometh not with observation (Luke 17:20); yet there is no doubt that this rebirth will happen sooner or later, and we will begin a new life, a life in Christ.

St. Barsanuphius of Optina

NEW MARTYR CHRYSANTHOS OF XENOPHONTOS. Chrysanthos was an elderly monk from the Xenophontos Monastery on Mount Athos. Beyond the monastery record of his martyrdom, his life is unknown to us. The manuscript reads: "On 10 April, the day of the Bright Resurrection of the Lord, our Elder Chrysanthos met his end by the sword in the Queen of Cities by a Hagarene for the sake of piety." This happened in Constantinople in 1821. On the same day, Ecumenical Patriarch Gregory V was martyred.

COMMEMORATIONS: Gregory V, Patriarch of Constantinople; Terence, Africanos, Maximos, Pompeios, Zeno, Alexander, Theodore, and 33 others, at Carthage; Prophetess Huldah (Olda); Chrysanthos of Xenophontos, Mt. Athos; James (Iakovos), Aza, and Abdicius of Persia; Martyrs of Kvabtakhevi Monastery; George of Cyprus, at Acre (Palestine); Misael, Archbishop of Ryazan; Demos at Smyrna; Anastasia, abbess of Uglich and 34 nuns with her; Martyrs Beocca, Hethor, and companions, at Chertsey Abbey; Martyrs under the Danes.

APRIL 11

Matthew 22:15-23:39
Matthew 24:36-26:2

*J*oy is thankfulness, and when we are joyful, that is the best expression of thanks we can offer the Lord, Who delivers us from sorrow and sin.

† *Elder Thaddeus of Vitovnica*

MARTYRS PROCESSUS AND MARTINIAN OF ROME. When Apostles Peter and Paul were imprisoned in Rome, Processus and Martinian were pagan jail guards. Hearing the Apostles' preaching and seeing their miracles, they believed in Christ and accepted Holy Baptism in a spring that miraculously flowed in the prison. Then Peter and Paul were freed, and as they traveled on the Appian Way, Jesus appeared to Peter, who asked Christ where He was going. Jesus said, "I'm going to Rome to be crucified afresh." So Peter and Paul returned to Rome, where they were arrested again and jailed. When the jailer Paulinus learned what Processus and Martinian had done, he demanded that they renounce Christ, but instead, they confessed Him. Therefore, they were beaten with rods, burned with fire, and thrown in prison. Three days later, the jailer lost his sight and died. When his son went to the city ruler, he demanded that Processus and Martinian be put to death. They were beheaded by the sword together with St. Paul.

COMMEMORATIONS: Antipas of Pergamus; Processus and Martinian of Rome; Barsanuphius of Tver; Pharmuthius of Egypt; Euthymius and Chariton of Syandema; Callinicus of Cernica; Tryphaina and Matrona of Cyzicus; Jakov (James) of Zheleznoborovsk, and his fellow-ascetic St. James; Guthlac of Crowland; Philip, Bishop of Gortyna; Domninus, Bishop of Salona, and 8 soldiers with him; Appearance of the Mother of God at Pochaev, *The Footprint*.

APRIL 12

John 12:17-50; Matthew 26:6-16

*T*here is no spiritual death from which one cannot be resurrected by the Divine power of the risen and ascended Lord Christ; there is no torment, there is no misfortune, there is no misery, there is no suffering which the Lord will not change either gradually or all at once into quite compunctionate joy because of faith in Him.

St. Justin Popovich

VENERABLE AKAKIOS THE NEW OF KAVSOKALYVA. The monk Akakios visited several monasteries and sketes on Mount Athos, seeking spiritual advice and a place to settle. With the guidance of his spiritual father, Elder Galaction, Akakios settled at Kavsokalyva, where he had many divine visions of St. Maximos the Hut-burner. In order to conquer the flesh, Akakios practiced the two virtues of fasting and vigil. Instead of bread, he ate dry grass that he crushed with a piece of marble, and he slept only a half-hour per day. He continued these ascetic exploits despite his old age and illness. God granted him the gift of unceasing mental prayer and divine revelations. One day the abbot handed Akakios his own staff and said, "Father, take the staff and be the Superior for all these brethren until your last breath." Akakios accepted the staff, and from that day, he no longer needed a walking cane. St. Akakios died peacefully in 1730, at around 100 years old.

COMMEMORATIONS: Deposition of the Sash of the Most Holy Theotokos from Zela to Constantinople; Basil the Confessor, Bishop of Parium; Hieromartyr Artemon; Virgin Anthusa of Constantinople; Isaac the Syrian of Spoleto, Italy; Zeno, Bishop of Verona; Menas, David, and John of Palestine; Sergius II, Patriarch of Constantinople; Basil, Bishop of Ryazan; Akakios the New of Kavsokalyvia Skete, Mt. Athos; Martyrs Demes, Protion, and those with them; *Murom* and *Belynich* Icons of the Mother of God.

Holy Thursday
Strict Fast

APRIL 13

1 Corinthians 11:23-32; Matthew 26:1-20
John 13:3-17; Matthew 26:21-39
Luke 22:43-44; Matthew 26:40-27:2

*O*ur Lord and Creator suffered, endured His Passion, and died alone for us. We who broke the law; we the traitors; we who utter insults and blasphemies; we who have given ourselves up to the enemy; we deserve to be spat upon; we deserve to be mocked, insulted, buffeted, beaten, tortured, to die for all eternity. But our Lord and God out of infinite love died in our place. The servant sinned; the Lord suffered the punishment. The servant erred; the Lord was scourged. The servant stole; the Lord offered compensation. The servant was indebted; the Lord paid the debt. And in what manner did He pay it? Not in gold and silver but with His disgrace, His wounds, His blood, His death on the cross.

St. Tikhon of Zadonsk

ST. MARTIN THE CONFESSOR, POPE OF ROME. Pope Martin battled the emperor over a heretical stance in the seventh century. The emperor had come to believe in Monothelitism, which taught that Christ had two natures but one will, contrary to Orthodox dogma that He had two wills, human and divine. Trying not to overstep his power in the political realm, Martin stated that any layman or clergyman would be excommunicated for espousing this belief. The emperor expected that Martin would acquiesce to his beliefs, but when he refused, he was summoned to Rome and held captive there for two years. Then he and his group were tried and sentenced to death. The patriarch intervened for the pope, and the sentence was exchanged for exile to a frozen land, where St. Martin died the following year.

COMMEMORATIONS: Martin the Confessor, Pope of Rome; Quintilian, Maximus, and Dada of Dorostolum; Eleutherius of Persia; Zoilus of Rome; Herman of Svyatogorsk; Martyrius, Patriarch of Jerusalem; Martius of Clermont; Stephen of Izhevsk; Anastasia, foundress of Protection Convent in Kiev; Martyr Theodosius; Guinoch of Buchan; Barnabas, Archbishop of Archangelsk.

APRIL 14

1 Corinthians 5:6-8; Matthew 27:62-66

*W*hatever is loosened by the spiritual father is loosened by God as well. Everything that is forgiven by God's representative is forgiven by the Lord also… When a person confesses voluntarily, with humility and self-knowledge, he feels happiness, alleviation, and jubilation in his soul. This is a clear indication that his sins have been forgiven. And once our sins have been forgiven, then all our fear, uneasiness, and uncertainty concerning the other life vanishes.

† *Elder Ephraim of Arizona*

VENERABLE MARTYR CHRISTOPHER THE SABBAITE. St. Stephen the Melodist, the nephew of St. John of Damascus, was an eyewitness to the slaughter of the Holy Fathers of the Great Lavra of St. Savvas in the seventh century. He recorded that Martyr Christopher had converted to Orthodoxy a few years earlier and was baptized and tonsured at the Great Lavra of St. Savvas, outside Jerusalem. Over time, this monastery had been attacked several times by the Saracens, who were demanding gold and church vessels, and they slaughtered many monks. Christopher was slandered by the chief councilor of the Saracens three days before Holy Friday and was killed by the sword.

COMMEMORATIONS: Apostles Aristarchus, Pudens, and Trophimos of the Seventy; Thomais of Alexandria; Ardalion the Actor; Euthymius the Wonderworker; Azat the Eunuch and 1,000 Martyrs in Persia; Christopher of St. Sabbas Monastery; Anthony, John, and Eustathius of Vilnius (Lithuania); Demetrios of Peloponnesus, at Tripoli; Tassach, Bishop of Raholp (Ireland); Sergius Trofimov of Nizhni-Novgorod and companion; Pachomius of Gledin, Bishop of Roman; Commemoration of Sts. Raphael, Nicholas, Irene, and the other Newly Revealed Martyrs of Lesvos; *Vilna* Icon of the Mother of God.

APRIL 15

Romans 6:3-11; Matthew 28:1-20

*L*et us then not be ashamed to confess the Crucified. Be the cross our seal, made with boldness by our fingers on our brow and in everything; over the bread we eat and the cups we drink, in our comings and in our goings out; before our sleep, when we lie down and when we awake; when we are traveling, and when we are at rest.

St. Cyril of Jerusalem

MARTYR SUCHIAS AND SIXTEEN COMPANIONS IN ARMENIA. These seventeen saints were dignitaries serving in the court of the Albanian ruler in the second century. When they escorted the ruler's daughter to the capital of Armenia, Bishop Chrysos, who Apostle Thaddeus had ordained, instructed them in the Christian faith. They believed in Jesus Christ, and Chrysos baptized them in the Euphrates River in Mesopotamia. When this happened, they saw a vision of Jesus Christ. When Chrysos died, Suchias became their spiritual leader, and the seventeen went to a desolate place for solitude and prayer. They followed the spiritual discipline of fasting, eating whatever vegetation was available and drinking spring water. When the new ruler of Albania heard this, he sent his aide Barnapas along with soldiers to entreat the group to return to their former lives. When this failed, Barnapas had them nailed to the ground, burned, and dismembered. Their relics remained unburied and incorrupt for two centuries. Finally, they were buried, and a monastery and church were built over their graves. Later, a healing spring of water began to flow there.

COMMEMORATIONS: Suchias of Iberia and 16 companions; Crescens of Myra; Anastasia and Vasilissa of Rome; Daniel of Achinsk, Siberia; Mstislav-Theodore, Prince of Kiev; Pausilipus of Thrace; Ruadhan, founder and abbot of Lorrha, Ireland; Paternus (Padarn), Bishop of Llandbadam Fawr; Ananias Lampardes, Metropolitan of Lacedaemon; Leonidas, Bishop of Athens.

*T*he all gracious God today bestowed upon us gifts, too great to be adequately expressed in words. Therefore, let us all rejoice together, and while rejoicing, let us praise our God… For I ask, what was given to us for our salvation that was not given to us by the Holy Spirit? He freed us from slavery, adopted and called us to the freedom of the children of God. From this fountain (i.e., the Holy Spirit) flow prophecies, the grace of healing, and all the other gifts and fruits with which the Church is wont to adorn herself.

St. John Chrysostom

MARTYRS LEONIDAS, CHARISSA, NIKE, GALINA, KALLIDA, NUNEKHIA, VASILISSA, AND THEODORA. Leonidas and these seven women were Christians from third-century Peloponnesus in Greece during the reign and persecutions of Emperor Decius. During Holy Week, they were arrested and brought before Governor Venoustos in Corinth. Seeing that Leonidas was unshakeable in his Christian faith, he gave orders to suspend and lacerate his body. Then he ordered that he be cast into the sea with the seven holy women. On the way to the boat, Charissa recalled how the Prophetess Mariam, the sister of Moses and Aaron, led the women in song as they fled from Egypt. The other women chanted with Charissa until they arrived at the sea. Having stones tied to them, the saints were cast into the depths of the sea one day before Pascha.

COMMEMORATIONS: Virgin Martyrs Agape, Irene, and Chionia in Illyria; Irene of Corinth; Leonidas, Charissa, Nike, Galina, Kallida, Nunekhia, Vasilissa, and Theodora; John, Fool-for-Christ of Verkhoturye; Christopher of Dionysiou, Mt. Athos; Michael of Smyrna; Nicholas the Deacon of Mytilene; Fructuosis of Braga in Iberia; Theodora-Vassa, Princess of Novgorod; Felix, Januarius, Fortunatus, and Septiminus of Lycaonia; Amphilochios Makris of Patmos; *Ilyin Chernigov* Weeping Icon of the Mother of God.

April 17

Acts 1:12-17, 21-26; John 1:18-28

℘he sign of the Cross has been the most powerful weapon against the temptations of the demons, from the time of the ancient ascetics to the present day. The most horrible of the devil's devisings vanish into nothing, like smoke, when man traces the sign of the Cross over himself. Thus, it is a sign of the Lord Jesus Christ's love for mankind that the Cross—at one time a sign of criminality and shame—became, through His Crucifixion and Resurrection, the repository of all victorious power and might.

St. Nikolai Velimirovich

ST. AGAPITUS, POPE OF ROME. Agapitus was raised with every virtue during the sixth-century reign of Emperor Justinian. He was elevated through the hierarchy and became Pope of Rome. Agapitus journeyed to Constantinople to meet Emperor Justinian, and along the way, he met a man who could neither speak nor walk, being mute from birth. Taking him by the hand, Agapitus prayed and cured his legs. After receiving the Holy Mysteries, the man was also able to speak. When Agapitus arrived in Constantinople, he went to the gate of the city, called Golden, and there saw a blind beggar. Placing his hands on the man's eyes, he immediately regained his sight. Because of his virtues and the miracles that he worked, the emperor received him with honor. While he was there, he exiled Patriarch Anthimus, who was unworthily elevated to the throne because he had accepted the Monophysite heresy. In his place, Agapitus elevated to Patriarch, a priest named Menas. St. Agapitus died peacefully in Constantinople.

COMMEMORATIONS: Agapitus, Pope of Rome; Makarios Notaras, Metropolitan of Corinth; Symeon, Bishop of Persia, and with him: Abdechalas, Ananias, Usthazanes, Fusicus, Ascitrea, and Azat; Acacius II, Bishop of Melitene; Adrian of Corinthus in Persia; Ephraim the Great of Atsquri, Georgia; Paisius, Fool-for-Christ of Kiev; Zosimas of Solovki; Elias of Makeevka, Ukraine; Donnan of Eigg and those with him (Scotland); Uncovering of the relics of St. Alexander of Svir.

APRIL 18

Acts 2:14-21; Luke 24:12-35

*S*eas dry up, mountains collapse, but the glory of Christ remains forever.

St. Gabriel Urgebadze of Georgia

VENERABLE ANASTASIA OF KIEV. Anastasia was the Grand Duchess Alexandra Petronova, and during her lifetime of 62 years, she accomplished prolific works of kindness in Russia. She converted to Orthodoxy at eighteen and married Grand Duke Nikolai Nikolaevitch in St. Petersburg. Anastasia established a hospital, a clinic, a girls' orphanage, and a school for training medics. She was also the director of the council of 23 children's orphanages, housing 5,000 children. During the Russo-Turkish War, she used her personal funds to organize a team of medics. Anastasia founded the Holy Protection Convent in Kiev and settled there. She was tonsured after her husband's death. At the convent, she established a free pharmacy, a school and orphanage for girls, a hospice for terminally ill women, and a refuge for the blind. The convent could only house 150 nuns, but there were 400 applicants. Anastasia also worked as a physician's assistant during surgeries and tended to patients recovering. When a typhus epidemic struck Kiev, she organized several specialized hospitals. But then her health began to worsen, and she required surgery. After a great deal of suffering, St. Anastasia reposed on the Tuesday of Bright Week in the year 1900. Great crowds of people attended her funeral, and she was buried near the altar of the convent she had founded.

COMMEMORATIONS: Sabbas the Commander; John, disciple of St. Gregory of Decapolis; Cosmas of Chalcedon, and Auxentius; Publius of Egypt; Euthymius of Karelia, and Anthony and Felix; Athanasia of Aegina; John the Tailor; Basil the Georgian; Tamara of Cheboksara; Alexis of Ekaterinburg; Nicholas, Basil, and the lay people of Gorodets; Molaise of Leighlin; Tounom, the Arab emir who confessed Christ; Miracle of the pillar at the Holy Sepulcher; *Maximov* Icon of the Mother of God; (Bright Tuesday: Sts. Raphael, Nicholas, and Irene, and Olympia, of Mytilene).

APRIL 19

*B*rethren and fathers, at Christ's resurrection creation too, putting away its winter gloom, like a deadness puts out fresh shoots and as it were comes to life again. And yes, we see the earth wearing green, the plants flourishing, the animals skipping around, the sea tamed, and everything being changed for the better. But I must explain why I have said this. If inanimate and irrational creatures are made radiant and lovely by the resplendent resurrection, how much more ought we, who have been honored with reason and the image of God, make ourselves bright by our life and give off sweet fragrance by the spirit. For one who strives after virtue is truly the sweet fragrance of Christ.

St. Theodore the Studite

VENERABLE GEORGE THE CONFESSOR, BISHOP OF PISIDIA.
George was dedicated to God from childhood. Because of his extraordinary virtue, he was ordained bishop of Pisidia, during the ninth-century reign of Leo the Armenian. The iconoclasts embarked on their heresy to remove all icons from the churches and prohibit their veneration. They sent letters to every bishop, including George, ordering them to gather in Constantinople. St. George disagreed with the heretics; therefore, he was condemned to exile, where he suffered many hardships until the end of his life.

COMMEMORATIONS: Tryphon, Patriarch of Constantinople; George the Confessor, Bishop of Antioch; Theodore of Perga in Pamphylia, his mother Philippa, and Dioscorus, Socrates, and Dionysius; Symeon the Barefoot of Philotheou; Agathangelos of Esphigmenou; Victor (Ostrovidov) of Vyatka; Nicephorus of Katabad; Paphnutius of Jerusalem; Joasaph (Bolotov), Enlightener of Alaska; Alphege, Archbishop of Canterbury; Matrona the Blind of Moscow; Uncovering of the relics of St. Joachim, founder of Opochka Monastery, Pskov.

APRIL 20

There is only one Creator of man and of woman, one dust from which both have come, one image [of God], one law, one death, one resurrection.

St. Gregory the Theologian

ST. JOASAPH, ABBOT OF METEORA. Joasaph was the son of the pious ruler of Epirus and Thessaly in the mid-fourteenth century. From an early age, he often went to churches and monasteries on Mount Athos and Meteora and constantly attended Divine Liturgy and other services. When his father died, Joasaph inherited the Royal Throne and the title of Tsar. He left Mount Athos and went to his kingdom, where he immediately began to find ways to be rid of his royal power, and he handed it over to his relative. Joasaph retired to the Platylithos Monastery at Meteora to be with his spiritual father, St. Athanasius, who tonsured him a monk. Before Athanasius died, he appointed Joasaph the new abbot, and he continued and completed his elder's works. His sister, Maria Angelina, gave a substantial part of her fortune to Joasaph, and he built many cells, a monastic infirmary, and water cisterns. Along with St. Athanasius, he is numbered among the founding fathers of the monastery. During his tenure, St. Joasaph helped Meteora achieve the highest point in their history.

COMMEMORATIONS: Apostle Zacchaeus, Bishop of Caesarea; Theodore Trichinas of Constantinople; Gregory, Anastasius I, and Anastasius II, Patriarchs of Antioch; Victor, Zotikos, Zeno, Acindynos, Christopher, Theonas, Caesarios, Antoninos, and Severian of Nicomedia; John the Ancient of Old Lavra; Joasaph and Athanasius of Meteora; Alexander of Oshevensk; Gabriel of Zabludov, Poland; Theodosius of Kolomna; Betran and Theotimos I, Bishops in Scythia Minor; Caedwalla, King of the West Saxons; Translation of the relics of St. Nikolai Velimirovich; *Cyprus* and *Keepiazh* Icons of the Mother of God; (Bright Thursday: St. Anastasia of Kiev; St. Michael the Mavroudis).

Bright Friday
Life-giving Spring of the Theotokos
Fast-free

APRIL 21

Acts 3:1-8; John 2:12-22

*E*ntreat the Mother of Light, the immaculate Theotokos, to help you, for she is the greatest means of consolation after God. When a person calls upon her holy name, he immediately senses her help. She is a mother; when she was on earth, as a human being and fellow-sufferer she suffered the same things we do, and for this reason, she has great sympathy for pained souls and swiftly comes to help them.

† *Elder Ephraim of Arizona*

ST. MAXIMIANOS, ARCHBISHOP OF CONSTANTINOPLE. Maximianos was the son of wealthy and noble parents in fifth-century Rome. He was pious, well educated, and had a good reputation among the Christians. He led a monastic life even before becoming a priest. Patriarch Sisinios of Constantinople ordained him to the priesthood. When Nestorius was deposed from the see of Constantinople, Maximianos was chosen by unanimous vote of the emperor, clergy, and the people. However, the Syrians were not invited to the consecration because they regarded Nestorius' removal as uncanonical. Maximianos participated in many negotiations to heal the split with the Syrians, but he died before this happened. After two years and five months as Patriarch, St. Maximianos died peacefully on Great Thursday.

COMMEMORATIONS: Januarius, Bishop of Benevento, with Proclus, Sosius, Festus, Desiderius, Gantiol, Eutychius, and Acutius, at Pozzuoli; Maximianos, Archbishop of Constantinople; Anastasius of St. Catherine's on Mt. Sinai; James of Stromynsk; Alexandra the Empress, wife of Diocletian and her servants Isaakios, Apollo, and Kodratos of Nicomedia; Niphon, Bishop of Novgorod; Maelruba of Apur Crossan, Ireland; Beuno of Clynnog Fawr, Wales; Basil Martysz of Teratyn (Poland); Alexis of Bortsumany, Nizhni-Novgorod; John Noultzos, in Kastoria; Uncovering of the relics of St. Theodore of Sanaxar Monastery; *Mozdok* Icon of the Mother of God; (Bright Friday: *Syriac* Wonderworking Icon of the Mother of God of Ghighiu Monastery).

APRIL 22

𝒧et Christ not be missing from your heart.
St. Amphilochios Makris of Patmos

HOLY APOSTLE BARTHOLOMEW (NATHANIEL) OF THE TWELVE.
With Apostle Philip, Bartholomew preached the Gospel in Syria and Asia
Minor. Apostle Philip's sister, Mariam, traveled with them, and they suffered many hardships and tribulations. In Hieropolis, the Apostles healed
and baptized Stakhios, who had been blind for forty years. When news of
this spread throughout the city, many sick and demon-possessed went to
them for healing and Holy Baptism. But when the governor heard that his
people were turning away from pagan worship, he gave orders to arrest these
Apostles. Thinking there were magical powers in their clothes, they stripped
Bartholomew and Philip, but Mariam appeared like a fiery torch, and no one
dared touch her. Philip and Bartholomew were sentenced to crucifixion. When
Apostle Philip was nailed to the cross upside down, an earthquake erupted,
and a fissure swallowed up the governor, pagan priests, and many others.
The pagans quickly took down the apostles, but Philip had already given up
his spirit. Bartholomew and Mariam were released. Mariam preached the
word of God in Likaoneia, where she peacefully reposed. Bartholomew went
to India, where he translated the Gospel of Matthew and converted many
pagans. He worked miracles in Great Armenia and healed the daughter of the
emperor Polimios. The emperor, his family, and the people from ten cities in
that country accepted Baptism. However, through the intrigues of the pagan
priests, Bartholomew was seized by the emperor's brother, Astiag. He had
Bartholomew crucified upside down, yet even from the cross, he did not cease
preaching Christ. Bartholomew's skin was flayed, and then he was beheaded.

COMMEMORATIONS: Apostles Nathaniel, Apelles, Luke, and Clement; Theodore the Sykeote; Leonidas of Alexandria; Platon of Banja Luka;
Vitalis of Abba Seridus; Epipodius of Lyons; Martyr Nearchus; Ananias
of Malles; Sabbas of Gornji Karlovac; Gregory the Gravanos; Ekaterina of
Piukhtitsa; Vsevolod of Rostov; (Bright Saturday: St. Kali the Philanthropist of Asia Minor).

APRIL 23

Acts 12:1-11; John 20:19-31

*A*s the most effective prayer the Church Fathers use the short phrase, 'Lord Jesus Christ, have mercy on me.' This prayer is the key to the spiritual life. It is a prayer that cannot be taught either by books, or by spiritual fathers or by anyone else. Its sole teacher is divine grace.
St. Porphyrios of Kavsokalyvia

KING SOLOMON I OF IMERETIA. As king of eighteenth-century western Georgia, Solomon was an excellent strategist. His father was Alexander V, King of Imereti (Western Georgia). Solomon succeeded him and quickly took action against the renegade nobles, and they, in turn, staged a coup. Solomon soon regained the crown and began a series of reforms to stabilize his kingdom, which had been torn apart by civil wars. On three different occasions, he defeated attacking Ottoman armies. Solomon also forged an alliance with his relative who ruled eastern Georgia, and together they joined a war with the Ottoman Empire. Finally, the Ottomans were forced to sign a treaty with Solomon. He ruled for 32 years. When he died in 1784, he was buried at the Gelati Monastery. King Solomon was canonized by the Georgian Orthodox Church in 2016. He came to be known as Solomon I the Great.

COMMEMORATIONS: George the Great Martyr; Anatolios and Protoleon, soldiers converted by the martyrdom of St. George; Glykerios the Farmer, Athanasius the Magician, Valerius, and Donatus, at Nicomedia; Gerontios and Polychronia, parents of St. George; George of Cyprus, at Ptolemais; Solomon I of Imeretia; George of Shenkursk, Fool-for-Christ; Egor (George) of Russia; George of Spas Chekriak; Sergius of Nabroz; John, priest; Lazarus the Shepherd of Bulgaria, at Pergamus; Iberius (Ibar) of Beggerin; Therinus of Bothrotus in Epirus; Adalbert Voitech, Bishop of Prague.

APRIL 24

A man who gives in to his passions is like a man who is shot at by an enemy, catches the arrow in his hands, and then plunges it into his own heart.

St. Dorotheos of Gaza

NEW MARTYR NICHOLAS AT MAGNESIA. Nicholas lived in the eighteenth-century town of Yaya Koy in Asia Minor during the Turkish domination. His father was the head shepherd for the Aga Kara Osumano-glu, and Nicholas assisted him. When Nicholas was twenty-two years old, he was preparing to be married on the Sunday after Pascha, and he traveled to the city to formally ask permission from his father and the Aga. However, he dressed in Muslim shoes and fez for this journey, which only Muslims are permitted to wear. Nicholas and his family were Orthodox Christians. When some of the servants saw Nicholas' clothing, they took him to the Aga. He told Nicholas that someone of another faith was not permitted to wear these items, and he was asked if he dressed this way to become a Muslim. Nicholas replied, "May I never deny my faith." He said that he dressed that way because his father was the Aga's servant. The Aga gave orders to beat him, but only lightly. Nicholas remained steadfast and said, "It is not possible for me to deny the faith which I believe, not with sticks or beatings but even if you inflict upon me painful death." Nicholas was offered honors and riches, but he responded, "I see my death before my eyes and there is no way I will ever deny it." He was beaten without mercy and put in prison, where he thanked God for being able to witness for Him. Martyr Nicholas died three days later.

COMMEMORATIONS: Savvas Stratelates and 70 soldiers; Sabbas the Commander, the Goth; Elizabeth the Wonderworker; Thomas, Fool-for-Christ; Pasicratos, Valentine, and Julius, at Dorostolum; Eusebius, Neon, Leontius, Longinus, and others; Xenophon of Xenophontos; Alexander of Lyons; Innocent, on the Mount of Olives; Sabbas and Alexis of the Kiev Caves; Nicholas of Magnesia; George in Anatolia; Joseph the Confessor; Symeon, Elias, and Sava, of Ardeal; Doukas of Mytilene; Branko of Veljusa; Wilfrid of York; Egbert of Iona.

St. Mark the Evangelist
Fast-free
1 Peter 5:6-14; Luke 10:16-21

*W*e should realize that, as long as we're in sin, that is, transgressing against Christ's divine commandments, we can be as pious as we like, read all the prayers of the saints, the various hymns and the canons all day every day, it will get us nowhere. Since the Lord Himself said, as a reproof and complaint: 'Why do you call me "Lord, Lord" but not do as I say?' In other words: 'As long as you live in breach of my commandments, there's no point in directing lots of long prayers towards me.' Only one prayer is pleasing to Him: that is the practical prayer which consists in abandoning, with all our soul and forever, every breach of His holy commandments and becoming firm in His fear, carrying out every righteous task with spiritual joy and genuine love.

St. Maximos the Confessor

ST. RUSTICUS, ARCHBISHOP OF LYON. Rusticus and his brother St. Viventiolus were sons of a nobleman in fifth-century Lyon, in the south of France, and their grandfather was St. Eucherius. Rusticus served for many years as a magistrate. He was married and had three children. At 39 years of age, he succeeded Lupicinus as Bishop of Lyon and served in that capacity for seven years. Shortly after his consecration, St. Rusticus sent financial aid to Pope Gelasius I.

COMMEMORATIONS: Holy Apostle and Evangelist Mark; Stephen, Patriarch of Antioch; Macedonias II, Patriarch of Constantinople; Aninanus, second Bishop of Alexandria; Sylvester, abbot of Obnora Monastery; Martyr Nike, who believed in Christ through St. George; 8 martyred anchorites; Basil of Poiana Marului, Romania; Mella of Doire-Melle in Ireland; Rusticus, Archbishop of Lyon; Repose of Elder Philotheos Zervakos of Paros; Commemoration of the Consecration of the Church of the Apostle Peter next to Hagia Sophia in Constantinople; *Constantinople* Icon of the Mother of God.

WEDNESDAY

Abstain from meat and dairy products, and fish.
Acts 4:13-22; John 5:17-24

APRIL 26

*L*et nothing visible or invisible hinder me, through jealousy, from attaining to Jesus Christ. Come fire, come cross, come whole herds of wild beasts, come drawing and quartering, scattering of bones, cutting off of limbs, crushing of the whole body, all the horrible blows of the devil—let all these things come upon me, if only I may be with Christ.

St. Ignatius of Antioch

ST. STEPHEN, BISHOP OF PERM. Stephen was a Russian Orthodox Christian in the fourteenth century. Having been inclined to prayer since his youth, he became a monk at the Monastery of St. Gregory the Theologian in Rostov. He was inspired to bring Christianity to the pagans in Perm. So he learned the language, constructed an alphabet, and translated from the Greek Church service books in preparation for his journey. He was ordained to the priesthood and set off as a missionary with the blessing of his metropolitan. With patience and much labor, the people began to come to him for Holy Baptism. He had a church built, and it prospered. St. Stephen became the first bishop of Perm. He had replaced idol worship with Christianity in a distant, foreign land. He lived into old age and died in Moscow.

COMMEMORATIONS: Stephen, Bishop of Perm; Glaphyra of Nicomedia; Basil of Amasea; Andrew and Anatole, disciples of St. Euthymius the Great; George of Cyprus; Ioannicius of Devic; Nestor the Silent; Cyril, Cindeus, and Tasie of Axiopolis; Righteous Justa; Richarius, in Picardy; Kalandion of Tamassos; Leo of Samos; New Martyrs of Novo Selo, Bulgaria.

APRIL 27

*P*ut up with that person who grieves you and creates temptations. Put up with him joyfully. Pray for him every day. Always try to do good to him, to commend him, to speak to him with love, and God will work His miracle and he will reform. Then our Christ will be glorified, the devil, who sets up all the stumbling-blocks, will be foiled. Force yourself especially to stop criticizing and lying. Your penance is to do one komboskini (prayer rope) every day for this person who hates you, so that God may enlighten him to repent, and do ten more metanoias (prostrations) daily for one month. If this person does something against you, overlook it, be patient. Let yourself be wronged, but do no wrong; let yourself be slapped, but do not slap; let yourself be criticized, but do not criticize. When you do all of this, then the Son of God, along with the Father and the Holy Spirit, will dwell in your soul. Fight the good fight; overlook the deeds of this person just as Christ has overlooked your sins.

† *Elder Ephraim of Arizona*

ST. POLLION THE READER OF CIBALIS IN PANNONIA. Pollion was a Church reader in Cibalis, the present-day city of Vinkovci, Croatia. According to the *Roman Martyrology, d*uring the persecutions of Emperor Diocletian, Pollion suffered interrogation from the Prefect Probus, but he refused to abandon Christianity. St. Pollion was put to death outside the city walls.

COMMEMORATIONS: Eulogios the Hospitable; Symeon the Kinsman of the Lord; Floribert of Luik; John the Confessor of Cathares Monastery; Elias (Ardunis) of Mt. Athos; Seraphim of Phanar; Stephen of the Kiev Caves; Lollion the Younger; Pollion the Reader of Cibalis; Nicon of St. Gerasimus; Machalus of the Isle of Man; Burning of the relics of St. Sava I of Serbia by the Turks; Glorification of New Hieromartyr St. Hilarion (Troitsky), Archbishop of Verey.

**Abstain from meat and
dairy products, and fish.**
Acts 5:1-11; John 5:30-6:2

APRIL 28

*F*aith is indiscriminate acceptance of the things heard, and assurance
of the things preached with God's grace.

St. Basil the Great

ST. CYRIL, BISHOP OF TUROV. Cyril was from a wealthy family in
twelfth-century Turov. He eagerly read the sacred books, in both Russian
and Greek, and deeply understood them. Cyril refused his inheritance
and chose to become a monk at the Saints Boris and Gleb Monastery in
Turov. He struggled at prayer and fasting, and he taught the brethren the
importance of obedience to one's spiritual elder. Otherwise, the monastic
vow is unfulfilled, and therefore the monk cannot be saved. Cyril redoubled
his ascetic struggles by living on a pillar, like St. Symeon the Stylite. Here
he contemplated Holy Scripture, and many visitors sought his spiritual
advice. As his fame spread, he was chosen to be the Bishop of Turov, and
he defended the Church from heresy. Because of his love for solitude, Cyril
retired from his See and devoted himself to spiritual writing. His contem-
poraries called him a "Russian Chrysostom." St. Cyril believed that his task
was to discern the true and hidden meaning of Holy Scripture. He also
said that his job was to proclaim the Word of God. He praised and blessed
those who attended church.

COMMEMORATIONS: Memnon the Wonderworker; Nine Martyrs
at Cyzicus—Theognes, Rufus, Antipater, Theostichus, Artemas, Magnus,
Theodotus, Thaumasius, and Philemon; Dada, Maximus, and Quintilian at
Dorostolum; Auxibius II, Bishop of Soli in Cyprus; Cyril, Bishop of Turov;
Basil Kishkin of Glinsk; Cyril, founder of Syrinsk Monastery (Karelia);
Cronan, abbot of Roscrea Monastery, Ireland; Cyriacus, abbot of Kargopol;
Tibald of Pannonia; Commemoration of the Miracle at Carthage of Africa.

APRIL 29

*T*he brilliance of the Christian faith is witnessed by the gifts of the Holy Spirit that are given to the person who believes in Christ. We find these divine gifts abundantly poured upon all the faithful who have been baptized in the name of the Savior Jesus Christ. He who was previously unlearned becomes filled with the Holy Spirit, and the spirit of wisdom and understanding rests upon him. Yesterday he was undistinguished and one of the multitude; today he is someone important with knowledge, and one of the few destined for the Kingdom of Heaven. Yesterday he was ignorant, today he is full of understanding and truth. Yesterday he was deluded in his pursuits, today he is endowed with purpose and strength. Yesterday he was oblivious to God, today he is filled with knowledge and Godly fear.

St. Nektarios of Pentapolis

ST. BASIL OF OSTROG. Filled with love for the Church from his youth, Basil became a monk in the country of Herzegovina in the seventeenth century. He developed a reputation for wrestling with progressively more difficult ascetic labors. He was elected bishop of Zakholm and Skenderia but continued to live in a monastery. When the Turks overran the area, he moved to Ostrog, where he lived out his life in peace and prayer for his people. His relics remained whole and incorrupt and continue to produce innumerable miracles of healing, not only to those in the faith but also to people of other beliefs. St. Basil's memory is commemorated there every year.

COMMEMORATIONS: Jason and Sosipater of the Seventy, with Saturninus, Jakischolus, Faustianus, Januarius, Marsalius, Euphrasius, Mammius, Virgin Cercyra, and Christodolus the Ethiopian; Zeno, Eusebius, Neon, and Vitalis, converted by Apostles Jason and Sosipater; John Kaloktenes the New Merciful One; Basil of Ostrog; Martyrs Quintian and Atticus; Secundellus in Gaul; Diodorus and Rhodopianus in Anatolia; John Tolaius, Patriarch of Alexandria; Arsenius of Suzdal; Nicetas of Synnada; John of Romania; Nectarius of Optina; Holy Martyrs of Lazeti (Georgia); Nicephorus of Sebaze.

Sunday of the Myrrhbearing Women
Fast-free

APRIL 30

Acts 6:1-7; Mark 15:43-16:8

*L*et us consider how we should glorify God. We cannot glorify Him in any way other than that in which He was glorified by the Son; for in the same way as the Son glorified the Father, the Son in turn was glorified by the Father. Let us, then, diligently use these same means to glorify Him who allows us to call Him 'our Father in heaven', so that we may be glorified by Him with the glory that the Son possesses with the Father prior to the world (cf. Jn. 17:5). These means are the cross, or death to the whole world, the afflictions, the trials and the other sufferings undergone by Christ. If we endure them with great patience, we imitate Christ's sufferings; and through them we glorify our Father and God, as His sons by grace and as coheirs of Christ.

St. Symeon the New Theologian

ST. DONATOS, BISHOP OF EUREIA IN EPIRUS. Donatos was a wonderworking bishop from Eureia, Albania, in the fourth century. He once raised a man from the dead so that he might defend his widow from the extortion of a moneylender. The man had repaid the loan before he died, but the lender tried to collect a second time from the widow. The prayers of Donatos caused rain to fall during a drought, caused a spring to flow from dry ground, and healed the daughter of Emperor Theodosius the Great of an unclean spirit simply by arriving at the palace. One day Donatos went with his clergy to a spring of undrinkable brackish water. When he arrived, Donatos first cast a huge snake from the water, and it died. Then he blessed the spring and drank from it.

COMMEMORATIONS: Apostle James, the brother of St. John the Theologian; Maximus of Ephesus; Clement the Hymnographer; Ignatius (Brianchaninov), Bishop of the Caucasus; Maximus of Ephesus; James, his wife, and son Alexis of Plotava; Donatos of Eureia; Eutropius and Estelle of Saintes; Erconwald of London; Endelienta of Cornwall; Translation of the relics of St. Argyre of Prusa; Translation of the relics of St. Theodore of Byzantium.

MAY 1

$\mathcal{L}$et me recall a wise custom of the ancient Holy Fathers: when greeting each other, they did not ask about health or anything else, but rather about prayer, saying "How is your prayer?" The activity of prayer was considered by them to a be a sign of the spiritual life, and they called it the breath of the spirit. If the body has breath, it lives; if breathing stops, life comes to an end. So it is with the spirit. If there is prayer, the soul lives; without prayer, there is no spiritual life.

St. Theophan the Recluse

ST. BREAGA OF CORNWALL. The life of St. Breaga clearly illustrates the role of women in successfully spreading Orthodoxy. John Leland, the father of local history in England, wrote about her life. Breaga was from late-fifth to early sixth-century Ireland. She became a nun and studied at a monastery founded by St. Brigid of Kildare. Later she was sent along with seven other male and female preachers to Cornwall. Some of them were soon murdered by a cruel ruler, Tewdwr Mawr. Breaga survived and built churches, and her endeavors were successful in the face of fierce pagan opposition. She had traveled all over Cornwall, and converts would gather at places of worship that she had created. St. Breaga was greatly venerated after her death for many hundreds of years, and her relics were famous for working miracles.

COMMEMORATIONS: Prophet Jeremiah; Panaretus of Paphos; Philosophos of Alexandria; Maria of Merambelos; Isidora of Tabenna; Tamara of Georgia; Nicephoros of Chios; Ultan of Fosse; Macarius of Kiev; Batas of Nisibis; Zosimas of Kumurdo; Michael of Chalcedon; Euthymius, Ignatius, and Acacius of Serres; Paphnutius of Borovsk; Gerasimus of Boldino; Luke of Glinsk; Brieuc, in Brittany; Breaga of Cornwall; Symeon of Trier; Romanus of Raqqa; Asaph of Llanelwy; Walpurga of Germany; Commemoration of the Dreadful Earthquake at Sinai.

**Removal of the Relics of
St. Athanasius the Great
Fast-free**
Hebrews 13:7-16; Matthew 5:14-19

*W*e must see God in the faces of our children and give God's love to our children. The children should learn to pray. And in order for children to pray they must have in them the blood of praying parents. This is where some people make the mistake of saying, 'since the parents are devout and pray, meditate on Holy Scripture and bring up their children in the nurture and admonition of the Lord, it is natural that they will become good children.' But nevertheless, we see the very opposite result on account of coercion. It is not sufficient for the parents to be devout. They mustn't oppress the children to make them good by force. We may repel our children from Christ when we pursue the things of our religion with egotism.

St. Porphyrios of Kavsokalyvia

MARTYRS HESPERUS AND ZOE, AND THEIR SONS KYRIAKOS AND THEODULUS. This Christian family was from Asia Minor during the second-century reign of Hadrian. They were slaves to an idol-worshipping merchant, Catallus. The family was treated horribly. They were given orders to do things against their faith and were not permitted to pray or chant. To celebrate his son's birth, Catallus invited all his slaves to dine at his table, thereby forcing them to eat foods sacrificed to the idols. The family refused to eat, so a large furnace was heated, and the four saints were thrown in to burn to death so that nothing would remain of them. The following day, they opened the furnace and found all four martyrs in the position of prayer, and a beautiful fragrance filled the air. Emperor Justinian had their holy relics taken to Constantinople.

COMMEMORATIONS: Hesperus, Zoe, and their sons; Athanasius III Patellarios; Boris-Michael of Bulgaria; Athanasius of Syandem; Jordan the Wonderworker; Basil of Kadom; Matrona the Blind (Greek Calendar); Translation of the relics of St. Athanasius the Great.

**Abstain from meat and
dairy products, and fish.**
Acts 8:18-25; John 6:35-39

MAY 3

*P*eople are blind and do not see what takes place in church during
the Divine Liturgy. Once I was serving and I could not make the
Great Entrance because of what I saw. I suddenly felt someone
pushing me by my shoulder and guiding me toward the holy
prothesis. I thought it was the chanter. I turned around and saw a
huge wing that the Archangel had laid on my shoulder, and that he
was guiding me to make the Great Entrance. What amazing things
take place in the alter during the Divine Liturgy! ... Sometimes
I cannot handle it, and so I pass out in a chair, and thus some
concelebrants conclude that I have got something wrong with my
health, but they do not realize what I see and hear.

St. Iakovos Tsalikis of Evia

ST. ECUMENIUS THE WONDERWORKER, BISHOP OF TRICCA.

Ecumenius was known as an exceptional interpreter of the Holy Scriptures.
He authored several commentaries on St. Paul's Epistles, the Acts of the
Apostles, the Catholic epistles, and the Apocalypse. He was greatly influ-
enced and guided by the writings of St. John Chrysostom. Ecumenius was
a man of high moral character. He was elevated to the Episcopal throne of
Tricca in Thessaly. He died peacefully.

COMMEMORATIONS: Timothy the Reader and his wife Maura of
Antinoe in Egypt; Peter, Bishop of Argos; Ecumenius, Bishop of Tricca;
Diodoros and Rodopianos the Deacon of Aphrodisia; Ansfried of Utrecht;
Mamai, Catholicos of Georgia; Xenia of Peloponnesus; Paul of Vilnius,
Lithuania; Holy 27 Martyrs; Eupraxia and Juliana of Conception Monas-
tery in Moscow; Gregory, Bishop of Rostov; Irodion of Romania; Theo-
phanes of Vatopedi; Theodosius of the Kiev Caves Monastery; Ahmet the
Calligrapher of Constantinople; Michael and Arsenius the Georgians;
Glywys of Cornwall; Sergius of Buzuluk; Translation of the relics of St.
Luke of Mt. Steirion; *Svensk* Icon of the Mother of God.

MAY 4

*S*eek purity. Do not listen to evil things about anyone. Stop your own mean thoughts. Stay away from any lie. Never fear to tell the truth. Just pray first and ask the Lord to bless you.

† *Elder Nikolai Guryanov*

STARO RUS ICON OF THE MOTHER OF GOD. The Staro Rus icon of the Mother of God is the largest portable icon in the world and is so named because of its time spent in Staro Rus. The Greeks had taken it to that city due to Turkish and Tatar threats, and it remained there until the sixteenth century. In 1570, a plague struck the town of Tikhvin, and it was revealed to a resident that if the Staro Rus Icon was sent there, the pestilence would end. The icon was carried throughout Tikhvin, and the plague ceased. Over two hundred years later, in 1787, unable to have the original icon returned to Staro Rus, a priest ordered a copy to be made, and this was brought to Staro Rus. But the people of Staro Rus greatly desired the return of the original. Eighteen years later, the people again petitioned its return, which was still not granted. Several more attempts were denied in later years. Finally, 180 years after the first petition, the wonderworking icon was returned with a grand procession. During Soviet rule, the original icon and its copy were ravaged, and the silver covers were removed. The original icon disappeared during the war years. Finally, the icon copy was returned to Staro Rus, and now it is revered as miraculous.

COMMEMORATIONS: Silvanus of Gaza and 40 Martyrs; Nikephoros the Hesychast of Mt. Athos; Pelagia of Tarsus in Asia Minor; Hilary the Wonderworker; Erasmus of Formia in Campania; Aphrodisius, Leontius, Anthony, Valerian, Macrobius, and others, at Scythopolis; Athanasius of Corinth; Nicephorus of the Medicium; Dimitry Lyubimov of Gdov; Alphanov Brothers: Nicetas, Cyril, Nicephorus, Clement, and Isaac of Novgorod; Monica of Tagaste; Florian and 40 companions at Lorsch, Austria; Ethelred, King of Mercia; Conleth of Kildare; New Martyr Vasily Martysz; Synaxis of the Venerable Fathers of Mount Sinai; Translation of the relics of St. Lazarus and St. Mary Magdalene; *Staro Rus* Old Russian Icon of the Mother of God.

MAY 5

*G*od forebears all our infirmities, but He cannot bear one who constantly murmurs, so He punishes him in order to correct him.

† *Elder Justin Pârvu of Romania*

VENERABLE ADRIAN OF MONZA. When Adrian came of age, he obliged his parents and agreed to marry, but he became seriously ill before the wedding. During his illness, he had a vision of a solitary church situated between two rivers, and he heard a voice, "Here is thy place." When he recovered, he took monastic vows and went in search of the church. Along the way, he spent time in several monasteries. Finally, Adrian found the church just as he had seen it in the vision, but the spring rains had flooded it. Still, Adrian and several monks that had come with him decided to settle there. Later an elder visited there and advised them to go live under the spiritual guidance of monk Therapont of Monzensk, which they did. There they founded a monastery at the River Monza near Kostroma. They ate by the work of their hands. St. Adrian died peacefully in 1610, and his relics were buried together with those of Elder Therapont in the church they founded.

COMMEMORATIONS: Great Martyr Irene of Thessalonica; Martyrs Neophytos, Gaius, and Gaianus; Barlaam of Serpukhov; Martin and Heraclius of Illyria; Eulogius the Confessor of Edessa; Adrian of Monza Monastery; Ephraim of Nea Makri; Efthymios, Bishop of Madytos in Thrace; Hydrock of Cornwall; Hilary of Arles; Translation of the relics of St. Aldhelm, Bishop of Sherborne; Martha of Monemvasia (Greek Calendar); Uncovering of the relics of St. James of Zhelezny Borok Monastery; *Inexhaustible Cup* Icon of the Mother of God.

MAY 6

*S*eek to distinguish yourself from others only in your generosity. Be like gods to the poor, imitating God's mercy. Humanity has nothing so much in common with God as the ability to do good.
St. Gregory of Nazianzus

VENERABLE GEORGE OF GOMATI. George was from nineteenth-century Halkidiki, Greece, during their enslavement to the Turks. He was a miller by trade and had a wife and children. He would grind the wheat for free for the poor and give flour to the needy. Such was his philanthropy. Because of the military movements of the enemy, he told his family to stay in the village for safety. However, they did not listen, and George returned to find his family gone and his mill in ruins. Brokenhearted, he went to live as a hermit in a cave and dedicated his life to God with unceasing prayer and fasting. George ate only mountain greens. He would descend from his cave by night and leave greens and wood outside the doors of pregnant women, the sick, and the poor. He also took care of the gardens and vineyards of the poor. But when the people no longer saw George, they found him in his cave dead. His body and the entire area around his cave were fragrant. The people and the priest took him to the village cemetery for burial, but along the way, the saint's body became so heavy that they could no longer move it. The priest said this was a sign, and they buried George there. Later, a chapel was built over his tomb. St. George began to work many miracles, especially to heal the pain of children's ears.

COMMEMORATIONS: Barbarus the Soldier, Bacchus, Callimachus, and Dionysius, in Morea; Barbarus the former robber; Mamas, Pachomius, and Hilarion, monks; Martyrs Danax, Mesiurs, Therin, and Donatus; Job the Long-Suffering; Job of Pochaev; Micah of Radonezh; Demetrios of Peloponnesus; Seraphim of Mt. Domvu; Sophia of Pontus; Edbert of Lindisfarne; Sinaites of Serbia: Romilus, Romanus, Sisoes, Martyrius, Gregory, Zosimas, and Gregory; George of Gomati; Translation of the relics of St. Sava I of Serbia and St. Pachomius of Nerekhta; (1st Saturday of May: St. George of Gomati; St. Gervasios of Gomati, the Athonite).

MAY 7

Acts 26:1, 12-20; John 5:1-15

$\mathscr{B}$e careful not to despise one of the least of these who are scorned and sick in this world. For this contempt and affront of yours doesn't stop at those unfortunate fellows, but ascends through them to the presence of the Creator and Fashioner, whose image they bear. You will be greatly astonished in that day, if you see the Holy Spirit of God resting in them more than in your heart.

St. Joseph the Hesychast

HOLY SIX VIRGIN MARTYRS OF GEROPLATONOS IN HALKIDIKI. When the Greek Revolution began in Halkidiki in 1854, sixty-five Turks were killed. But this effort failed, and thirty Greek notables were massacred. The destruction extended throughout Halkidiki. In Geroplatonos, seven girls were locked inside a mill surrounded by Turks. They demanded these Christian girls to change their religion. One acquiesced and married a Turk, but the other six were burned alive. Traces of the fire can still be seen in the mill today. The girls' last names were: Mizouli, Karakasi, Lemoni, Tsami, Paschou, and Nestora.

COMMEMORATIONS: Commemoration of the Appearance of the Sign of the Precious Cross over Jerusalem; Domitianus, Bishop of Maastricht; Quadratus (Codratus), Rufinus, and Saturninus of Nicomedia; Acacius the Centurion at Byzantium; Nilus, founder of Sora Skete; John of Zedazeni in Georgia and 12 disciples; Thaddeus of Urbnisi; Pachomius the Russian of Usaki; John Psychaites the Confessor; John of Beverley, Bishop of York; Martyr Maximos, in Asia; Repose of St. Alexis Toth in America; Translation of the relics of St. Euthymius the Great; Finding of the relics of St. Nilus the Myrrhgusher of Mt. Athos; Zhirovits and Lubech Icons of the Mother of God; (Third Sunday of Pascha: St. Tamara, Queen of Georgia; St. Seraphim, Archbishop of Phanarion and Neochorion; St. Elias Ardunis of Mt. Athos; All Saints of Thessalonica); (1st Sunday of May: All Saints of Gortyna and Arcadia in Crete; Six Virgin Martyrs of Geroplatonos in Halkidiki, Greece).

*T*he faster you acquire a virtue, the easier it is lost. The more slowly and laboriously you acquire it, the more steadfastly it remains; just like that squash plant that grew tall and said to the cypress tree, "See how much I've grown in just a few days! You've been here for so many years and haven't grown much at all!" "Yes," said the cypress tree, "but you still haven't seen storms, heat waves, and cold spells!" And after a little while, the squash plant dried up, while the cypress tree remained where it was. This is also how a spiritual man is. Both during a storm and during times of peace he remains the same. Why? Because the long period of time has created stability. When he first renounced the world, his spiritual condition was unstable, but with time, the grace of God gradually worked out his salvation and freedom from the passions. Thus, a person needs to force himself today, and the grace of God will start acting by itself tomorrow.

† *Elder Ephraim of Arizona*

ST. IDUBERGA, FOUNDRESS OF NIVELLES. Iduberga was the daughter of a count of Aquitaine. She married the mayor of the palace, and they had two daughters. When her husband died, Iduberga was advised by St. Amandus to establish a convent at Nivelles in Belgium. She dedicated herself and all her assets to this effort. The first nuns came to the monastery from Ireland. Before her death, Iduberga arranged for her daughter Gertrude to succeed her as abbess. Later, St. Iduberga's relics were carried in procession every year with the relics of the other saints of Nivelles.

COMMEMORATIONS: Synaxis of St. John the Theologian; Arsenios the Great; Pimen the Faster of the Far Caves; Macarius of Ghent; Milles the Hymnographer; Arsenius the Lover of Labor; Arsenios of Varnakova; Iduberga of Nivelles; Zosima and Adrian of Volokolamsk; Hierax of Egypt; Wiro of Utrecht; Plechelm and Otger of Odilienberg; Victor of Milan; Soldier Martyrs slain by the sword; Translation of the relics of St. Arsenius of Novgorod; Miracle wrought by the icon of the Mother of God of Cassiope.

MAY 9

*P*rayer is food for the soul. Do not starve the soul, it is better to let
the body go hungry.

St. Joseph of Optina

VENERABLE JOSEPH OF OPTINA. Joseph was born to simple, pious
parents in the Ukraine province of Kharkov. They would read the Lives of
the Saints to their six children, who they raised in obedience and the fear
of God. Joseph was a happy and affectionate child. When he was eight
years old, he had a vision of Panagia one day as he was playing. Another
time, his house was spared from burning to the ground after praying to
the Panagia. Joseph became an orphan at eleven. He lived unhappily with
various families, taking odd jobs. Then Joseph visited his sister, a nun,
and he decided to live with the Elders of Optina. When St. Ambrose first
saw him, he prophesied good things for him. Joseph struggled in perfect
obedience and humility, renouncing his own will and judging no one. For
the next 30 years, he became the cell attendant to St. Ambrose and slept in
the elder's reception room. Joseph read the wisdom of the elders in the four
books of the *Philokalia* and would share this with those seeking advice. In
keeping with the traditions of the ancient fathers, Joseph never spoke or
offered advice unless asked. He considered unsolicited advice as idle talk.
He eventually became the confessor of the Optina Monastery and the
primary consultant for the Shamordino Convent. Joseph stopped eating
and nourished himself only with the Holy Mysteries towards the end of
his life, but he was conscious and lucid until the end. When he died, his
smiling face shone radiantly. That night and in the following days, Joseph
appeared to some of the monks in their dreams. His relics were taken to the
monastery church of St. Mary of Egypt and buried at the feet of his elder,
St. Ambrose. The intercessions of St. Joseph still work miracles.

COMMEMORATIONS: Isaiah the Prophet; Christopher of Lycia, with
Callinica, Aquilina, and 200 soldiers; Epimachus of Pelusium; Gordion at
Rome; Maximus III of Jerusalem; Nicholas of Vuneni; Joseph of Optina;
Shio of Mgvime; Ieronymos of Simonopetra.

Mid-Pentecost
Abstain from meat and dairy products.
Acts 14:6-18; John 7:14-30

*I*f you would know of the Lord's love for us, hate sin and evil thoughts, and day and night pray fervently. The Lord will then give you His grace, and you will know Him through the Holy Spirit, and after death, when you enter into paradise, there too, you will know the Lord through the Holy Spirit, as you knew Him on earth.

St. Silouan the Athonite

TRANSLATION OF THE RELICS OF MARTYR BASIL OF MANGAZEA. Basil was a pious young man in late sixteenth-century Yaroslavl. He was filled with Christian meekness and humility and had a love for church services. He went to the Russian village of Mangazea in Siberia, where he found work in a merchant's shop. The shop owner did not believe in God and did not care for Basil's religious inclinations, so he treated Basil poorly. While in church one day during the Paschal season, thieves robbed the shop. The merchant went to the governor, saying that Basil was one of the thieves. Basil was arrested and tortured to make him confess his guilt, but he continued to proclaim his innocence, which enraged the merchant, who struck Basil on the head, and he died. The governor gave orders to bury the body in a swamp. After forty-two years, a Christian named Shiryaev removed the relics from the swamp, and the holy relics were found incorrupt. A chapel was built over Basil's grave. Because of the many miracles taking place there, the people began to pray to St. Basil for healing. He is credited with healing blindness, sick children, palsy, those in immediate danger, and those about to commit suicide. In 1670 the saint's relics were placed in the Holy Trinity Monastery near Turakhanov, then in 1787, a new stone church was built at the monastery, and the holy relics were transferred there.

COMMEMORATIONS: Apostle Simon the Zealot; Alphaeus, Philadelphus, Cyprian, Onesimus, Erasmus, and 14 others, in Sicily; Simon, Bishop of Vladimir; Hesychius the Palantine of Antioch; Simon of Yurievets; Lawrence, of Mt. Pilion; Eustathius the Youth; Conleth of Kildare; Synesius of Irkutsk; Lawrence of Egypt; Comgall of Bangor; Translation of relics of St. Basil of Mangazea; *Kiev-Bratsk* Icon of the Mother of God.

MAY 11

Acts 10:34-43; John 8:12-20

*S*eek the simplest in all things, in food, clothing, without being ashamed of poverty. For a great part of the world lives in poverty. Do not say, "I am the son of a rich man. It is shameful for me to be in poverty." Christ, your Heavenly Father, Who gave birth to you in the baptistery, is not in worldly riches. Rather he walked in poverty and had nowhere to lay His head.

St. Gennadius of Constantinople

HIEROMARTYR JOSEPH, METROPOLITAN OF ASTRAKHAN. Joseph was a seventeenth-century monk at the Astrakhan Trinity Monastery in Russia. At age fifty-two, he was made Archimandrite and later the first Metropolitan of Astrakhan. The city fell under the control of the Cossacks. One day during an uprising of the townspeople, Joseph was martyred because he refused to give allegiance to the head of the Cossacks. Two priests of the Astrakhan cathedral, Cyril and Peter, were eyewitnesses to the torture of St. Joseph, and they recorded the events leading to his martyrdom. The priests took the body of Joseph, dressed in episcopal vestments, and laid him in a prepared grave. However, St. Joseph was taken to a chapel the following day, where he remained unburied for nine days. Then he was placed in a tomb at the cathedral, and soon miracles began to happen.

COMMEMORATIONS: Cyril and Methodius, Equal-to-the-Apostles; Mocius of Amphipolis; Nicodemus of Pech, Serbia; Dioscorus the New and Argyros of Thessalonica; Sophronius of the Kiev Caves; Rostislav of Greater Moravia; Cathan of Bute; Joseph of Astrakhan; Olympia and Euphrosyne of Karyes, Mytilene; Mayeul of Cluny; Asaph of Llanelwy, North Wales; Acacius of Lower Moesia; Theophylactus of Stavropol; Christesia, called Christopher, of Gareji; Bassus of Persia; Alexander of Kharkov; Commemoration of the founding of Constantinople.

MAY 12

Acts 10:44-11:10; John 8:21-30

*W*here our hearts are, there our actions are as well. If our hearts are pure, holy, and filled with a passionate love for the Lord Jesus Christ, then all our deeds, all our thoughts, all our social and political views, all our philosophy will be imbued with these feelings, these holy ordinances of our hearts.

St. Luke the Physician of Simferopol

ST. PHILIP OF AGIRA, SICILY. In the writings of St. Athanasius, he maintains that Philip of Agira was a saint of the first century, born in the year AD 40, in Cappadocia, modern-day Turkey. He was known as an apostle to the Sicilians and was the first Christian missionary to visit there. Little else is known about him. He died at the age of sixty-three and is the patron saint of Agira, Sicily, and the city of Haz-Zebbug, Malta. St. Philip is one of the patron saints of the United States Army Special Forces and is also known for his power to accomplish exorcisms. His relics were discovered in the church dedicated to him in Agira.

COMMEMORATIONS: Germanus, Patriarch of Constantinople; Sabinos, Bishop of Cyprus; Pancratius of Rome; Epiphanios, Archbishop of Cyprus; Polybius of Cyprus, Bishop of Rinocyria in Egypt; Athanasia of Smolensk Hodigitria Convent; Philip of Agira, Sicily; Theodore of Cythera; John of Serres; John of Wallachia, at Constantinople; Dionysius and Anthony, Archimandrite of St. Sergius Lavra; Glorification of St. Hermogenes, Patriarch of Moscow and All Russia; Synaxis of the Sofroniev-Molchensk Monastery (Ukraine).

MAY 13

*P*eople often cast aspersions against priests. But priests are people, as well. If one person makes a mistake in life, that doesn't mean that everybody's to blame. A priest might err, as well, but that's not the fault of all other priests. 'Don't judge, that you be not judged', says Christ. Because one day we'll be judged by the same measure by which we judged others. Who are we to judge? Let us pray that God will illumine every person. As much as we can, let's forgive.

St. Iakovos Tsalikis of Evia

ST. MACARIUS OF GLUSHITSA MONASTERY. Macarius was from Rostov, Russia. At twelve years of age, he was given over to the Monk Dionysius, the abbot of Glushitsa Monastery in Vologda. A rare purity of soul distinguished Macarius. He was ordained to the priesthood and later chosen as the new abbot. St. Macarius was buried at his monastery in the fifteenth century. His memory is also celebrated on October 12 with other Glushitsa saints.

COMMEMORATIONS: Glyceria and Laodicius, at Heraclea; Sergios the Confessor; George the Confessor of Constantinople, his wife Irene, and children; Pausicacius of Synnada; Alexander of Rome; Nicephorus of Ephapsios Monastery; John, Euthymius, George, and Gabriel of Iveron; Servatius of Maastricht; Alexander of Tiverias; Leander of Seville; Macarius, Amphilochius, and Tarasius of Glushitsa; Glyceria of Novgorod; Basil, Christopher, Alexander, Macarius, and Sergius of Moscow; Translation of the relics of St. Macarius of Kanev; Synaxis of the 103 New Martyrs of Cherkassy; Commemoration of the monks of Iveron Monastery martyred in the 13th century (Georgia); Consecration of the Church of Theotokos Pantanassa.

Sunday of the Samaritan Woman
Fast-free

MAY 14

Acts 11:19-30; John 4:5-42

*C*hrist never made a single comment about the human body. He did not say to Zacchaeus, "How short you are!" He did not say to Judas, "How ugly you are!" He did not say to the paralytic, "How paralytic you are!" He did not say to the leper, "You smell bad!" Christ would always speak to what was real and true in people— that is, to their souls. It was the Soul speaking to souls, it was the Soul healing souls.

St. Nikolai Velimirovich

MARTYR MAXIMOS. Maximos was a third-century merchant and a pious Christian. He led many pagans to faith in Christ and Holy Baptism during the reign and persecutions of Emperor Decius. Once when the pagans gathered to offer a human sacrifice to their God, Maximos was unable to bear the sight of this spectacle. He rushed at them, loudly denouncing their idols, calling them soulless creations. The pagans stoned St. Maximos to death.

COMMEMORATIONS: Isidore of Chios; Serapion the Sindonite; Leontios, Patriarch of Jerusalem; Aprunculus of Clermont; Maximus, under Decius; Nicetas, Bishop of Novgorod; Alexander, Barbarus, and Acolythus in Constantinople; Alexander of Kentoukellai; Isidore, Fool-for-Christ of Rostov; Mark of Crete; Nicetas, recluse of the Kiev Caves; John-Raiko of Bulgaria; Anthony, with 40 monks, 1,000 laymen, and Daniel, with 30 monks and 200 laymen; Andrew, abbot in Tyumen; Matthew of Yaransk; Therapon, Bishop of Cyprus; Martyr Maximos; Uncovering of the relics of St. Tikhon, Bishop of Zadonsk; *Yaroslavl* (Pechersk) Icon of the Mother of God.

MAY 15

Seek for a lifeline near to God. Contain your material needs because they create huge burdens and anxieties.

St. Paisios the Athonite

VENERABLE SILVANOS OF TABENNISI. Silvanos had worn the monastic habit for twenty years, having once been an actor. In the beginning, he was exceedingly vigilant of his soul, with fasting, prayer, and humility, but he grew lax and fearlessly spoke improper quips from the theater. Exasperated by this and other antics, the monastery abbot Pachomios ordered Silvanos to be stripped of the monastic habit. Silvanos asked forgiveness with multiple petitions and promised to mend his ways. Pachomios forgave him, and Silvanos became a model of every virtue of piety for all the brothers to see. He achieved absolute humility and unceasing tears, even when he was eating. When the others asked him why he could not stop the tears, Silvanos replied that when he saw holy men waiting upon him, the very dust of whose feet he was not worthy, should he not mourn for himself, a man from the theatre. Silvanos said," I know my sins, indeed, for which, even if I could give my soul, there is no grace for me." Eventually, Pachomios told all the brothers that Silvanos had so completely subjugated the devil and slain him by his great humility that the devil would never be able to approach him. He said, "Nothing so weakens the demon as humility coming from active power of the whole soul." When St. Silvanos died, the abbot testified that a multitude of holy angels took his soul with great rejoicing and psalmody.

COMMEMORATIONS: Pachomios the Great; Euphrosynus of Pskov and Serapion; Barbarus the Myrrhgusher; Isaiah of Rostov; Isaiah of the Kiev Caves; Andrew the Hermit; Silvanus and Pachomius of Nerekhta; Silvanos of Tabennisi; Dymphna of Geel; Hallvard of Husaby; Arethas of Valaam; Pachomius of Chernigov, Abercius, Nicholas, and Vladimir; Achilles of Larissa; Jacob of Putna; Panegyrios of Cyprus; Kali of Asia Minor; Martyrdom of Crown Prince St. Demetrius of Moscow; Translation of the Sacred Head of Apostle Titus; *Acheiropoieton* Icon of Christ in Kamouliana.

MAY 16

*T*he athlete is tested by the stadium, the captain by the storm and tempest, the general by the battle, the magnanimous by misfortune, and the Christian by temptation.

St. Basil the Great

MARTYR PETER THE KALYVITE AT BLACHERNAE. Peter was the first victim of the iconoclast movement in the year 762. A ban on religious images was started by Emperor Leo III and accompanied by widespread destruction of icons and persecution of the supporters of the veneration of icons. Peter was called "Kalyvite," meaning hut dweller. Emperor Constantine V Copronymos whipped Peter to death in the hippodrome at St. Mamas. Peter had accused Constantine of impiety and being a new Valens, an emperor in favor of the Arian heresy, and called him a Julian, a pagan emperor. Constantine had Peter's body thrown in a river, but his sister retrieved his body and buried it.

COMMEMORATIONS: Theodore the Sanctified of Egypt; Nicholas I Mystikos, Patriarch of Constantinople; Abdas and Abdiesus, bishops, with 38 Martyrs, in Persia; Peter of Blachernae; George II, Bishop of Mytilene; Nicholas of Metsovo; Isaacius, Symeon and Bachthisoes of Persia; Martyr Papylinos; Alexander, Archbishop of Jerusalem; Euphemia near Neaorion; Cassian and Laurence, abbots of Komel; Ephraim of Novgorod; Musa of Rome; Bardas of Petra; Brendan the Voyager, abbot of Clonfert; Carantoc of Carhampton; Theodore, Bishop of Vrsac in Banat, Serbia; Vukasin of Klepci, Serbia; Matthew of Yaransk; Silas, Paisios, and Nathan of Putna; Monk-Martyrs of the community of St. Sava the Sanctified.

MAY 17

A chaste body is more precious before God than a pure offering. These two, humility and chastity, prepare a tabernacle in the soul for the Holy Trinity.

St. Isaac the Syrian

MARTYRS SOLOCHON, PAMPHAMER, AND PAMPHALON. Solochon was a soldier in the imperial army led by the tribune Campanus during the fourth-century persecutions of the emperors Maximian and Diocletian. Campanus and his regiment were sent to the city of Chalcedon. All the soldiers were required to offer sacrifice at a pagan temple. Solochon, Pamphamer, and Pamphalon refused to sacrifice and confessed to worshipping Jesus Christ. Campanus gave orders to subject them to torture. Pamphamer and Pamphalon died, but Solochon remained alive. The angry torturer tried to force his mouth open with a sword to pour in idol-worship blood, but instead, Solochon bit the sword with his teeth and cut off a part of it. He also broke the bonds with his teeth and stood before the torturer, glorifying God. Then he heard a voice from heaven encouraging him to endure to the end. He was beaten again and dragged over sharp stones, but he remained steadfast. He was suspended by one hand for three hours, with a heavy stone tied to his leg. When they finally cut the ropes, Solochon stood on his feet. Filled with anger, the torturer thrust a stylus deep into his ear, and he was left for dead. But Christians carried him to the home of a pious woman and fed him. He exhorted them to stand firmly for the faith. Then St. Solochon prayed, lifting his eyes to heaven, and gave up his soul.

COMMEMORATIONS: Andronicus of the Seventy, and Junia; Solochon, Pamphamer, and Pamphalon at Chalcedon; Nektarios and Theophanes of Barlaam; Athanasios the New of Christianopolis; Nicholas of Sofia; Andronicus the Gravedigger; Euphrosyne of Moscow; Melangell of Wales; Jonah of Odessa; New Martyrs of Batak; Translation of the relics of St. Adrian of Ondrusov; Commemoration of the Fall and Burning of Jerusalem by the Persians.

MAY 18

Acts 14:20-15:4; John 9:39-10:9

*P*eople say that if you feel no inclination to pray, it is better not to pray; but this is crafty, carnal sophistry. If you only pray when you are inclined to, you will completely cease praying; this is what the flesh desires. 'The Kingdom of Heaven suffers violence' (Mt. 11:12). You will not be able to work out your salvation without forcing yourself.

St. John of Kronstadt

ST. ELGIVA OF SHAFTESBURY. Elgiva was the queen of Edmund the Magnificent, King of England, in the mid-tenth century. A robber killed Edmund only five years after his enthronement. Elgiva became adviser and ennobler of the whole kingdom, consoler of the Church, and supporter of the needy and oppressed. She would discharge the penalties of culprits and give a beautiful garment to the first poor person she saw. Eventually, St. Elgiva became a nun at the convent of Shaftesbury, where she died peacefully.

COMMEMORATIONS: Peter of Lampsakos with Dionysia, Andrew, Paul, Christina, Heraclios, Paulinos, and Venedimos, at Euridinos; Tecusa and others, of Ancyra; Stephen the New, Patriarch of Constantinople; Theodore, Pope of Rome; Christina of Athens; Euphrasia of Nicaea; Symeon, Isaac, and Bachtisius of Persia; Potamon of Heraclea; Anastaso of Lukada; Martinian of Areovinthus; Martyr Julian; Theodore in Orenburg; David and Tarichan of Georgia; Elgiva of England; Macarius, apostle to the Altai; Damian of Serbia; John of Korma; Commemoration of all Orthodox Martyrs slain under the Emperor Valens.

**Abstain from meat and
dairy products, and fish.**
Acts 15:5-12; John 10:17-28

*S*hould we fall, we should not despair and so estrange ourselves from
the Lord's love. For if He so chooses, He can deal mercifully with
our weakness. Only we should not cut ourselves off from Him or feel
oppressed when constrained by His commandments, nor should we
lose heart when we fall short of our goal...let us always be ready to
make a new start. If you fall, rise up. If you fall again, rise up again.
Only do not abandon your Physician, lest you be condemned as
worse than a suicide because of your despair. Wait on Him, and
He will be merciful, either reforming you, or sending you trials, or
through some other provision of which you are ignorant.

St. Peter of Damascus

ST. JOHN-IGNATIUS, PRINCE OF UGLICH. Prince John was the
nephew of Tsar Ivan Vasilievich, also known as Ivan the Terrible. From his
youth, the prince was devout and God-fearing, and he became known as a
miracle worker. Ivan the Terrible had John and his brother imprisoned for
thirty-two years. However, before he died, John became a monk, taking the
name Ignatius. Sometime later, when Ivan the Terrible approached Metropolitan Philip for a blessing, Ivan was chastised for slaughtering Christians
and innocent people. Ivan had Philip killed by suffocation.

COMMEMORATIONS: Patrick, Bishop of Prusa, and presbyters Acacius, Menander, and Polyenus; John, Conon, Jeremias, Cyril, Theoctistus,
Barnabas, Maximus, Theognostus, Joseph, Gennadius, Gerasimus, Mark,
and Herman of Cyprus; John, Bishop of the Goths; Kyriake and Theotima
of Nicomedia; Demetrius Donskoy of Moscow; Akolouthos of the Thebaid; Memnon, Wonderworker; Cornelius, abbot of Komel; Onuphrius,
Archbishop of Kursk; Cornelius of Paleostrov and Olonetsk; John (Ignatius), Prince of Uglich; Sergius of Shukhtom; Dunstan, Archbishop of
Canterbury; Valentin (Lukianov) of Moscow; Synaxis of the Hieromartyrs
of Kharkov; Translation of the relics of St. Julian and St. Julias the Missionaries from Aegina.

MAY 20

Acts 15:35-41; John 10:27-38

*N*ot every act of prayer is prayer. Standing at home before your icons, or here in church, and venerating them is not yet prayer, but the "equipment" of prayer. Reading prayers either by heart or from a book, or hearing someone else read them is not yet prayer, but only a tool or method for obtaining and awakening prayer. Prayer itself is the piercing of our hearts by pious feelings towards God, one after another—feelings of humility, submission, gratitude, doxology, forgiveness, heart-felt prostration, brokenness, conformity to the will of God, etc. All of our effort should be directed so that during our prayers, these feelings and feelings like them should fill our souls, so that the heart would not be empty when the lips are reading the prayers, or when the ears hear and the body bows in prostrations, but that there would be some qualitative feeling, some striving toward God. When these feelings are present, our praying is prayer, and when they are absent, it is not yet prayer.

St. Theophan the Recluse

VENERABLE THALASSIOS THE MYRRH-GIVER OF LIBYA. Thalassios was a talented writer and abbot of a monastery in Libya during the seventh century. He often wrote to his friend St. Maximos the Confessor concerning difficulties in his spiritual life. In writing about the inner spiritual effort, he dealt with the struggle against the passions. Thalassios believed that self-love is the mother of all evils. To abolish this is to be free from every evil, but nurturing self-love gives birth to all the passions, including lust, then finally, in the end, bitterness follows. St. Thalassios died peacefully, and his relics produced streams of fragrant myrrh.

COMMEMORATIONS: Thalaleos with Alexander and Asterios, at Aegae; Lydia of Philippi; Thalassios the Myrrhgusher of Libya; Zabulon and Susanna, parents of St. Nina; Stephen of Piper; Asclas of Egypt; Dovmont-Timothy, Prince of Pskov; Niketas, John, and Joseph of Nea Moni in Chios; Ethelbert of East Anglia; Austregiselus of Bourges; Mark the Anchorite of Athens; Recovery of the relics of St. Alexis, Metropolitan of Moscow.

SUNDAY

Sunday of the Blind Man
Fast-free

MAY 21

Acts 26:1, 12-20; John 9:1-38

*A*sk with tears, seek with obedience, knock with patience. For thus he who asks receives, and he who seeks finds, and to him that knocketh it shall be opened.

St. John Climacus

ST. CHRISTOPHER, PATRIARCH OF ANTIOCH. Peter was from an Orthodox family in tenth-century Baghdad. Because of his excellent penmanship and eloquence in Arabic, he was employed by the ruler of Aleppo, Syria, Sayf al-Dawla, who made him secretary to one of his emirs. At the time, the Catholicos, something like a metropolitan, died in the town of Shash. Christopher led a delegation from Baghdad to Antioch to help elect a new one. During this same time, the Patriarch of Antioch died. The clergy and the people of Antioch were most impressed by Christopher, and when they consulted with Sayf al-Dawla, he naturally approved Christopher to be the new Patriarch. Christopher tried to live as an example of monastic piety from this time. He would pray before dawn, kept vigil every Saturday night until the Sunday Liturgy, ate a simple meatless diet, and never ate before nightfall. He demonstrated his administrative wisdom as he fought against simony and corruption among bishops and clergy. Christopher also arranged a reduction in the tax imposed on non-Moslems and paid the tax for the poor from the coffers of the Patriarchate. He also built schools to train young people for the Church. Because of his great concern for the poor, he was called a new St. Nicholas. Christopher also defended the correctness of Orthodox practices, to the point of having his life threatened by the Sayf al-Dawla. When Syria and Palestine had fallen into political, economic, and social chaos, St. Christopher's enemies killed him.

COMMEMORATIONS: Emperor Constantine and Helen, his mother; Basil of Ryazan; Constantine, Michael, and Theodore, of Murom; Cassian the Greek; Secundus and those with him; Cyril of Rostov; Pachomios of Patmos; Hospicius of Trier; Helen of Dechani; Agapitus of Markushev; Christopher I of Antioch; Meeting of the *Vladimir* Icon of the Mother of God; *Zaonikievsky, Oransk,* and *Krasnogorsk* Icons of the Mother of God.

*P*eople hate the truth for the sake of whatever it is they love more than the truth. They love truth when it shines warmly on them, and hate it when it rebukes them.

St. Augustine of Hippo

NEW MARTYR PAUL OF PELOPONESE. Paul was born to poor and virtuous Christians near Kalyvrta of Peloponnesus. At age nine, he moved to Patras, and his relatives took him in. He became a shoemaker and returned home at the age of twenty-three. He established his own business and made a modest living. When the Turkish property owner raised the rent beyond his means, Paul soon went into debt and then debtor's prison. However, he was freed when he agreed to convert to Islam. Soon afterward, his conscience condemned him and regretted what he had done. He moved to the Great Lavra Monastery on Mount Athos and befriended another monk named Timothy. After some time, Paul took monastic vows. Paul and Timothy worked to help maintain a high level of Orthodox spirituality among the villagers that visited. Paul decided to return to his native city to do the same work there. He spent the first forty days in seclusion at a local monastery and then began his missionary work of helping and comforting those in need. The Turkish authorities arrested him, but Paul said that he had exchanged the copper of their faith for the gold of his faith. St. Paul was charged with treason and burned to death.

COMMEMORATIONS: Commemoration of the Second Ecumenical Council; Melchisedec, King of Salem; John-Vladimir, King of Serbia; Basiliskos, Bishop of Comana; Donatus, Bishop of Thmuis, with Macarius and Theodore; James of Borovichi (Novgorod); Markella and Codratus; Sophia the Healer; Zachariah of Prusa; Paul and Demetrius of Tripoli, near Kalavryta; Maxim, Bishop of Serpukhov; Castus and Aimilius of Carthage; Kali of Asia Minor.

MAY 23

Acts 17:19-28; John 12:19-36

*H*ave no confidence in your own virtuousness. Do not worry about a thing once it has been done. Control your tongue and your belly.
St. Pambo of Nitria

VENERABLE MICHAEL THE CONFESSOR, BISHOP OF SYN-NADA. Michael endured fifty years of exile in desolation and want for his eloquent defense of the icons before the emperor Leo the Armenian. From his youth, Michael desired a monastic life. He entered a monastery on the coast of the Black Sea, together with the future bishop of Nicomedia, St. Theophylaktos. Once, during a time of harvest, the prayers of the two monks brought an abundance of needed rain. Michael was given the honor and title of confessor because of his outstanding service as a priest. Patriarch Tarasios then ordained him bishop of the city of Synnada in Asia Minor. He gained the love of the faithful, and the emperor took notice. In the year 787, Michael was present at the Seventh Ecumenical Council of Nicaea. At the request of the emperor, he also negotiated peace talks. When the heretic Leo the Armenian ordered the destruction of all icons, Michael was brought before him. Not fearing torture, Michael said he would not fulfill the order to remove all icons from the churches. Leo banished and imprisoned Michael in the city of Eudokiada, where he died in the year 821. The head of St. Michael is housed in the Lavra of St. Athanasios of Mount Athos, and part of his holy relics are at the Iversk monastery.

COMMEMORATIONS: Michael the Confessor, Bishop of Synnada; Mary Cleopa the Myrrhbearer; Michael the Black-robed of St. Sabbas Monastery; Salonas the Roman; Paisius, abbot of Galich; Martyr Seleucus; Damiane (Demetrius) of Gareji, Georgia; Euphrosyne, Princess of Polotsk; Ioannicius I, Archbishop of Serbia; Desiderius, Bishop of Vienne; Donatian and Rogatian of Nantes; Theodore of Murom; Translation of the relics of St. Joachim of Ithaca; Uncovering of the relics of St. Leontios, Bishop of Rostov; Uncovering of the relics of St. Abramius of Rostov; Synaxis of All Saints of Rostov and Yaroslavl; Repose of Archimandrite Athanasios Mitilianos; *Thou Art the Vineyard* Icon of the Mother of God.

It is the Cross that saved mankind! Not God's justice or His miracles, but His Cross! When Jesus was crucified, Satan was defeated.

† *Elder Arsenie Papaciac of Romania*

VENERABLE KYRIAKOS OF EVRYCHOU THE WONDER-WORKER.

Kyriakos was born into a Christian family in the village of Evrychou, Cyprus, around the third or fourth century. At an early age, he developed a love for Christ at a time when monasticism and asceticism began to blossom in the deserts of Palestine and Egypt. His hermitage in Evrychou became a center for missionary work around that region, and pilgrims would seek his advice. His holy life and the miracles his prayers caused during his life and to this day convinced the people that he was a saint. A few years ago, St. Kyriakos appeared in a vision to a patient in Larnaca suffering from a brain tumor. He prayed in the church of St. Kyriakos and was healed. The iconography in the saint's chapel is from the fifteenth and sixteenth centuries, and a service to him was composed in the year 2000. Even though he is not mentioned by any Cypriot chroniclers nor in the Synaxaristes, tradition and the ancient church outside his village of Evrychou bear testimony to his holy life.

COMMEMORATIONS: Meletios Stratelates with Stephen, John and 1,218 soldiers with women and children, including Serapion of Egypt, Callinicus the Magician, Theodore, Faustus, Marciana, Susanna, Palladia, Cyriacus and Christian, and 12 tribunes, all suffering in Galatia; Gregory, Archbishop of Novgorod; Symeon Stylites (the Younger) of Wondrous Mountain; Vincent of Lerins; Nicetas the Stylite, Wonderworker of Pereyaslavl-Zalesski; Martha, abbess of Monemvasia; Sava Brancovic; Kyriakos of Evrychou, Cyprus.

*T*he Book of Psalms contains everything useful that the other books have. It predicts the future, it recalls the past, it gives directions for living; it suggests the right behavior to adopt. It is, in short, a jewel case in which have been collected all the valid teachings in such a way that individuals find remedies just right for their cases.

St. Basil the Great

NEW MARTYRS OF PIVA. In 2017 the Synod of the Serbian Orthodox Church canonized the Piva Martyrs. These included 1,290 innocent people from various villages of the Piva region of Montenegro, Serbia. They were massacred over six days in 1943 by the Nazi "Prinz Eugen Division," and 549 of these were children and those under twenty years of age. The Rite of Canonization was celebrated by a great number of clergy and hieromonks and attended by descendants and relatives. Bishop Joanikije called the largest site of execution in the village of Dola the "Serbian Golgotha." He said that the Church has felt the power of their intercession, thus becoming protectors of the people.

COMMEMORATIONS: Third Finding of the Precious Head of St. John the Baptist; Martyr Celestine; Olbian, monk; Mary of Ustiug (mother of John of Ustiug); Therapontus, Bishop of Cyprus; Innocent of Kherson; Aldhelm, Bishop of Sherborne; Thaddeus of Svyatogorsk Monastery; Zenobius, Bishop of Florence; Dionysius, Bishop of Milan; New Martyrs of Piva; Synaxis of Saints of Volhynia: Yaropolk, Stephen, Macarius, Igor, and Juliana; Translation of the relics of St. Anthimos Arethiotis; Commemoration of the reunion of 3,000,000 Uniates with the Orthodox Church at Vilna in 1831; Commemoration of the Finding of the Sacred Icon of Great Martyr Demetrios the Myrrhgusher; *The Helper of the Sinners* Koretsk Icon of the Mother of God; (On Holy Ascension: Holy Georgian Martyrs of Persia).

**Abstain from meat and
dairy products, and fish.**
2 Corinthians 4:6-15; Matthew 11:2-15

*W*hen we pray we are all beggars before God. We stand before the
great householder bowed down and weeping, hoping to be given
something; and that something is God Himself.

St. Augustine of Hippo

ST. AUGUSTINE, ARCHBISHOP OF CANTERBURY. Augustine was
from sixth-century Italy and was a disciple of St. Felix. St. Gregory Dialogos
chose Augustine to lead a mission of forty monks to evangelize the people
of Britain. King Ethelbert, a pagan, and Bertha, his Christian wife, welcomed them and restored the ancient church of St. Martin in Canterbury
for them. The king promised to supply all their needs and permit them to
preach Christianity. Later, Augustine converted the king and thousands
of his people. He was consecrated Archbishop of Britain and was the first
Archbishop of Canterbury. He evangelized the country with zeal and built
Christ Church, the present-day Cathedral at Canterbury. He founded
the monastery of Sts. Peter and Paul where Augustine, the archbishops
of Canterbury, and the kings of Kent are buried. He founded the diocese
of London and Rochester, a school in Canterbury, and helped the king
write the earliest Anglo-Saxon laws. However, all of St. Augustine's efforts
were not successful. He could not unite with the existing Celtic Christian
community because they would not give up their ancient traditions. His
tombstone reads in part, "with the help of God, and aided by miracles,
guided King Ethelbert and his people from the worship of idols to the
Faith of Christ."

COMMEMORATIONS: Apostles Carpos and Alphaeus, of the Seventy;
Abercius and Helen, children of Apostle Alphaeus; Alexander of Thessalonica; Synesios, Bishop of Karpasia, Cyprus; Augustine of Canterbury,
evangelizer of England; Milan Banjac and Milan Golubovic of Drvar, Serbia; Translation of the relics of St. George of Kratovo and Sofia, Bulgaria;
Uncovering of the relics of St. Macarius, abbot of Kolyazin.

MAY 27

Acts 20:7-12; John 14:10-21

*P*atient endurance kills the despair that kills the soul; it teaches the soul to take comfort and not to grow listless in the face of its many battles and afflictions.

St. Peter of Damascus

ST. MELANGELL OF POWYS. Melangell was a seventh-century Irish princess. Her father, the king, arranged for her to marry, but she fled to the countryside for solitude and prayer. About fifteen years later, when Prince Brochwel of Powys and his friend were hunting rabbits with their hounds, the rabbits hid under Malangell's cloak, and the hounds turned and fled. Struck by her beauty, Brochwel hoped to marry her, but when he heard her story, he gave her land where she could live her monastic life. Melangell's fame spread, and other women gathered around her, and a monastic community grew based on prayer and works of mercy for the poor and needy. Melangell lived there thirty-seven years and was often seen surrounded by rabbits. After her death, pilgrims would travel from afar, and her tomb became a place of healing. Brochwell charged his successors to protect the site for those in need of healing and a place of refuge for small animals, and it remained so for centuries. But during the Reformation, it was desecrated, but the saint's relics were well hidden. Renovation work began in the late 20th century, and St. Melangell's relics were discovered and properly enshrined.

COMMEMORATIONS: Hieromartyr Helladius, bishop in the East; John the Russian; Therapontus, Bishop of Sardis; Venerable Bede; Therapon of White Lake (Belozersk); Martyrs Alypius and Eusebiotus; Michael of Parekhi, Georgia; Basil Khakhuli, son of King Bagrat III of Georgia; Julius the Veteran at Dorostolum, Moesia; Therapontus, monk of Monza Monastery; Lazarus the Clairvoyant of Pskov Caves Monastery; Melangell of Powys; Translation of the relics of St. Nilus of Stolben Island; Translation of the relics of St. Cyprian, St. Photius, and St. Jonah, Metropolitans of Kiev; (Last Saturday of May: Synaxis of All Saints of Boeotia).

Fathers of the First Ecumenical Council
Fast-free

Acts 20:16-18, 28-36; John 17:1-13

*L*et us enter into the church of God with the fear of God, with a pure heart, laying aside all passions and every worldly care, and let us stand in it with faith and reverence, with understanding attention, with love and peace in our hearts, so that we may come away renewed, as though made heavenly, so that we may live in the holiness natural to heaven, not binding ourselves by worldly desires and pleasures.

St. John of Kronstadt

HIEROMARTYR EUTYCHIUS, BISHOP OF MELITENE. During the Christian persecutions of the pagan Romans, Bishop Eutychius voluntarily presented himself to the ruler of the city, where he proclaimed Jesus Christ as the true God. He also belittled and spat at the pagan idols. Because of this, he endured many torments and was drowned at sea. As they were binding his hands and securing him in a leather sack, St. Eutychius continued preaching the faith. Later, when his relics were recovered, they became a source of miraculous healings.

COMMEMORATIONS: Niketas the Confessor, Bishop of Chalcedon; Eutychius, Bishop of Melitene; Crescens, Paul, and Dioscorides of Rome; Germanus, Bishop of Paris; Ignatius, Bishop of Rostov; Heliconis and Dapni of Thessalonica; Gerontius, Metropolitan of Moscow; Demetrios (Mitros) of Tripoli; Helen of Diveyevo; Macarius, Dionysius, Nicholas, Ignatius, and Peter; Heraclius of Turkistan; Rodion (Fyodorov) of St. Sergius Lavra; Domnica of Kherson; Andrew, Fool-for-Christ of Constantinople; Sophronius of Bulgaria; William of Languedoc (Gaul); *The Consoler of Angry Hearts* and *Unbreakable Wall* Icons of the Mother of God; (Last Sunday of May: Neomartyrs of Eurytania; the co-workers of the Apostle Paul; Finding of the Icon of Holy Great Martyr St. Demetrios the Myrrhgusher).

MAY 29

*E*nvy is a food of the mind, corrupting it with poisonous juices, and ceasing not to torment it miserably with the thought of a neighbor's happy success.

St. John Cassian

VIRGIN MARTYR THEODOSIA OF CONSTANTINOPLE. Four centuries after her martyrdom, St. Theodosia of Tyre appeared in a vision to a woman who was fervently praying for a child. St. Theodosia told her that she would give birth, and the child was to be named Theodosia. At an early age, young Theodosia was dedicated to God. She lived in the monastery of the holy Martyr Anastasia in Constantinople and became a devout nun. When her parents died, they left her much wealth. She spent part of the money to commission gold and silver icons of Jesus, the Theotokos, and St. Anastasia. The rest she gave to the poor. Theodosia became an activist when another iconoclast period intensified under Emperor Leo the Isaurian. She led a demonstration to the city gates, where an icon of Christ was about to be removed by an imperial guard. The group surged forward, toppling the ladder he was standing on and killing him. Because of this, many were beheaded, and the monks involved were tortured for eight months. Theodosia led a group of women to the impious Patriarch Anastasius, who Leo gave the office after deposing Patriarch Germanus. They threw stones at Anastasius, and as a result, the women were beheaded except for Theodosia, who was martyred when an imperial guard plunged a ram's horn through her throat. St. Theodosia died the same day as St. Theodosia of Tyre, four centuries earlier.

COMMEMORATIONS: Commemoration of the First Ecumenical Council; Alexander of Alexandria; Theodosia of Constantinople; Theodosia of Tyre; John of Thessalonica; Euthymios of Zela; Luke of Simferopol; Constantine XI, emperor; Olbian of Aneus, and Symphoros, Callistos, and Macedonios; Andrew Argentes of Chios; John of Ustiug; Cyril, Carellus, Primolus, Phinodus, Venustus, Gissinus, Alexander, Tredentius, and Jocunda, at Caesarea; Commemoration of the Fall of Constantinople; *Surety of Sinners* Icon of the Mother of God in Moscow.

MAY 30

*O*ur whole life goes on in a bustle. The mind is in the midst of worldly thoughts and temptations. Little by little it will be able to remember God in such a way that it will think about Him without thinking and remember Him without remembering. So long as your mind keeps moving. As long as you have this drive that pushes you forward, do not be afraid, your boat is still traversing the sea of life under the shadow of the Cross. Don't be afraid of possible storms. No voyage can be accomplished without bad weather, the least so the journey of life.

St. Barsanuphius of Optina

ST. FELIX, POPE OF ROME. Felix was a Roman, and he was chosen to succeed Pope Dionysius in the mid-third century. He was the first to condemn the heresy of the excommunicated Bishop Paul of Samosata. This heresy stated that Jesus was born as an ordinary man and was later imbued with the Word of God. Felix sought the help of the pagan emperor Aurelian to settle this theological dispute. He decided in favor of Felix, who was also recognized by the bishops of Italy and the city of Rome. St. Felix erected a basilica on the Via Aurelia. It was said that he died peacefully and is buried in his basilica.

COMMEMORATIONS: Isaac the Confessor, founder of the Dalmatian Monastery; Emilia, mother of St. Basil the Great (Greek Calendar); James, monk of Starotorzhok Monastery in Galich; Martyr Natalius; Barlaam of Caesarea in Cappadocia; Martyrs Romanus, Meletius, and Euplius; Macrina, grandmother of St. Basil the Great; Hubert, Bishop of Liege; Venantius of Gaul; Walstan of Bawburgh; Felix I, Pope of Rome.

**Abstain from meat and
dairy products, and fish.**
Acts 23:1-11; John 16:15-23

MAY 31

*R*emembering a sin we have committed does not mean that the
sin has not been forgiven. This remembrance of our sins is only a
warning to us lest we become proud and sin again. In fact, we—
not God—are the ones who cannot forgive ourselves. We cannot
forgive ourselves because of our pride. A genuine sign that a sin
has been forgiven is the fact that it has not been repeated, and we
are at peace. It is also important how we spend the last years of our
lives. A God-pleasing life in old age blots out the sins of youth.

† *Elder Thaddeus of Vitovnica*

VIRGIN MARTYR PETRONILLA OF ROME. It is believed that Petronilla of Rome may have been a convert of St. Peter the Apostle and that he
cured her of palsy. The details of her life are unknown other than she was
a Virgin Martyr of Rome during the persecutions of Domitian. The sixth-
and seventh-century lists of the tombs of the most highly venerated Roman
martyrs mention St. Petronilla's grave on the Via Ardeatina, where there is a
basilica dedicated to her. A painting of St. Petronilla was discovered in the
late nineteenth century, and it shows her receiving a deceased person into
heaven. The inscription carved on her sarcophagus reads, "of the golden
Petronilla, the sweetest maiden."

COMMEMORATIONS: Hermeias at Comana; Marus the Magician, who
converted witnessing the martyrdom of St. Hermias; Hierotheus, Bishop
of Nikolsk, and Seraphim Nikolsky; 5 Martyrs of Ascalon; Eustathius,
Patriarch of Constantinople; Martyrs Eusebius and Charalampus; Philosophos of Alexandria; Philotheus, Metropolitan of Tobolsk; Philosophus
Ornatsky, with Nicholas and Boris, in St. Petersburg; Winnow, Mancus,
and Myrbad of Cornwall; Petronilla of Rome; First translation of the relics
of St. Philip, Metropolitan of Moscow and All Russia; Finding of the relics
of St. Nicholas the Deacon of Mytilene; (Wednesday after Holy Ascension:
St. Dodo of Davit-Gareji Monastery, Georgia).

St. Anthony dearly loved spending time on his mountain. Once, he was pressed by those in need. At the insistence of the Governor of the region, he finally went down to the city, and after having said a few words about salvation and about how we ought to act, he hastened to return to the mountain.

The Governor, however, demanded that he delay his return.

"I cannot spend time here in the city," St. Anthony replied.

To persuade the Governor of this, he gave the following charming illustration: "Just as fish die when they linger on dry land, so monks are destroyed when they extend their stay with you and spend time with you. I must hasten back to the mountain, then, just as the fish must to the sea, lest by lingering I forget to keep watch over my inner self.

The Evergetinos
Volume III of the First Book

JUNE 1

People talk a lot and often for a long time, and as if their ideas should serve the good; but how much wrong, seductive and empty pours from their lips. No need to trust all the words of the people. People themselves often suffer for the words that they themselves have said, and repent of them.

St. John Maximovitch

ST. WITE OF DORSET. St. Wite is one of the most beloved and visited saints in Dorset, on the English Chanel, where there were numerous monasteries and churches. She is venerated by today's Orthodox living in the United Kingdom. Many miracles still occur by the prayers of St. Wite near her relics and her holy well, which is located one mile south of her relics. Wite was from ninth-century Charmouth, only a few miles from where her relics are kept. It is possible that she maintained fires and beacons on the cliffs to protect sailors. She was martyred by pagan Danes who made regular raids on English monasteries. During the bloody Reformation and the Cromwellian atrocities, nearly all the relics, shrines, icons, statues, and stained glass were destroyed, but St. Wite's tomb and relics were undisturbed. Her tomb was rediscovered in 1900, and on her leaden coffin was inscribed, "Here lie the relics of St. Wite." Her shrine has three oval holes in it, where pilgrims place their sick limbs in the hope of healing. Many testimonies show that St. Wite's well is famous for healing eye diseases and other ailments.

COMMEMORATIONS: Justin the Philosopher, and those with him at Rome: Justin, Chariton, Charita, Euelepistus, Hierax, Paeon, Liberianus, and Justus; Thespesius of Cappadocia; Metrios the Farmer of Myra; Dionysius of Glushitsa; Onuphrius of Kharkov; Firmus of Magus; Shio the New, David, Gabriel, and Paul of Gareji, Georgia; Justin Popovic of Celije in Serbia; Martyr Neon; Ronan of Locronan; Agapitus of the Kiev Caves; Pyrros the Virgin; Wistan of Mercia; Caprais of Lerins; Wite of Dorset; Deliverance of the Island of Lefkada from the Plague of 1743; (Thursday after Holy Ascension: St. Davit of Gareji and St. Lukiane (Georgian)).

FRIDAY

Leavetaking of Holy Ascension
Abstain from meat and
dairy products, and fish.

JUNE 2

Acts 27:1-28:1; John 17:18-26

*T*he Jesus Prayer is work common to angels and humans. With this prayer people attain to the life of the angels in a short time. The prayer is the source of all good works and virtues and drives the dark passions far away from man. In a short time it makes a man capable of acquiring the grace of the Holy Spirit. Acquire it, and before you die you will have acquired an angelic soul. The prayer is divine rejoicing. No other spiritual weapon can so effectively restrain the demons. It burns them as fire burns a wick.

St. Paisius Velichovsky

NEW MARTYR CONSTANTINE THE FORMER HAGARENE. Constantine was a Muslim from nineteenth-century Mytilene. He contracted smallpox at age fifteen, which caused him to lose his eyesight. With permission from his mother, a pious Orthodox Christian woman took him to a church, bathed him with holy water, and he was cured. Sometime later, he went to Mount Athos and received Holy Baptism. But a desire was born in him to become a martyr for Christ. The elder recommended that he spend forty days in solitude praying and fasting for God's will. After this time, he was granted the blessing to suffer for Christ, and he went back to Smyrna and confessed his faith in Christ. For over forty days, Constantine was interrogated and fiercely tortured. He was finally hanged when he could not be forced or persuaded to deny his Orthodox Christian faith.

COMMEMORATIONS: Nikephoros the Confessor, Patriarch of Constantinople; John the New of Suceava, at Belgorod; Pothinus, Bishop of Lyons; Sanctus, Maturas, Attalus, Blanding, Biblis, Ponticus, Alexanders, and others, at Lyon; Marinus of Constantinople, son of St. Mary the New; Constantine the former Hagarene, at Constantinople; Nicholas the Pilgrim; Marcellinus and Peter of Rome; Nicephorus of Milet; Demetrius of Philadelphia; Andrew of Nizhegorod; Martyr Asprocastron; Erasmus of Formia in Campania, and 20,000 Martyrs; 38 Martyrs; A mother and 3 children; Odo of Canterbury; Marino, known as Baanes; Uncovering of the relics of St. Juliana, Princess of Vyazma; *Kiev-Bratsk* Icon of the Mother of God.

*A*s it is not to be imagined that the fornicator and the blasphemer can partake of the sacred Table, so it is impossible that he who has an enemy, and bears malice, can enjoy the holy Communion. I forewarn, and testify, and proclaim this with a voice that all may hear! 'Let no one who hath an enemy draw near the sacred Table, or receive the Lord's Body! Let no one who draws near have an enemy! Do you have an enemy? Draw not near! Do you wish to draw near? Be reconciled, and then draw near, and touch the Holy Thing!'

St. John Chrysostom

ST. HIERIA OF NISIBIS. Hieria was a pagan by birth. She married a Roman senator, but he died after only seven months. After hearing about the nun Febronia at a monastery in Nisibis, she went there to seek salvation. For an entire night, Hieria spoke with Febronia and was instructed in the faith. She went home and urged her parents to abandon idolatry and accept Christ. When the persecutions of Diocletian began at the end of the third century, Febronia was arrested. She refused to deny her faith and was fiercely tortured. When Hieria learned that Febronia was at the judge's tribunal, she went there and railed against the torturers and shouted at the judge. He had her arrested but released her when he learned that she was a senator's widow. Hieria grieved Febronia's death, and after witnessing the horrors of St. Febronia's martyrdom, she received Holy Baptism, as did her parents, many pagans, and soldiers. Hieria left her home, renounced the world, gave her wealth to the convent, and lived the rest of her days in toil at the monastery. St. Hieria died peacefully in the year 312.

COMMEMORATIONS: Lucillian, at Byzantium, with Hypatios, Paul, Claudius, Dionysios, and Virgin Paula; Athanasius of Cilicia; Lucian, Maxianus, Julian, Marcellinus, and Saturninus, at Beauvais; Achilles of Alexandria; Barsabus of Ishtar, and 10 companions; Hieria of Mesopotamia; Chlotilda of France; Joseph III of Thessalonica; Cyprian Nelidov; Kevin of Glendalough; Pappos of Kythrea; Isaac of Cordoba; Dorotheos Proios of Adrianople; Gregory of Derkoi; *Yugsk* Icon of the Mother of God.

*B*lessed is the one who is fired by the fear of God, ever having in himself the fervor of the Holy Spirit, and who has burned up the thorns and thistles of the thoughts.

St. Ephraim the Syrian

ST. OPTATUS, BISHOP OF MILEVUM IN NUMIDIA. Once, a schism in Africa was created by a small group of heretics known as the Donatists, who stated that Church clergy must be faultless for their prayers and sacraments to be effective. Their champion was a bishop named Parmenian, who was well-versed in the art of sophistry and wrote five books to explain their heretical views. Bishop Optatus defended the true faith while pointing out the follies of the Donatists. He wrote six books against Parmenian about the year 370. The Donatist schism was born during the Christian persecutions of Diocletian when Christians who feared torments delivered holy scriptures to be burned by their persecutors. The Church later offered these people clemency if they would subject themselves to a public course of repentance. But many bishops admitted penitent priests without insisting on this condition, to which Donatus and other zealots took offense. Optatus said that this anger was the mother of the schism, ambition was the nurse, and covetousness was the champion to defend it. Seventy bishops, mostly Numidians, espoused this heresy. The Pope condemned the schismatics, and the emperor enacted laws against the Donatists. Some Donatist fanatics pretended to devote themselves to martyrdom by throwing themselves into rivers and even compelled strangers to murder them. This lasted for over 100 years, but St. Optatus had already given this movement a mortal blow with his books against Parmenian.

COMMEMORATIONS: Metrophanes, Patriarch of Constantinople; Andronicus of Perm; Basil of Chernigov; Mary and Martha, sisters of St. Lazarus; Concordios of Spoleto; Alonius of Scetis; Frontasius, Severinus, Severian, and Silanus of Gaul; Astius of Dyrrachium; Zosimas of Cilicia; Sophia of Thrace; Optatus of Milevum; Methodius of Peshnosha; Eleazar and Nazarius of Olonets; Titus of Byzantium; John of Monagria.

MONDAY

Feast of the Holy Spirit
Fast-free

Ephesians 5:8-19; Matthew 18:10-20

JUNE 5

*R*evere every work, every thought of the Word of God, of the writings of the Holy Fathers, and amongst them, the various prayers and hymns which we hear in Church or which we read at home, because they are all the breathing and words of the Holy Spirit.

St. John of Kronstadt

ABBA DOROTHEOS OF PALESTINE. In his youth, Dorotheos was so immersed in his secular studies that he did not know what he ate or drank or if he slept. He was so absorbed in reading that even his friends could not distract him. As a monk, he had an even greater zeal for studying the virtues. He was a disciple of St. John the Prophet in the Palestinian monastery of Abba Serid. One of his first obediences was to welcome pilgrims, and Dorotheos would hear about their burdens and temptations. Then he attended to the needs of those in the infirmary. He cared for them as if his salvation depended on them. He drove himself to exhaustion and still felt he was not doing enough. Dorotheos wrote prolifically. His writings include 21 Discourses, various Letters, 87 questions with written replies from St. Barsanuphius the Great and St. John the Prophet, 30 Talks about Asceticism, and written Guidances of the Monk Abba Zosima. Dorotheos also read the advice of the St. Basil the Great, St. Gregory the Theologian, and St. Gregory of Nyssa. The works of St. Dorotheos are found in monasteries worldwide and are considered preliminary reading for anyone entering the spiritual path.

COMMEMORATIONS: Dorotheos, Bishop of Tyre; Dorotheos of Gaza; 10 Martyrs of Egypt: Marcian, Nicander, Hyperechius, Apollonius, Leonides, Arius, Gorgias, Selenias, Irene and Pambo of Egypt; Christopher of Rome; Conon of Rome; Constantine of Kiev; Illidius of Clermont; Dorotheus at Chiliokama; Agapius and Nicodemus of Vatopedi; Dorotheus of Thebes; Theodore of the Jordan; Theodore Yaroslavich; Peter of Korisha; Boniface of Mainz; Mark of Smyrna; Nicholas of Vladimirskoye; John of Valaam; Uncovering of the relics of St. Jonah and St. Bassian of Solovki; Translation of the relics of St. Igor-George of Kiev; *Igor* Icon of the Mother of God.

JUNE 6

Romans 1:1-7, 13-17; Matthew 4:23-5:13

*E*ven before you call, God hears you.

St. Paisios the Athonite

VIRGIN MARTYRS ARCHELAIS, THECLA, AND SUSANNA, AT SALERNO. During Diocletian's third-century persecutions, these three nuns lived in a small monastery near Rome. They cut their hair, dressed as men, and set off to a remote area in Campagna. Once there, they continued to pursue asceticism in fasting and prayer. Through their prayers, God granted them the gift of healing. They healed the local people and converted many pagans. When the governor heard this, he had them arrested and ordered Archelais to sacrifice to idols or be tortured and killed. She said it was folly to worship statues, and when she was thrown to hungry lions, they merely lay at her feet. The following day, Archelais was suspended, her skin lacerated, and hot tar poured on her wounds, but she prayed more loudly. Then a radiant light shone over her, and a voice said, "Fear not, for I am with you." They wanted to crush her with a huge stone, but an angel of God threw it aside, and it crushed the torturers instead. Then the soldiers were commanded to behead the three nuns, but they feared even touching them. Thereupon, Saints Archelais, Thecla, and Susanna said to the soldiers, "If ye fulfill not the command, ye shalt have no respect from us." The holy martyrs were beheaded.

COMMEMORATIONS: Bessarion the Great of Egypt; 5 Virgin Martyrs of Caesarea in Palestine: Martha, Mary, Cyria, Valeria, and Marcia; Virgin Martyrs Archelais, Thecla, and Susanna, at Salerno; Attalos the Wonderworker; Hilarion the New; Justus, Patriarch of Alexandria; Anoub of Egypt, the Worker of Signs; Martyr Gelasius; Amandus, Amantius, Alexander, Lucius, Alexander, Alexandria, Donatus, and Peregrius in Scythia Minor; Claudius of Besancon, Gaul; Raphael of Optina Monastery; Jonah of Klimetsk; Paisius of Uglich; Jonah, Bishop of Perm; Jarlath of Cluainfois (Ireland); *Pimen* Icon of the Mother of God.

JUNE 7

Romans 1:18-27; Matthew 5:20-26

*P*rayer is … the prosperity of the household, … the wedding crown of spouses.

St. Gregory of Nyssa

VENERABLE ANASTASIOS GORDIOS. Anastasios was one of the most important scholarly clerics during the Turkish occupation of Greece in the seventeenth century. He was a disciple of St. Eugenios the Aitolos, who kept the authentic Orthodox spirit alive in those times of ignorance. Anastasios was his most brilliant student at the school of the Hellenic Museum of Agrafa. He received monastic tonsure and was ordained to the priesthood. Then he was sent abroad to study in Italy for five years and returned to his homeland in Greece even though he was offered higher pay in foreign countries, saying that he must help his motherland. Anastasios settled in a small monastery and was a distinguished teacher. Later, many of his students distinguished themselves as great teachers in their own homelands. In addition to teaching, Anastasios spent time writing, preaching, and building schools and churches. His reputation spread throughout central Greece, and people constantly sent him letters with questions and other issues. He responded to everyone with care. Anastasios died peacefully at the age of 75 and was buried next to his teacher St. Eugenios at the Monastery of St. Paraskevi. His relics emit a beautiful fragrance and are a source of miracles.

COMMEMORATIONS: Marcellinus, Bishop of Rome, and those with him: Sisinius and Cyriacus, deacons, Aproniun, Saturninus, Smaragdus, Largus, Pappias, Maurus, Crescentian, Priscilla, Lucina, and Princess Artemia; Cyria, Valeria, and Marcia, of Caesarea; Theodotos of Ancyra; Lykarion of Hermopolis; Daniel of Scetis in Egypt; Sebastiane the Wonderworker; Potamiane of Alexandria; Aesia and Susanna of Taormina; Panagis Basias of Cephalonia; Anthony of Kozha Lake; Zenaidos of Caesarea; Stephen and Anthimos of Constantinople, of the Fervent Ones; Martyrs Tarasius and John; Colman, Bishop of Dromore, Ireland; Andronicus, Archbishop of Perm; Repose of St. Anastasios Gordios; Synaxis of All Saints of Ivanovo.

THURSDAY

JUNE 8

**Translation of the Relics of
St. Theodore the Commander**
Fast-free
Ephesians 2:4-10; Matthew 10:16-22

*W*e must live with one hand holding onto Heaven.
† *Elder Timothy Sakkas of Holy Spirit Monastery, Greece*

**VENERABLE MARTYRS THEOPHANES THE ELDER AND
PAISIOS OF MESSOLONGHI.** Paisios lived at the Skete of Saint Anna
on Mount Athos and was a calligrapher, copying the works of the Holy
Fathers. He had also memorized the entire Psalter. Theophanes was his
unlettered elder who had a calm and sweet character. They were both Kollyvades Fathers. The Kollyvades were concerned with restoring traditional
practices of Orthodoxy and were opposed to unwarranted innovations. At
this time, a heated controversy began as to whether memorial vigils should
be held on Saturdays, which was ecclesiastical tradition, or on Sunday, a
day of Resurrection and joy unfit for memorials. There was such hatred
for the Kollyvades monks on Mount Athos by 1773 that some sought to
murder them. Some monks slandered Theophanes and Paisios, then hired a
bandit named Markos to murder them by drowning. Markos severely beat
Theophanes and Paisios in the view of the other monks, who showed no
sympathy. He hung ropes with heavy stones around their necks and then
cast them into the sea. The two martyrs prayed for the world and their
murderer before they died. Markos later learned that he had been lied to
by the monks. In rage and with a sword in hand, he went to the Skete of
Saint Anna and demanded ten purses of silver coins, or he would kill all
the monks. Afterward, thirty Kollyvades monks left Mount Athos. The
Holy Community of Mount Athos later condemned the accusers of the
Kollyvades Fathers.

COMMEMORATIONS: Ephraim of Antioch; Nicander and Marcian at
Dorostolum; Athre of Nitria; Naukratios the Studite; Naukratios of Caesarea;
Kalliope, at Rome; Theophanes at Constantinople; Medardus of Noyon;
Theodore of Rostov; Zosimas of Phoenicia; Theophilus of Luga; Melania
the Elder; Barlaam and Herman of Russia; Theodore of Kvelta; Paul the
Confessor; Martyrs Mark and Nikandros; Chlodulf of Metz; Theophanes and
Paisius of Messolonghi; Translation of the relics of St. Theodore Stratelates.

JUNE 9

Romans 2:14-28; Matthew 5:33-41

*D*emons watch over us like fishermen, and carefully watch our thoughts. What we are in our thoughts, similar ones present their dreams to us.

St. Paisius Velichkovsky

ST. COLUMBA OF IONA. Columba was born to a prominent family in Ireland. His name means "Dove of the Church." At a young age, he became a monk and was a student of St. Finnian of Clonard. For almost twenty years, Columba traveled as a missionary throughout Ireland, where he founded the monasteries of Derry and Durrow. He founded the famous monastery of Iona on the coast of Scotland. It became the center of operations for the conversion of the Scots and Picts. And there, he baptized the King of the Picts and later a King of the Scots. This monastery became a great center of learning from which monasticism spread throughout Northern Europe. Columba was a true scholar and writer, and he loved solitude. He radiated love and was known for his booming voice and love of nature. When he built his monastery, he made sure not one tree was cut down. Columba developed a reputation for miracles and prophecies. Toward the end of his life, he spent much of his time transcribing books. St. Columba died peacefully on Iona in 597.

COMMEMORATIONS: Cyril, Archbishop of Alexandria; Holy 5 Virgins: Thecla, Mariamne, Martha, Mary, and Ennatha in Persia; Alexander, Bishop of Prusa; 3 Virgin Martyrs of Chios; Righteous Cyrus; Martyr Ananias; Cyril, founder of White Lake (Belozersk); Primus and Felician of Rome; Alexander, founder of Kushta (Vologda); Cyril of Velsk (Vologda); John of Shavta; Raphael of Moldavia; Columba of Iona; Baithene of Tiree; Alexius Mechev of Moscow.

*S*o, brethren, 'rejoice in the Lord,' [Phil. 4:4] not in the world. That is, rejoice in the truth, not in the wickedness; rejoice in the hope of eternity, not in the fading flower of vanity. That is the way to rejoice. Wherever you are on earth, however long you remain on earth, 'the Lord is near, do not be anxious about anything' [Phil.4:4].

St. Anthony the Great

VENERABLE CANIDES OF CAPPADOCIA. Canides was the son of pious parents and lived in fourth-century Cappadocia. His mother did not eat any foods with fat during her nine-month pregnancy. When he was born, Canides would only feed on his mother's right breast and not at all from the left. At about seven years of age, he went to a mountain and lived in a small cave. He prayed and fasted, eating only raw vegetables with no salt once per week. Because of the cave's location on a downward slope, water would seep into his cave, making it constantly wet, and this caused the hair on his head and beard to fall out. After seventy-three years of asceticism, St. Canides died peacefully.

COMMEMORATIONS: Theophanes and Pansemne of Antioch; Timothy, Bishop of Prusa; John Maximovitch, Metropolitan of Tobolsk; Asterius, Bishop of Petra; Alexander and Antonina at Constantinople; Bassian, Bishop of Lodi in Lombardy; Canides of Cappadocia; Neaniskos the Wise of Alexandria; Mitrophan, the first Chinese priest, and the Chinese New Martyrs of the Boxer Uprising, at Peking and other places in 1900; Alexios of Bithynia; Silouan of the Far Caves in Kiev; Apollo, bishop; Landry, Bishop of Paris; Savvas the Stageiritis; Tamar, abbess of St. Seraphim-Znamensky Skete (Moscow); Translation of the relics of St. Basil, Bishop of Ryazan; Synaxis of the Saints of Siberia and Saints of Ryazan.

SUNDAY	**All Saints Sunday** **Fast-free**
JUNE 11	Hebrews 11:33-12:2 Matthew 10:32-33, 37-38, 19:27-30

*W*e ought to have the most lively spiritual union with the heavenly inhabitants, with all the saints, apostles, prophets, martyrs, prelates, venerable and righteous persons, as they are all members of one single body, the Church of Christ, to which we sinners also belong with the living Head of which is the Lord Jesus Christ. This is why we call upon them in prayer, converse with them, thank and praise them. It is urgently necessary for all Christians to be in union with them, if they desire to make Christian progress; for the saints are our friends, our guides to salvation, who pray and intercede for us.

St. John of Kronstadt

NEW MARTYR ZAFEIRIOS OF HALKIDIKI. During the Turkish occupation of Greece in 1820, a revolution broke out in Halkidiki. Many Orthodox families fled to Mount Athos to escape the slaughter. The Russian Athonite Monastery of Saint Panteleimon notes: The Pasha of Thessalonica captured Mount Athos and much suffering occurred. They found seventy children there and took them to Thessalonica to convert them to their religion. Only Zafeirios stood firm in his faith, and they martyred him. According to Monk Moses of Mount Athos, even though Zafeirios is unknown in the Synaxaria, he is still honored with the Synaxis of the Athonite Fathers.

COMMEMORATIONS: Holy Apostles Bartholomew and Barnabas; Niphon, Patriarch of Constantinople (Romania); Barnabas of Vetluga; Barnabas of Vasa in Cyprus; Martyr Theopemptus and 4 with him; Arcadius of Vyazma; Zafeirios of Halkidiki; Uncovering of the relics of St. Ephraim of New Torzhok; Commemoration of the appearance of Archangel Gabriel to a monk on Mt. Athos and the revelation of the hymn "It is Truly Meet" (Axion Esti); *It is Truly Meet* Icon of the Mother of God.

Fast of the Holy Apostles Begins
Abstain from meat and dairy products.

JUNE 12

Romans 2:28-3:18; Matthew 6:31-34, 7:9-11

It is difficult, brothers, to argue with the atheist, it is difficult to talk with the insane, it is difficult to convince the embittered. Godless, mad and embittered is hard to convince by words. They are easier to convince by deeds. Let them see your good works and praise God (1 Pet 2: 12). To someone who wants to argue with you, do a good deed, and you will win the argument. One thing of mercy will teach the insane and will please the angry more successfully than many hours of conversation. The devil causes you to long disputes and fruitless conversations, and from good deeds runs. Do a good deed in the Name of Christ—the devil will run away.

St. Nikolai Velimirovich

VENERABLE ONOUPHRIOS OF KORONISIA. According to local tradition from the small island of Koronisia off Epirus, Greece, Onouphrios was a pious and humble monk from the Monastery of the Nativity of the Theotokos sometime during the seventeenth or eighteenth century. He was so humble that his fellow monks would laugh at him, but two miracles changed their perception. First, they saw Onouphrios using his monastic cassock as a boat when he returned from a nearby island. Second, after he prayed about it, his beard grew to reach the ground like his patron St. Onouphrios of Egypt. A church was built over his grave, and his relics are in the chapel. Near the church is a well that he dug, and it remains in use to this day. St. Onouphrios is the patron saint of the island.

COMMEMORATIONS: Onuphrius the Great; Onuphrius of Malsk; Onuphrius and Auxentius of Vologda; Onuphrios of Koronisia; Antonina of Nicaea; Amphianos in Cilicia; Olympius in Thrace; Julian of Dagouta; John the Soldier; John of Trebizond; Peter of Mt. Athos; John Tornike of Mt. Athos; Stephen of Komel; Timothy of Egypt; Arsenius of Konev-its; Bassian and Jonah of Solovki; Cunera of Rhenen; Synesios, Benedict, Timothy, and Paul of Thessalonica; Glorification of St. Anna, Princess of Kashin; Uncovering of the relics of St. John of Moscow, Fool-for-Christ; Synaxis of All Saints of St. Onuphrius Monastery at Jablechna (Poland).

Abstain from meat and dairy products.

JUNE 13

Romans 4:4-12; Matthew 7:15-21

*T*he Holy Spirit teaches us to love our enemies in such way that we pity their souls as if they were our own children.

St. Silouan the Athonite

ST. JAMES, WHO WAS BEGUILED TO WORSHIP THE DEVIL.

James had such love for Christ and so little regard for the things of the world that he sold everything and gave it to the poor. He lived a life of poverty, fasting, and prayer. In this way, James won the people's praise, which caused him to develop an inflated ego. He followed his self-will and undertook difficult struggles without the blessing and advice of a wise and experienced elder. A demon once appeared to him as an angel, saying that Christ was very pleased with him and that he was now equal to the Apostle Paul and that he would return that night to reward him. In his delusion, James accepted all this and made ready. When Satan arrived at midnight, James fell to the ground and worshipped him. Satan mocked him and struck him on the head, but he vanished when James made the sign of the Cross. James fell into despair and went to visit a certain elder for advice. Before he could speak a word, the elder told him that Satan had deceived him. He advised James not to live alone any longer and go to a cenobitic monastery in humility and obedience to an elder. James lived on this straight and narrow path for seven years. Because of his newfound humility and obedience, St. James became a great wonderworker.

COMMEMORATIONS: Aquilina of Byblos in Lebanon; Eulogius, Patriarch of Antioch; Anna and her son John of Constantinople; Antonina of Nicaea; Diodoros of Emesus; Antipater, Bishop of Bostra in Arabia; Triphyllios of Leukosia; Andronicus, disciple of St. Sergius of Radonezh, and Sabbas, abbots of Moscow; Anthimus the Georgian, Metropolitan of Wallachia; Alexandra, foundress of Diveyevo Convent; Philotheos of Sklataina; John Triantaphyllides, presbyter of Chaldia; James, who was beguiled by the devil; Synaxis of New Martyrs and Confessors of Zaporozhie (Ukraine); Finding of the relics of St. Nicholas of Karyes of Lesvos; *Lugansk* Icon of the Mother of God.

JUNE 14

The feeling of self-importance is deeply hidden, but it controls the whole of our life. Its first demand is that everything should be as we wish it, and as soon as this is not, so we complain to God and are annoyed with people.

St. Theophan the Recluse

NEW HIEROMARTYR ARCHPRIEST ALEXANDER PARUSNIKOV.

His father was a priest in the nineteenth-century Russian village of Troitsko-Ramenskoye. Alexander enrolled in Moscow's Technical College, but before he graduated, his father asked him to replace him as the village priest, so he entered the seminary. He married Alexandra, and they had ten children. His parishioners loved him for his kindness, and he never refused anyone who requested a service. The Soviet Regime brought persecution against the Russian Orthodox Church. Alexander and his family were classified as those deprived of rights. Except for the donations from his parishioners, food was almost impossible to get. Many of their children died of tuberculosis. The children who did survive were not permitted to be fed with the other schoolchildren. When their cow was taken away, they offered a service of thanksgiving to St. Nicholas the Wonderworker. From that time, a basket would appear on their porch every day with a bottle of milk and two loaves of bread, which continued for a long time. In 1938 Fr. Alexander was arrested. During his trials, his teeth were knocked out. He wrote to his family, "Do not weep for me; it is God's will." He was executed by firing squad. Hieromartyr Alexander was added to the host of New Martyrs and Confessors of Russia in 2001.

COMMEMORATIONS: Elisha the Prophet; Methodius, Patriarch of Constantinople; Niphon of Kavsokalyvia, Mt. Athos; Julitta of Tabennisi in Egypt; John, Metropolitan of Euchaita; Cyril, Bishop of Gortyna in Crete; Methodius, abbot of Peshnosha; Sabbas, Fool-for-Christ of Vatopedi, Mt. Athos; Elisha of Solovki; Joseph, Bishop of Thessalonica; Mstislav-George, Prince of Novgorod; Alexander Parusnikov of Troitsko-Ramenskoye; Synaxis of the Saints of Diveyevo.

THURSDAY

Abstain from meat and dairy products.

JUNE 15

Romans 5:10-16; Matthew 8:23-27

*P*ray for those who want to work but can't because they are sick. Pray for the healthy who need work but can't find any.

St. Paisios the Athonite

ST. THEOPHAN, ELDER OF THE ROSLAVL FORESTS AND OPTINA. The Venerable Optina Elder Moses recollected the following: At first, Theophan served in the Black Sea Cossack army in the late eighteenth century. He received monastic tonsure and labored with zeal in extreme non-acquisitiveness, meekness, fasting, prayer, and prostrations. At last, when Theophan was about to die, he was asked if he feared anything and if his soul was calm. He said, "I joyfully desire to be delivered from this life." He made the sign of the Cross and gave up his soul in the arms of Venerable Anthony of Optina. Anthony said he forgot to ask for Elder Theophan's prayers before his death. Forty days later, Theophan appeared to Anthony in a dream and promised to pray for him. Anthony said about Elder Theophan, "In life this elder had such a face shining with grace that I lacked the spirit to look him straight in the eyes, but only secretly looked at him from the side." St. Theophan's grave is still revered by pilgrims today.

COMMEMORATIONS: Prophet Amos; Apostles Stephanas, Achaicus, and Fortunatus, of the Seventy; Augustine, Bishop of Hippo, and his mother Monica; Dulas of Cilicia; Cedronus, Patriarch of Alexandria; Ephraim II of Serbia; Jonah of Moscow; Modestus, Vitus, and Crescentia at Lucania; Doulas the Passion-bearer; Hesychius the Soldier; Lazar, Tsar of Serbia; Gregory and Cassian of Avnezh; Orsiesius of Tabennisi; Michael, first Metropolitan of Kiev; Martyr Grace; Symeon of Novgorod; Spyridon, Patriarch of Serbia; Abraham of Auvergne; Sergius and Barbara of Oyatsk; Jerome of Stridon; Theophan of Roslavl Forests and Optina; Job of Ugolka; Synaxis of New Martyrs of Serbia; *Marianica* Icon of the Mother of God.

JUNE 16

Romans 5:17-6:2; Matthew 9:14-17

The Jesus prayer gives you so much sweetness, so much joy. It's short, but it's got so much power. So much, that you say: 'Even if I go to hell, I'm not afraid. I'll just say the prayer there, as well.'

St. Ephraim of Katounakia

ST. TYCHON THE WONDERWORKER, BISHOP OF AMATHUS.
Tychon was born to pious parents in fourth-century Cyprus, and from his birth, he was dedicated to God. When he was a young boy, he once gave the poor all the bread from his father's bakery. His father chastised him, but the boy said he was letting God borrow the loaves of bread, and as soon as he said these words, the storehouse overflowed with grain. After studying Holy Scripture, Tychon became a Reader. Because of his pure and blameless life, he was ordained Deacon and later was elevated to Bishop of Amathus by St. Epiphanios. Tychon destroyed many pagan Greek idols and temples and converted the remaining idol-worshipers in Cyprus. St. Tychon's biggest miracle is as follows. A vine clipping that he planted took root and miraculously sprouted leaves, bloomed, and produced ripe and sweet grapes in June. After his repose, on his feast day, the vine would be filled with unripe grapes, which is typical for the time of year, but during the Divine Liturgy, the grapes would become fully ripened. And in no other area of the island do grapes ripen on the 16th of June, the day of the St. Tychon's commemoration.

COMMEMORATIONS: Tychon the Wonderworker, Bishop of Amathus in Cyprus; Tigrius and Eutropius of Constantinople; Mnemonios, Bishop of Amathus; Mark the Just of Apollonia; 5 Martyrs of Nicomedia; 40 Martyrs of Rome; Kaikhosro the Georgian; Tikhon of Krestogorsk; Hermogenes, Bishop of Tobolsk, and Euphremius, Michael, Peter, and Constantine; Tikhon of Lukh; Tikhon of Kaluga and Medin; Moses of Optina, founder of Optina Skete; Translation of the relics of St. Theophan the Recluse; Synaxis of the Theotokos at Maranakios.

JUNE 17

Romans 3:19-24; Matthew 7:1-8

The Lord calls to him all sinners; He opens His arms wide, even to
the worst among them. Gladly He takes them in His arms, if only
they will come to Him.

St. Macarius of Optina

**ST. BOTOLPH, ABBOT AND CONFESSOR OF IKANHOE, ENG-
LAND.** Botolph was from early seventh-century Britain and became a
monk in Gaul, which is modern-day France, as a young man. The sisters of
the king of East Anglia met Botolph in Gaul when the king sent them to
learn the monastic discipline. When they heard that Botolph intended to
return to Britain, they asked their brother to grant Botolph land to build a
monastery. But Botolph asked the king for land not owned by any man so
no one would lose any ground for his sake. Botolph chose a desolate place
in Ikanhoe. The demons who lived there tormented Botolph with horrible
apparitions, threats, and turmoil, but he drove them away with prayer and
the sign of the cross. He established the monastic rule from Gaul and worked
signs and wonders. He also had the gift of prophecy and was known for
the sweetness of his disposition. Toward the end of his life, he had a painful
sickness, but he bore it with thankfulness and patience while continuing to
instruct his spiritual children. He died peacefully at about the age of seventy,
and his relics were later found incorrupt and exuding a sweet fragrance.

COMMEMORATIONS: Joseph and Pior the Anchorites, disciples of St.
Anthony the Great; Manuel, Sabel, and Ishmael of Persia; Philoneides, Bishop
of Kurion in Cyprus; Aetius the Eunuch, Enlightener of Ethiopia; Isauros,
Basil, Innocent, Felix, Hermias, Perigrinos, Rufus, and Rufinus, of Apollonia; Ananias the Iconographer of Novgorod; Ismael of Russia; Shalva of
Akhaltsikhe, Georgia; Nectan of Hartland; Botolph of Ikanhoe (Boston, England) and Adolph the Confessor; Nicander of Yaroslavl; Hypatius of Rufinia-
nos; Martyrs of Atchara, Georgia; Uncovering of the relics of the Alfanov
Brothers of Novgorod: Nicetas, Cyril, Nicephorus, Clement, and Isaac.

Second Sunday of Matthew
Abstain from meat and dairy products.
Romans 2:10-16; Matthew 4:18-23

JUNE 18

The parish must become an ascetic focal point. But this can only be achieved by an ascetic priest. Prayer and fasting, the Church-oriented life of the parish, a life of liturgy: Orthodoxy holds these as the primary ways of effecting rebirth in its people.

St. Justin Popovich

MARTYR ALENA OF BELGIUM. Alena was born near Brussels, Belgium, in the seventh century. She was baptized without the knowledge of her pagan parents. She secretly attended church services, giving her parents various excuses for her absence. One day her father had his guards follow her, and they witnessed Alena entering a chapel in Vorst. Her father decided that she had been bewitched into a conversion and ordered that she be arrested, but she resisted. During the struggle, her arm was severed, and St. Alena died. An angel appeared and took the severed arm to the chapel where she worshipped and placed it on the altar. Witnessing this miracle, her parents converted to Christianity.

COMMEMORATIONS: Marina the Virgin of Bithynia; Leontius, Hypatius, and Theodulus at Tripoli in Syria; Aitherios of Nicomedia; Leontius the Myrrh-flowing of Dionysiou Monastery, Mt. Athos; 2 Martyrs of Cyprus; Leontius, canonarch of the Kiev Caves; Nicanor (Morozkin) of Spas-Ruzsky; Leontius of Phoenicia; Erasmus, monk; Amand of Bordeaux; Alena of Belgium; Kalogeros the Anchorite with Gregory and Demetrios; Uncovering of the relics of St. Victor (Ostrovidov), Bishop of Glazov; *Bogoliubsk-Zimarovsk* and *Piukhtitsa* Icons of the Mother of God; (2nd Sunday after Pentecost: Olga of Kwethluk; Finding of the Relics of St. Basil of Ryazan; Synaxis of the Saints of Ryazan and Siberia; Synaxis of the Saints of North America).

Apostle Jude, Brother of our Lord
Abstain from meat and dairy products.
Jude 1:1-25; John 14:21-24

*T*here is a depression that is the result of many sins, of a heavy conscience and of a profound grief. This is because the soul is covered with many injuries and descends under the weight of them into the depth of depression. There is another type of grief that comes to us from haughtiness and vanity, when one supposes that he has not merited his sudden fall. The one observing closely will discover the characteristics of each: the one coldly yields to apathy while the other in depression still holds on to his struggle, which is not in agreement with his state. The first is treated by moderation and hope. The latter is treated by a humble heart and the practice of not condemning anybody.

St. John Climacus

VENERABLE PAISIUS OF HILANDER AND BULGARIA. Paisius was born to a pious family in eighteenth-century Bulgaria. His brother Lawrence was the abbot of Hilander Monastery on Mount Athos, and his other brother was a great benefactor of Orthodox monasteries and churches. Paisius went through monastic training at the Rila Monastery and then went to his brother at Hilander and took monastic tonsure. There he studied Holy Scripture and was ordained a priest. During this time, Bulgaria was under foreign oppression, and Paisius wrote a book, "History of the Slavo-Bulgarians," upholding the Christian faith of the Bulgarian nation, and it rekindled the lamp of Orthodoxy. It is unknown how or where St. Paisius died. The Bulgarian Orthodox Church canonized him in 1962. Many institutes, schools, and the state university bear his name.

COMMEMORATIONS: Apostle Jude, the Brother of the Lord; Paisios the Great of Egypt; Paisius the Bulgarian of Hilander, Mt. Athos; Holy Myrrhbearer Mary, mother of Apostle James; Zosimas the Soldier at Antioch; Macarius of Petra; John the Solitary of Jerusalem; Romuald of Ravenna; Job, Patriarch of Moscow; Zeno of Egypt; Barlaam of Shenkursk; Parthenius of Russia, bishop; Asyncretus, martyred at the Church of Holy Peace by the Sea in Constantinople.

Abstain from meat and dairy products.

JUNE 20

Romans 7:14-8:2; Matthew 10:9-15

The Lives of the Saints are holy testimonies of the miraculous power of our Lord Jesus Christ.

St. Justin Popovich

ST. NAHUM THE WONDERWORKER, ENLIGHTENER OF BULGARIA. Nahum's story was written by St. Nicodemus the Hagiorite. Nahum lived during the time when Saints Cyril, Methodius, and Clement, the Equal-to-the-Apostles, were all taking the Orthodox faith to the misled nation of Bulgaria. Nahum wandered with them throughout all the cities. They were persecuted by the unbelievers and enemies of Christ, being flogged and reviled. In order to translate the Old and New Testament from Greek into the Bulgarian (Slavic), Cyril, Methodius, and Clement first developed an alphabet. Pope Hadrian of Rome gave them authority to do so, having seen the many miracles and revelations that God worked through them in Rome. Just looking at the sick immediately healed them. Nahum was younger than the three others and was more fervent in his zeal. Upon leaving Rome, Nahum, Methodius and his disciples went to the land of the Germans, where many heresies had spread, and they had blasphemed against the Holy Spirit. Again, they were flogged, tormented, and imprisoned. While they were praying in prison, a great earthquake shook the entire area. They were freed from their bonds, and the prison doors opened of their own accord. The saints returned to Bulgaria to preach Christ. The sacred relic of St. Nahum produces miracles for those who hasten to it with faith.

COMMEMORATIONS: Callistus I, Patriarch of Constantinople; Studius of the Studion; Methodios of Patara; Lucius the Confessor; Paul, Cyriacus, Paula, Felicilana, Thomas, Felix, Martyrius, Vitaly, Crispinus, and Emilius in Tomi; Nicholas Cabasilas of Thessalonica; Nahum of Ochrid; Gleb of Vladimir; Minas of Polotsk; Florentina of Spain; Govan of Pembrokeshire; Stanislav Nasadil in Slovakia; Finding of the relics of St. Raphael of Lesvos; Translation of the relics and garments of Apostles Luke, Andrew, and Thomas, Prophet Elisha, and Martyr Lazarus in the Church of the Holy Apostles in Constantinople; *Directress* Icon of the Mother of God of Xenophontos.

JUNE 21

That a soul is truly intelligent and virtuous is shown in a man's look, walk, voice, smile, conversation and manner…Its God-loving mind, like a watchful doorkeeper, bars the entrance to evil and shameful thoughts.

St. Anthony the Great

NEW HIEROMARTYR BASIL KALAPALIKES. Basil was from mid-nineteenth-century Kastoria in northern Greece, in the region of Macedonia. He was a married priest with three children. In 1902 unbelievers burst into his parish church while serving Vespers and shot him before the altar. He was seriously wounded, but when he came out of the church, he was stabbed, beaten with rods and axes, and mercilessly injured to death. He was recognized only by his beard and sacred robes. Basil was buried behind the sanctuary. After his continuous appearances to the faithful, his relics were uncovered in 1987. His skull was found with skin and hair, and his right hand was in the form of giving a blessing. Then the holy relics were reburied. In 2014 they were unearthed again and were accompanied by a beautiful fragrance as witnessed by clergy and faithful. They remain fragrant to this day. In 2020 the Ecumenical Patriarchate canonized St. Basil with six other New Martyrs from Kastoria.

COMMEMORATIONS: Terence, Bishop of Iconium; Julian of Tarsus; Theodore of Starodub; Julian of Egypt, with Anthony, Anastasius, Celsius, Basilissa, Marcianilla, 20 prison guards, and 7 brothers; Aphrodisios in Cilicia; Demetria of Rome; Julius and Julian of Novara; Archil II and Laursab II, of Georgia; Nicetas of Nisyros; Cormac of the Sea; Raoul of Bourges; George (Lavrov) of Kaluga; Basil Kalapalikes, in Chiliodendrou; Finding of the *Panagia Eleusa* Icon of the Mother of God in Xyniada.

JUNE 22

*T*he essence of sin consists not in the infringement of ethical standards but in falling away from the divine eternal life for which man was made and to which, by his very nature, he is called.

St. Sophrony of Essex

ST. ANASTASIA OF SERBIA. Anastasia was of royal lineage. She was born in 1125, the daughter of the Byzantine Emperor, thereby Greek by birth. She married the pious Grand Prince Stefan Nemanja of Serbia. Their marriage solidified political and religious ties between the Kingdom of Serbia and the Byzantine Empire. In the early years of Anastasia's marriage, they had two sons. Desiring another child, they fervently petitioned the Lord, and at fifty years old, she gave birth to her last child, Sava. Saint Sava was the most beloved figure in Serbian history, and his mother saw the beginning of the Serbian Orthodox culture and civilization. When Sava was seventeen, he went to Mount Athos, and Anastasia never saw him again. When she was 71 years old, she took monastic vows and went to a monastery known as Petcovaka. Stefan became a monk, went to Mount Athos, and joined his son at Hilander Monastery. St. Anastasia reposed peacefully at age 75, four months after the death of her husband. She was buried at the Studenica Monastery.

COMMEMORATIONS: Paulinus, Bishop of Nola; Eusebius, Bishop of Samosata; Zenas and Zenon of Philadelphia in Arabia; Pompianos, Galacteon, Juliana, and Saturninos of Constantinople; Basil of Patalaria Monastery; Athanasius, Bishop of Chytri, Cyprus; Anastasia of Serbia, mother of St. Sava; Alban, Protomartyr of Britain; Gregory, Metropolitan of Wallachia; 1,480 Martyrs of Samaria in Palestine; Aaron of Britain.

JUNE 23

Romans 9:6-19; Matthew 10:32-36, 11:1

*A*nger does not do the work of God and does not bear the fruit of love. When you're angry, the Spirit of God is not present, neither is the spirit of love; it's the spirit of pride and vainglory that is present.

† *Elder Paisius of Sihla*

STS. JOSEPH, ANTHONY, AND IOANNICIUS, ABBOTS OF ZAON-IKIEV MONASTERY. Monk Joseph was a pious peasant from the Vologda region in sixteenth-century Russia. For a long time, he suffered from an illness of eyesight. Joseph fervently prayed for healing from Christ, the Mother of God, and the saints, particularly the holy Unmercenaries Cosmas and Damian. St. Cosmas revealed to Joseph that he should go into the forest to a swampy place, and there he would find an icon of the Mother of God from which he would receive healing. In gratitude, Joseph cleared a part of the forest there and built a chapel, in which he placed the icon. He settled nearby, and afterward, with the blessing of Bishop Anthony of Vologda the Zaonikiev monastery was founded. The monastery expanded, and the number of monks grew. Out of humility, Joseph refused to become the abbot, and instead, he recommended St. Anthony to be the abbot. Joseph was perceived as a Fool-for-Christ because of his strict ascetic exploits, such as going barefoot in freezing weather. St. Joseph died peacefully at age 83 and was buried in his monastery. Later, St. Ioannicius became the monastery abbot.

COMMEMORATIONS: Eustochius, Gaius, Probus, Lollius, and Urban of Ancyra; Agrippina of Rome; Joseph, Anthony, and Ioannicius of Vologda; Dionysius of Polotsk; Leonty, Maximus, and Mitrophan of Russia; Artemius of Verkola; Aristocles, Demetrianos, and Athanasios of Cyprus; Nicetas of Thebes, with Theodore, Gregory, and Daniel; Etheldreda of Ely; Fomar (Tamara) of Moscow; Barbaros the Pentapolitis; Translation of the relics of St. Michael of Klops; Translation of the relics of St. Herman of Kazan; Synaxis of All Saints of Vladimir; Synaxis of the New Martyrs of Crete; Meeting of the *Vladimir* Icon; Pskov *Umileniye* and *Zaonikiev* Icons of the Mother of God.

Nativity of St. John the Baptist
Abstain from meat and dairy products.
Romans 13:11-14:4
Luke 1:24-25, 57-68, 76, 80

*I*n order to attain a fruitful life of prayer, we should not expect blessings to fall upon us suddenly. Rather, we should make our way through with slow but sure steps. We need a long, disciplined struggle. We need patience and constraint. It is enough to make progress however slow that progress may seem, or however pitch-black the world around us and around our faith may appear. Mere progress in the life of prayer and intimacy with God is a sure sign that we will reach our goal. It is proof positive that the light must appear, however long it may be hidden from us. Once it appears, the fruit of our laborious struggle and our faith and patience will materialize. When we constraint ourselves in our struggle, when we expend our sweat and tears, when we contend with our doubts and whispers—walking on in spite of the darkness that shrouds everything in us, our own eyes may not see in ourselves anything but weakness. The eyes of God, however, see precious and valuable signs of growth: "Blessed are those who have not seen and yet believe" (Jn 20:29); "For God is not so unjust as to overlook your work and the love which you showed for His sake" (Heb 6:10).

† *Fr. Matthew the Poor*

ST. NICETAS, BISHOP OF REMESIANA. Nicetas taught the southern Slavic people the Christian faith in the fourth- and the fifth-century Roman province of Dacia Mediterranea, present-day Bela Palanka in the Pirot District of Serbia. He wrote six volumes, *Instructions for Candidates for Baptism,* and liturgical hymns. St. Paulinus of Nola lauded his friend St. Nicetas in a poem about how he taught and brought to the faith the barbarians.

COMMEMORATIONS: Nativity of St. John the Baptist; Synaxis of the Righteous Zacharias and Elizabeth, parents of St. John the Baptist; Athanasios of Paros; Michael, Great Prince of Tver; John of Solovki; John and James of Novgorod; John the Hermit; Anthony of Dymsk; Panagiotes of Caesarea; Nicetas of Remesiana; Gerasimus of Astrakhan and Enotaeva.

Third Sunday of Matthew
Abstain from meat and dairy products.
Romans 5:1-10; Matthew 6:22-33

The evil one cannot comprehend the joy we receive from the spiritual life; for this reason he is jealous of us, he envies us and sets traps for us, and we become grieved and fall. We must struggle, because without struggles we do not obtain virtues.

St. Maximos the Confessor

PANAGIA MEGALOMATA ICON OF THE MOTHER OF GOD IN SKIATHOS. The Panagia Megalomata Icon of the Mother of God resided in the Church of the Panagia in Skiathos, Greece, which is in the northern Aegean Sea. Megalomata means "large-eyed." Traditionally, its feast was celebrated on the Saturday of the Akathist Hymn. The chapel was built between the sixteenth and seventeenth centuries, but eventually, it collapsed and turned into ruins. In 2010 the silt was cleaned away, revealing the entrance and altar area. Following the discovery, an all-night vigil was held, and today the annual Vigil is celebrated on the last Sunday of June. The Panagia Megalomata Icon is now housed in the Cathedral Church of the Three Hierarchs in Skiathos.

COMMEMORATIONS: Febronia of Nisibis; Gallicianus the Patrician; Symeon of Sinai; 7 martyred brothers: Orentius, Pharnacius, Eros, Firmus, Firminus, Cyriacus, and Longinus, near Lazica; Nikon of Optina; Dometius and Dionysios of the Monastery of the Forerunner, Mt. Athos; Theoleptos, Metropolitan of Philadelphia; Cyprian of Svyatogorsk Monastery; Methodius of Nivritos; George of Attalia; Peter and Febronia of Murom; Procopios of Varna & Mt. Athos, in Smyrna; Orosia of Spain; Adelbert, archdeacon; Virgin Martyrs Leonida, Liby, and Eutropia of Syria; Moluac of Lismore (Scotland); *Panagia Megalomata* Icon of the Mother of God in Skiathos.

JUNE 26

*T*he candles lit before icons of saints reflect their ardent love for God for Whose sake they gave up everything that man prizes in life, including their very lives, as did the holy apostles, martyrs and others. These candles also mean that these saints are lamps burning for us and providing light for us by their own saintly living, their virtues and their ardent intercession for us before God through their constant prayers by day and night. The burning candles also stand for our ardent zeal and the sincere sacrifice we make out of reverence and gratitude to them for their solicitude on our behalf before God.

St. John of Kronstadt

DIRECTRESS ICON OF NEAMT MONASTERY. The Wonderworking Icon of the Mother of God from Neamt Monastery is the oldest known icon in Romania, valuable both spiritually and historically. It is a copy of an icon of the Mother of God written in the year 35. On the reverse side is an icon of Great Martyr St. George. Patriarch St. Germanos took the icon to Constantinople and gave it to the Heleopatra Monastery. When the iconoclast persecution began in 714 by Byzantine Emperor Leo the Armenian, the icon was hidden and secretly sent to Pope Gregory III in Rome. It remained in St. Peter's Basilica in Rome for about a century. Pope Sergius II returned the icon to the Heleopatra Monastery, and it remained there for over 500 years. In the early fifteenth century, it was taken to the Neamt Monastery, where it remains today. However, during an Ottoman invasion in 1822, the icon was threatened again, but it was hidden underground in the Rusu Mountains with other sacred objects.

COMMEMORATIONS: David of Thessalonica; John, Bishop of Gothia; Dionysius of Suzdal; David of St. Anne's Skete; Anthion, monk; Perseveranda of Spain; Brannock of England; Translation of the relics of St. Nilus of Stolobny and St. Tikhon of Lukhov; Appearance of the *Tikhvin*, *Of the Seven Lakes*, *Of Neamts*, and *Of Lydda* Icons of the Mother of God.

TUESDAY   **Abstain from meat and dairy products.**

JUNE 27

Romans 10:11-11:2; Matthew 11:16-20

*T*he angels—and especially our guardian angels—distance themselves
and flee from man when he is not careful! However, when man
prays, he receives fragrance and grace from God, and his guardian
angel also prays by his side and petitions, "My God, hear this person's prayer. Give him what he is asking." When prayer is further
accompanied by tears and offered with true repentance, the guardian angel rejoices because he is accompanying and watching over
such a beautiful soul, and he has boldness before God.

† *Elder Ephraim of Arizona*

NEW HIEROMARTYR GREGORY NIKOLSKY OF KUBAN. Gregory
was a Russian priest in the Astrakhan Diocese and was actively involved in
a missionary society. He also enjoyed time spent in solitary prayer at a local
monastery. At 61 years of age, Gregory began to serve St. Mary Magdalene
Hermitage in the Kuban Governorate that bordered the Caspian Sea. There
he headed the women's department of the Kuban correctional shelter and
cared for wounded soldiers at the monastery's hospital. He was also a church
builder, teacher, and zealous pastor. His diocese often gave him awards. In
1918 the Bolsheviks captured Kuban and carried out regular massacres
of the clergy. Fr. Gregory was arrested just as he had finished serving the
Divine Liturgy. They severely beat him, and they shot him when he tried
to cross himself.

COMMEMORATIONS: Joanna the Myrrhbearer; Sampson the Hospitable; Kirion II, Catholicos-Patriarch of All Georgia; Crescens, Maximus,
and Theonest of Mainz (Germany); Martin of Turov; Anectus of Caesarea;
Severus of Interocrea; Pierios of Antioch; Gregory Nikolsky of Kuban;
Serapion of Kozha Lake; George of Mt. Athos and Georgia; Martyrs Marcia and Mark; Luke (Mukhaidze) of Holy Cross Monastery in Jerusalem;
Uncovering of the relics of the Optina Elders.

JUNE 28

Romans 11:2-12; Matthew 11:20-26

*T*he enemy of men, the devil and his angels, the demons, know very well how to whisper into our ear and to pass on to us evil under the guise of the good and to hypnotize our conscience. If that which passes into our mind corresponds to our hidden desires and our passions, then very easily they will be understood by our heart. We must resist their evil works. We can do this more easily if we manage to think of how much these things that we hear correspond with the Will of God and if we shut our ears to the devil.

St. Luke of Simferopol

TRANSLATION OF THE RELICS OF HOLY AND WONDER-WORKING UNMERCENARIES AND MARTYRS CYRUS AND JOHN. The lives of Saints Cyrus and John are commemorated on January 31. The title "Unmercenary" was given to Christian saints who, during their life, healed without accepting payment for their services. Saints Cyrus and John were martyred in Alexandria during the reign of Diocletian in the year 311. Their relics were buried in a mass grave at St. Mark the Apostle's in Canopus. In the fifth century, an angel of the Lord appeared to St. Cyril of Alexandria, commanding him to transfer the relics of these saints to Manuphin. Everyone feared this city because of the evil spirits dwelling in the pagan temple. St. Cyril destroyed it and built a church dedicated to the Saints Cyrus and John. Through their prayers, many remarkable miracles and healings took place. In 634, the holy relics were transferred to Rome.

COMMEMORATIONS: Paul the Physician of Corinth; Sennuphius the Standard-bearer of Egypt; Sergius and Herman of Valaam; Serenus, Plutarchus, Heraclides, Heron, Raiso and others in Alexandria; Venerable Magnus; Sergios the Magistrate of Paphlagonia; Xenophon of Novgorod; Donatus of Libya; Austell of Cornwall; 3 Martyrs of Galatia; 70 Martyrs of Scythopolis; Moses the Anchorite; Martyr Papias; Heliodorus of Glinsk Hermitage; Martyr Macedonius; Finding of the relics of St. Cyrus and St. John the Unmercenaries; *Of the Three Hands* Icon of the Mother of God.

JUNE 29

2 Corinthians 11:21-12:9; Matthew 16:13-19

*he fact that the Scriptures often make use of identical or very similar phrases is due, says St. John Chrysostom, not to repetitiveness or prolixity, but to the desire to imprint what is said on the heart of the reader.

St. Peter of Damascus

HOLY APOSTLE PAUL. Paul had once vowed to wipe out belief in Jesus Christ, but the Lord called him. He was largely responsible for the inception and growth of Christianity. Jesus Himself converted the Pharisee Paul on the road to Damascus on his deadly mission to capture and imprison Christians. He was a brilliant speaker and writer, and with zeal, he taught the new religion throughout the ancient Eastern world. He became known as the 'Apostle to the Gentiles.' Jesus Christ was so much a part of him that he said, "I live, yet not I but Christ liveth in me." He worked toward a union between Christians and Jews in Jerusalem but was almost killed for it. He tried for two years to develop Rome as a base to spread Christianity. While under house arrest in Rome, he wrote his letters to the Philippians, Ephesians, Colossians, and Philemon. In the year 64, St. Paul was beheaded by Emperor Nero for confessing Christ. He was martyred after Apostle Peter, and their relics were placed in the same place. Apostle Paul authored almost half of the twenty-seven books of the New Testament.

COMMEMORATIONS: Holy and All-Praised Apostles Peter and Paul; Mary, mother of John-Mark, nephew of Apostle Barnabas, at Jerusalem; Cassius of Narni; Cocha of Ros-Bennchuir in Ireland; Uncovering of the relics of St. Nicander of Pskov; *Kasperov* Icon of the Mother of God.

FRIDAY

JUNE 30

Synaxis of the Twelve Holy Apostles
Abstain from meat and
dairy products, and fish.
1 Corinthians 4:9-16; Matthew 9:36, 10:1-8

$\mathscr{B}$ut mark both their faith, and their obedience... For though they were in the midst of their work... when they heard His command, they delayed not, they procrastinated not, they said not, 'let us return home, and converse with our kinfolk,' but 'they forsook all and followed,' even as Elisha did to Elijah. Because such is the obedience which Christ seeks of us, as that we delay not even a moment of time, though something absolutely most needful should vehemently press on us. Wherefore also when some other had come unto Him, and was asking leave to bury his own father, not even this did He permit him to do; to signify that before all we ought to esteem the following of Himself.

St. John Chrysostom

NEW MARTYR MICHAEL PAKNANAS THE GARDENER, OF ATH-ENS. During Greece's occupation by the Turks in 1771, the eighteen-year-old Michael was arrested at the city gates of Athens. Because he was carrying farm tools, he was suspected of aiding the Greek guerillas, the pasha's nemesis. Michael was imprisoned for a month while they created a list of charges against him. He was told all charges would be dropped if he denied his faith and converted to Islam. Michael's only response was that he would not become a Turk. While the Athenians pleaded for his release, he was taken to the place of execution, where they struck his neck with the sword. St. Michael demanded they strike harder for his faith.

COMMEMORATIONS: Synaxis of the Holy Twelve Apostles: Peter, Andrew, James, John, Philip, Bartholomew, Thomas, Matthew, James the son of Alphaeus, Jude the brother of James, Simon the Zealot, and Matthias; Basilides the Soldier; Stephen of Omsk; Gelasius of Rimet; Peter of Sinope; Peter, Prince of the Tatar Horde; Erentrude of Salzburg; Andrew of Bogoliubsk; Michael Paknanas the Gardener; Martial of Limoges; Dinar of Khereti; Nicander of Yaroslavl; Theogenes of Kazakhstan; Milan Popovic of Rmanj; Alexander of Munich; Peter of Ordinsk; Martyr Meleton; Glorification of St. Sophronius, Bishop of Irkutsk and All Siberia.

**St. Cosmas & St. Damian
the Holy Unmercenaries
Fast-free**

1 Corinthians 12:27-13:8; Matthew 10:1, 5-8

He who lives according to God's will has no worries.
† *Elder Thaddeus of Vitovnica*

MARTYR POTITUS OF SARDINIA. Potitus was born into a pagan family in second-century Sardinia. He learned about the Christian faith and received holy Baptism when he was thirteen years old. This upset his father, and he tried with entreaties and threats to dissuade his son from this new faith. However, they talked about the truth of the Christian faith and the falseness of the idols, and Potitus' father was so impressed with his son's firmness that he also came to believe in Christ. Potitus traveled through many areas teaching about Christ, and God granted him the gift of working miracles. In Epiros, there lived a senator's wife named Kyriake, who suffered from leprosy. She sent for Potitus and asked him to heal her, and he said that if she believed in Christ, she would be healed. As soon as Kyriake received Baptism, she was made well, and this caused her husband and the whole household to believe and be baptized. Then Potitus went to Mount Gargano and lived in solitude among the animals. But he was found there by the servants of Emperor Antoninus. They asked Potitus to return to heal the emperor's daughter, who was possessed. The demon had spoken through the girl, saying that only Potitus could expel him. The girl was freed through Potitus' prayers, but the emperor turned on him, saying his gods had healed her. Potitus insisted that it was through the power of Jesus Christ, and when he refused to sacrifice to the pagan gods, he endured horrible tortures. Finally, he was beheaded. Many wonders took place that day, and two thousand people were converted to Christianity.

COMMEMORATIONS: Cosmas and Damian the Unmercenary Physicians; Potitus of Sardinia, Italy; Peter the Patrician; Gallus, Bishop of Clermont; Eparchius the Recluse of Gaul; Basil, founder of the Monastery of the Deep Stream; 25 Martyrs at Nicomedia; Leo the Hermit; Nicodemus of Svyatogorsk; Leontius, Bishop of Radauti; Servanus (Serf), apostle of Western Fife, East Scotland; Julius and Aaron of Wales; Constantine of Cyprus, and those with him; Juthwara of England; Second translation of the relics of St. John of Rila from Turnovo to Rila; (1st Saturday of July: St. Melo of Kos).

SUNDAY

JULY 2

Fourth Sunday of Matthew
Fast-free

Hebrews 9:1-7; Matthew 8:5-13

*K*eep this word of the Lord near: *'Everyone who humbles himself will be exalted, and everyone who exalts himself will be humbled'* (Luke 14:11). Do not judge yourself with prejudice, nor examine yourself with partiality. If you think you possess some good, do not count this to your credit while purposely overlooking your misdeed—extolling yourself on account of the good things you accomplished today, and pardoning yourselves for the bad things you did yesterday and long ago. Instead, whenever the present causes you to exalt yourself, recall the past, and you will put an end to any stupid self-inflation.

St. Basil the Great

NEW MARTYR LAMPROS OF SAMOTHRACE. Lampros was from the early nineteenth-century island of Samothrace in the northern Aegean Sea. He and five other youths, including Manual, Theodore, George, Michael, and George, were forcibly converted from Christianity at a young age. Later, Lampros returned to his Orthodox Christian faith. For this, he was martyred in 1835 in the village of Makri in Alexandroupoli, across from Samothrace. The other five youths returned to their Christian faith and were martyred a few months earlier in Makri.

COMMEMORATIONS: Placing of the Honorable Robe of the Most Holy Theotokos at Blachernae; John Maximovitch, Archbishop of Shanghai and San Francisco; Juvenal, Patriarch of Jerusalem; Juvenal, Protomartyr of America and Alaska; Photius, Metropolitan of Kiev and All Russia; Quintus of Phrygia; Basil, Patriarch of Jerusalem; Stephen the Great of Moldavia; Lampros of Samothrace; Monegunde of Gaul; Paul, Bilonus, Theonas, and Heron, at Thessalonica; Swithun of Winchester; Oudoceus of Llandaff; Uncovering of the relics of St. Sergius Florinsky, of Estonia; *Pozai, Theodotiev, Of Akhtyra,* and *The Root of Jesse* Icons of the Mother of God.

JULY 3

Those who are in Hades desire only one thing from Christ: to live for five minutes in order to repent.

St. Paisios the Athonite

MILK-GIVER ICON OF THE MOST HOLY MOTHER OF GOD OF HILANDER. The icon is located at the Hilander Monastery on Mount Athos. It was housed at the Lavra of St. Savvas the Sanctified, near Jerusalem in the sixth century. Just before his death, Savvas told the brotherhood that a pilgrim with the same name as himself would visit the Lavra after some time, and he was to be given the miraculous icon. He also said that as the man approaches his tomb, Savvas' staff will fall at his feet. This prophecy was passed down among the brethren for over six hundred years. In the thirteenth century, St. Savas of Serbia visited the monastery. When he came to the tomb of St. Savvas the Sanctified, the saint's staff fell. The brotherhood asked the man who he was, and when he said he was the archbishop of Serbia, he was given the saint's staff, the Milk-Giver Icon, and the Icon of the Three Hands, which St. John of Damascus prayed in front of when his hand was cut off. Because John venerated the holy icons, the iconoclasts cut off his hand, and the Mother of God miraculously healed him. Archbishop Savas took the icon to the Hilander Monastery on Mount Athos, where it remains to this day.

COMMEMORATIONS: Hyacinth of Caesarea, and Theodotus and Theodota; Diomedes, Eulampius, Asclepiodotos, and Golinduc of Caesarea; Anatolios, Patriarch of Constantinople; Anatolios of Laodicea, and Eusebius; Symeon the Stylite; Anatolius of the Near Caves; Anatolius of the Far Caves; Isaiah the Solitary; Martyrs Mark and Mocius; Alexander of the Unsleeping Ones; John and Longinus of Yarenga; Basil and Constantine of Yaroslavl; Gerasimos of Carpenision; Nicodemus of Kozha Lake; John 'Iron Cap' of Moscow; Germanus of the Isle of Man; George of the Black Mountain; Joachim of Notena; Basil of Novgorod; Michael, Herodion, Basil, and Thomas of Solvychegodsk; Jacob of Hamatoura; Repose of St. Basil, Bishop of Ryazan; Second translation of the relics of St. Philip, Metropolitan of Moscow; *Milk-Giver* Icon of the Mother of God of Hilander.

JULY 4

Romans 14:9-18; Matthew 12:14-16, 22-30

No matter how just your words may be, you ruin everything when you speak with anger.

St. John Chrysostom

ST. ANDREW RUBLEV THE ICONOGRAPHER. Andrew is considered Russia's greatest iconographer. He was born in the fourteenth century near Moscow. While still a young man, he visited the Trinity-St. Sergius Lavra and was greatly impressed by St. Sergius of Radonezh, whom he met there. Andrew later became a novice at that monastery after the death of St. Sergius. Under the new abbot St. Nikon, Andrew received the blessing to live at the monastery founded by St. Andronicus. He was tonsured a monk and learned to write icons by Theophanes the Greek and the monk Daniel, who became Andrew's friend. Andrew's first work was when he decorated icons for the Cathedral of the Annunciation of the Moscow Kremlin with Theophanes and Prochorus of Gorodets. Next, Andrew and Daniel painted the frescoes in the Dormition Cathedral in Vladimir. After the Tatars destroyed the Monastery of the Holy Trinity, St. Nikon asked Andrew and Daniel to paint the new church at the reconstructed monastery. This is where Andrew wrote his most famous icon, the Hospitality of Abraham. After Daniel's death, Andrew painted his last work at Moscow's Andronikov Monastery in the Savior Cathedral. Daniel appeared to Andrew and urged him to join him in Paradise. St. Andrew died peacefully at the age of seventy in the year 1430.

COMMEMORATIONS: Theodore, Bishop of Cyrene, with Cyprilla, Aroa, and Lucia; Donatus, Bishop of Libya; Hieromartyrs Theophilus and Theodotus; Righteous Menignos; Andrew, Archbishop of Crete; Asclepias the Wonderworker; Martha, mother of St. Symeon Stylites the Younger; Innocent and Sabbatios and 30 others in Sirmium; Andrew the Russian of Cairo; Euthymius of Suzdal; Nilus of Poltava; Andrew of Bogoliubsk; Michael Choniates of Athens; Ulrich of Augsburg; Andrew (Rublev), iconographer of Moscow; Sava, Bishop of Gornji Karlovac and George Bogich of Nasice, and Bogoljub Gakovic of Plaski; Holy Royal Martyrs of Russia (Old Calendar); *Galatea* Icon of the Mother of God.

St. Athanasios of Mount Athos
Strict Fast

Galatians 5:22-6:2; Matthew 11:27-30

*O*bedience and dependency are recognized duties and constitute the first step to our progress. As a proof, God the Son has kept this before everything else. "There is nothing less than the Splendor of the Father." Therefore, as an unquestionable duty, it cannot be the subject of choice. Without obedience, which means total dependency on the life-giving Son of God, one cannot be freed from the power of death.

St. Joseph the Hesychast

VENERABLE LAMPADOS THE WONDERWORKER OF IRENO-POLIS. Lampados gave himself over to the ascetic way of life from his early youth. With prayer and watchfulness, he brought his flesh under submission. He shone forth and enlightened those around him who were darkened by their passions and deceived by the demons. God granted him the gift to work miracles during life and after death to those who hastened to him for his protection. Later, the holy relics of St. Lampados were found in a cave.

COMMEMORATIONS: Athanasios of Mt. Athos and his 6 disciples; Cyprian of Koutloumousiou, Mt. Athos; Stephen, Bishop of Rhegium, and Bishop Suerus, Agnes, Felicitas, and Perpetua; Anna at Rome; Athanasius, disciple of Sergius of Radonezh; Basil and 70 Martyrs of Scythopolis; Theodosius of Cherepovets; Athanasius of Jerusalem; Lampados of Irenopolis; Elizabeth Romanova and Nun Barbara, and with them John, Igor, Constantine, Sergius, Vladimir, and Theodore; Agapitus of Optina Monastery; Morwenna of Morwenstow; Synaxis of 23 Saints of Lesvos; Uncovering of the relics of St. Sergius of Radonezh; *Economissa* Icon of the Mother of God.

JULY 6

Romans 15:17-29; Matthew 12:46-13:3

*M*others who are always standing over their children and pressurizing them, that is, over-protecting them, have failed in their task. You need to leave the child alone to take an interest in its own progress. Then you will succeed. When you are always standing over them, the children react. They become lethargic and weak-willed and generally are unsuccessful in life. This is a kind of over-protectiveness that leaves the children immature.

St. Porphyrios of Kavsokalyvia

HOLY MARTYR QUINTUS OF PHRYGIA. The pious Quintus was a Christian from third-century Phrygia, a Roman province in Asia Minor. He later moved to an area called Neolida, and there he did many charitable acts and his prayers healed those possessed by unclean spirits. The district governor demanded Quintus to offer sacrifice to the pagan idols, but then the governor fell to the ground in a demonic fit until Quintus prayed and healed him. The grateful governor rewarded Quintus and released him. Then he traveled to Pergamum, not far from the Aegean Sea. Along the way, he was captured by pagans who began to torture him for his Christian faith, but an earthquake destroyed their pagan temple. The frightened pagans stopped their torture until the arrival of the new governor Klearchos. He gave orders to break the saint's legs, and by the grace of God, Quintus was healed. After this, St. Quintus lived another ten years, continuing to help others and working many miracles.

COMMEMORATIONS: Synaxis of Apostles Archippos, Philemon, and Onesimus; Sisoes the Great; Marinus, Martha, Audifax, Abbacum, Cyrinus, Valentine, and Asterios; Astius of Dyrrachium; Lucy at Rome, and 24 companions; Cyril of Hilander; Simon of Ufa; Sisoes of the Kiev Caves; Isaurus, Innocent, Felix, Hermias, Basil, Peregrinus, Rufus, and Rufinus of Apollonia; Martyrs Alexander, Epimachos, and Apollonius; Theodore of Moscow; Euthymius of Optina; Barnabas of Gethsemane Skete; Monenna of Ireland; Goar, missionary; Quintus of Phrygia; Synaxis of the Saints of Radonezh; Uncovering of the relics of St. Juliana Olshansky.

FRIDAY

St. Kyriake the Great Martyr
Strict Fast

Galatians 3:23-4:5; Mark 5:24-34

JULY 7

*P*rayer is our very breath.

† *Elder Sergei of Vanves*

GREAT MARTYR KYRIAKE OF NICOMEDIA. Kyriake was born through the prayers of parents who had been childless. Her goal in life was to preserve her virginity and be a bride of Christ. But an idol-worshipping magistrate wanted Kyriake for his son. When she explained her desire, he reported her to Emperor Diocletian. Her parents were also arrested, and when her father Dorotheos told Diocletian that his deities did not fashion heaven and earth, they were sent away and later beheaded. Kyriake was sent to Diocletian's son-in-law Maximian. He flattered her and promised to betroth her to royalty if she would venerate the gods. She replied that no torment could separate her from the love of Christ. She was bullwhipped, but with Christ's help, she did not feel any pain. The shamed emperor sent her to the eparch Hilarion in Chalcedon, who had the reputation of being a wild beast. She was suspended and burned with torches. That night in prison, Jesus appeared to her and said, "Fear not O Kyriake, the tortures for My grace shall be with you, and shall deliver you from every temptation." Then Christ healed her wounds and vanished. The following day, Hilarion marveled at her, but she told him that Christ, the true God, had restored her. She then asked to go to the temple of his gods. She prayed to Christ, and immediately an earthquake caused the idols to fall. Hilarion stood in the ruins, blaspheming the God of the Christians. Suddenly, a lightning bolt struck him in the face, killing him. The new governor, Apollonios, attempted to burn Kyriake, but rain quickly put out the fire. He sent hungry lions after her, but they became tame and fell at her feet. Then he sentenced her to death. Before the soldiers could behead her, St. Kyriake prayed and surrendered her soul.

COMMEMORATIONS: Kyriake of Nicomedia; Acacius of Sinai; Hieromartyr Eustathius; Epictetus and Astion; Peregrinus, Lucian, Pompeius, Hesychius, Pappias, Saturninus, and Germanus; Pantaenus of Alexandria; Thomas of Mt. Maleon; Evangelos of Tomi; Euphrosyne of Moscow; New Martyr Polycarp; Vlasios of Akarnania; Willibald of Eichstatt; Hedda of the West Saxons; Maelruin of Tallaght.

SATURDAY

St. Procopius the Great Martyr
Fast-free

JULY 8

1 Timothy 4:9-15
Luke 6:17-19, 9:1-2, 10:16-21

The door of repentance is open to everyone, and it is not known who will enter it first—whether you, the condemning one, or the one condemned by you.

St. Seraphim of Sarov

VENERABLE THEOPHILOS THE MYRRHGUSHER OF MOUNT ATHOS. Theophilos was a well-educated ascetic from Mount Athos. The Patriarch of Constantinople once directed him to travel to Alexandria to ascertain the truth of the miracles taking place there by Patriarch Joachim. Convinced that Joachim could move a mountain with his prayers and drink poison without harm, he reported this and returned to Mount Athos. Theophilos lived in the monasteries of Vatopedi and Iveron and then in a cell at the Church of St. Basil near Karyes, the capital city of Mount Athos. Through his prayers, he became passionless and remained silent. He also refused an appointment to become archbishop of Thessalonica. Finally, when he was about to die, he directed his disciple to drag his dead body to a stream and throw it in. Later, his body was recovered and placed in his cell, where he had struggled. The relics of St. Theophilos soon gushed fragrant myrrh.

COMMEMORATIONS: Procopius of Caesarea in Palestine, and with him: Theodosia, his mother, tribunes Antiochus and Nicostratus, and 12 women of senatorial rank; Anastasios at Constantinople; Theophilos the Myrrhgusher of Pantocrator Monastery; Mirdat, King of Kartli, Georgia; Procopius, Fool-for-Christ of Ustiug (Vologda); Procopius, Fool-for-Christ of Usya; Martyr Abdas; Edgar the Peaceable of England; Sunniva and companions on Selja Island, Norway; Hieritha (Urith) of Chittlehampton; Translation of the relics of St. Demetrius of Basarabov, Bulgaria; Appearance of the *Kazan* Icon of the Mother of God; *Our Lady of Sitka, Of Tender Feeling*, Ustiug *Annunciation*, and *Peschanskaya* Icons of the Mother of God.

Fifth Sunday of Matthew
Fast-free

JULY 9

Romans 10:1-10; Matthew 8:28-9:1

The devil, having failed in all his other schemes, tempts us with thoughts of despair.

St. Peter of Damascus

REPOSE OF PRIEST ILIE LACATUSU OF ROMANIA. Father Ilie had a degree in theology from Bucharest University, and he served as a parish priest and a missionary in Odessa. He was arrested with a group of other priests and sent to hard labor, where he became grievously ill. After two years, he was released but was arrested again five years later and sent to a labor camp in the Danube Delta. At the end of January 1962, they took the prisoners to a freezing lake with a thicket of reeds in the middle, where they were ordered to wade into the waist-deep, ice-cold waters to cut the reeds. Father Ilie encouraged the group to go into the lake rather than be shot. Their clothes froze as they cut the reeds until noon, but then, by the prayers of Father Ilie, a July-like sun warmed the air to over 75 degrees. Two years later, in 1964, Father Ilie was released and placed under house arrest and worked as a bricklayer. Later he served as a priest in some of the villages. To this day, the elderly worshippers remember his kindness and mercy toward the poor. When four of his children died, Father Ilie accepted this as God's will. He retired in 1978, but his life of hardship had worn him down, and he fell critically ill. As he lay dying in a hospital, he requested that his wife be buried next to him upon her death, which would occur fifteen years later. Just as he had prophesied. At her funeral, Father Ilie's body was found fragrant and incorrupt. His holy relics have performed many miracles at the Dormition of the Theotokos-Giulesti Cemetery in Bucharest.

COMMEMORATIONS: Procopius of Caesarea, with Theodosia, Antiochus, Nicostratus, and 12 women; Anastasios at Constantinople; Theophilos the Myrrhgusher; Mirdat of Kartli; Procopius of Ustiug; Procopius of Usya; Martyr Abdas; Edgar the Peaceable; Sunniva and companions on Selja Island; Appearance of the *Kazan* Icon of the Mother of God; *Our Lady of Sitka, Of Tender Feeling, Ustiug Annunciation*, and *Peschanskaya* Icons of the Mother of God.

JULY 10

Romans 16:17-24; Matthew 13:10-23, 43

*A*ll our success in Christian life depends on how we subjugate our own will to the will of God.

St. John Maximovitch

SYNAXIS OF ALL SAINTS OF VATOPEDI MONASTERY. According to tradition, Mount Athos was given to the Panagia by her Son. When the Theotokos first arrived at the Holy Mountain with the Apostle John, the place where they walked ashore was where the Monastery of Vatopedi was founded. St. Gregory Palamas said that when St. Peter the Athonite was visiting Vatopedi as a pilgrim in the fourteenth century, he was saddened to see a woman caring and serving in the church and dining area. He assumed that the monks received women in that monastery, but then he learned from the abbot of Zographou Monastery that the woman he saw was the Most Holy Theotokos. There are seven wonderworking icons of the Theotokos within Vatopedi Monastery. St. Ephraim of Katounakia says that Vatopedi is the throne of Mount Athos. From the fourth to the tenth centuries, pirates would destroy this monastery. In the tenth century, St. Athanasios the Athonite sent three rulers to re-establish the ruined monastery. Today there are more than 66 known saints of Vatopedi Monastery. St. Gregory Palamas and St. Maximos the Greek, illuminator of the Russians, matured here. Also, the Honorable Belt of the Theotokos is one of the monastery's greatest treasures.

COMMEMORATIONS: Deposition of the Precious Robe of the Lord at Moscow; 45 Martyrs at Nicopolis; 10,000 Fathers of Scetis; Anthony of the Kiev Caves; Bianor and Silvanus of Pisidia; Apollonios of Sardis; Silouan of the Far Caves; Evmenios and Parthenios of Crete; Joseph of Damascus, and companions; Athanasios of Pentaschoinon; Synaxis of All Saints of Vatopedi; Synaxis of St. John the Theologian in Beatus; Translation of the relics of St. Gregory, Bishop of Assos; *Konevits* Icon of the Mother of God.

TUESDAY

St. Euphemia the Great Martyr
Fast-free

JULY 11

2 Corinthians 6:1-10; Luke 7:36-50

*D*iscernment is greater than all other virtues.

† *Elder Justin Pârvu of Romania*

NEW VENERABLE MARTYR NECTARIUS OF VRYOULLA. Nectarius was from a poor Orthodox Christian family in nineteenth-century Vryoulla in Asia Minor. He was seventeen when his father died, so he and six other Orthodox Christian young men hired themselves out to a wealthy Muslim to tend his camels. When a plague struck the area of Ephesus, these seven men, together with other Muslim camel attendants, fled to the countryside. Soon, they began to believe that their parents and all Orthodox Christians would not survive the plague, so they decided to join the Muslim faith so they might be sustained. Much later, they learned that the epidemic had ended, and they returned to the city, where Nectarius was surprised and pleased to see his mother alive. But when she saw him dressed as a Muslim, she shunned him with anger. He left there hurt and went to see an uncle in Smyrna who gave him western clothes and sent him to Constantinople to escape. However, Nectarius returned to Smyrna, and with the counsel of an Athonite monk, he went to live on Mount Athos and became a monk. As time passed, he nurtured a desire to become a martyr, and he would often ask the elders for their permission. However, they were reluctant to approve until finally, he did receive their blessing and went before a judge in his hometown, where he announced his return to Orthodoxy. The judge told him to leave and think well because torments would await him, but St. Nectarius was adamant. He was imprisoned and finally beheaded. His relics were thrown down a dry well.

COMMEMORATIONS: Euphemia of Chalcedon; Olga, Equal-to-the-Apostles; Cindeos of Pamphylia; Januarius and Pelagia of Nicopolis; Nicodemus of Elbasan and Mt. Athos; Nicodemos of Hilander and Vatopedi, Mt. Athos; Arcadius of Vyazemsk; Nectarius of Vryoulla, Asia Minor; Cyril of Paros; Leo of Mandra; Drostan of Old Deer; Sophrony of Essex; New Hieromartyrs of Serbia (1941–1945); Translation of the relics of St. Barbara from Constantinople to Kiev.

JULY 12

1 Corinthians 2:9-3:8; Matthew 13:31-36

*D*on't accept thoughts that cause you frustration, lest you render useless the gifts God has given you. The truer you look at things, the more peace and tranquility you will have, the healthier you will be and the more you will stop taking medicine. Sadness disarms a person. It sucks all the juices of mental and bodily strength and does not let you do anything. It poisons the soul and makes disorder in the body. It hits the most sensitive spots of the body, causes fear and wears a man down. The poison of despondency can bring down not only a person with a weak body, but also very strong.

St. Paisios the Athonite

MONK-MARTYR SIMON, FOUNDER OF VOLOMSK MONASTERY. Simon was born into a peasant family from Volokolamsk in the sixteenth century. After visiting many Orthodox monasteries, he became a monk at the age of twenty-four. He lived in solitude for five years, eating only vegetables he had grown. Others who were also seeking quietude gathered near him, so Simon asked the tsar for assistance to build a monastery, which he named in honor of the Holy Cross. Here he served as the abbot and was an example to the other monks struggling in all virtues. But one day St. Simon was found brutally murdered in his monastery. He was buried in the church he founded, and his relics have produced many miracles.

COMMEMORATIONS: Proclus and Hilarion of Ancyra; Andrew the Commander, Heraclius, Faustus, Menas, and others; Mamas, near Sigmata; Serapion, Bishop of Vladimir; Serapion the New, at Alexandria; Veronica, who was healed by the Lord; Michael of Maleinus; Arsenius of Novgorod; Simon of Volomsk Monastery; Theodore and John of Kiev; John and Gabriel of Mt. Athos; Paisios the New of Mt. Athos; Translation of the relics of Momcilo Grgurevic of Serbia; Translation of the relics of St. Anthony of Leokhnovo Monastery; *Of the Three Hands* of Hilander, Mt. Athos, and *Prodromitissa* Icons of the Mother of God.

Synaxis of Archangel Gabriel
Fast-free
Hebrews 2:2-10; Luke 10:16-21

*N*othing so provokes God to anger as the division of the Church.
St. John Chrysostom

HELIOPHOTOI SAINTS OF CYPRUS. In the abandoned Turkish-Cypriot village of Agio Heliophotoi, there is a chapel dedicated to the Heliophotoi Saints. According to tradition, 300 Alamanni Christian refugees went to Cyprus after the Second Crusade, where the waves destroyed their boat during a storm. These saints scattered over the island to continue to live as hermits. Five of them went up to the Mountain Koroni and set up their hermitage in two caves and made a water spring that still exists there. Their sheep and goats multiplied into many hundreds, and the animal pens remain to this day and are known as the "Holy Pens of the Heliophotoi Saints." The Cypriots would visit the saints often for spiritual advice, and in return, the saints would feed the poor of the region. When the island's sovereign learned about the saints, he asked them to deny Christ. When they refused, they were whipped without mercy, cutting their flesh, and finally, they were beheaded. The faithful buried them in their caves. The saints were found after many years due to the many miracles, and they still take place today. A village priest once visited the saints to seek healing for his hands that were filled with warts. He noticed that a large part of the saints' relics was missing. In a dream, he saw the five martyrs who asked him to make a wooden box and collect the remains of their relics. The priest returned with the box, and as he began to collect the relics, his hands were healed.

COMMEMORATIONS: Synaxis of the Holy Archangel Gabriel; Stephen of St. Sava's; Sarah of Seeds; Mary Golinduc of Persia; Julian of Cenomanis; Martyr Serapion; Marcian of Iconium; Alamannia, in Cyprus; Heliophotus, Epaphrodites, Ammon, and 2 others, of Cyprus; Onesiphoros of Anarita in Paphos; Mildred of Minster; Juthwara of Cornwall; Just of Cornwall; Alexander of Munich; Translation of the relics of Martyrs Anthony, John, and Eustathius, of Vilnius, Lithuania.

JULY 14

*O*ne must try to be meek and humble, and then the yoke of Christ that you have taken up will be easy and light. Take care of the sick, as Christ did, and for this you'll receive salvation and be rid of the ruthless passions while on earth. Don't abandon that sick person, or the Lord will send another, kinder person to do it, and you'll lose the reward prepared for you. The enemy is attacking you all the more, for your obedience is not to his liking; or perhaps he in his slyness has noticed that it will soon come to a finish and wishes to deprive you of the reward. If one seeks to receive gain for what he does, for what can such a one be rewarded? But he who readily works for Christ freely will receive a hundred times more from Him and inherit eternal life.

St. Joseph of Optina

ST. JOSEPH THE CONFESSOR, ARCHBISHOP OF THESSA-LONICA. During the reign of the iconoclast Leo the Armenian in the ninth century, Joseph was exiled three times because of his zealous defense of the icons. He was the brother of St. Theodore the Studite. Joseph also received the title "Studite," especially when he is mentioned with his brother. They composed canons that are sung during Holy Week. During his exiles, St. Joseph was imprisoned in dark dungeons, and he endured tribulations, hunger, and thirst. He died in exile.

COMMEMORATIONS: Apostle Aquila of the Seventy, and St. Priscilla; Justus at Rome; Joseph, Archbishop of Thessalonica; Heraclius, Patriarch of Alexandria; Onesimos of Magnesia; Hellius of Egypt; John of Merv; Marcellinus of Utrecht; Nicodemos of Mt. Athos; Stephen of Makhrishche Monastery; Martyr Aquila; Longinus of Svyatogorsk Monastery; Constantine Oprisan of Jilava, Romania; Procopius of Sazava in Bohemia; Emmanuel, Anezina, George, and Maria of Melissourgio of Kissamos; Uncovering of the relics of St. Theophilos of Kiev.

St. Cyricus and his mother St. Julitta
Fast-free

1 Corinthians 13:11-14:5; Matthew 17:24-18:4

If your heart has been softened either by repentance before God or by learning the boundless love of God towards you, do not be proud with those whose hearts are still hard. Remember how long your heart was hard and incorrigible... Seven brothers were ill in one hospital. One recovered from his illness and got up and rushed to serve his other brothers with brotherly love, to speed their recovery. Be like this brother.

St. Nikolai Velimirovich

FINDING OF THE HONORABLE HEAD OF ST. MATRONA OF CHIOS. Matrona was a renowned ascetic from Chios, Greece. She is commemorated on October 20. Because of the many miracles that her prayers caused long after her falling asleep, crowds of people continued to make a pilgrimage to the small church that housed her wonderworking relics to receive healing from her. For this reason, it was decided to enlarge the church. When they dug into the church foundation, they opened her tomb and realized a wonderful fragrance exuded from her head. Her relics showed all the signs of having been touched by God. Many miracles occurred at that moment. A paralyzed man could walk, another with a speech impediment could speak clearly, and many other miracles were also wrought. The Orthodox Church has dedicated this second day to St. Matrona.

COMMEMORATIONS: Julitta and Cyricus of Tarsus; Equal-to-the-Apostles Great Prince Vladimir, Enlightener of Russia; Abudimus of the isle of Tenedos; Donald of Ogilvy, and his 9 virgin daughters, nuns of Abernathy (Scotland); Asiya of Tanis in Syria; Zosima of Alexandrov (Vladimir); Job of Malaya Ugolka; Martyr Lollianus; Commemoration of the Miracle of St. Barbara in Polydendri in Attica; Finding of the head of St. Matrona of Chios; Translation of the relics of St. Swithun, Bishop of Winchester.

**Sunday of the Holy Fathers of the
Fourth Ecumenical Council**
Fast-free
Titus 3:8-15; Matthew 5:14-19

The Eucharist is like a fire that inflames us, that, like lions breathing
fire, we may retire from the altar being made terrible to the devil.
St. John Chrysostom

FIVE VENERABLE MARTYRS OF LEIPSOI. The information we have
regarding these five saints comes from the Monastery of St. John the Theologian on Patmos and local tradition. Leipsoi is a Greek island south of
Samos. In the year 1088, this island was given to St. Christodoulos by
Emperor Komnenos. The first ascetics arrived in 1550 from Patmos. They
built a church, dug a well, planted wheat and vines for the bread and wine
of the Eucharist, and they planted olive trees to get oil for their lamps.
Their hermitage attracted other monks and even a few Kollyvades Fathers
from Mount Athos. Later, five of these monks were killed by pirates and
others, including Monk Neophytos of Amorgos, Monk Jonah of Leros,
Monk Neophytos the Fazos, Monk Jonah of Nysiros, and Monk Parthenios of Philipopolis. A service was written for these five saints who were
canonized in 2002.

COMMEMORATIONS: Athenogenes, Bishop of Heracleopolis, and 10
disciples; Antiochus of Sebaste; 15,000 Martyrs of Pisidia; Julia of Carthage; Ardalion of Kasli; John of Turnovo; Theodotus of Glinsk; Seraphim,
Theognostus, and others of Alma-Ata; Helier of Jersey; James of Barnaul,
with Peter, John, Theodore, and John; Matrona of Anemnyasevo; Anastasios
and Euxitheos of Thessalonica; Basil of Novgorod; 5 Martyrs of Leipsoi;
Commemoration of the Fourth Ecumenical Council.

MONDAY

JULY 17

St. Marina the Great Martyr
Fast-free

Galatians 3:23-4:5; Mark 5:24-34

*D*o not run away from poverty or sorrows; such things lift our prayer to heaven.

† *Evagrius of Pontus*

ST. TIMOTHY OF SVYATOGORSK, THE FOOL-FOR-CHRIST. In the region of Voronezh, Russia, south of Moscow, in the mid-sixteenth century, there lived a 15-year-old shepherd named Timothy, who everyone considered a holy fool. Once as he grazed his flock near the Lugovitsa River, he suddenly saw the Eleousa Icon of the Mother of God in the air, which was in the Veronezh church of St. George. The same vision appeared a second time on Mount Sinica, but this time, Timothy heard a voice saying that the grace of God would shine on that mountain in six years. Timothy did not tell anyone about the visions. Six years later, he went to Mount Sinica and saw the Hodigitria Icon of the Mother of God standing on the bough of a pine tree. Timothy made a small hut and spent forty days in continuous fasting and prayer. Then he heard a voice from the icon commanding him to go to the suburbs of Voronezh and tell the clergy and people to go to Mount Sinica for the icon on a specific day, which he did. When clergy and many faithful reached the place of Timothy's first vision at Lugovitsa River, the healing of the sick began to take place. And on Mount Sinica, when they started prayers and the reading of the Gospel, the mountain suddenly lit up with an unusually bright light, and an unspeakable fragrance filled the air. Some tried to remove the icon from the tree, but it rose by an invisible force and descended into Timothy's hands. They placed the Hodigitria Icon in the St. George Church of Voronezh, next to the Eleousa Icon of the Mother of God.

COMMEMORATIONS: Marina of Antioch; Scillitan Martyrs: Speratus, Cittinus, Narzalis, Felix, Veturius, Acyllinus, Laetantius, Januaria, Generosa, Donata, Secunda, and Vestina; Timothy of Svyatogorsk; Euphrasius of Ionopolis; Holy Royal Martyrs: Tsar Nicholas II, Empress Alexandra, Alexis, Olga, Tatiana, Maria, and Anastasia, and others; Eugene Botkin, the Passion-bearer; Irenarchus of Solovki; Leonid of Ustnedumsk; Kenelm of Mercia; Marcellina, sister of St. Ambrose; *Svyatogorsk* Icon of the Mother of God.

JULY 18

1 Corinthians 6:20-7:12; Matthew 14:1-13

*W*hen the love of God is completely overwhelming, it binds the lover not just to God but to everyone else too.

St. Thalassios the Libyan

VENERABLE NEW MARTYR BARBARA YAKOVLEVA. Barbara became a nun at the age of thirty at the Saints Martha and Mary Convent in Moscow in 1910. She had served as the maid to Grand Duchess Elizabeth Feodorovna. The Grand Duchess, Barbara, and other women were all tonsured together on the same date. They became well known throughout Moscow for their acts of charity. They took food to the poor, created a home for women with tuberculosis, established a hospital and an orphanage, and houses for the disabled, pregnant women, and the elderly. Their efforts spread to other cities in Russia. Barbara was accessible to everyone, affectionate, and courteous. In 1918, following the Russian Revolution, Barbara accompanied the Grand Duchess when she was arrested and exiled, not wanting to leave her abbess. They were clubbed in the back of the head and thrown into a mine shaft, followed by grenades. For a while, hymns could be heard coming from the bottom of the shaft. They were martyred the day after Tsar Nicholas and his family were murdered. The bodies of Grand Duchess Elizabeth and Barbara were later discovered and eventually buried in the Holy Land, in the upper church of St. Mary Magdalene.

COMMEMORATIONS: Hyacinth of Amastris; Martyrs Dasius and Maron; Paul, Chionia (Thea), and Valentina in Caesarea of Palestine; Emilian of Silistra in Bulgaria; Athanasius of Klysma, Egypt; Stephen II, Archbishop of Constantinople; Pambo, hermit of Egypt; Cozmas of Georgia; John the Confessor, Metropolitan of Chalcedon; Pambo, recluse of the Kiev Caves; Apollinarius (Mosalitinov) of Verkhoturye; Leontius, abbot of Karikhov (Novgorod); Barlaam of Bald Mountain, near Antioch in Syria; Fredrich, Bishop of Utrecht; John the Long-suffering of the Kiev Caves; Martyr Marcellus; New Martyr Barbara Yakovleva; *Tolga* Icon of the Mother of God.

JULY 19

1 Corinthians 7:12-24; Matthew 14:35-15:11

*D*epression is a spiritual cross. It is sent to help penitents who do not know how to repent... One must either learn to repent and offer the fruits of repentance; or else bear this spiritual cross with humility, meekness, patience and great gratitude to the Lord, remembering that the bearing of this cross is accounted by the Lord as the fruit of repentance.

St. Maria of Gatchina

RIGHT-BELIEVING PRINCESS JELENA LAZAREVA OF SERBIA.

Jelena was born in the mid-fourteenth century to Great-Martyr Tsar Lazar of Serbia. At the age of thirty, she married the ruler of the state of Zeta, modern-day Montenegro. After seventeen years of marriage, he died, and Jelena governed the state along with her son Balsa III. She once resisted a military invasion from the Venetians, and Balsa declared Orthodox Christianity the official state religion, despite the strong influence of another religion. Jelena also restored the abandoned Church of St. George that her husband had built, and next to it, she founded the Church of the Holy Mother of God, where she was later buried. St. Jelena is also known as a writer, for her correspondence with her spiritual father, monk Nikon of Jerusalem.

COMMEMORATIONS: Macrina, sister of St. Basil the Great; Theodore the Sabbaite; Abba Diocles of *The Paradise*; Dios of Antioch; Paisius of the Kiev Caves; Victor of Glazov; Militsa (Eugenia), Princess of Serbia; Stephen Lazarevic, King of Serbia; Jelena Lazareva of Serbia; Romanus Olegovich of Ryazan; Sophronius of Svyatogorsk; Synaxis of All Saints of Kursk; Commemoration of the Miracle of St. Haralambos in Filiatria of Messenia; Translation of the relics of St. Seraphim of Sarov; Seraphim-Diveevsk *Tenderness* Icon of the Mother, before which St. Seraphim reposed.

JULY 20

James 5:10-20; Luke 4:22-30

*N*o matter how much we may study, it is not possible to come to know God unless we live according to His commandments, for God is not known by science, but by the Holy Spirit. Many philosophers and learned men came to the belief that God exists, but they did not know God. It is one thing to believe that God exists and another to know Him. If someone has come to know God by the Holy Spirit, his soul will burn with love for God day and night, and his soul cannot be bound to any earthly thing.

St. Silouan the Athonite

MARTYR SALOME OF JERUSALEM AND KARTLI, WHO SUFFERED UNDER THE PERSIANS. Because of her outspoken defense of Christ, Persians arrested Salome in the thirteenth-century Monastery of the Holy Cross in Jerusalem. The Synaxarion of her monastery tells us that she gave in to the threats and denied Christ at first. Later, however, she repented and publicly confessed Christ as Son of God and Savior of the world. The Persians tortured and beheaded St. Salome, then burned her holy relics.

COMMEMORATIONS: Elias (Elijah) the Prophet; Elias and Flavius II, Patriarchs of Jerusalem and Antioch; Lydia, Alexis, and Cyril of Russia; Elias Chavachavadze of Georgia; Philosoph Omalsky, and those with him; Salome of Jerusalem and Kartli; Abraham of Galich; Deacon Juvenal; Alexis Medvedkov of Ugine, France; Elias Fondaminsky, Priest Demetrius Klepinine, George Skobtsov, and Nun Maria Skobtsova of Paris; Tikhon, George, Cosmas, John, Sergius, Theodore, Alexander, George, Euthymius, and Peter, at Voronezh; Ethelwida, widow of King Alfred the Great; Uncovering of the relics of St. Athanasius of Brest.

JULY 21

1 Corinthians 7:35-8:7; Matthew 15:29-31

To repent is not to look downwards at my own shortcomings, but upwards at God's love, it is not to look backwards with self-reproach, but forward with trustfulness.

St. John Climacus

ST. PRAXEDES AT ROME. Praxedes was the daughter of Christian Roman Senator Pudens, who is mentioned in one of St. Paul's letters to Timothy. She was also the sister of St. Pudentiana, who helped Praxedes in her endeavors. The sisters built a baptistry in their father's house to baptize pagans. This was a time of Christian persecutions by the emperor Marcus Antoninus in the first century. Praxedes contributed to the care and comfort of the Christians. She hid many Christians in her home while encouraging others to keep firm in the faith. She would also lovingly bury the relics of the martyrs. Pudens and Pudentiana predeceased Praxedes, and she also died at the age of sixteen. The writings say she was possibly martyred. Her body was laid next to her father and sister in the catacombs of Priscilla near the Via Salaria. The Church of St. Praxedes was built on the site of her former house in Rome.

COMMEMORATIONS: Symeon of Emesa and his fellow faster John; Parthenius, Bishop of Radobysdios; Acacius of Constantinople; Eleutherius of "Dry Hill"; Justus, Matthew, and Eugene of the 13 who suffered at Rome with Trophimos and Theophilos; Victor of Marseilles; Bargabdesian at Arbela; Paul and John, near Edessa; Raphael and Parthenios of Old Agapia Monastery (Romania); Onuphrius the Silent of the Kiev Caves; Zoticus of Comana; Onesimus of the Kiev Caves; 3 Martyrs of Melitene; Simo Banjac, Milan Stojisavljevic, and his son Milan of Glamoc, Serbia; Praxedes at Rome; Arsenia of Ust-Medveditsky; Manuel II Palaiologis, Emperor of the Romans; Uncovering of the relics of St. Anna of Kashin; *Armatia* Icon of the Mother of God.

St. Mary Magdalene the Holy Myrrhbearer
Fast-free
1 Corinthians 9:2-12; Luke 8:1-3

*N*ever sleep before saying evening-prayers, lest your heart should become gross from ill-timed sleep, and lest the enemy should hinder it by a stony insensibility during prayer.

St. John of Kronstadt

VENERABLE CORNELIUS OF PEREYASLAVL. Cornelius was a novice of the Elder Paul in the Lukyanovsk wilderness near Pereyaslavl. He then became an eager and obedient novice at the Monastery of Saints Boris and Gleb in Pereyaslavl. He never sat down to eat with the brethren but ate only the leftovers three times per week. He was never seen sleeping on a bed. After five years, Cornelius took monastic vows. The other monks thought he was foolish, and they often insulted him. His elder blessed him to live alone in a cell apart from the monastery to pray and fast. So severe were his efforts that brought the purity of heart, that the monks once found Cornelius barely alive. After recovering, he returned to the monastery, working in the church, the refectory, and the garden, where he would give the exceptional apples to visitors. His body became withered from fasting, but Cornelius never ceased working. With his own hands, he built a well for the brethren. For thirty years, Cornelius lived in complete silence for the sake of prayer. The monks even thought that he had become deaf and dumb. Before his death, Cornelius confessed, received Holy Communion, and took the Great Angelic Schema. After nine years, during the construction of a new church, the relics of St. Cornelius were found incorrupt. St. Dimitri of Rostov, who also saw the saint's relics, composed a Troparion and Kontakion to St. Cornelius.

COMMEMORATIONS: Myrrhbearer and Equal-to-the-Apostles Mary Magdalene; Cyril I, Patriarch of Antioch; Marcella of Chios; Cyprian, Fool-for-Christ of Suzdal; Cornelius of Pereyaslavl; Menelaos of France; Wandregisilus of Caux (Gaul); Michael Nakaryakov of Usolye.

JULY 23

It is possible to offer fervent prayer even while walking in public or strolling alone or seated in your shop...while buying or selling... or even while cooking.

St. John Chrysostom

NEW MARTYR ANDREW ARGUNOV. Andrew was born into a peasant family in Russia in 1904. When his father died, the family fell into dire need. Still, Andrew managed to educate himself, and he worked as a handicraftsman to produce toothbrushes. He was chairman of the parish council and sang in the choir. In 1933 a local collective farm was organized, but since the farm declared itself godless, Andrew did not join. During the next three years, the communists took away everything he owned, and the authorities demanded that he hand over 60 kg of meat each year, which he could not do. Also, the authorities wanted to dismantle a brick fence around the church to use the bricks for a new power plant. Andrew defended the wall and verbally attacked them. In 1937 they imprisoned him for selling toothbrushes and again later for building a log house without permission. He was charged as a counter-revolutionary and for spreading slander against the Soviet regime, to which he pleaded not guilty. St. Andrew was sentenced to eight years of hard labor but died in custody less than a year later. He was buried in an unknown grave and was canonized by the Russian Orthodox Church in 2005.

COMMEMORATIONS: Ezekiel the Prophet; Trophimos, Theophilos, and 13 others, in Lycia; Anna (Hannah), mother of Prophet Samuel; 8 Martyrs of Carthage; Nectarius of Yaransk; Anna of Leucadia; Apollonius at Rome; 250 Martyrs killed by the Bulgarians; John (Jacob) of Neamts; Apollinarius of Ravenna; Theodore Ushakov; Pelagia of Tinos; Vitale of Ravenna; Thyrsos, Bishop of Karpasia; New Martyr Andrew Argunov; Repose of St. John Cassian the Roman; Translation of the relics of St. Herman (Germanus) of Kazan; Translation of the relics of St. Phocas, Bishop of Sinope; Commemoration of the Miraculous Appearance of Mother of God at Pochaev; *The Joy of All Who Sorrow* of St. Petersburg and *Pochaev* Icons of the Mother of God.

JULY 24

*J*esus is the Christ, one of the Holy Trinity, and you will become
no less than his heir.

St. Thalassios the Libyan

GREAT MARTYR CHRISTINA OF TYRE. In third-century Tyre, Christina's pagan father had a tower built and he locked her in it and placed idols there so she could sacrifice. As she observed the beauty of the sun and stars, her natural wisdom led her to believe in the One God. Finally, an angel of God instructed her, and she devoted herself to prayer and fasting. When Christina told her parents of the One God, her father told her to worship many so as not to offend any gods. Later she smashed the idols, for which he had her beaten. He had her flesh lacerated, but it was as though she did not feel it. When a torture wheel with fire was brought, she prayed, and the fire scattered and burned the pagans. She was left in prison to starve, but angels fed and healed her. She was thrown into the sea, and by this means receiving from the Lord Holy Baptism, but angels rescued her and put her on dry land. When her father saw her, he condemned her to beheading, but he died that night. A few days later, the new governor, Deon, had her boiled in oil, but again God protected her. He took her to Apollo's temple, where her prayers caused the idols to be smashed. Deon died that night from distress, and three thousand souls believed and converted to Christianity. The next governor, Julian, had her burned in a furnace for six days, but she emerged unharmed. Then two soldiers were ordered to stab her, and St. Christina gave up her spirit. Julian went home and died with great suffering.

COMMEMORATIONS: Christina of Tyre; Boris and Gleb of Russia; Pachomius, abbot; Hilarion of Tvali; Bernulphus, Bishop of Utrecht; Theophilos of Zakynthos; Athanasius of Nicaea; Polycarp of the Kiev Caves; John Kalinin of Olenevka; Bogolep, child schemamonk of Cherny Yar; Declan of Ardmore (Ireland); 17 New Martyrs of Mgarsk Monastery (Poltava); Alexander of Bolshaya Rechka; Martyrs Capito and Hymenaeus; Martyr Hermogenes; Christiana of Termonde; George, Archbishop of Mogilev; Serbian New Martyrs of Prebilovci (Herzegovina).

**Dormition of St. Anna,
Mother of the Theotokos
Fast-free**

Galatians 4:22-27; Luke 8:16-21

It is not the clever, the noble, the polished speakers, or the rich who win, but whoever is insulted and forbears, whoever is wronged and forgives, whoever is slandered and endures, whoever becomes a sponge and mops up whatever they might say to him. Such a person is cleansed and polished even more. He reaches great heights. He delights in the theoria of mysteries. And finally, it is he who is already inside paradise, while still in this life.

St. Joseph the Hesychast

ST. CHRISTOPHER, ABBOT OF SOLVYCHEGODSK. Christopher was a novice and student under the direction of Longinus, the abbot of the Koryazhemsk Monastery in the sixteenth century. After Longinus died, Christopher stayed another ten years, and then he settled alone along the banks of a tributary of the Large Koryazhemka. When novices came to Christopher for spiritual guidance, he founded a monastery. He built a church in honor of the miraculous Hodegitria Icon of the Mother of God, which he had brought with him, and many healings took place from it. This monastery was famous for its strictness and curative spring, where Anastasia, the wife of Ivan the Terrible, was healed. In 1572 St. Christopher left that monastery and secretly settled in an unknown place. It is uncertain when he died.

COMMEMORATIONS: Dormition of St. Anna, mother of the Most Holy Theotokos; Sanctus, Maturus, Attalus, Blandina, Vivlia, Vetius, Egapathus, Ponticus, Alexander, and others, at Lyons; Olympiada the Deaconess of Constantinople; Eupraxia of Tabennisi; Vukosav Milanovic and Rodoljub Samardzic of Kulen Vakuf, Serbia; Theodore Tonkovid of Lovets (Pskov); Gregory Kallides of Thessalonica and Heraclea; Christopher of Solvychegodsk; Macarius of Zheltovod and Unzha; Synaxis of the Holy 165 Fathers of the Fifth Ecumenical Council.

St. Paraskevi the Martyr of Rome
Abstain from meat and
dairy products, and fish.
Galatians 3:23-4:5; Mark 5:24-34

*L*et us humble ourselves because a proud man cannot be saved. Let us weep for our sins here, so we can rejoice forever in the next life, for after we leave this world everyone will forget us. Let us not hope in men, but only in God.

† *Elder Paisius of Sihla*

HIEROMARTYRS HERMOLAUS, HERMIPPOS, AND HERMOCRATES. Hermolaus and his companions were priests in Nicomedia during the fourth century. They went in hiding after Maximian had burned to death twenty thousand Christians. They ceaselessly taught the pagans the Christian faith. Panteleimon (Great Martyr Panteleimon) was a pagan boy who worshipped the idols. One day, Hermolaus passed by Panteleimon and told him to stop by his house for a conversation. He explained to the boy the falseness and vanity of worshipping the pagan gods. Panteleimon continued to visit Hermolaus every day, and soon he was baptized. Panteleimon was arrested for being a Christian and was to stand trial. In the meantime, the night before the trial, God revealed to Hermolaus that he would suffer for Him and receive a martyr's crown. The following day, Hermolaus, Hermippos, and Hermocrates were arrested. They refused the offer to sacrifice to the idols; instead, they confessed their faith in Jesus Christ. Suddenly, there was an earthquake, and the idols in the temple collapsed. Filled with wrath, Maximium had the priests tortured and then beheaded.

COMMEMORATIONS: Paraskevi of Rome; Jerusalem of Byzantium; Hermolaus, Hermippos, and Hermocrates at Nicomedia; Oriozela of Reuma in Byzantium; Ignatius of Mt. Stirion; Sava III, Archbishop of Serbia; Gerontios, founder of St. Anne Skete; Ioannikios the New of Muscel (Romania); Theodosius of the Caucasus; Isaac of Svyatogorsk; Moses the Hungarian of the Kiev Caves; Jacob, Enlightener of Alaska; *Emvolon* Icon of the Mother of God, in Constantinople.

St. Panteleimon the Great Martyr
Fast-free
2 Timothy 2:1-10; John 15:17-16:2

*L*et us only fear God, not men, no matter how evil they may be.
St. Paisios the Athonite

HOLY SEVEN APOSTLES OF BULGARIA: STS. CYRIL, METHO-DIOS, CLEMENT, NAHUM, SAVA, GORAZD, AND ANGELARIUS.
These saints each have their own feast day, but today they are celebrated together. When Cyril and Methodios died in Moravia, some of their disciples fled to Bulgaria to escape persecution. However, some were enslaved and taken to Venice until Emperor Basil the Macedonian had them returned to Constantinople. Clement and his companions were marched to the border and beaten along the way. Angelarius died from his wounds. Clement and Nahum led the missionary activity in Bulgaria. King Boris welcomed them, giving them state support and encouragement for their sacred work. They had two main educational centers with training schools for preparing priests for the Church and for disseminating and translating from Greek to Old Slavonic Christian literature. Nahum was the head of one school, and Clement was sent to Ochrid in southwestern Bulgaria to establish a school. Local administrators and the military were put under his submission. Clement personally trained over 3,500 priests and teachers. In a short time, the Greek language in the liturgy was replaced with the local Bulgarian language and understood by the entire Bulgarian population.

COMMEMORATIONS: Great Martyr and Healer Panteleimon; the blind man healed by St. Panteleimon; Clement of Ochrid; Angelarius, Gorazd, Nahum, and Sava of Bulgaria; Anthousa of Mantinea, and 90 sisters; 153 Martyrs of Thrace; Christodoulos of Kassandra; Ambrose (Gudko) of Sarapul; Joasaph of Moscow; Nicholas Kochanov, Fool-for-Christ; Righteous Manuel; Aurelius, Sabigotha, Felix, Liliosa, and George the Sabbaite, at Cordoba; Glorification of St. Herman of Alaska.

JULY 28

*M*oments of pain and sacrifice are actually a time of blessings. Behind every cross there follows a resurrection.

† *Elder Ephraim of Arizona*

MARTYR AKAKIOS THE YOUNGER. During the third-century persecutions of Roman Emperor Licinius, the young man Akakios confessed he was a Christian, so he was suspended and lacerated. Then he was sent to Governor Terentius, who threw him into a boiling cauldron of oil, pitch, and tallow, but he was unharmed by divine grace. Then he was made to run behind the governor's chariot as they traveled to the distant city of Apollonia. Once there, they took Akakios to a temple to worship the idols, but by his prayers, they shattered. They handed the saint over to a tribune, and when he again confessed his faith, he was given a merciless beating. They placed him before a hungry lion, but it would not harm him. He was beaten again and thrown into a cauldron of asphalt and pitch. Yet again, he remained unharmed. The tribune approached the cauldron, suspecting it had not been brought to a boil, and he was quickly burned to ashes. After this, Akakios was sent in heavy chains to Ionia, and they took him to a pagan temple to sacrifice. Instead, Akakios commanded that the idols fall to the ground, and they shattered. And this happened again in another temple. St. Akakios was beheaded, but milk flowed from his neck instead of blood.

COMMEMORATIONS: Apostles Prochorus, Nicanor, Timon, and Parmenas; Paul of Xeropotamou; Julian of Dalmatia; Eustathius of Ancyra; Akakios of Apamea; Irene Chrysovolantou of Cappadocia; Ursus and Leobatius of Gaul; Anastasius of Ancyra; Anthony of Rostov; George the Builder of Iveron; Pitirim of Tambov; Samson of Dol; Basil of Sarov; Ignatius of Jablechna; Moses of the Kiev Caves; Translation of the relics of St. John the New Chozebite; Synaxis of All Saints of Tambov; Smolensk *Hodigitria*, *Suprasl* (Poland), *Grebensk*, and *Yugsk* Icons of the Mother of God.

JULY 29

Romans 13:1-10; Matthew 12:30-37

*W*hat pleasure and joy we feel when we find some necessary and valuable object which was lost! Now picture how pleased our Heavenly Father is with the sight of His lost child, the sinner who is found, the lost sheep brought to life again… "I say to you that likewise there will be more joy in heaven over one sinner who repents than over ninety-nine just persons who need no repentance" (Luke 15:7). My lost brothers and sisters, return from the way of destruction to the Heavenly Father. "Repent, for the Kingdom of Heaven is at hand" (Mt.3:2; 4:17).

St. John of Kronstadt

ST. ROMANUS, FOUNDER OF KIRZHACH MONASTERY. Romanus was a student of St. Sergius of Radonezh. Sergius and Romanus built a church in the forest of Vladimir in honor of the Annunciation of the Theotokos, and they established a new monastery there. Romanus became the abbot and was ordained to the priesthood by St. Alexei, Metropolitan of Moscow. With great enthusiasm, he fulfilled the precepts of his teacher St. Sergius. Romanus was a zealous ascetic, an excellent and demanding instructor, and he was an example to emulate. He was also known as a Wonderworker. St. Romanus died peacefully in the late fourteenth century.

COMMEMORATIONS: Kallinikos of Gangra; Theodota and her 3 sons, in Bithynia; Theodota of Asia Minor; Benjamin and Berius of Constantinople; Constantine III Leichoudes, Patriarch of Constantinople; Seraphima of Antioch; Bessarion, Bishop of Smolyan; John the Soldier at Constantinople; Constantine and Cosmas of Kosinsk; Mamas in Darii; Romanus of Kirzhach; Eustathius of Mtskheta; Lupus of Troyes; Theodosius the Younger, emperor; Basiliscus the Elder; Bogolep of Black Ravine; Olav of Norway; Anatole of the Caucasus Mountains; Seraphim and Theognostus at Kazakhstan; Pachomius of Kazakhstan; Daniel Kushnir of Mlievich (Ukraine).

JULY 30

*B*e careful of some spiritual fathers and teachers, who pretend to teach you virtues and repentance but introduce voluptuousness, by doing away with the fasts and discouraging youth from asceticism, temperance and from reading Patristic texts, and also speak against the monastic life. What harm this brings to pious young men is useless to mention, for I have seen many, who were enticed by these deceptive exhortations, become unwitting victims.

St. Daniel of Katounakia

HIEROMARTYR VALENTINE, BISHOP OF INTERAMNA. Valentine was a third-century bishop in Italy. His prayers healed the brother of a Roman tribune. Because of this, the tribune sent to Bishop Valentine, Cherimon, the son of the eminent pagan philosopher Craton. Cherimon was grievously ill. He had been so cramped that his head was stuck between his knees. Valentine spent a whole night in prayer, and in the morning, Cherimon was found healed. Because of this, Craton and his entire household received Baptism, and Cherimon became Valentine's disciple. Later, Valentine baptized the son of a Roman eparch, but this angered the eparch, who tortured and beheaded St. Valentine and some of Craton's pupils.

COMMEMORATIONS: Apostles Silas, Silvanos, Crescens, Epenetos, and Andronikos, of the Seventy; Julitta at Caesarea; Valentine, Bishop of Interamna, and Proculus, Ephebus, Apollonius, and Abundius; Polychronius of Babylon, and Parmenius, Helimenas, Chrysotelus, Luke, Mocius, Abdon, Sennen, Maximus, and Olympius; Stephen (Vladislav) of Serbia; Anatole II of Optina; Alexander the Chanter; Angelina Brancovich of Serbia; Tsotne Dadiani the Confessor of Mingrelia; Uncovering of the relics of St. Herman of Solovki; Synaxis of the Saints of Samara; *Okonsk* Icon of the Mother of God.

MONDAY   **Fast-free**

JULY 31

1 Corinthians 11:31-12:6; Matthew 18:1-11

*E*ase and idleness are the destruction of the soul, and they can injure…more than demons.

St. Isaac the Syrian

TRANSLATION OF THE SACRED RELICS OF THE HOLY APOSTLE PHILIP TO CYPRUS. Apostle Philip is commemorated on two other dates on the Church calendar, June 14 and June 30. Jesus initially selected Philip, saying, "Follow thou Me" (Jn. 1:43). After Pentecost, Philip taught in Asia and Western Asia Minor along with Apostle Bartholomew and Philip's sister Mariamne. Philip endured prison, stoning, and the whip. His ankles were drilled, and they put a rope through the holes so they could drag him. Finally, in the year 71, the Greek pagans crucified Philip in Hierapolis, and he died. Later, parts of his relics were sent to Constantinople, Florence, and Rome. The Apostle Philips's skull was translated to Cyprus, to the village of Arsinoe, and this date commemorates this event. A large and beautiful church dedicated to Apostle Philip was built in the twelfth century. And to this day, a portion of his skull is in the church where many miracles have occurred. The church also houses many old and valued icons, vestments, and sacred vessels. The village is called Arsos, and Apostle Philip is the patron saint.

COMMEMORATIONS: Joseph of Arimathea; Julitta, at Caesarea in Cappadocia; Eudokimos of Cappadocia; John the Exarch of Bulgaria; Germanus of Auxerre; 12 Martyrs of Rome; Dionysios of Vatopedi; Benjamin, Sergius, George, and John of Petrograd; Basil of Kineshma; Neot, in Cornwall; Arsenius of Ninotsminda; Anonymous New Martyr from Crete; Consecration of the Church of the Most Holy Theotokos of Blachernae; Translation of the relics of Apostle Philip to Cyprus.

It is not right to say that our surroundings or the circumstances of our life do not allow us to save our souls. Of course, one cannot close one's eyes to the fact that today's life is quite different to what it was seventy or eighty years ago; it is more complex, and it has also become more corrupt. But the Apostle says, *Where sin aboundeth, there doth grace much more abound* (cf. Rom. 5:20), i.e., if sin increases, the person desiring salvation experiences an increase in the help of the grace-filled power of the Lord that his soul might not be crushed by all that surrounds him, but that it remain faithful to God and be saved.

† *Philaret the New Confessor*

Procession of the Precious Cross
Dormition Fast Begins
Strict Fast

AUGUST 1

Hebrews 11:33-12:2
Matthew 10:16-22

*N*ever be jealous of wealth… Always live modestly and humbly.
St. George Karslides

ST. EUSEBIUS, BISHOP OF VERCELLI. Eusebius was born in late third-century Sardinia. Together with his mother, they moved to Rome after his father's martyrdom. Eusebius later became a Reader, and because of his holiness, he was consecrated the first bishop of Vercelli. He was inspired by the work *Life of St. Anthony* and founded something that resembled a monastic community in Vercelli. He devoted his energy to training his clergy in piety and zeal, which inspired the creation of many similar communities in other areas. Later a Synod was convened for the heresy of Arianism and to condemn Athanasius of Alexandria, who opposed the heresy. When Eusebius refused to condemn Athanasius, he was exiled to the see of an Arian bishop, whom Eusebius called his jailer, and later to the Thebaid in Egypt, where he was dragged through the streets and persecuted. Still, he never gave up defending the True faith. When a new emperor was elected, all the exiled bishops were freed. Eusebius attended the Synod of Athanasius, which confirmed the divinity of the Holy Spirit and the Orthodox doctrine on the Incarnation. When Eusebius returned to Vercelli, he and Hilary of Poitiers fought to defeat Arianism in the Western Church. The Alexandrian priest, Arius, denied the divinity of Christ, claiming that Christ was created by the Father, and was neither co-eternal with the Father nor consubstantial.

COMMEMORATIONS: Procession of the Life-giving Cross; Feast to the All-Merciful Savior and the Most Holy Mother of God; Holy Seven Maccabees: Abimus, Antonius, Gurias, Eleazar, Eusebonus, Alimus, and Marcellus, and their mother Solomonia, and their teacher Eleazar; 9 Martyrs of Perge: Leontios, Attos, Alexander, Cindeos, Mnsitheos, Kyriakos, Menaios, Katounos, and Eukleos; Timothy of Priconissus; Nicholas, Enlightener of Japan; Eusebius of Vercelli; Basil of Chernigov; Elesa of Kythera; Papas the New; Martyr Eleazar; Martyrs Theodore and Polyeuctus; Anthony the New of Beroia; Menas, Menais, and others of England; Sidwell of Exeter.

**Translation of the Relics of
St. Stephen the First Martyr
Strict Fast**

Acts 6:8-7:5, 47-60; Mark 12:1-12

*T*ry to pray attentively. If you become distracted, reproach yourself, "open yourself to God," and again force yourself to say the words of the prayer mindfully. Your heart will gradually soften and at times will respond with compunction and perhaps even tears. Give these moments wholly to prayer and do not heed the enemy who will find a thousand reasons for you to stop praying and to occupy yourself with something else. The thought that "distracted prayer can be counted for sin," is from the devil. He tries by all means to divert one from prayer, knowing what good can result from it.

† *Abbot Nikon Vorobiev*

MARTYR PHOCAS. Phocas suffered many insults on Christ's behalf in the fourth century. It is believed that he was martyred at Antioch and is buried in Syria. Those bitten by a snake hasten to touch the entrance of the courtyard where St. Phocas is buried. And those with faith are healed of the infection and poisonous venom. It is said that even if the person is already distended and swollen from the snake bite when they are carried into the courtyard, they receive healing.

COMMEMORATIONS: Theodore of the Dardanelles; Friardus of Gaul; Basil of Moscow, Fool-for-Christ; Marco of Belavinsk; Justinian of Byzantium and Theodora; Stephen, Pope of Rome, and companions; Martyr Phocas; Basil of Kuben Lake; Platon of Chasovo; Etheldritha of England; Alexis of Uzine; Fotou the Cypriot; Translation of the relics of Sts. Dada, Maximus, and Quintilian, at Dorostolum in Moesia; Translation of the relics from Jerusalem to Constantinople of St. Stephen the Protomartyr.

AUGUST 3

1 Corinthians 14:6-19
Matthew 20:17-28

*W*e need to notice our mistakes and fight to correct them. Surely, a person cannot succeed spiritually if he allows his mistakes to slip unnoticed or makes nothing of his shortcomings when others tell him about them.

St. Paisios the Athonite

MARTYR OLYMPIOS THE PREFECT. In the years 614 and 615, during an ongoing war with the Western Roman Empire, the Sassanid Persian army invaded Asia Minor and reached Chalcedon, a city across the Bosporus from Constantinople. According to the Armenian historian Sebeos, the Roman Emperor Heraclius had agreed to stand down and allow the Roman Empire to become a Persian client state. The prefect Olympios, the prefect Leontios, and Anastasios, a presbyter of Hagia Sophia, were appointed to pursue peace. Olympios delivered a letter from the Roman Senate and people expressing the submission of their emperor. However, the head of the Persians was so confident that he could seize the entire Roman empire that he kept Olympios and the others imprisoned and let them die in captivity. St. Olympios died confessing his Christian faith and refusing to worship the sun.

COMMEMORATIONS: Dalmatos, Faustus, and Isaac of the Dalmatian Monastery; Salome the Myrrhbearer; Stephen, Pope of Rome; John, abbot of Patalaria Monastery; Theodora of Thessalonica and her daughter Theopisti of Aegina; Cosmas, hermit of Palestine; Olympios the Prefect; Anthony the Roman of Novgorod; Theocleto the Wonderworker of Optimaton; Rajden of Tsromi, Georgia; Nine Kherkheulidze brothers, with their sister and mother and 9,000 Martyrs of Marabda, Georgia; Trea of Ardtrea.

AUGUST 4

*W*hat does God seek of men, and what does He give them? He seeks repentance and gives forgiveness of sin. He seeks little and gives all. Men have only to repent of the committing of sin and stop sinning, and they will receive all from God, all indeed! Not only that which their hearts are able to desire, but more, much more. All is promised to the sinless. The sinless will be inheritors of the Kingdom of God, sons of God, children of light, children of immortality, companions of the angels, brothers of Christ. The sinless will have abundant life, abundant peace, wisdom, power and joy. The sinless will have all, for all is promised to them.

St. Nikolai Velimirovich

TRANSLATION OF THE RELICS OF MARTYR IA OF PERSIA. Ia was a Christian living in Persia during the reign of the Emperor Sapor II. She was one of 9,000 Christians who were arrested and taken to the city of Bisada. The chief of the Persian sorcerers demanded that Ia renounce Christ. When she refused, she was repeatedly tortured, imprisoned, and finally beheaded. According to tradition, the sun darkened at the hour of her beheading, and a sweet fragrance filled the air. Her body was left for the vultures, but Christians ransomed her and gave her a proper burial. St. Ia's holy relics were later transferred to Constantinople, where several churches were dedicated to her.

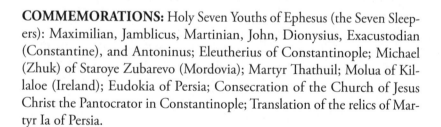

COMMEMORATIONS: Holy Seven Youths of Ephesus (the Seven Sleepers): Maximilian, Jamblicus, Martinian, John, Dionysius, Exacustodian (Constantine), and Antoninus; Eleutherius of Constantinople; Michael (Zhuk) of Staroye Zubarevo (Mordovia); Martyr Thathuil; Molua of Killaloe (Ireland); Eudokia of Persia; Consecration of the Church of Jesus Christ the Pantocrator in Constantinople; Translation of the relics of Martyr Ia of Persia.

SATURDAY

AUGUST 5

Forefeast of the Transfiguration
Abstain from meat and
dairy products, and fish.
1 Peter 1:1-2:10; Matthew 15:32-39

In the spiritual life there is no "tomorrow"—save the soul now!
† *Monk Simeon of Mt. Athos*

NEW HIEROMARTYR SIMON (SHLEEV), THE FIRST EDINOV-ERIE BISHOP. The Edinoverie is a section of Old Believers that were reunited with the Russian Church, and they maintain the Old Rites of the ancient Church. Simon dedicated his entire life to defending the Edinoverie and healing the Russian schism during the seventeenth century. Simon attended the Kazan Theological Academy, and his dissertation defended the Edinoverie. But the new hierarch of the Kazan Diocese considered the Edinoverie schismatics. Simon was sent to an Edinoverie church in St. Petersburg and a bright period of his ministry began there. At this time, the Edinoverie hoped to get their own like-minded bishop, but there was a movement toward reunification. Father Simon started publishing the journal "The Truth of Orthodoxy," which touched on the most pressing issues of the times. In the journal, he wrote, "To be Orthodox, it is not enough to understand and teach Orthodoxy, but you must live it." He opened a school at the parish for catechetical and educational work, and candidates for the priesthood were prepared. More than 400 people were studying there. Following the death of his wife, Simon took monastic vows. He humbly accepted his elevation to Bishop of the Edinoverie. The faithful loved him, and he was accessible, kind, and selfless. He interceded for those who came under trial for religious or political reasons. Bishop Simon was murdered for political reasons.

COMMEMORATIONS: Eusignius of Antioch; Pontius at Cimella in Gaul; Nonna, mother of St. Gregory the Theologian; Fabian and Antherus, Popes of Rome; John Jacob of Neamt, the Chozebite; Cantidius, Cantidian, and Sibelius of Egypt; Eugenius the Aitolos; Job the Gorge-dweller on the Mezen River; Eudocia Shikova of Puzo, with Daria, Daria, and Maria of Diveyevo; Euthymios I, Patriarch of Constantinople; Simon (Shleev), Bishop of Ufa; Chrestos of Preveza; Oswald, King of Northumbria; Soleb of Egypt; Afra of Augsburg, Germany; Uncovering of the relics of St. Arsenios the New of Paros.

Transfiguration of our Lord Jesus Christ
Abstain from meat and dairy products.
2 Peter 1:10-19; Matthew 17:1-9

*P*rayer is a security, it is a guard, it is the oxygen of the soul. We ask for things, but we don't kneel, we don't raise our hands, to bring the light down, to light the way.

† *Elder Ephraim of Arizona*

NEW MARTYR FATHER NIKOLAI ZAVARIN. Nikolai was born into the family of a priest. He became a cantor and teacher in several parish schools. Amid heavy persecutions against the Church in Russia in 1926, he was ordained to the priesthood. In 1931 he was imprisoned for nonpayment of taxes in arrears but was later acquitted. One year later, he was arrested again for anti-Soviet activities and again released after a year. The Soviets tried many times to close his parish, but together with his parishioners, they found ways to keep it open. Finally, in 1937 Fr. Nikolai and his daughter were arrested for organizing a counter-revolutionary group. He was asked if he had any weapons, and Nikolai responded that the Gospel and religion, in whose name he fights, were his weapons. He would not admit guilt or accuse anyone, including false witnesses. He was shot on August 19, 1937. His canonization service was held in his church, where he served for eleven years. An icon of St. Nikolai was carried out of the altar when the Holy Synod's decision to include Fr. Nikolai among the New Martyrs and Confessors of the Russian Church was read by the bishop. He said that the main task of the Church is to glorify God, and Fr. Nikolai was a humble and little-known pastor who was an example of deep faith in Christ and courage. Knowing his fate, he continued to serve and preach the Gospel.

COMMEMORATIONS: Transfiguration of our Lord and Savior Jesus Christ; Theoctistus, Bishop of Chernigov; Abbacum of Thessalonica; New Martyr Nikolai Zavarin; Dimitri (Lyubimov), Archbishop of Gdov, and Nicholas Prozorov, Andrew Zimin, Sergius Tikhomirov, Domnik, Lidia, and Mary Zimin, of Russia; New Virgin Martyr Eudocia, near Sarov; New Martyr Maxim Sandovich (Polish Orthodox Church); Justus and Pastor of Complutum.

AUGUST 7

1 Corinthians 15:12-19
Mark 9:2-9

In the mercy of God, the little thing done with humility will enable us to be found in the same place as the saints who have labored much and been true servants of God.

St. Dorotheos of Gaza

MARTYRS MARINUS THE SOLDIER AND ASTERIUS THE SENATOR, AT CAESAREA. Marinus was a third-century Roman Christian soldier during the reign and persecutions of Emperor Valerian. When Marinus was promoted to the rank of centurion, he refused to offer a sacrifice to the pagan gods, and for this, he was cruelly tortured and beheaded. Asterius, a Roman senator who was also a Christian, witnessed the beheading of Marinus. He took off his senatorial clothing and wrapped the saint's body with them. Then he carried the martyr on his shoulders to the burial site. During a pagan feast, an offering was made to the idol, but to everyone's astonishment, the demon in the idol made the sacrifice vanish. When Asterius prayed, he expelled the demon, and the sacrifice reappeared, thus ending the pagan festival. St. Asterius was beheaded for giving the relics of St. Marinus a proper burial.

COMMEMORATIONS: 10,000 Ascetics of Thebes; Narcissus, Patriarch of Jerusalem; Marinus and Asterius the Senator at Caesarea; Sozon of Nicomedia; Horus of the Thebaid; Nicanor of Mt. Callistratus; Hyperechius of *The Paradise*; Potamia of Alexandria; Dometius of Persia and 2 disciples; Mercurius of Smolensk; Dometios of Philotheou; Theodora of Sihla; Anthony of Optina; Pimen the Much-ailing; Theodosius the New of Argos; Nikanor the Wonderworker; Mikallos of Akanthou; Pimen, faster of the Kiev Caves; Joseph of Kapsa; Victricius of Rouen; Irene and Pulcheria of Constantinople; Alexander, Peter, Michael, John, Demetrius, Alexei, Elisha, and Athanasius, of Moscow; Paphnutius the Mute; *Valamo* Icon of the Mother of God in Finland.

TUESDAY   **Strict Fast**

AUGUST 8   1 Corinthians 15:29-38
                                Matthew 21:23-27

*R*eal love resembles the candle flame. As you light more little can-
dles, the initial flame remains whole. It is not at all diminished.
And each new little candle has as much flame as the other ones do.
† *Elder Epiphanios Theodoropoulos of Athens*

TWO MARTYRS OF TYRE. Like many other Egyptian Christians, these
two martyrs were sent to Palestine to labor in the mines and were tortured
under the persecutions of Emperor Maximinus. They were scourged with
innumerable stripes and thrown before leopards, bears, wild boars, and
bulls that were goaded with a red-hot iron. Even though the saints were
naked and waving their arms to attract the beasts, an invisible force hin-
dered them. This continued for some time, and the spectators were amazed.
Though they were not even twenty years of age, these contestants for the
faith stood fearless and in deep prayer. Yet, if someone from the outside
approached the beasts to incite them, the bull would toss them into the air
and mangle them. Other wild beasts were let loose that might prove more
effective, but they would not harm the saints. Finally, the Two Martyrs of
Tyre were slain with the sword, and their relics were cast into the sea.

COMMEMORATIONS: Gregory of Sinai; Myron, Bishop of Crete; Eleu-
therius and Leonides of Constantinople, and many infants; Emilian the
Confessor, Bishop of Cyzicus; Gormizdas of Persia; Gregory, iconographer
of the Kiev Caves; Gregory, Wonderworker of the Kiev Caves; Anastasius of
Radovishte in Strumica; Philaret of Ivanovo; 12 Ascetics of Egypt; Euthym-
ius of Georgia; Triandaphillos of Zagora; 2 Martyrs of Tyre; Zosimas the
Sinaite of Tumana Monastery, Serbia; Martyr Styracius; Joseph of Tolga;
Nicholas of Pokrovskoye; Nicodemus of Kostroma; Theodosios of Oroboi;
Kallinikos, Metropolitan of Edessa; Translation of the relics of Sts. Zosimas,
Sabbatius, and Herman of Solovki; Uncovering of the relics of St. Barlaam
of Chikoisk Monastery (Siberia); *Tolga* Icon of the Mother of God.

Strict Fast

Acts 1:12-17, 21-26
Matthew 21:28-32

In the hearts of the meek the Lord finds rest, but a turbulent soul
is a seat for the devil.

St. John Climacus

NEW MARTYR MARGARET, ABBESS OF MENZELINSK. In the early
twentieth century, Margaret was the abbess of the Prophet Elijah monastery
in Menzelinsk, Kazan Diocese. She was strict and demanding but at the same
time loving, and the monastery prospered. It had kitchen gardens, beehives,
fruit trees, workshops for writing icons, and gold weaving. There was even a
rare photographic laboratory. In 1918, during the Russian Revolution, the
White armies left Kazan, and Abbess Margaret decided to escape the power
of the Bolsheviks. At the wharf, St. Nicholas appeared to her in a vision and
said, "Why are you running from your crown?" She returned to her monastery, sensing that she would soon suffer for the faith. She asked for her coffin
to be prepared and gave instructions to be buried immediately following the
funeral. The next day during a service, she was dragged out of church. Her
request to commune the Holy Mysteries was denied, and she was shot. Abbess
Margaret was quickly buried behind the altar following the service. The next
day the same soldiers brought a Muslim mullah to be shot, wanting to bury
him in the same grave as the abbess. However, seeing that Margaret was
already buried, they left. Russian elder, St. Ambrose of Optina, had prophesied about the monastery and all that would happen there, including its
closure. In the 1970s, during a dig on the monastery grounds, St. Margaret's
coffin was found. Her relics were found incorrupt with a cross on her chest.

COMMEMORATIONS: Apostle Matthias; Herman of Alaska; 10 Mar-
tyrs at the Chalke Gate: Julian, Marcian, John, James, Alexius, Demetrius,
Photius, Peter, Leontius, and Maria the Patrician; Psoes of Egypt; Anthony
of Alexandria; Macarius of Oredezh Monastery; Philaret Humilevsky of
Chernigov; Felim of Kilmore; Nathy of Achonry; Ignatius Bazyluk of
Poland; Euthymios, Metropolitan of Rhodes; Margaret of Menzelinsk;
Synaxis of the Saints of Solovki; Glorification of St. Herman of Alaska;
Finding of the *Acheiropoeton* Icon of Christ in Kamouliana.

AUGUST 10

*Y*ou ask by what path to go towards God. Go by the path of humility; by humbly enduring the difficult circumstances of life, by humbly enduring the sicknesses that are sent by the Lord, by humbly hoping that you will not be abandoned by the Lord, by the Quick Helper and by the loving Heavenly Father; by humble prayer for help from on high, for the driving away of despondency and feelings of hopelessness by which the enemy of salvation endeavors to bring us to despair, which is ruinous for a man and deprives him of divine grace, and which withdraws God's mercy from him.

St. Nectarius of Optina

ST. AGILBERTA, ABBESS OF JOUARRE. Agilberta was a nun and the second abbess of the seventh-century Jouarre Abbey, founded by her relatives Ebrigisil and Ado. Her brother, Agilbert, was bishop of Paris and her sister was the third abbess of Jouarre. Agilberta is a French Benedictine saint, and she is venerated by the Roman Catholic Church and the Antiochian Orthodox Church. She is buried in the crypt at Jouarre in one of three well-preserved sarcophagi that are of interest because they follow the Roman burial tradition. The abbey is located in the département of Seine-et-Marne.

COMMEMORATIONS: Archdeacon Lawrence and Pope Sixtus II, Felicissimus, and Agapitus, deacons, and others with them; Hippolytus of Rome and 18 Martyrs with him, including Concordia, Irenaeus, and Abundius; Romanus, soldier of Rome; 6 Martyrs of Bizin; Bertram, King of Mercia; Lawrence, Fool-for-Christ of Kaluga; Blaine of the Isle of Bute; Heron the Philosopher; Agilberta of Jouarre; Synaxis of New Martyrs and Confessors of Solovki.

AUGUST 11

Instead of grumbling at God for not giving you what you want, better thank Him for not giving you what you deserve.

St. John Chrysostom

ST. MANETHA OF GOMEL. Manetha was diagnosed with cerebral palsy as a baby, and the doctors said she would never walk. Despite this, she grew up cheerful and active. She often saw her mother praying in front of the icons. One time, an elder was begging, and Manetha handed him some bacon. He then told her mother, "Your nun gave me lard." Manetha soon became a nun. She would embroider towels for the churches in that area, feed every visitor, and comfort them. She exuded love, benevolence, friendship, and cheerfulness. God granted her the gift of prophecy and miracle-working. During the Second World War, she was often asked about the fate of husbands and fathers. Her main advice was consistent prayer, repentance, mercy, and reading the Akathist of the Mother of God. Though Manetha was ashamed to take donations, she accepted them so she could feed others. Her favorite Psalms were the 26th, 50th, 90th, and 17th kathisma. Several times in a dream, she saw the Mother of God, and this would give her happiness. But many times, she was visited by evil spirits, and she chased them away with her woolen prayer rope. To find a suitable spouse for marriage, she advised turning to the Mother of God and St. Nicholas, and reading twelve times "Theotokos, Virgin, rejoice" and "The Symbol of Faith" every morning and evening. St. Manetha died peacefully in 1984.

COMMEMORATIONS: Euplus of Catania; Niphon II, Patriarch of Constantinople; Theodore and Basil of the Kiev Caves; Taurinus of Evreux, Gaul; Susanna, with Gaius, Pope of Rome and Gabinus the priest; Maximus, Claudius and his wife, Praepedigna, and their sons Alexander and Cuthias; Anastasios Paneras of Asomaton, and Demetrios Begiazis of Lesvos; Theodore (Theodosius), Prince of Ostrog; John the Recluse of Svyatogorsk; Passarion of Palestine; Martyrs Neophytus, Zeno, Gaius, Mark, Macarius, and Gaianus; Blaan, Bishop of Bute, Scotland; Manetha of Gomel; Commemoration of the Miracle of St. Spyridon against the Hagarenes on Corfu.

Abstain from meat and dairy products, and fish.

AUGUST 12

Romans 15:30-33
Matthew 17:24-18:4

*L*et us not grieve when we make a slip, but when we become hardened by it.

St. Isaac the Syrian

ST. EUMENIUS, ARCHBISHOP OF ZHITOMIR AND OVRUCH.

Eumenius was from the late nineteenth-century Odesa Province in Ukraine. He graduated from the Church teachers' school and entered the Holy Trinity Monastery in Kiev at the age of twenty-two. Over the next ten years, he moved to a few monasteries and settled at St. Michael's Golden-Domed Monastery in Kiev, where he took monastic vows. He also graduated from the St. Petersburg Theological Academy. In 1930, Eumenius was arrested by decision of the local Troika and was sent to a concentration camp for 16 years. He returned to the Kiev Caves Lavra as a monk after his release. In 1954 he was consecrated a bishop and took over the administration of the Chernivtsi Diocese. Later he was elevated to the rank of archbishop. God granted him the gift of miracleworking both during his life and after. There was a protodeacon named Boris who, without telling anyone, had thoughts of becoming a priest. Eumenius abruptly told him, "Get rid of those foolish thoughts. You serve in the cathedral and only in the cathedral." Also, one night after his prayers, Eumenius saw the Mother of God leave the church and ascend heavenward. The date of his repose was revealed to him, and on that day, he washed, anointed himself with holy oil, and asked those with him to read the Canon at the Departure of the Soul. When they finished, he lay down on his bed, crossed himself, and said, "Into Thy hands do I commit my spirit, O Lord," and peacefully reposed.

COMMEMORATIONS: Alexander of Comana; Palamon of Egypt; Martyrs Pamphilus and Capito; 12 Soldiers Martyrs of Crete; Sergius and Stephen, monks; Anicetus and Photius of Nicomedia; Gerontius, Serapion, Germanus, Bessarion, Michael, Simeon, and Otar of Garesja; Molaise of Devenish; Jambert of Canterbury; Seigine of Iona; Muredach (Murtagh) of Killala; Eumenius of Zhitomir; Barlaam, Anthony, Sergius, Elijah, and many others of the Belogorsk St. Nicholas Monastery (Perm).

AUGUST 13

Tenth Sunday of Matthew
Abstain from meat and
dairy products, and fish.
1 Corinthians 4:9-16
Matthew 17:14-23

*L*et us scatter our love selflessly to all, without regards to the way they act towards us.

St. Porphyrios of Kavsokalyvia

VENERABLE DOSITHEUS THE SUBMISSIVE. Dositheus had never heard the word of God, and he lived in luxury and indulgence. But one day, he desired to go to Jerusalem to visit the holy places. When he had come to Gethsemane, the Theotokos stood beside him and told him of the punishment that awaited the wicked, and she gave several other instructions. He asked what he needed to do to be saved, and she said, "Fast, do not eat meat, and pray often, and you will be saved from the tortures." Then she vanished. Dositheus kept the commandments that she had given him. Several of his friends took him to the monastery of Abba Dorotheos. There he could only explain that he wanted to be saved. Abba Dorotheos helped him curtail his appetite for food and reduce his unkind talk. He made Dositheus realize that to whoever he was speaking, he was speaking to Christ Himself. Dositheus never carried out his own will in anything; he practiced total obedience. After five years in the monastery, he developed tuberculosis. As he lay dying, God enlightened one of the elders that no evil remained in Dositheus. Dositheus asked the abbot several times for permission to give up his soul, and when he finally received it, he gave up his spirit. One day, a great elder visited the monastery, and he asked God to show him which monks from that monastery were in heaven with the angels. His vision showed him ancient elders and a young man. When he described the young man to the brethren, they knew it was St. Dositheus.

COMMEMORATIONS: Tikhon of Zadonsk; Dorotheos of Gaza; Maximos the Confessor; Xenia-Irene of Hungary; Dositheus of Thawaitha; Eudocia the Empress; Empress Irene (Xene) of Constantinople; Serid (Seridus) of Gaza; Radegunde of Poitiers; Wigbert of Hersfeld; Seraphim (Zvezdinsky) of Dmitrov; Benjamin of Petrograd, Sergius, and others; Transfer of the relic of St. Maximos the Confessor; *Of the Passion, Minsk, Of the Seven Arrows,* and *The Softening of Evil Hearts* Icons of the Mother of God.

AUGUST 14

It is not suffering for the sake of the Faith which is painful; what is hard to bear is to fail to fight its battle. The athlete does not so much complain of being wounded in the struggle as of not being able even to secure admission into the stadium.

St. Basil the Great

TRANSLATION OF THE RELICS OF ST. ARCADIUS OF VYAZMA AND NOVY TORG. Arcadius was from a pious family that taught him prayer and obedience. He was a gentle boy, prudent, and perceptive. His ascetic exploit was to be a Fool-for-Christ. He would beg for alms and sleep anywhere the end of the day had found him. Arcadius was aloof from worldly vanity, and when he prayed in church, he often wept from spiritual joy and tenderness. When he foretold events that would take place in the future, they would come to pass. When he gave advice, it was always sound. His mentor was St. Ephraim the Wonderworker of Novy Torg. These two traveled together, and they founded a church and monastery. Arcadius became a monk there under the spiritual direction and obedience to St. Ephraim. Arcadius never missed a liturgy, and he was always first to arrive. He lived there in prayer, fasting, and silence until his peaceful death many years later, in 1077. The prayers of Arcadius wrought miracles during his life and after his death. In 1672 his holy relics were reburied in a stone crypt of Saints Boris and Gleb Cathedral in Novy Torg.

COMMEMORATIONS: Forefeast of the Dormition; Prophet Micah; Ursicius at Nicomedia; Nazarius, Herman, Hierotheus, Simon, and Bessarion, of Georgia; Marcellus of Apamea; Symeon of Trebizond; Luke the Soldier; Basil of Chernigov, with Matthew and Alexis; Fachanan of Ross Carbery; Matthew and Eleutherius of Smolensk; Eve of Penza; Translation of the relics of St. Arcadius of Vyazma and Novy Torg.

Dormition of the Most Holy Theotokos
Fast-free

AUGUST 15

Philippians 2:5-11
Luke 10:38-42, 11:27-28

If '*precious in the sight of the Lord is the death of His saints*' (Ps. 116:15), and '*the memory of the just is praised*' (Prov. 10:7 LXX), how much more fitting is it for us to celebrate with highest honors the memory of the ever-virgin Mother of God, the Holy of Holies, through whom the saints receive their hallowing? That is exactly what we are doing today by commemorating her holy passing away, through which, having been made a little lower than the angels (cf. Ps. 8:5), she rose incomparably higher than the Angels, Archangels, and all the heavenly powers above them, because of her nearness to the God of all, and the marvels written of old which were accomplished in her.

St. Gregory Palamas

GALICH-CHUKHLOMSK TENDERNESS ICON OF THE MOTHER OF GOD. In the mid-fourteenth century, the monk Abraham moved to the shore of Galich Lake near a mountain to pursue his ascetic life. He prayed to the Mother of God to bless his efforts. Suddenly, a bright light appeared on the mountain nearby, and he heard a voice saying, "Abraham, come up the mountain, where is set an icon of My Mother." Abraham went up there, and he found the icon on a tree. He built a chapel at that spot and placed the icon within it. Later, the Galich Prince Demetrius asked Abraham to bring the icon, so he rowed across the lake accompanied by a crowd of people and clergy. He took the icon to the cathedral, and on that day, many people were healed by it. The prince gave Abraham money to build a monastery, and later, he founded several more.

COMMEMORATIONS: Dormition of the Theotokos; Chrestos of Ioannina; Alexis, archpriest of Petrograd; Stephen, elder of Vyatka; Priest Paul Szwajko and Presbytera Joanna of Graboviec (Poland); Macarius the Roman and his disciple Chariton of Novgorod; Tarcisius the Acolyte; Remembrance of the Love of God for Mankind; Synaxis of the Panagia Fidousa in Kefallonia; *Diasozousa, Chajnicke, Semigorodnaya,* and *Galich-Chukhlomsk Tenderness* Icons of the Mother of God.

WEDNESDAY

AUGUST 16

Translation of the Image of
Our Lord and Savior Jesus Christ
Strict Fast
1 Timothy 3:13-4:5
Luke 9:51-57, 10:22-24, 13:22

*ust as man dies when he stops breathing, so too, does the soul die
without continuous and endless prayer.

St. Joseph the Hesychast

ST. TIMOTHY, BISHOP OF EURIPOS. Timothy had deep faith and spiritual gifts, so the Bishop of Orion in Evia sent him to Athens to study for the priesthood. After graduation, Timothy worked with the bishop, where he learned temperance, fasting, watchfulness, prayer, and meditation on the Scriptures. He became a monk and later was ordained to the priesthood. When the bishop died, Timothy was chosen to replace him. Then he was elevated to Metropolitan of Euripos, Greece. During his episcopacy, the city was under Ottoman rule, which forced churches to convert to mosques. Timothy strongly protested this decision, so the pasha had him expelled. Seeking to live a hesychastic life, Timothy finally settled at the Mount of Penteli, which monks and robbers occupied. He battled the three enemies of humankind: the world, the flesh, and the devil. Some robbers became monks, and Timothy built a monastery and guided them. When pirates kidnapped the governor's son, Timothy prayed, and a storm forced the pirates to shore, thus saving the boy. When a property dispute arose between Timothy and Mother Philothei of Athens, who was a protectress of oppressed women and virgins, Timothy abandoned the property. He lived the rest of his days in a cave on the island of Kea, where he reposed peacefully in 1590. St. Timothy's sacred skull produced healing myrrh, and it was taken in procession to Athens to end a pandemic, and on the island of Aegina, it halted death and destruction.

COMMEMORATIONS: Diomedes of Tarsus; Joseph the Hesychast; Anthony the Stylite; Cherimon of Egypt; Akakios of Liti; Romanus the Sinaite; Nicodemus of Meteora; 33 Martyrs of Palestine; Apostolos of St. Lawrence; Gerasimos of Cephalonia; Joachim of Osogovo; Eustathius II of Serbia; Nilus of Erikoussa; Christopher of Guria; Raphael of Banat; Stamatius of Demetrias; Constantine Brancoveanu of Wallachia and his sons, Constantine, Stephen, Radu, and Matthew, and Ioannicius, counsellor; Joseph of Varatec; Timothy of Euripos.

AUGUST 17

2 Corinthians 4:1-12
Matthew 24:13-28

*E*arthly life is fleeting. You won't notice how it flashes by. But by this life, the eternal lot of your soul will be determined. Do not forget this not even for a moment.

St. Philaret of New York

MARTYRS STRATON, PHILIP, EUTYCHIANOS, AND CYPRIAN OF NICOMEDIA. Nicomedia, current-day Izmit, Turkey, is about sixty miles east of Constantinople. It was the capital city of the Eastern Roman Empire, where Emperor Diocletian resided. These four Christian saints would go to the theater in Nicomedia to teach and convert the pagans, and their efforts proved successful. On one occasion, the pagan governor visited the theater and found it nearly empty. He learned that the spectators that evening were with Straton, Philip, Eutychianos, and Cyprian and were being taught to forsake the pleasures of this life. They were brought before the governor and confessed their faith in Christ. Then they were thrown to wild animals in the same theater but remained unharmed. The four martyrs were tortured, but they remained steadfast and would not abandon Christ. Then they were burned alive.

COMMEMORATIONS: Straton, Philip, Eutychianos, and Cyprian of Nicomedia; Paul and Juliana of Syria; Patroclus of Troyes; Myron of Cyzicus; Thyrsus, Leucius, and Coronatus, at Caesarea; Alypius the Iconographer of the Kiev Caves; James the Deacon; Agapius at Thermes; Elias the Younger; Demetrius of Samarina; Macarius of Mt. St. Auxentius; Theodoretus, Enlightener of the Laps; Tveli of Georgia; Archilleus of Stavropol; Pimen of Ugresh; Philip of Vologda; Jeroen at Noordwijk; George the Pilgrim; *Armatia* and *Svensk* Icons of the Mother of God.

AUGUST 18

2 Corinthians 4:13-18
Matthew 24:27-33, 42-51

*W*hen the door of the steam baths is continually left open, the heat inside rapidly escapes through it; likewise, the soul, in its desire to say many things, dissipates its remembrance of God through the doors of speech, even though everything it says may be good. Thereafter the intellect, though lacking appropriate ideas, pours out a welter of confused thoughts to anyone it meets, as it no longer has the Holy Spirit to keep its understanding free from fantasy. Ideas of value shun verbosity, being foreign to confusion and fantasy. Timely silence, then, is precious, for it is nothing less than the mother of the wisest thoughts.

St. Diadochos of Photiki

NEW MARTYR GEORGE OF KASTORIA, THE FORMER HAGARENE. George was from late-eighteenth to early-nineteenth-century Kastoria, Greece. He went to Ioannina seeking work, and there he saw St. Demetrios of Samarina enduring martyrdom, which inspired George to embrace the Orthodox faith. He departed there and went to the town of Acarnania, where he lived a quiet, Christian life. However, one day a former acquaintance recognized him and tried to persuade him to return to his former religion. When he and those with him saw that George was steadfast, they submitted him to harsh torture, including the insertion of molten iron into his intestines, after which he died.

COMMEMORATIONS: John of Rila; Christodoulos the Philosopher; Florus and Laurus of Illyria, with Maximos, Patroklos, and a multitude of paupers; Sophronios of St. Anne's Skete; Juliana, near Strobilus; Leo, in Lycia; Hermes, Serapion, and Polyaenus of Rome; Emilian of Trebia, with Hilarion, Dionysius, Hermippus, and 1,000 others; Barnabas and Sophronius of Mt. Mela; Christopher of Mt. Mela; Demetrius the Vlach; John and George, Patriarchs of Constantinople; Matthew of Crete; Agapios of Galatista; Agapios and Porphyrios of Santorini; Augustine of Orans; George of Kastoria; Nicholas of Nizhni-Novgorod; Constantine of Kappua; Translation of the relics of St. Arsenios the New of Paros; *Sumela* Icon of the Mother of God.

AUGUST 19

1 Corinthians 1:3-9
Matthew 19:3-12

*A*t any moment, every soul can expect the telegram from heaven to break off all relations with earthly things, to seal the time of this "fair" to render an exact count of his spiritual trading, and to seal his eternal fate either in the heights of heaven or the depths of hell. Ah, When I reflect upon this, what can I say! May the all compassionate God be merciful to my wretched soul, which has nothing but it's indifference and unreadiness. My mind stops when it contemplates the absolute truth about salvation.

St. Theophan the Recluse

ST. CREDAN OF EVESHAM. Credan was the eighth-century abbot of the Benedictine Abbey at Evesham, England, as attested to by the charters of King Offa of Mercia. However, there are no details of Credan's life. Because of this, there was suspicion of Credan's sainthood several hundred years later, in the year 1077, by the new Norman abbot. After consulting with Archbishop Lanfranc, a three-day fast was ordered. While St. Credan's relics were put through an ordeal of fire, they chanted seven penitential psalms and appropriate services. According to legend, the holy relics survived and shone like gold when moved to a place of devotion.

COMMEMORATIONS: Andrew Stratelates and 2,593 soldiers with him in Cilicia; Timothy, Agapius, and Thecla of Palestine; Pitirim, Bishop of Perm; Theophanes, Wonderworker of Macedonia (Mt. Athos); Credan, abbot of Evesham; Mochta of Britain; Namadia of France; Uncovering of the relics of St. Gennadius, abbot of Kostroma; *Of the Don* Icon of the Mother of God.

AUGUST 20

Eleventh Sunday of Matthew
Fast-free
1 Corinthians 9:2-12
Matthew 18:23-35

*L*et us understand that God is a physician, and that suffering is a medicine for salvation, not a punishment for damnation.

St. Augustine of Hippo

ST. OSWIN, KING OF DEIRA. Oswin was the son of the seventh-century apostate king, Osric of Deira, in current-day Yorkshire, England. Oswin later became King of Deira, and to the north, his cousin Oswy became King of Bernicia. They became bitter rivals. Oswin was handsome, courteous, generous, and humble, and this endeared him to all people, and the nobles throughout England willingly served him. He once gave Bishop Aidan a fine horse for his travels throughout the diocese, but the bishop gave the horse to a poor man. Oswin chastised him, but when the bishop asked Oswin if the horse was more valuable than a child of God, Oswin became so filled with compunction that he knelt at the bishop's feet and begged forgiveness. He said that he would never again question the bishop's charity. The bishop later commented that he had never seen a king so humble, and the nation would soon lose him, as they were not worthy. Oswin ruled well for seven years. However, animosity grew between the two kings. They both raised armies, but when Oswin saw that he would be defeated, he disbanded his army and hid at a friend's home, but the friend betrayed him to Oswy. Oswin was assassinated in the year 651, and his relics were buried in a chapel built under a rock at a Tynemouth monastery. As centuries passed, Oswin's burial site was forgotten. In the eleventh century, a man named Edmund, who lived at the monastery, saw Oswin in a dream and was instructed to unearth the relics and bury them in a more fitting place. Many miracles occurred during and after the unearthing of St. Oswin's relics.

COMMEMORATIONS: Samuel the Prophet; Philip of Heraclea, with Severus, Memnon, and 37 soldiers, in Thrace; Lucius the Senator; Heliodorus and Dosa in Persia; Photina, at the Church of Blachernae; Hierotheus, Enlightener of Hungary; Stephen I, King of Hungary; Theocharis of Neopolis; Reginos and Orestes of Cyprus; Oswin of Deira; Philibert of Jumieges.

MONDAY

AUGUST 21

Holy Apostle Thaddaeus
Fast-free
2 Corinthians 5:10-15
Mark 3:13-21

*L*et us stare at our salvation straight in the eyes, no matter how alarming and embarrassing it is. Let us correct our life. Let us thank God from the depth of our heart, and let us offer Him praise and doxology because we are still alive and we can amend the matters related to our soul and prepare ourselves.

† *Elder Ephraim of Arizona*

NEW MARTYR ARCHPRIEST THEODORE KALLISTOV. Theodore was from the family of a deacon in mid-nineteenth-century Penza Governorate, located in the Volga region of Russia. He graduated from Penza Seminary, married, and began as a psalm reader before his ordination to the priesthood. Theodore served in various churches and was involved in spiritual and secular education. He had fourteen children. Finally, in 1916 he became the priest at the Cathedral of the Lifegiving Trinity in Troitsk. But in the 1930s, the Soviet authorities did all they could to close the church. Father Theodore was detained and accused of anti-Soviet activities, to which he pleaded not guilty. Then he was sentenced to three years' exile in Western Siberia, and the church was closed. When he was released, he reopened the church, but it was closed again under the pretext of tax delinquency two years later. Yet again, he reopened the church, but in 1937 he was arrested, and he admitted to no charges. St. Theodore was shot for anti-Soviet terrorist agitation and calling for a revolution.

COMMEMORATIONS: Holy Forefathers Abraham, Isaac, and Jacob; Thaddeus, of the Seventy; Vassa of Edessa, with Theognios, Agapios, and Pistos; Avitus of Clermont; Theocleta of Asia Minor; Sarmean, Catholicos of Georgia; Symeon of Samokovo; Isaiah of Mt. Athos; Donatus, Romulus, Silvanus, and Venustus of Romania; Abramius of Smolensk, and Ephraim; Abramius of the Kiev Caves; Cornelius of Paleostrov, and Abramius; Raphael of Serbia; Ignatius of Optina; Martha of Diveyevo; Hardulph of Breedon; Jacob of Serbia; New Martyr Theodore Kallistov; Commemoration of the Appearance of the Theotokos at Panteleimon Monastery.

AUGUST 22

2 Corinthians 5:15-21
Mark 1:16-22

*L*ike the animals who labor and sweat in a mill with their eyes blindfolded, we go about the mill of life always going through the same motions and always coming back to the same place again. I mean that round of hunger, satiety, going to bed, getting up, emptying ourselves and filling ourselves, one thing constantly follows the other, and we never stop going round in circles until we get out of the mill.

St. Gregory of Nyssa

ST. BOGOLEP OF ST. PAISIUS OF UGLICH MONASTERY. Bogolep was a disciple of St. Paisius of Uglich during the late fifteenth and early sixteenth centuries. Before he became a monk, he was a bread baker, and he continued this obedience at his monastery. He became a priest-monk and later was tonsured into the Schema. One day Bogolep went to the river Volga for water, and there he beheld an icon standing on the shore, and it shined with a heavenly light. It was the wonderworking Icon of the Protection (Pokrov) of the Most Holy Mother of God. Bogolep quickly ran back to the monastery and related what he had seen to his elder. All the monks accompanied the icon back to the monastery.

COMMEMORATIONS: Agathonicus of Nicomedia and his companions: Zotikos, Theoprepios, Akyndinos, Severian, Zeno, and others; Eulalia and Felix of Barcelona; Athanasios, Bishop of Tarsus; Anthousa of Syria and Martyrs Charesimos and Neophytos; Bogolep of Uglich Monastery; Isaac I of Optina Monastery; Macarius, Bishop of Orel, with Andrew, Alexis, Theodore, John, Hierotheus, John, Hilarion, and Gorazd; Martyrs Irenaeus, Or, and Oropsios; Ephraim, Bishop of Selenginsk and John Vostorgov; Symphorian of Autun; Sigfrid, abbot of Wearmouth; *Prusa* and *Georgian* Icons of the Mother of God.

WEDNESDAY

AUGUST 23

Leavetaking of the Dormition
Strict Fast

Philippians 2:5-11
Luke 10:38-42, 11:27-28

A marriage done just for pleasure has no meaning. *Marriage means reaching together into eternity.*

† *Elder Arsenie Papaciac of Romania*

VENERABLE CALLINICUS, PATRIARCH OF CONSTANTINOPLE.
Callinicus was a priest in the late seventh century at the church of the Most Holy Mother of God in Blachernae. Because of his virtues, he was ordained Patriarch of Constantinople. At this time, the cruel Emperor Justinian II wanted to build a palace next to the church of the Mother of God. He demanded the blessing of Callinicus to tear down the church, but Callinicus responded that he only gave blessings to build churches. Regardless, Justinian tore the church down. Justinian was removed from the throne, imprisoned, and his nose was cut off. But after ten years, he escaped, gathered an army, and reentered Constantinople. He had made an oath before the Honorable Cross, the Gospel, and the Holy Mysteries that he would not harm anyone. However, he killed citizens and beheaded the emperor. Justinian captured Callinicus, removed his eyes, tongue, and nose, and sealed him in a stone wall. After forty days, the wall collapsed, and Callinicus was found barely alive. Four days later, he died. The Apostles Peter and Paul appeared in a dream to Pope John VI and directed him to bury St. Callinicus in the Church of the Apostles at Rome.

COMMEMORATIONS: Irenaeus, Bishop of Lyons; Irenaeus, Bishop of Sirmium; Callinicus, Patriarch of Constantinople; Pothinos, Bishop of Lyons; Victor of Marseilles; Eutychius and Florentius of Nursia; Nicholas the Sicilian, who struggled on Mt. Neotaka in Euboea; 38 Martyrs of Thrace; Lupus, slave of Demetrios of Thessalonica; Haralambos of Crete; Anthony, Bishop of Sardis; Ebba the Younger, abbess of Coldingham, Northumbria, and her companions; Ephraim (Kuznetsov), Bishop of Selenginsk, John Vostorgov of Moscow, and Nicholas Varzhansky; Tydfil of Wales.

AUGUST 24

*W*hoever lives in the past is as if dead. Whoever lives in the future in his imagination is naive, because the future belongs only to God. The Joy of Christ is found only in the present, in the Eternal Present of God.

† *Gerontissa Gavrilia of Leros*

ST. MARTYRIUS, ARCHBISHOP OF NOVGOROD. Martyrius was from twelfth-century Stara Rus, in Poland. He was chosen to replace St. Gregory at the Novogord cathedral and was soon elevated to the rank of archbishop in Kiev. He became a prolific and tireless builder of churches, having built six within three years. One church was built by Princess Elena because of the following miracle. There was a certain pious man of Novgorod who attended church every day, and one day, he returned home, fell asleep, and dropped a prosphora that was stamped with the image of the Theotokos. Smelling the bread, the dogs ran up to it but jumped away, driven off by an invisible power. In the year 1199, on his way to Vladimir, Martyrius died. His body was taken to Novgorod, to the Sophia Cathedral he had built. About 270 years later, before the defeat of Novgorod, there was a sign on the saint's tomb - blood appeared. St. Martyrius was canonized in the early sixteenth century.

COMMEMORATIONS: Cosmas of Aitolia, Equal-to-the-Apostles; George Limniotes the Confessor of Mt. Olympus; Eutychios, disciple of St. John the Theologian; Serapion of St. John the Baptist Monastery at Garesja, Georgia; Cyra of Persia; Arsenius of Komel; Tation at Claudiopolis; Maxim Sandovich of the Lemkos, Poland; Ouen, Archbishop of Rouen (Gaul); Athanasius II, Patriarch of Jerusalem; Seraphim of Grodno; Aristokles of Moscow and Mt. Athos; Martyrius, Archbishop of Novgorod; Holy Martyrs of Utica, called The White Mass; Commemoration of the Appearance of the Most Holy Theotokos to St. Sergius of Radonezh; Translation of the relics of St. Dionysios of Zakynthos; Translation of the relics of St. Peter, Metropolitan of Kiev and Moscow; *Petrovskaya* (Of St. Peter of Moscow) Icon of the Mother of God.

*ℒive simply, love generously, care deeply for the needs of your
neighbor, speak softly… And leave the rest to God.*

St. Luke of Simferopol

HOLY APOSTLE TITUS, BISHOP OF GORTYNA. Titus, one of the
Seventy Apostles, and Apostle Paul were a powerful and effective team that
laid much of the foundation for Christianity. Titus was born to an illustrious pagan father in Crete. However, he pursued a virtuous life, not passions
and vices like the other pagans. When he was twenty years old, he heard
a voice in a dream that told him to seek after that which would save him.
This caused him to begin learning about the teachings of the prophets of
God. When news reached Crete about a Great Prophet in Palestine and the
miracles He was working, he decided to journey to Jerusalem. Titus saw
Jesus, heard his preaching, and believed in Him, and he witnessed Christ's
suffering and Crucifixion. Titus received Holy Baptism from the Apostle
Paul and became his closest disciple. He accompanied Paul on his missionary journeys and helped establish new churches. Apostles Paul and Titus
converted whole nations. Titus was made Bishop of Crete. When Paul was
imprisoned in Rome, Titus went there to be of service. After Paul's death,
Titus returned to Crete, and God granted him the gift of wonderworking.
Apostle Titus died peacefully at the age of ninety-seven.

COMMEMORATIONS: Apostle Titus of the Seventy; Menas, Patriarch
of Constantinople; John II the Cappadocian and Epiphanios, Patriarchs
of Constantinople; Gennadios, Patriarch of Constantinople; Barses and
Eulogius of Edessa; Protogenes of Carrhae; Gregory of Utrecht; John of
Karpathos; Aredius of Limousin; Genesius of Arles; Constantia of Paphos;
Ebba the Elder; Moses (Kozhin) of Solovki; Lucilla and Nemesius, at Rome;
Synaxis of the Hierarchs of Crete: Andrew the Wonderworker, Eumenius
of Rome, and Cyril of Gortyna; Translation of the relics of Apostle Bartholomew from Anastasiopolis to Lipari; Translation of the relics of St.
Hilda of Whitby; Translation of the relics of St. Luke of Adrianople.

AUGUST 26

Hebrews 10:32-38
Matthew 20:29-34

*W*hich is better? To be meek, humble, peaceful and to be filled with love, or to be irritable, depressed, and to quarrel with everyone? Unquestionably the higher state is love.

St. Porphyrios of Kavsokalyvia

VENERABLE ADRIAN OF ONDRUSOV. Adrian owned a wealthy estate near the monastery of St. Alexander of Svir. Once while deer hunting, he encountered St. Alexander, and after this, he would often go to him for guidance and would take bread to the monks. Finally, Adrian became a monk at the Valaam Monastery, and he settled in a solitary place at Lake Ladoga. There he built a church in honor of St. Nicholas the Wonderworker. However, a gang of robbers led by Ondrusa lived nearby. When Ondrusa encountered Adrian, he ordered him off that land, but Adrian negotiated a settlement, offering to intercede before God on Ondrusa's behalf. Soon after, another gang captured Ondrusa, chained him, and was preparing to torture him to death. Suddenly, Adrian appeared to him and said that because of the mercy he had shown the monks, he was now free through the mercy of God. Adrian vanished, and Ondrusa found himself unchained and in another area. He quickly went to the monastery and begged Adrian to accept him as one of the brethren, and he finished his life there in repentance. Later, Adrian went to Moscow to become the godfather of Anna, the daughter of Tsar Ivan the Terrible. On his way home, robbers killed him. Two years passed, and Adrian appeared in a vision to a few elders and told them of his death. The brethren found St. Adrian's incorrupt relics in a swamp and buried them in a wall of the church of St. Nicholas, which he had built.

COMMEMORATIONS: Adrian, Natalia, and 23 companions of Nicomedia; Tithoes of the Thebaid; Ibestion the Confessor; Adrian of Ondrusovsk; Cyprian of Storozhev; Zer-Jacob of Ethiopia; Maria of Diveyevo; Nectarius of Yaransk; Roman of Moscow; Joasaph of India; Abenner the King, father of St. Joasaph; Adrian of Poshekhonye; Bassian of Alatyr; Martyr Adrian.

SUNDAY

AUGUST 27

Twelfth Sunday of Matthew
Fast-free
Ephesians 6:10-17
Matthew 19:16-26

*W*hen the most sacred Body of Christ is received and eaten in a proper manner, it becomes a weapon against those who war against us, it returns to God those who had left Him, it strengthens the weak, it causes the healthy to be glad, it heals sicknesses, and it preserves health. Through it we become meek and more willing to accept correction, more longsuffering in our pains, more fervent in our love, more detailed in our knowledge, more willing to do obedience, and keener in the workings of the charismata of the Spirit. But all the opposite happens to those who do not receive Communion in a proper manner.

St. Gregory the Theologian

VENERABLE POEMEN THE GREAT. Poemen was a sixth-century ascetic of Egypt. One time, during winter, he was visited by the monk Agathonikes, who was seeking guidance. Agathonikes spent the night in an adjoining cave, and in the morning, he complained that he had suffered from the cold during the night. Poemen said that he also was uncovered, but a lion came to him and slept alongside him, warming him. Poemen explained that it was revealed to him that one day he would be devoured by wild beasts. Before he became a monk, Poemen had tended sheep, and one day his dogs attacked a man and killed him. He went on to say that he could have saved him, but he did not. Three years later, St. Poemen was torn apart by wild beasts.

COMMEMORATIONS: Poemen the Great of Egypt; Sabbas of Benephali; Hosius (Osia) the Confessor; Martyr Anthusa; Liberius, Pope of Rome; Caesarius, Bishop of Arles; Kuksha, Pimen, and Nicon of the Kiev Caves; Phanourios the Newly-Revealed of Rhodes; Poemen of Palestine; Michael Voskresensky with 28 other Martyrs, and Stephen Nemkov with 18 other Martyrs, of Nizhni-Novgorod; Methodius (Ivanov) of Sukovo; Praulius, Archbishop of Jerusalem; Commemoration of the Baptism of Djan Darada, the Ethiopian eunuch, by St. Philip; (Last Sunday of August: Synaxis of All Evrytanian Saints; Synaxis of the Three Saints of Ypati).

AUGUST 28

2 Corinthians 8:7-15
Mark 3:6-12

*D*o not reproach anyone for their sins, but consider yourself responsible for everything, even for your neighbor's sins.

† *Elder Justin Pârvu of Romania*

VENERABLE MOSES THE ETHIOPIAN. Moses was from fourth-century Egypt. During his youth, he had committed a murder and was banished. Moses gathered a fierce band of robbers, and they terrorized the countryside. Everyone feared his name. One day he attacked a monastery. When he burst into the abbot's cell, the abbot's composure and piercing look unnerved Moses to the point of regret and remorse for his past life. He asked to stay at the monastery, where he wept for a long time. He lived in obedience and continual repentance. For six years, he tried to defeat the demon of lust by fasting, all-night vigils, and carrying water from the well to each brother. One day, as he was kneeling near the well, the demons struck him upon his back. He lay crippled in his cell for a year. Abba Isidore told him that the passions had left him, and now he had power over the demons. Moses spent many years in monastic exploits, and he acquired deep humility. The governor visited the monastery one time, wanting to meet the famed Moses, but Moses went to hide in his cell. However, he encountered the governor's servants along the way, who asked him where they could find Moses. Moses answered, "Go on no further to this false and unworthy monk." The servants returned to the monastery where the governor was waiting and told him about those words. When they described the monk's appearance, they knew that it was Moses himself. At the age of 75, Moses warned his monks to flee the monastery because barbarians were coming to murder them. St. Moses and six monks were killed.

COMMEMORATIONS: Hezekiah, King of Judah; Anna the Prophetess; Moses the Black of Scetis; Queen Shushaniki (Susanna) of Georgia; Martyrs Diomedes and Laurence; Amphilochius of Vladimir; 33 Martyrs of Nicomedia; Theodore, Prince of Ostrog; Sergius of Zilantov, with Laurence, Seraphim, Theodosius, Leontius, Stephen, Gregory, Hilarion, John, and Sergius; Acacius of Miletus; Savva of Krypetsk; Synaxis of the Venerable Fathers of the Far Caves in Kiev.

If it is necessary to confess and do penance to receive forgiveness of sins, Holy Communion is just as necessary for the remission of sins. As with a festered wound, first one removes any worms, afterwards one cuts away the putrefied flesh and lastly puts on an ointment, that it might be healed; and if you do this you are restored to your former condition. Thus if you sin, with confession you remove the worms, and with penance you cut away the putrid parts and you follow this with Holy Communion, which is the ointment, and you are healed. For if he is not given Holy Communion, the wretched sinner will return to his former state and will become, in the end, someone worse than before.

St. Nicodemus the Hagiorite

ST. ARCADIUS THE WONDERWORKER, BISHOP OF ARSINOE.

Arcadius was from the village of Arsinoe, on the island of Cyprus. He was born to godly and prosperous parents. His brother was St. Theosevios (October 12). Arcadius was sent to Constantinople by his parents to receive his higher education. When he returned, his brilliance and virtues were seen by all. When the bishop died, Arcadius was chosen to succeed him, and he shepherded his flock in a God-pleasing manner. St. Arcadius did many miracles during his life and after his death. He died peacefully.

COMMEMORATIONS: Beheading of St. John the Baptist; Arcadius, Bishop of Arsinoe, Cyprus; Basil I the Macedonian; Candida and Gelasia of Constantinople; Peter, Metropolitan of Krutitsa; Alexander, abbot of Voche of Galich; Anastasius of Bulgaria; Theodora, nun of Thessalonica; Sebbi, King of the East Saxons; Theodore Ivanov of Tobolsk; Sabina of Rome; Translation of the relics of St. Joseph the Sanctified of Samaka; Commemoration of all Orthodox soldiers killed on the field of battle.

AUGUST 30

2 Corinthians 9:12-10:7
Mark 3:20-27

A spiritual father, like a signpost, merely indicates the way; but you yourself must follow the path.

St. Nikon of Optina

ST. RUMON (RONAN), BISHOP OF TAVISTOCK. Rumon was originally from Ireland. Because of his knowledge of the Holy Scriptures, he was ordained bishop. He later moved to Lesser Britain. Grallon, the king of the Britons, would visit him. There was also a religious peasant that would see Rumon almost every day. The peasant's wife, Keban, became jealous because her husband was becoming more of a monk than a husband. She began to spread a vicious rumor, saying that Rumon would change into a wolf and kill the neighbor's sheep and cattle at each full moon. She also accused him of killing and eating her five-year-old daughter, whom she had hidden away. But soon after, the little girl choked on some food and died. When King Grallon heard these rumors, he sent for him. As the king's two fierce dogs were about to attack Rumon, he made the Sign of the Cross, and the dogs lay at his feet. The king asked for his forgiveness. He then told them what Keban had done and where the girl now lay. Keban begged forgiveness, and through his prayers, Rumon raised the little girl from the dead. But Keban was relentless, and now she said that he wanted to sleep with her. Therefore, Rumon moved far away from that area. A religious man gave him hospitality, and he lived there until his death. Knowing that Rumon's body would be carried away by the faithful, the man cut off one of the saint's arms for a relic. The next night, the man awoke, finding that his own arm was missing. He quickly returned the saint's arm and miraculously his own arm was restored. Many miracles were wrought at St. Rumon's grave.

COMMEMORATIONS: Alexander, John, and Paul the New, Patriarchs of Constantinople; Felix of Thibiuca; Martyrs Fortunatus, Septiminus, and Januarius; Fantinus of Calabria; 16 Martyrs of Thebes; 6 Martyrs of Melitene; Sarmata of Egypt; Vryaene of Nisibis; Eulalius of Cyprus; Alexander of Svir; Barlaam of Moldavia; John of Rasca; Alexander of Voch; Christopher of Palestine; Fiacrius of Breuil; Ignatius of Moscow.

Placing of the Sash of the Theotokos
Fast-free
Hebrews 9:1-7
Luke 10:38-42, 11:27-28

*Y*ou ask how to lay the beginnings of repentance—if you wish to begin repentance, look at the woman sinner: she washed Christ's feet with her tears (Luke 7:38). Tears wash away sins of every person. But a person acquires tears by internal efforts, through the diligent study of the Holy Scripture, through patience, meditation on the Last Judgment and eternal shame, and through self-denial, just as the Lord said: *"If anyone desires to come after Me, let him deny himself, and take up his cross, and follow Me,"* (Mt. 16:24). To deny one's self and to take up the cross—means to sever your own will in everything and regard yourself as nothing.

St. Barsanuphius the Great and St. John the Prophet

HIEROMARTYR CYPRIAN, BISHOP OF CARTHAGE. Cyprian was born around the year 200 in the city of Carthage. He was the son of a rich pagan senator. He married and became a teacher of philosophy and rhetoric. He left his wife when he became a Christian and absorbed himself solely in the study of the Gospels. He also worked at perfecting his faults. Because of this, he was ordained a priest and then bishop. He wrote against idolatry and Judaism, and he commended almsgiving, virginity, prayer, patience, and martyrdom. When St. Cyprian was beheaded during the persecutions of Valerian, he left the executioner gold pieces.

COMMEMORATIONS: The Placing of the Venerable Sash of the Most Holy Theotokos; Cyprian, Bishop of Carthage; 4 Martyrs of Perga; Gennadius Scholarius, Patriarch of Constantinople; Paulinus, Bishop of Trier; 7 Virgin Martyrs of Gaza; 366 Martyrs of Nicomedia; John, Metropolitan of Kiev; Aidan, Bishop of Lindisfarne; Martyr Menas and others; Miron Rzhepik of Sergiev Posad.

There are two facets to humility. The first is composed of you regarding your brother as more sensible than yourself and more superior to you, or according to the advice of the Holy Fathers, "regard yourself as being lower than everybody." The second is comprised in ascribing your self-imposed meritorious ordeal to God—this is the complete form of humility of the Saints. It is born naturally in the soul through fulfilling the commandments. Because it is like the branches of a tree that sag downwards when they have abundant fruit on them. However, branches that have no fruit strive upwards and grow straight up. There are trees in existence that will not bear fruit unless their branches are bent downwards: if somebody attaches a stone to them so that they grow toward the ground, they yield fruit. Similarly with the soul, when it becomes humble, it brings forth fruit, and the more fruit it produces, the humbler it becomes. The closer the Saints get to God, the more they realize their sinfulness.

St. Isaac the Syrian

FRIDAY

Ecclesiastical New Year
Abstain from meat and
dairy products, and fish.

SEPTEMBER I

1 Timothy 2:1-7; Luke 4:16-22

*W*hile we are living improperly, we fear all kinds of things. When we recognize God, there occurs a fear of His judgment. But when we start to love God, all fears vanish.

St. Isaac the Syrian

ST. GILES (AEGIDIUS), MONASTIC FOUNDER. Giles would end up playing a significant role in the spiritual history of Europe. He was born into a noble Greek family in mid-seventh-century Athens. As a young man, he gained a reputation for sanctity, but fearing pride, he fled to southern France and into the deep forests of Nimes. He lived there for years in total solitude, conversing only with God. As it happened, there was a doe that was so comfortable around Giles that she let him milk her. But one day, some hunters happened upon her, and she fled to Giles. An arrow meant for the deer struck Giles, crippling him for life. It was accidentally fired by the king, who was horrified. Even so, Giles became the king's spiritual father. News of the hermit Giles spread, and soon he was asked to establish a monastery. A town sprung up around it, and many disabled beggars went there for alms. Giles became the patron saint of people with disabilities, beggars, and anyone seeking a good confession. He died peacefully in the early eighth century. St. Giles is revered all over Europe and by the British and Baltic peoples. He is also one of the Fourteen Holy Helpers and was initially invoked as protection against the Black Plague.

COMMEMORATIONS: Church New Year; Symeon the Stylite, and his mother Martha; 40 Virgin Martyrs and Ammon the deacon, at Heraclea; Venerable Evanthia; Nicholas Kourtaliotis of Crete; Joshua the Son of Nun; Callista, Evodus, and Hermogenes at Nicomedia; Angelis of Constantinople; Meletios the Younger; Symeon of Lesvos; Verena of Zurzach (Switzerland); Haido of Stanos; Aegidius (Giles), along the Rhine; Dionysius Exiguus of Rome; Commemoration of the Great Fire at Constantinople about AD 470; Synaxis of the Most Holy Theotokos in Miasena Monastery; Synaxis of Panagia Katapoliani in Tinos; *Chernigov-Gethsemane, Of Alexandria, All-blessed One,* and *Avgustovskaya* Icons of the Mother of God.

SEPTEMBER 2

*T*he one great and indispensable requirement for unanimity and concord is this: the imitation of God and of the things divine. It is to these alone that the soul, created in God's image, must steadfastly gaze; in order that—by becoming as much like them as possible—it may preserve, to the greatest extent, its noble status.

St. Gregory the Theologian

VENERABLE FATHERS ANTHONY AND THEODOSIUS, FOUNDERS OF THE KIEV CAVES LAVRA. According to the *Primary Chronicle,* Anthony was an eleventh-century Orthodox monk from Esphigmenou Monastery on Mount Athos. He returned to Kiev as a missionary of monastic tradition and chose to live in a cave that overlooked the Dnieper River. Disciples soon went to live around him, and a community grew. Prince Iziaslav I of Kiev gave the whole mountain to those monks. Architects from Constantinople built the monastery, which became the Kiev Caves Lavra. Theodosius copied the monastic Rule of St. Theodore the Studite, which spread to all the monasteries of the Russian Orthodox Church. The names of Saints Anthony and Theodosius are often listed together, but each has his own feast day as well.

COMMEMORATIONS: Mamas of Caesarea, and his parents, Theodotus and Rufina; John the Faster; Eleazar, son of Aaron, and Righteous Phineas; Anthony and Theodosius of the Kiev Caves; Justus of Lyon; Holy 10 Martyrs; Barsanuphius of Kyrilov, John Ivanov, and Seraphima of Therapontov Convent, and Anatole, Nicholas, Michael, and Philip; Damascene of Glukhov, Herman of Vyaznikov, and Stephen Yaroshevich; Aeithalas and Ammon of Thrace; Hieu of Tadcaster; Kosmas the Hermit of Crete; *Kaluga* Icon of the Mother of God.

Thirteenth Sunday of Matthew
Fast-free

1 Corinthians 16:13-24
Matthew 21:33-42

SEPTEMBER 3

I ... see a new craftiness in the devil. He causes people to think that if they make a vow to God and fulfill it, if they go on some pilgrimage, then they are alright spiritually. You see hordes of people going to monasteries and shrines with tall candles and extravagant offerings, ostentatiously making the sign of the cross, even weeping a little, and feeling content. They do not repent, do not confess, do not correct or change their way of life ... and this is quite pleasing to the devil.

St. Paisios the Athonite

ST. CONSTANTINE THE NEW OF CONSTANTINOPLE. Constantine was the oldest son of Roman Emperor Heraclius, and he was crowned co-emperor of the Eastern Roman Empire. Constantine married the daughter of his father's first cousin, making the couple second cousins and the marriage incestuous. But this paled in comparison to Heraclius marrying his own niece, Martina. When his father died, Constantine became senior emperor, and his half-brother, Martina's son, reigned with him. However, Martina was accused of poisoning Constantine, and she and her sons were banished to Rhodes. Knowing that he was dying, Constantine sent more than two million gold coins to the army to be distributed to the soldiers to ensure the succession of his sons after his death. But while Heraclius was still king, he declared the heresy of Monothelitism as the imperial form of Christianity, and the Patriarch of Constantinople and all the bishops subscribed to this. This heresy claimed that Christ had only one will, divine, and not two, divine and human. Under his reign, Constantine suppressed this edict. He died after only four months as emperor, making him the shortest reigning Eastern Roman emperor.

COMMEMORATIONS: Anthimos, Bishop of Nicomedia, with others; Aristion of Alexandria; Emperor Constantine the New; Ioannicius II of Serbia; Vasilissa of Nicomedia; Theoctistus of Palestine; John "the Hairy" of Rostov; Phoebe, deaconess; Remaclus of Maastricht; Polydoros of Cyprus; Translation of the relics of St. Nektarios of Aegina in 1953.

SEPTEMBER 4

2 Corinthians 12:10-19
Mark 4:10-23

*E*xercise restraint, which is superior to silence.

St. Pachomios of Chios

ST. HERMIONE. Hermione was one of Apostle Philip's four daughters. She became a physician, and the Christians hastened to her for healing by her prayers, but she was taken to Emperor Trajan, who persecuted Christians. He tried to separate her from her faith, but when he could not, he had her struck on the face for a long time, but she was comforted by a vision of Christ. When Trajan saw her unchanging mind, he gave up and released her. She built a guesthouse, where she cared for the mentally and physically sick. Following Trajan's death, the new emperor Hadrian sent for Hermione. He had her flogged and ordered nails to be driven into her feet, and she was placed in a cauldron of boiling tar. She prayed for God to give her strength, and as soon as she entered the cauldron, immediately the fire was extinguished, and she remained unharmed. Hadrian became angrier and had a second cauldron prepared. When he saw her standing in it as if it were cool, he got up from his throne and touched the cauldron, and immediately the skin and nails of his hand came off. Then he placed her in a heated furnace, but an angel of God scattered the flames, burning those standing nearby. Hadrian took her to the temple of idols, where thunder shattered the statues when she prayed. The enraged emperor gave orders to behead her. He sent two executioners, Theodoulos and Timothy, but along the way, their hands withered, and they believed in Christ. They repented and asked her to pray so that they may give up their souls before her, and they reposed. Then St. Hermione gave up her spirit in the same place. Christians took up their sacred relics and buried them in Ephesus.

COMMEMORATIONS: Prophet Moses; Aaron the Priest; Babylas of Antioch; Babylas of Nicomedia and 84 children; 3,628 Martyrs at Nicomedia; Sarbelus and Bebaia of Edessa; Hermione and Timothy and Theodoulos; Charitina of Amisus; Symeon of Garesja; Martyr Sarbelus; Jerusalem of Berroia and her sons; Petronius of Egypt; Anthimus the Blind; Parthenius of Kiziltash; Gregory of Shliserburg, Sergius of Narva, and Stephen of Nikolskoye; Gorazd of Prague.

Holy Prophet Zacharias
Fast-free
2 Corinthians 12:20-13:2
Matthew 23:29-39

A tree is known by its fruits, a man by his deeds. A good deed is never lost; he who sows courtesy reaps friendship, and he who plants kindness gathers love.

St. Basil the Great

MARTYRDOM OF HOLY PASSION-BEARER GLEB OF RUSSIA. Gleb was one of the first Russian martyrs in the early eleventh century. He is also called a Passion-Bearer. After the murder of his brother St. Boris, Svyatopolk the Accursed sent his younger brother Prince Gleb a message with false information about their father and thus using deceit to murder yet another possible claimant to the Kiev throne. The unsuspecting Gleb hastened off towards Kiev. The assassins came upon Gleb's boat, and one of their cohorts slit Gleb's throat. He was buried in a desolate place in the year 1015. Another brother, Yaroslav, found Gleb's grave about four years later, and his incorrupt relics were transferred and buried alongside his brother, St. Boris. Later, the relics of the brothers were transferred to the church of St. Basil the Great, where many miracles were worked. They have rendered powerful help to their native land during the years of grievous tribulation. In the year 1240, just before the Nevsky battle, Boris and Gleb appeared in a vision to one of St. Alexander Nevsky's soldiers, and they aided the Russians during the battle. There are numerous accounts of miracles witnessed at their tombs and the victories won through their help. Many churches and monasteries were built throughout Russia to honor them.

COMMEMORATIONS: Holy Prophet Zacharias and Righteous Elizabeth, parents of St. John the Forerunner; Urban, Theodore, Medimnos, and 77 companions at Nicomedia; Abdas, Hormizd, and Sunin of Persia; Athanasius of Bretsk; Juventinus and Maximinus at Antioch; Gleb of Russia, in Holy Baptism David; Alexis Belkovsky, Archbishop of Great Ustiug; Neophyte and Meletios of Stanisoara Monastery; Bertin (Bertinius) of France; Appearance of Apostle Peter to Emperor Justinian at Athira, near Constantinople.

Commemoration of the Miracle Wrought by Archangel Michael
Abstain from meat and dairy products, and fish.
Hebrews 2:2-10; Luke 10:16-21

*B*esides the path of repentance, there is no other path that returns to salvation.

St. Ignatius Brianchaninov

MARTYRS EUDOXIUS, ZENO, MACARIUS, AND 1,104 SOLDIERS MARTYRS. Eudoxius was a military commander in the Roman army under Emperor Maximian. Many Christians fled to other lands to avoid persecution, and Eudoxius and his family fled to Melitene. The governor there sent soldiers to find him, but they did not recognize him because he was not wearing his military uniform. Eudoxius fed the soldiers and invited them into his home to rest there that evening. The next day he told them who he was, and because of the hospitality he gave them, the soldiers offered to conceal him, but he refused. He instructed his wife Basilissa to celebrate his death and not mourn him. The governor tried to convince Eudoxius to sacrifice to the idols, but instead, he denounced the folly of anyone who worshipped soulless idols. Eudoxius threw his military belt at the governor's face, and 1,000 Christian soldiers did the same. Eudoxius was tortured and led to his execution. Along the way, he told his friend Zeno that they would enter heaven together. With these words, Zeno immediately proclaimed Christ and was beheaded. St. Eudoxius and all the soldiers were beheaded. Basilissa buried Eudoxius where he had instructed. He appeared to his wife, instructing her to tell Macarius, their house steward, that he and Zeno awaited him. Zeno declared that he was a Christian and was martyred.

COMMEMORATIONS: Commemoration of the Miracle of the Archangel Michael at Chonae; Romulus and 11,000 Soldiers with him, in Armenia; Eudoxius, Zeno, Macarius, and 1,104 soldiers with them, in Melitene; David of Hermopolis in Egypt; Archippus of Hierapolis; Kalodote, Faustus, Makarios, Andrew, Kyriakos, Dionysios, Andrew, Pelagia, Thekla, Theoktistos, and Sarapabon, in Alexandria; Eleutherius of Spoleto; Lygeri of Chios; Bega, first abbess of Copeland in Cumbria; Magnus of Fussen; *Kiev-Bratsk* Icon of the Mother of God.

SEPTEMBER 7

Galatians 1:1-3, 20-24; 2:1-5
Mark 5:1-20

You are unable to stop the mouth of one who calumniates his neighbor? At least keep yourself from having anything to do with him. Know that if fire comes forth from you and burns others, God will demand an accounting from your hands for the souls that are burned by your fire. If, on the other hand, though you do not give off fire, yet you agree with the one who ignited it and take pleasure in this, you will be reckoned his accomplice in the Judgment.

St. Isaac the Syrian

HOLY APOSTLE EVODOS OF THE SEVENTY. Evodos was one of the Seventy Apostles chosen by Jesus Christ to go two by two before Him into the cities. Apostle Peter consecrated him the first Bishop of Antioch. Evodos is credited with first using the name "Christians" to describe the followers of Christ. He was a man filled with virtues, and he preached with a great voice. He wrote about the life of the Holy Theotokos and a work titled "The Beacon." Both were destroyed during the persecution of Christians. Some sources say St. Evodos died in peace, while others say he was a martyr. Apostle Peter consecrated Saint Ignatios, the next Bishop of Antioch.

COMMEMORATIONS: Apostles Evodos and Onesiphoros of the Seventy; Sozon of Cilicia; Cassiane the Hymnographer; Eupsychius of Caesarea; Luke and Peter the Cappadocian of the Deep Stream; Symeon and Amphilochius of Pangarati; John of Verkhne-Poltavka; Alexander and Andrew; Macarius of Kanev; John of Novgorod; Cloud of Nogent-sur-Seine; Eugene of Nizhni-Novgorod; Leo of St. Alexander Nevsky; Sozon of Cyprus; Daniel of Katounakia.

Nativity of the Mother of God
Abstain from meat and dairy products.
Philippians 2:5-11
Luke 10:38-42, 11:27-28

*W*hen you see an icon of the Theotokos with the infant Christ in her arms, do you know what you are looking at? Heaven and earth! Heaven is Christ, Who is above the heavens; He is the Creator of heaven and earth. And the Mother of the Lord represents all the people on the face of the earth, for she was chosen from among us. She was born from both royal and priestly lineage. The arms of the Mother of the Lord are more powerful than the shoulders of the Cherubim and the most blessed Thrones. Who does she hold in her arms? Do you know? She holds the One Who made heaven and earth, all things visible and invisible!

† *Elder Cleopa of Romania*

KHOLMSK ICON OF THE MOTHER OF GOD. Bishop James the Emaciated passed down the tradition that credits the writing of the Kholmsk Icon to the Evangelist Luke, the Physician. This icon was brought from Greece to Russia, along with many other icons from Constantinople, as gifts to Equal-to-the-Apostles Prince Vladimir when he received Baptism. When the Tatar (Mongol) Horde invaded and pillaged the city of Kholm in southwest Poland, the jeweled frame was taken, and the icon was damaged and thrown down. Two gashes remained on the icon: one on the shoulder of the Panagia and the other on her right hand. According to tradition, those who damaged her icon lost their eyesight, and their faces became distorted. The miraculous signs worked by the Kholmsk Icon are recorded in a book by Archimandrite Ioannikes Golyatovsky, titled "The New Heaven."

COMMEMORATIONS: Nativity of the Mother of God; Sophronius of Achtaleia; Martyrs Rufus and Rufianus; Martyrs Severus and Artemidorus; Lucian of Alexandrov; Athanasios of Thessalonica; Serapion of Pskov; Arsenius of Konevits; John and George-John of Georgia; Ina of Wessex and Ethelburga; Alexander, at Solovki; Icon of Sophia, the Wisdom of God (Kiev); *Kholmsk* Icon of the Mother of God.

SEPTEMBER 9

*T*hree things bring salvation to man: faith, works, and contemplation. For firstly, one believes from hearing; secondly, one does the commandments; and thirdly, one is granted union with God and enjoys with contemplative faith what he formerly believed with faith from hearing.

St. Maximos of Corinth

COMMEMORATION OF THE THIRD ECUMENICAL SYNOD. In the year 431, the Third Ecumenical Council was held in Ephesus with 200 bishops in attendance. The Synod was convened to condemn the heretical teachings of Patriarch Nestorius of Constantinople. He asserted that Christ was two distinct persons—one divine and the other human. The Holy Church teaches that Christ is one Person (Hypostasis). In addition, Nestorius stated that the Mother of God should be called the "birth-giver of the man Christ" (Christotokos) and not the "Birth-giver of God" (Theotokos). Nestorius said that Jesus was born an ordinary man, and afterward, because of His sanctity of life, He was joined to the Godhead. He attempted to undermine the Christian faith on these points. A long while before the convening of the Third Ecumenical Council, St. Cyril, Archbishop of Alexandria, repeatedly tried to reason with Nestorius. He enlisted the support of other Orthodox bishops, but Nestorius continued his false teachings, which became widespread. Nestorius refused to attend the council that lasted about five weeks. In his absence, the Church Fathers condemned the heresy of Nestorius.

COMMEMORATIONS: Holy Ancestors of God Joachim and Anna; Severian of Sebaste; Theophanes the Confessor; Roufos of Thessalonica; Martyrs Chariton and Straton; Nicetas the Hidden; Joseph of Volotsk; Joachim of Opochka; Joachim of Suzdal; Onuphrius of Voronsk; Omer of Therouanne; Kieran of Clonmacnois; Bettelin of Crowland; Wulfhilda of Barking; Kyriakos of Tazlau; Onuphrius of Vorona; Commemoration of the Third Ecumenical Council; Synaxis of the Saints of Glinsk Monastery.

SEPTEMBER 10

Never remain in a state of sadness but strive to do something spiritual that will help to get you out of this state.

St. Paisios the Athonite

ST. CHRYSOSTOMOS OF SMYRNA. Chrysostomos was born in late nineteenth-century Tryglia, Greece. He was one of eight children. His father, Nikolaos, represented fellow Greek citizens in the Ottoman courts. Chrysostomos was educated in ecclesiastical matters, music, Greek, Turkish, and French. He also studied at Halki Theological School. He served as chancellor of the Great Church, Metropolitan of Drama, and later at the Metropolis of Smyrna. But Chrysostomos became involved in political issues against Bulgarian propaganda. He organized a large rally denouncing Bulgarian violence against the Greeks in Macedonia and the oppression of Greeks by the Ottomans. This alarmed the authorities, and he was removed from his metropolis several times only to be reinstated. Chrysostomos was an inspired leader of the Asia Minor Defense for the creation of an autonomous state. Throughout all of this, he refused to abandon his people in the face of grave danger. In the end, he was arrested and handed over to an angry mob of over one thousand. St. Chrysostomos was tortured to death. He was beaten and stabbed, and they gouged out his eyes, tore off his beard, and disfigured his face.

COMMEMORATIONS: Menodora, Metrodora, and Nymphodora at Nicomedia; Pulcheria, Empress of the Romans; Varypsavas in Dalmatia; Salvius of Albi; Joasaph of Kubensk; Theodoritus of Ryazan; Peter and Paul of Nicaea; Paul the Obedient of the Kiev Caves; Cassian of Spaso-Kamenny; Cyril of White Lake; Finnian of Ulster; Theodaard of Maastricht; Meletius of Kuzhba, Gabriel of Donskoy, and Warus of Lipetsk; Synaxis of the Holy Apostles Apelles, Lucius, and Clement of the Seventy; (Sunday before the Elevation: St. Chrysostomos, Metropolitan of Smyrna, and the Hierarchs with him).

MONDAY

SEPTEMBER 11

St. Theodora of Alexandria
Fast-free
Galatians 2:11-16
John 12:19-36

*O*ther people's sins are not your business. Sit and cry for your sins.
St. Gabriel Urgebadze

VENERABLE JOHN OF SVYATOGORSK. John longed to become a monk, and at the age of sixteen, he began to ask his parents to bless him to go, but they would not. He had a dream and saw monks who told him that it was God's will for him to join them. He secretly left home with one piece of bread and barefoot. He spent three months at a monastery until his father found him. He tied his legs with a rope and took him home, but after his father's death, his mother gave him the blessing. John was taught the Jesus Prayer, the basics of the monastic life, and the need to confess even his thoughts. But with extreme fasting and prayer, his health weakened, and he finally took to his bed, barely alive. In this condition, John heard the voice of the Savior, "Rise, and be half-healthy and serve for the good of the soul of your neighbors." He was appointed spiritual father for the pilgrims. As a humble confessor, he recognized mental illness and could heal with amazing ease. He also administered the Holy Mysteries to the sick in the surrounding villages. He healed the soul and body with prayer and anointing with holy oil from the miraculous icon of St. Nicholas. Some of the possessed would rush at him with blows and beatings. His prayer rule consisted of 1,200 Jesus Prayers during the day and 1,200 at night. He said that communion of the Holy Mysteries, even through our wretched preparation, makes us better by grace, renews us, and transforms us from the carnal into the spiritual. St. John died peacefully.

COMMEMORATIONS: Demetrius, Evanthia, and Demetrian at Skepsis; Ia (Violet) of Persia and 9,000 Martyrs; Theodora of Alexandria; Diodorus, Didymus, and Diomedes of Laodicea; Euphrosynos the Cook; Paphnutius the Confessor; Elias the Cave-dweller of Calabria; John of Svyatogorsk; Theodora of Vasta; Joseph of Zaonikieva; Deiniol, Bishop of Bangor; Translation of the relics of Sts. Sergius and Herman of Valaam; Glorification of St. Xenia of St. Petersburg, Fool-for-Christ; *Kaplunovka* Weeping Kazan Icon of the Mother of God.

**Leavetaking of the Nativity
of the Mother of God**
Fast-free

SEPTEMBER 12

*P*eople seek money, not for its practical usefulness, but because with it they can become slaves to pleasure. Three reasons for the love of money are pleasure, conceit, and lack of faith. Hedonists love money to spend it on their pleasures, the conceited want it to procure fame, those who are lacking in faith seek money to keep it hidden away out of fear of starvation, old age, or illness. The latter put their trust in their money rather than in God the creator of the universe, whose providence knows no bounds and reaches even the lowest of his creatures. But there are four kinds of people who put money aside. I have just mentioned three. There are, however, also those who restrict themselves to the administration of goods. Only these last are justified in accumulating money, on the assumption that their aim is to be always in the business of helping the needy.

St. Maximos the Confessor

HIEROMARTYR CORONATOS, BISHOP OF ICONIUM. It is said that asceticism is a prolonged martyrdom. Coronatos was already a very old man, an ascetic, and a bishop when Christian persecutions came to Nicomedia during the reigns of Emperors Valerian and Decius. All the other Christians had escaped the city except for Coronatos. One day, he was seized by the pagans and brought before the governor Perinius. After proclaiming his faith in Christ, Perinius had Coronatos bound, dragged through the city, then executed with a sword.

COMMEMORATIONS: Coronatos, Bishop of Iconium; Autonomos, bishop in Italy; Julian of Galatia, and 40 Martyrs; Andronicus of Atroa; Macedonius in Phrygia, and with him Tatian and Theodulus; Daniel of Thasos; Martyr Okeanos; Sacerdos, Bishop of Lyons in Gaul; Dositheus of Tbilisi, Georgia; Bassian of Totemsk; Theodore of Alexandria; Alexis, Fool-for-Christ of Elnat and Zharki; Athanasius, disciple of Sergius of Radonezh, and his disciple Athanasius; Kournoutas of Cyprus; Ailbhe (Elvis) of Emly; Translation of the relics of St. Symeon of Verkhoturye.

WEDNESDAY

SEPTEMBER 13

Forefeast of the Elevation of the Holy Cross

Abstain from meat and dairy products, and fish.

Hebrews 3:1-4
Matthew 16:13-19

*I*t is essential in these days to be able to protect ourselves from the influence of those with whom we come in contact. Otherwise we risk losing both faith and prayer. Let the whole world dismiss us as unworthy of attention, trust or respect—it will not matter provided that the Lord accepts us.

St. Sophrony of Essex

NEW MARTYRS OF JASENOVAC CONCENTRATION CAMP. There is a particular icon written as a witness to the genocide of the Serbs during the Second World War. The Jasenovac concentration camp is shown in the upper left-hand corner, with barbed wire and watchtowers. The churches of Jasenovac are shown centrally. They were destroyed twice; one burned to the ground with 500 Serbs inside. The upper right-hand corner shows one of the many caves that became graves for innocent people, and in the lower foreground is a river that carries the bodies of the tortured people. They were all killed for their Orthodox faith. On either side stand St. John the Baptist, the patron of the Jasenovac Church, and St. Sava, the patron saint of the Serbian people.

COMMEMORATIONS: Cornelius the Centurion; Seleucus of Galatia; Straton of Nicomedia; Cronides, Leontius, and Serapion of Alexandria; Theodotus of Alexandria; Hierotheos of Kalamata; Ketevan, Queen of Kakheti, Georgia; Elias, Zoticus, Lucian, Valerian, Macrobius, and Gordian at Tomis in Moesia; Peter of Atroa; John of Prislop (Romania); Meletios Pegas, Patriarch of Alexandria; Litorius of Tours; Cornelius of Padan-Olonets, with Dionysius and Misael; Maurilius, Bishop of Angers; New Martyrs of Jasenovac (Serbia); Commemoration of the Founding of the Church of the Resurrection (the Holy Sepulcher) at Jerusalem.

Elevation of the Holy Cross
Strict Fast
1 Corinthians 1:18-24
John 19:6-11, 13-20, 25-28, 30

It is easier to measure the entire sea with a tiny cup than to grasp the ineffable greatness of God with the human mind.

St. Basil the Great

WONDERWORKING ICON OF ST. VLASIOS IN TRIKALA, CORINTH. In Trikala, Corinth is the historic Monastery of St. Vlasios, which played an important spiritual role during Ottoman rule. It has a great miraculous tradition because of the wonderworking icon of St. Vlasios. A hermit discovered the icon around the thirteenth to fourteenth centuries. He saw an intense light emitting from a cave that was on a steep hillside. The icon is now encased in silver, and at the bottom is depicted the life of St. Vlasios. The monastery prospered with considerable land holdings and many monks during the eighteenth century. Later it was used as a school for children in the nineteenth century, and in the twentieth century, it became a convent. The miracles that continue to this day are numerous due to the icon, especially against severe illnesses and those with diseases of the throat and larynx. This is evidenced by the numerous offerings that adorn the icon and the number of pilgrims that travel there. They sleep on the church floor to receive the blessing of St. Vlasios and to receive healing.

COMMEMORATIONS: Exaltation of the Honorable and Life-Creating Cross; Placilla the Empress, wife of Theodosius the Great; Child-Martyr Valerian; Martyr Theokles; Maria of Tarsus; Cyprian, Bishop of Carthage; Makarios of Thessalonica; Papas of Lycaonia; Cormac, Bishop of Cashel in Ireland; Holy Fathers of the Sixth Ecumenical Council; Repose of St. John Chrysostom; Uncovering of the relics of Sts. Alexandra, Martha, and Helen of Diveyevo; *Lesna* Icon of the Mother of God; Wonderworking Icon of St. Vlasios in Trikala, Corinth.

St. Niketas the Great Martyr
Strict Fast

SEPTEMBER 15

Colossians 1:24-2:1
Matthew 10:16-22

Be attentive to your salvation while it is day; that is, you have to force yourself in every way to do every kind of good deed. I repeat, you have to force yourself because the Kingdom of Heaven is given to those who *'take it by force'* (Mt.11:12).

St. Joseph of Optina

VENERABLE PHILOTHEOS THE PRESBYTER AND WONDER-WORKER. Philotheos was born in a small village near Nicaea. He married, had children, prayed, and fasted. Due to his piety, the bishop ordained him to the priesthood. Because of his pure manner of life, God granted him the gift to work miracles. Just as Jesus said, "If you have faith as a mustard seed, you will say to this mountain, 'Move from here to there,' and it will move" (Matthew 17:20), so Philotheos moved a great rock with just a word. He changed river water to wine and did many other wondrous deeds. Philotheos died peacefully and was buried. A year later, two priests were sent to transfer the saint's relics to another place. When they went to lift his body, Philotheos stretched out his arms, grabbed the two priests by the shoulders, got up, and walked three steps to the place where his relics are today. The relics of St. Philotheos gushed myrrh.

COMMEMORATIONS: Niketas the Goth; Martyr Maximus; Bessarion I and Bessarion II of Larissa; Symeon of Thessalonica; Gerasimos of Sourvia; Philotheus of Asia Minor; Joseph of Alaverdi; Porphyrios the Mime; Joseph the New; 2 maidens slain by the sword; John of Crete; Nicetas, disciple of St. Sergius of Radonezh; Ignatius of Aleksievo-Akatov; Dimitry of Melitopol; Mirin of Paisley; Philotheos the presbyter, of Asia Minor; Uncovering of the relics of the Holy Protomartyr and Archdeacon Stephen.

SEPTEMBER 16

1 Corinthians 1:26-2:5
John 8:21-30

*O*ften our knowledge becomes darkened because we fail to put things into practice. For when we have totally neglected to practice something, our memory of it will gradually disappear.

St. Mark the Ascetic

GREAT MARTYR AND ALL-PRAISED EUPHEMIA. Proconsul Priscus governed Chalcedon in 288. A feast was decreed to the idol Ares and the demon within it. Euphemia and forty-eight other Christians did not attend but went into hiding. They were found and dragged before the proconsul, who flattered and threatened them to sacrifice to Ares. In chains, they suffered wound upon wound for nineteen days. All the Christians were sent to the dungeon, except Euphemia. Through kind words, promises, and gifts, Priscus tried to entice her. She said, "Although I am a woman by nature, my heart is more manly than yours." Angered, he had her body cut up and mangled on a torture wheel with knives. She prayed to Christ to come to her aid, and immediately, angels wrecked the wheel and healed her wounds. Everyone was amazed but called it sorcery. Preparing to cast her into a furnace, two attendants, Victor and Sosthenes, saw an angel of God part the flames and forbade them to touch Euphemia. They believed in Christ and were martyred. When two other attendants put Euphemia in the furnace, they were burned to ashes. Euphemia remained unharmed and prayed to God to receive her soul and end her suffering. A voice from heaven summoned her, and she surrendered her spirit. Then immediately, an earthquake destroyed the temples and city walls, and everyone fled.

COMMEMORATIONS: Euphemia the All-praised of Chalcedon; Cyprian, Bishop of Carthage; Victor and Sosthenes at Chalcedon; Dorotheos of Egypt; Ninian of Whithorn; Ludmilla, grandmother of St. Wenceslaus; Meletina of Marcianopolis; Isaac and Joseph at Karnu, Georgia; Kushka of Odessa; Procopius, abbot of Sazava in Bohemia; Cyprian, Metropolitan of Kiev and All Russia; Edith of Wilton; *Support of the Humble* Icon of the Mother of God.

SEPTEMBER 17

*T*he mill is always turning; the mind of man is always working—like a mill. Do you want to have good results? Put good material into the mill. Do you want to find compunction, tears, joy, peace, etc.? Put good thoughts into the mill of your mind—for example, thoughts about the soul, about the Judgement, the remembrance of death, and so on—and then you will get corresponding spiritual results! But if a person puts sinful thoughts into the mill of his mind, he will definitely have sin as a result. The material that will be given to the mind depends on the intentions of man. And these intentions will either be commended or censured. We should always strive to have salvific thoughts and beneficial images in our mind, so that we do not leave room for Satan to throw in his garbage—sinful thoughts and fantasies!

† *Elder Ephraim of Arizona*

HOLY 50 MARTYRS OF PALESTINE AND 100 MARTYRS OF EGYPT. In the year 310, idol-worshipping pagans captured these martyrs in Palestine. Because they confessed Jesus Christ, 50 martyrs were sentenced to die by fire. Two of these were Egyptian bishops, Paleus and Nilus, and two were rulers, Elias and Patermuthius. The 100 martyrs from Egypt had their eyes plucked out and their right feet and arms cut off. They were then put to work in the mines before killing them with the sword. In his writings, St. John Chrysostom praised these one hundred spiritual athletes for their courage and perseverance.

COMMEMORATIONS: Sophia and her daughters, Faith, Hope, and Love, at Rome; Heraclides and Myron of Cyprus; Maximos, Asclepiodotos, and Theodotos of Marcianopolis; Theodota at Nicaea, and Agathoklea; Lucy and Geminian of Rome; Innocent of Glinsk; Anastasios of Perioteron; Eusipius of Cyprus; Lambert of Maastricht; Joachim I the Pany; 100 Martyrs of Egypt; 50 Martyrs of Palestine; Martyrs Haralampus, Panteleon, and others.

SEPTEMBER 18

Galatians 4:28-5:10
Luke 3:19-22

The soul is greater than the body: the body becomes sick, and with that it is finished. But a spiritual sickness extends into eternity. Deliver us, O Lord, from such illness, and grant us healing.

St. Macarius of Optina

THE HEALER ICON OF THE MOTHER OF GOD. This icon was written in the country of Georgia around the fourth century at the time of St. Nino. Another icon with the same name is in the Alexeev women's monastery in Moscow, and many miracles have taken place before it at the end of the eighteenth century. St. Demetrius of Rostov relates the following story about this icon. A cleric at the Navarninsky church would always venerate the icon when he entered the church. He would pray, "Hail Virgin Theotokos full of grace, the Lord is with Thee. Blessed is the womb which bore Christ, and the breasts which nourished the Lord God, our Savior." After some time, he suffered from a terrible affliction where his tongue began to putrefy, and he passed out from the pain. When he came to himself, he recited his usual prayer. As soon as he finished his prayer, his guardian angel appeared at the head of his bed and with pity called on the Mother of God to heal him. Suddenly, she appeared and healed him, who was so devoted to Her. To everyone's amazement, he got out of bed and took his usual place at the church service. The miracle inspired the writing of 'The Healer' icon, which depicts the Mother of God standing at the sick mans bed.

COMMEMORATIONS: Ariadne of Phrygia; Eumenius, Bishop of Gortyna on Crete; Sophia and Irene of Egypt; Castor of Alexandria; Arcadius, Bishop of Novgorod; Bidzina, Shalva, and Elizbar princes of Ksani, Georgia; Romulus the Sinaite of Ravanica; Hilarion, elder of Optina Monastery; Amphilochius Skvortsov, Bishop of Krasnoyarsk; *The Healer* and *Staro-Rus* Icons of the Mother of God.

SEPTEMBER 19

Galatians 5:11-21
Luke 3:23-4:1

*W*hether you are on the road, or in bed, wherever you may be, pray. You are the temple of God; do not look for a place, you only need a spiritual disposition.

St. John Chrysostom

MARTYRS TROPHIMUS, SABBATIUS, AND DORYMEDON OF SYNNADA. During the third-century reign of Emperor Probus, Trophimus and Sabbatius arrived in Antioch on the day of a pagan feast to Apollo. The citizens were drinking and engaging in acts of defilement. The strangers were questioned before the ruler Atticus. In response to the imperial decree, Trophimus said the difference between piety and demon deception is like day and night. He was beaten, and his flesh scraped to the bone while he hung from a tree. Then he was imprisoned and questioned again. When asked his rank, he said, "My rank and honor and homeland and glory and wealth is Christ." He laughed when threatened with more torture. He was beaten until the ground was red with his blood. Because he also confessed Christ, St. Sabbatius was tortured with iron claws until there was no meat left on his bones, and he gave up his spirit. Trophimus was sent to Synnada shod in sandals with sharp nails in the soles. He was stretched out and scraped for many hours, and then he was put in prison. Dorymedon was a secret Christian and chief senator. Instead of attending a pagan festival, he went to the prison to attend to Trophimus. But he was brought before the governor, and he confessed Christ. He was beaten, pierced with iron skewers, and burned. Finally, St. Trophimus and St. Dorymedon were beheaded.

COMMEMORATIONS: Trophimus, Sabbatius, and Dorymedon of Synnada; Seguanos of Gaul; Theodore of Smolensk, and his sons David and Constantine; Alexis of Zosima; Zosimas of Cilicia; Theodore of Tarsus; Igor-George of Kiev; Constantine of Bogorodsk, with two Martyrs.

WEDNESDAY

SEPTEMBER 20

St. Eustathius the Great Martyr
Abstain from meat and
dairy products, and fish.

Ephesians 6:10-17
Luke 21:12-19

*T*o offend God and to stray from the straight path of His commandments is not unusual; all human nature easily slips and quite often falls into sin. However, to remain in evil is a grievous mistake, and we must be very careful, for woe unto us if we are found unrepentant at the time of our departure.

St. Daniel of Katounakia

HYPATIUS THE BISHOP AND ANDREW THE PRESBYTER. Hypatius and Andrew were educated in a monastery. Because of their constant fasts and humility, Hypatius became a monk and Andrew a priest. The archbishop of Ephesus appointed Hypatius the Bishop of the Church of Asia. When Emperor Leo the Iconoclast learned about them and that they were teaching everyone to venerate the icons, he sent for them. First, he imprisoned them and then tortured them. The saints were dragged on the ground until they were torn to pieces, their heads were scalped, and their beards covered in pitch. Finally, they were slaughtered, and their bodies were thrown to wild dogs to be devoured.

COMMEMORATIONS: Eustathius Placidas, his wife Theopistes, and their sons Agapius and Theopistus, of Rome; Martin, Pope of Rome, Theodore, Euprepius, and 2 named Anastasius, disciples of St. Maximos the Confessor; Hilarion the Cretan, of St. Anne's Skete; Michael and Theodore of Chernigov; John of Crete; Eustathius, Archbishop of Thessalonica; Meletios, Bishop of Cyprus; John of Putivl (Ukraine); Martyrs Artemidorus and Thalus; Oleg of Bryansk; John the Confessor of Egypt, and 40 Martyrs; Hypatius and Andrew, Confessors; Synaxis of the Saints of Bryansk.

SEPTEMBER 21

Ephesians 1:1-9
Luke 4:16-22

*T*his is the only straight path into the Kingdom of Heaven. Christ walked this path and calls us to follow Him. There never was and never will be any other path to salvation but this one, shown to us by Jesus! To the beginner this path may seem too narrow and steep. But it seems this way only because our understanding of divine blessings and happiness has become distorted. Many of us regard the bitter as sweet and the sweet as bitter. However, as we come closer to God, much of what seemed difficult or bitter before will become easy or sweet, and what seemed to please before will come to seem boring and harmful. Of course, there will be trying periods in our life when the path of ascension toward God will seem exceptionally difficult. Then we should think that for every step taken there are a thousand rewards being prepared. Sufferings along this path are momentary, but the rewards are eternal. Therefore, do not fear the path of Christ, for a smooth and wide path ends in hell, but a thorny and narrow one leads to Heaven.

St. Innocent of Alaska

MARTYR EUSEBIUS OF PHOENICIA. Of his own free will, Eusebius presented himself before the ruler of Phoenicia and declared that he was a Christian. He asked the ruler why he was persecuting Christians. Angered by the accusation, the ruler ordered that Eusebius be suspended and his flesh scraped. He was tortured even more when salt was added to his wounds. Eusebius gladly endured the tortures as if someone else was suffering and not himself. Not knowing what to do, the ruler ordered his beheading. St. Eusebius received a martyr's crown from heaven.

COMMEMORATIONS: Apostle Kodratos of the Seventy; Jonah the Prophet; Jonah the Sabbaite; Eusebios, Nestabus, Zeno, and Nestor the Confessor; Eusebius of Phoenicia; Priscus of Phrygia; Daniel of Shugh Hill; Theophan of Lipetsk, and Maurice of Yuriev-Polsky; Isaac and Meletios of Cyprus; Joseph of Zaonikiev; Hypatius of Ephesus; 6 Martyrs slain by the sword; Platon of Patmos.

SEPTEMBER 22

Ephesians 1:7-17
Luke 4:22-30

*T*he time of our earthly life is priceless; during this time we decide our eternal fate.

St. Ignatius Brianchaninov

HIEROMARTYR THEODOSIUS OF BRAZI MONASTERY. As a boy in the first half of the seventeenth century, Theodosius attended divine services with his parents at the Brazi Monastery. At eighteen, he became a novice at this monastery. Later he became a monk at the Bogdana Monastery. Because he was pious and intelligent and knew the Holy Bible and some writings of the Holy Fathers, he was ordained Bishop of Radauti and later was elected Metropolitan of Moldavia. It was written in *The Chronicles of the Land of Moldavia* that the ruler of Moldavia, Dumitrascu Voda Cantacuzino was one of the worst rulers in their history. He paid the mercenary Tatars to protect his throne with a considerable sum of money, which he collected from the poor and the monasteries. Theodosius went to the ruler and asked if perhaps he was the Antichrist. These Tatars robbed the Moldavians of their fortunes and tortured Theodosius, demanding money and church treasures. When he refused, they beheaded him. His relics were hidden but discovered several times. In 1842 a future abbot of the Brazi Monastery found a container of gold coins and a note written by Theodosius which said that whoever should find it was obligated to build a monastery and three sketes, and when the third skete was finished, his relics would be found. The abbot followed these instructions and discovered the relics of St. Theodosius that exuded an exquisite fragrance.

COMMEMORATIONS: Phocas, Bishop of Sinope; Peter the Tax Collector; 26 Martyrs of Zographou Monastery; Phocas the Gardener of Sinope; Macarius of Zhabyn; Theophanes the Silent of the Kiev Caves; Theodosius of Brazi; Paraskeva (Pasha) of Diveyevo; Emmeram, bishop in Gaul; Jonah of Yashezersk; Benjamin of Romanov; Cosmas of Zographou; Martyrs Isaac and Martin; Maurice and the Theban Legion, including Candidus and Exuperius, at Agaunum (Gaul); Synaxis of the Saints of Tula; *She Who is Quick to Hear* Icon of the Mother of God.

Conception of St. John the Baptist
Fast-free

SEPTEMBER 23

Galatians 4:22-27
Luke 1:5-25

*W*ith fear and reverence may you stand in church, for our Christ is present invisibly with the holy angels. The attentive and reverent He fills to the full with grace and blessing; the heedless He censures as unworthy.

† *Elder Ephraim of Arizona*

ETHNOMARTYR GREGORY THE KALAMARAS, METROPOLITAN OF ARGOS. Gregory was from eighteenth-century Kalamata, Greece. He served as the Metropolitan of several cities. In 1819 he was initiated into the Filiki Etaireia (Friendly Society), a secret organization to overthrow the Ottoman rule of Greece and establish an independent Greek state. Gregory was given the nickname Kalamaras, indicating that he was a scholar. He turned the Secondary School of Argos into a remarkable educational unit. However, it was burned and demolished by the Turkish-Albanians. When the Revolution was betrayed, Gregory and others were imprisoned in the basement of the Great Saragio of Tripoli, a sequestered living quarters used by wives and concubines in an Ottoman household. The prisoners remained there from March until September 1821. However, a contagious disease had spread among the malnourished prisoners, and Gregory died.

COMMEMORATIONS: Conception of St. John the Baptist; Xanthippe and Polyxenia of Spain; Rhais of Alexandria; Andrew, John, Peter, and Antoninus of Syracuse, martyred in Africa; Nicholas Pantopolos at Constantinople; John of Konitsa; Arsenius of Russia; Adamnan, abbot of Iona; Gregory the Kalamaras, Metropolitan of Argos; Glorification of St. Innocent, Metropolitan of Moscow, Enlightener of Alaska and Siberia; Herineus (Popkonstantinov) of Sofia (Bulgarian Calendar); *Slovensk* Icon of the Mother of God.

SUNDAY

First Sunday of Luke
Fast-free

SEPTEMBER 24

2 Timothy 3:10-15
Luke 5:1-11

To honor a saint is to imitate a saint.

St. John Chrysostom

PROTOMARTYR AND EQUAL-TO-THE-APOSTLES THECLA.
The Apostle Paul taught and worked miracles in Iconium. A betrothed eighteen-year-old Thecla went to hear his preaching, and for three days, she listened, neither eating, drinking, or sleeping, and she resolved to forsake her betrothed. Her mother and fiancé did not want her to listen to the words of Apostle Paul. When Paul was imprisoned, Thecla followed him, and the teachings continued. But when Thecla's mother heard this, she demanded that she be burned. Apostle Paul was beaten and then exiled. Thecla was cast into flames, but hail extinguished the fire, and she remained unharmed. Then she left that place searching for Paul, who she found living in a tomb. Together they went to Antioch. As soon as they entered the city, one of the rulers became enamored with Thecla, but she thwarted him. He had her taken to the governor, and she underwent many tortures, each time emerging unharmed. The governor freed her, and she settled in a cave outside the city of Seleucia. She battled the demons and lived a life of prayer and fasting. Thecla became famous for her virtues and the miracles she worked. When the sick came to her, she taught them about Christ and healed them. The physicians of Seleucia envied Thecla, so they sent some young men to violate her. When Thecla saw the men approaching, she called upon God, and a large stone split open to shelter her. Therein, St. Thecla died at the age of nineteen.

COMMEMORATIONS: Silouan the Athonite; Coprius of Palestine; Thecla of Iconium; Stephen the First-Crowned of Serbia; Dorothea of Kashin; David and Stephen of Serbia; Abraham of Mirozh; Nicander of Pskov; Galacteon of Vologda; Isarnus of Marseilles; Gabriel of Seven Lakes; Leontius of Vilnius; Theodosius of Manyava Skete (Ukraine); Arrival in America of the first Orthodox Mission: Herman, Juvenaly, and Peter the Aleut; *Of Mirozh* and *Of the Myrtle Tree* Icons of the Mother of God.

SEPTEMBER 25

Ephesians 1:22-2:3
Luke 4:38-44

*T*o him who hungers after Christ, grace is food; to him who is thirsty, a reviving drink; to him who is cold, a garment; to him who is weary, rest; to him who prays, assurance; to him who mourns, consolation.

St. Mark the Ascetic

VENERABLE EUPHROSYNE OF ALEXANDRIA. Euphrosyne was from fifth-century Alexandria, the only child of rich and illustrious parents. Her mother died, so her father, Paphnutius, raised her. He was a pious Christian who often visited a monastery and his spiritual father, the abbot. When Euphrosyne was eighteen, her father wanted her to marry, and the abbot gave father and daughter a blessing for the marriage. However, Euphrosyne longed for the monastic life. She secretly accepted monastic tonsure from a monk who had been passing by, and she decided to enter the same monastery she had visited her whole life. But she disguised herself as a man, thinking that her father would be searching for her in a women's monastery. She named herself Smaragdos and looked like a eunuch. Euphrosyne lived in a solitary cell in prayer, fasting, and good works, and she reached a high level of spiritual perfection. For thirty-eight years, she remained unknown to the brethren. Just as she was about to die, her father visited the monastery, and Euphrosyne revealed her identity to him and then died. Paphnutius gave his wealth to the poor and the monastery and became a monk. He spent the last ten years of his life laboring in his daughter's cell.

COMMEMORATIONS: Paphnutios and 546 companions in Egypt; Euphrosyne of Alexandria, and her father Paphnutius; Euphrosyne of Suzdal; Paul and Tatta, and Sabinian, Maximus, Rufus, and Eugene; Dositheos the Recluse; Paraskeva of Kostroma; Arsenius the Great; Finbar (Barry) of Cork; Cadoc of Llancarfan; Ceolfrith (Geoffrey) of Wearmouth; Translation of the relics of St. Herman, Archbishop of Kazan; Repose of St. Sergius of Radonezh; Commemoration of the Deliverance from the Great Earthquake in Constantinople in 447, and the child who heard the "Trisagion."

Repose of St. John the Theologian
Fast-free
1 John 4:12-19
John 19:25-27, 21:24-25

*W*e must try to always be in good spirits, always joyful, because the spirits of evil want us to be sad all the time.

† *Elder Thaddeus of Vitovnica*

ARRIVAL OF THE IVERON ICON OF THE MOTHER OF GOD IN GEORGIA. The Iveron Icon was kept in the home of a certain pious widow near Nicaea. During the iconoclast persecutions, soldiers went to her house, and one of them struck the icon with a spear, and blood flowed from it. To preserve the holy icon, the widow and her son put it into the sea. Standing upright on the water, it floated to Mount Athos. As it approached the shores of Athos, the monks saw a fiery pillar on the sea rising to the heavens. They went down to the shore and saw the icon of the Panagia standing upon the water. Meanwhile, Gabriel, a pious monk of Iveron Monastery, had a dream in which the Mother of God instructed him to get her icon. He walked across the water, took up the holy icon, and placed it in the church. The following day, and for several days after, the icon was found on the monastery's gates. The Theotokos revealed to Gabriel that She did not want to be guarded, but instead, She was their Protectress. The icon was installed on the monastery gates and was named "Portaitissa" or "Gatekeeper." The Mother of God promised Gabriel that the grace and mercy of Her Son toward the monks would continue as long as the icon remained at the monastery. It is believed that if the icon disappears from Mount Athos, it will be a sign of the end of the world. On September 26, 1989, a copy of this icon arrived in Tbilisi, Georgia, from the Iveron Monastery. This copy was written by the monks of Mount Athos as a symbol of love and gratitude to the Georgian people.

COMMEMORATIONS: Holy Apostle John the Theologian; Gideon of Israel; Martyr Heras; 5 Virgin Martyrs and Monastrion; Ephraim of Perekop; Nilus the Younger; Neagoe of Wallachia; Chera (Cyra); Translation of the Head of the First-Called Apostle Andrew; Arrival of the Iveron Icon of the Mother of God in Georgia.

SEPTEMBER 27

Ephesians 3:8-21
Luke 5:33-39

If a poor man comes to you asking for bread, there is no end of complaints and reproaches and charges of idleness; you upbraid him, insult him, jeer at him. You fail to realize that you too are idle and yet God grants you gifts. Now don't tell me that you actually work hard. If you call earning money, making business deals, and caring for your possessions "work," I say, "No, that is not work. But alms, prayers, the protection of the injured and the like—these are genuine work." You charge the poor with idleness; I charge you with corrupt behavior.

St. John Chrysostom

APOSTLES MARK, ARISTARCHUS, AND ZENAS OF THE SEVENTY. These Apostles were sent by Christ to various cities to teach the kingdom of God and to heal and cast out demons. After Pentecost, the apostles were assigned to territories, and many became their first bishops. Mark taught with Apostles Paul and Barnabas. Mark's mother, Mary, had a house in Jerusalem that became a church for all the apostles. Mark became the Bishop of Byblos. Aristarchus also traveled and taught with Paul and became the bishop of Syrian Apamea. Zenas, a lawyer, was the bishop in Palestinian Lydda. Apostle Paul writes about Mark, Aristarchus, and Zenas in the Acts of the Apostles.

COMMEMORATIONS: Mark, Aristarchus, and Zenas, of the Seventy; Callistratos and 49 Martyrs; Sabbatius of Solovki; Flavian I of Antioch; Philemon and Fortunatus; Epicharis of Rome; Martyr Gaiana; Aquilina of Thessalonica; Ignatius of the Deep Stream; Anthimos the Georgian of Wallachia; Archippus of Glinsk; Herman of Volsk; 15 Martyrs, at sea; Sigebert of East Anglia; Barry, disciple of St. Cadoc; Dimitri the New of Basarab; Rachel of Borodino; Peter Polyansky of Krutitsa.

THURSDAY

SEPTEMBER 28

St. Chariton the Confessor
Fast-free
2 Corinthians 4:6-15
Luke 6:17-23

If the demons threaten suddenly to appear in the air to stupefy you and ravish your mind, do not fear them and pay no attention at all to their threat. They merely try to frighten you to see whether you attribute some importance to them or hold them in utter contempt.

St. Nilus of Sinai

VENERABLE AUXENTIOS THE WONDERWORKER OF CYPRUS. By race, Auxentios was German, and he won great praise in battles and wars. He showed himself most terrible to his enemies, but to the soldiers under his command, he was gentle, kind, and beloved. When he told his soldiers that he wanted to leave the world to become a monk, they agreed to do likewise. They took a ship to Cyprus and scattered abroad, each to a dwelling of his own choosing. Auxentios settled in a cave and gave himself over to severe fasting and discipline, cleansing his soul and body. With unceasing prayer, he received the gift of healing. After some time there, he died peacefully. Many years later, his relics were found exuding a beautiful fragrance. The men from the surrounding two villages argued as to who would claim the relics of Auxentios. Finally, they decided to put the holy relics in a cart pulled by two oxen without a guide and let them go wherever the saint guided them. They went until they reached a spot and stood firm, and there, a church was built. The Church of St. Auxentios is now inaccessible to its Greek-Cypriot inhabitants since the Turkish invasion of 1974.

COMMEMORATIONS: Prophet Baruch; Chariton the Confessor; Mark the Shepherd and Alexander, Zosimas, Alphius, Nicon, Neon, Heliodorus, and 24 others in Pisidia; Eustathios the Roman and Kallinikos; Cyril and Maria, parents of Sergius of Radonezh; Chariton of Vologda; Herodion of Iloezersk; Faustus of Riez; Hilarion of Petushki, and Michaela Ivanova; Juliana, Princess of Olshansk; Alkison of Nicopolis; Annemund of Lyons; Martyr Alexander; Wenceslaus, Prince of the Czechs; Wenceslaus of Zenkovka; Auxentius the Alaman; Leoba of Tauberbischofsheim; Eustochium, daughter of St. Paula.

SEPTEMBER 29

Galatians 5:22-6:2
Luke 6:17-23

*𝒟*o not give way to your desires, but keep a tight rein on them, directing them exclusively to one chief aim—to remain within God's will and to proceed in accordance with God's will. For then your desires will all be good and righteous, and you will remain calm in every trial, finding peace in God's will. If you believe with all sincerity that nothing can happen to you except by God's will, and if you have no other desire but to be actively doing God's will, it is self-evident that no matter what happens to you, you will always have only what you desire.

St. Theophan the Recluse

MARTYR GUDELIA OF PERSIA. Gudelia was a Christian missionary in fourth-century Persia. She converted many fire-worshipping people to Christianity. The Persians finally discovered her during the reign and persecutions of Shapur II the Great. She was arrested, but she refused to worship fire. Gudelia was imprisoned for many years without food, yet God preserved her. The Persians abandoned the idea of starving her to death and tried again to coerce her to renounce Jesus Christ. She was scalped and then nailed to wood when she refused, and St. Gudelia surrendered her soul.

COMMEMORATIONS: Dada, Gabdelas, and Casdoa of Persia; Theophanes the Merciful of Gaza; Kyriakos the Hermit of Palestine; Gudelia of Persia; Mary of Palestine; 80 Holy Martyrs of Byzantium; Tryphon, Trophimus, and Dorymedon, and 150 Martyrs in Palestine; Onuphrius of Gareji; John of Riga in Latvia; Cyprian of Ustiug; Malachias of Rhodes; Holy Martyrs massacred at Strofades Monastery; Uncovering of the relics of St. John Maximovitch, Archbishop of Shanghai and San Francisco; Translation of the relics of St. Donatos of Euroea; Synaxis of the Saints of Poltava.

SEPTEMBER 30

If some shameful thought is sown in your heart as you are sitting in your cell, watch out. Resist the evil, so that it does not gain control over you. Make every effort to call God to mind, for He is looking at you, and whatever you are thinking in your heart is plainly visible to Him. Say to your soul: "If you are afraid of sinners like yourself seeing your sins, how much more should you be afraid of God who notes everything?" As a result of this warning the fear of God will be revealed in your soul, and if you cleave to Him, you will not be shaken by the passions; for it is written: *"They that trust in the Lord shall be as Mount Zion; he that dwells in Jerusalem shall never be shaken"* (Ps. 125:1. LXX). Whatever you are doing, remember that God sees all your thoughts, and then you will never sin.

St. Isaiah the Solitary

ST. MICHAEL I, METROPOLITAN OF KIEV AND ALL RUSSIA.
The Patriarch of Constantinople sent Michael to establish Christianity in tenth-century Russia, an imposing assignment for one man. However, in just four years, Michael baptized many people in the cities of Novgorod, Kiev, and Rostov. He ordained priests and bishops and built churches. He established a monastery in Kiev and even sent missionaries to other peoples, especially the Tatars and the Bulgars. St. Michael died peacefully. His incorrupt relics were transferred to the Dormition Church of the Caves in 1730.

COMMEMORATIONS: Gregory, Bishop of Greater Armenia; Ripsimia, Gaiana, and companions, in Armenia; Michael, Great Prince of Tver; Meletius, Patriarch of Alexandria; Honorius of Canterbury; Seraphim Zagorovsky of Kharkov; Martyr Mardonius; Martyr Stratonicus; 1,000 Martyrs; 2 female Martyrs; 70 male Martyrs; Gregory of Pelsheme; Alexandra Chervyakova of Moscow; Translation of the relics of St. Michael, first Metropolitan of Kiev.

The
2024
Daily Lives, Miracles, and Wisdom of the Saints & Fasting Calendar

Preorder Now at:
www.LivesoftheSaintsCalendar.com

You can also place your order by phone at 412-736-7840
or email OrthodoxCalendarCompany@gmail.com

According to the Fathers of the Church, sweetness of prayer is not to be achieved by man, it is God's gift, and during prayer we must not seek after it, but must only endeavor to eliminate everything that prevents us from being with God.

St. John of Kronstadt

Second Sunday of Luke
Holy Protection of the Mother of God
Fast-free

OCTOBER I

2 Corinthians 6:16-7:1; Luke 6:31-36

*A*ll my happiness and unhappiness are in thoughts and desires of my heart. If the thoughts of my heart are in accord with God's truth, with the will of God, then I am at rest, filled with divine light, joy and blessedness; if not, I am uneasy, filled with spiritual darkness that corrupts the soul, with heaviness and despondency. If I replace the false and ungodly thoughts of my heart by true and godly ones, then rest, blessedness, and joy return.

St. John of Kronstadt

ST. BAVO OF GHENT. Bavo was born to a Frankish noble family, and his father was mayor of the Palace of Austrasia. Bavo was a wild young aristocrat. He contracted a beneficial marriage and had a daughter. As a soldier, he led a disorderly and undisciplined life. After his wife's death, he heard a sermon by St. Amand about the emptiness of material things. He distributed his wealth to the poor and received monastic tonsure by St. Amand. Bavo then joined him in his mission travels throughout France and Flanders. On one occasion, Bavo met a man he had sold into slavery. He had the man lead him to the town jail, bound by a chain to atone for this deed. Bavo built a monastery on his grounds and later lived as a hermit, first in a hollow tree and then in a cell in the forest. He died peacefully at the monastery in Ghent, in what is today Belgium. St. Bavo is the patron saint of several towns. He is most often depicted as a knight with a sword and a falcon.

COMMEMORATIONS: The Protection of Our Most Holy Lady the Theotokos (Slavic Calendar); Apostle Ananias of the Seventy; Romanus the Melodist; John Kukuzelis the Singer; Gregory the Singer of Mt. Athos; Savas of Vishera; Bavo of Haarlem; Domninus of Thessalonica; King Mirian and Queen Nana, and Abiathar of Mtskheta, and Sidonia; Michael of Zovia Monastery, and 36 Fathers; Remigius of Rheims; Bavo of Ghent; Mylor of Brittany; Melchizedek I of Georgia; Alexis of Petrograd; Ismael of Strelna; Joseph and Kyriakos of Bisericani; Miracle of the Pillar with the Robe of the Lord under it at Mtskheta, Georgia; *Quick to Hear* and *Pokrov* (Pskov) Icons of the Mother of God.

MONDAY *Christ Jesus came into the world to save sinners, of whom I am the chief.* Fast-free

OCTOBER 2

1 Timothy 1:12-17; Luke 6:24-30

*W*ith perfect confidence we partake Holy Communion as of the Body and Blood of Christ. For in the figure of bread His Body is given to you, and in the figure of wine His Blood, that partaking of the Body and Blood of Christ you may become of one body and blood with Him ... Do not then think of the elements as bare bread and wine, they are, according to the Lord's declaration, the Body and Blood of Christ. Though sense suggests the contrary, let faith be your stay. Instead of judging the matter by taste, let faith give you an unwavering confidence that you have been privileged to receive the Body and Blood of Christ.

St. Cyril of Jerusalem

VENERABLE THEOPHILOS THE CONFESSOR. During the reign of Leo the Isaurian in the eighth century, a persecution raged against the holy icons and those who venerated them. The iconoclasts argued that God was invisible and infinite and therefore beyond human ability to depict in images. Theophilos boldly stood before Leo and called him an atheist, lawless, and a forerunner of the Antichrist. In a rage, Leo had Theophilos harshly beaten, then imprisoned and left hungry and thirsty. Finally, St. Theophilos was sent into exile, where he died.

COMMEMORATIONS: Cyprian and Justina of Nicomedia of Antioch, and Martyr Theoctistus, at Nicomedia; Cassian the Greek; Theophilos the Confessor; Anna of Kashin; Theodore Gavras of Atra; David and Constantine of Argveti; Damaris of Athens; Andrew, Fool-for-Christ of Constantinople; Cyprian of Suzdal, Fool-for-Christ; Hadji George of Philadelphia; Theodore Ushakov, admiral of the Russian Navy; Paisy Yanevts of Pec.

OCTOBER 3

Acts 17:16-34; Luke 6:37-45

If we pray from our heart every morning, the day will be stamped by our prayer.

St. Sophrony of Essex

HIEROMARTYR DIONYSIUS OF ALEXANDRIA, AND EIGHT MARTYRS WITH HIM. Dionysius was a heathen from third-century Alexandria. He was educated, wealthy, and had an excellent civil career. He once had a vision and heard a voice from heaven instructing him about the Christian faith. He became a Christian and student of the scholar Origen. Dionysius was later made the bishop of Alexandria during a time of civil unrest and persecution. The persecutions were preceded by a year of famine, plague, and civil war. When the persecutions began, Dionysius waited four days at his home to be arrested. Finally, God commanded him to leave there, and he and his companions were arrested and held in a private home. When a crowd rushed the house, the soldiers fled, and the crowds dragged the unwilling Dionysius to safety. Fearing death, many Christians made sacrifices to the pagan gods when they were called. Others were tortured until they complied. Dionysius forgave those who lapsed under torture. Still others, many of them women, were strong Christian witnesses and were torn apart, burned, or killed by the sword. Dionysius appeared before the governor and said that he would never cease worshipping the One God. Even though Dionysius and his group were persecuted and stoned, many pagans were brought to Christianity. They were sent to a desert and endured there for twelve years. But their afflictions continued, and they all died in prison, having defended the faith to the end. Their relics were reclaimed and given a Christian burial.

COMMEMORATIONS: Dionysius the Areopagite, with Rusticus and Eleutherius; John the Chozevite, Bishop of Caesarea; Dionysius, Bishop of Alexandria and 8 Martyrs; Agathangelus of Yaroslavl; Damaris of Athens; Dionysius of the Kiev Caves; Jerome of Aegina; Martyrs Theoctistus, Theogenes, and Theotecnus; Hesychius the Silent of Mt. Horeb; Hewald the White and Hewald the Black; Leodegarius (Leger) of Autun; 24 Patron Saints of Korea; Uncovering of the relics of St. Joseph, elder of Optina Monastery.

OCTOBER 4

Ephesians 5:25-33; Luke 6:46-7:1

If a man has no worries about himself at all for the sake of love toward God and the working of good deeds, knowing that God is taking care of him, this is a true and wise hope. But if a man takes care of his own business and turns to God in prayer only when misfortunes come upon him which are beyond his power, and then he begins to hope in God, such a hope is vain and false. A true hope seeks only the Kingdom of God…the heart can have no peace until it obtains such a hope. This hope pacifies the heart and produces joy within it.

St. Seraphim of Sarov

MARTYRS FAUSTUS, GAIUS, EUSEBIUS, AND CHAEREMON, THE DEACONS. During the third century, these four deacons were disciples of St. Dionysios of Alexandria. When St. Dionysios was exiled to Libya, Gaius and Faustus were sent with him, and they suffered much together for many years. They died as martyrs, Faustus, by beheading. Eusebius and Chaeremon would visit the martyrs in prison and bury any Christians who had no one to bury them. Eusebius became the bishop of Laodicea. After confessing their faith in Christ, Eusebius and Chaeremon were beheaded.

COMMEMORATIONS: Peter of Capitolias, Bishop of Bostra in Arabia; Hierotheos, Bishop of Athens; Domnina of Syria, with daughters Bernice and Prosdoke; Ammon of Egypt; Theodore of Tamassos, Cyprus; Adauctus and Callisthene of Ephesus; Gaius, Faustus, Eusebius, and Chaeremon of Alexandria; Jonah and Nectarius of Kazan; John Lambadistos of Cyprus; Helladius and Onesimus of the Near Caves; Ammon of the Far Caves; Peter Michurin of Siberia; Vladimir Yaroslavich of Novgorod, and his mother Anna; Evdemoz the Catholicos of Georgia; Stephen Stiljanovic of Serbia, and his wife Helen; Basil Tsvetkov of Ryazan; Barsanuphius Yurchenko of Kherson; Uncovering of the relics of St. Gurias, first Archbishop of Kazan and St. Barsanuphius, Bishop of Tver; Synaxis of the Saints of Kazan.

OCTOBER 5

Ephesians 5:33-6:9; Luke 7:17-30

If we use all means and all efforts to avoid death of the body, how much more must we seek to avoid death of the soul. For there is no obstacle for a man wishing to be saved, except negligence and laziness of soul.

St. Anthony the Great

FINDING OF THE RELICS OF VENERABLE EVDOKIMOS. Nothing is known about the life of Evdokimos. In fact, that was not his name in life. In 1840 at the Monastery of Vatopedi on Mount Athos, a wall in the cemetery narthex was buckling. When the monks went to dismantle the narthex roof, it collapsed, and the rubble covered the bones. As the workers reverently unearthed them, they uncovered an intensely fragrant relic of a monk found in a kneeling position and clutching an icon of the Theotokos Bematarissa (Queen of the Altar). His skeleton was still intact. Archbishop Chrysanthos said that this was proof that the spirit of God dwelt in this monk in life and death. They decided to name him Evdokimos, which means 'who was found to be highly esteemed.' They surmised that he must have known the hour of his death, went into the bone room, and died in prayer. The monks held an all-night vigil and composed a service to him. Many miracles have been credited to Evdokimos. Once while in light sleep, a monk suffering from tuberculosis was touched by St. Evdokimos and was healed.

COMMEMORATIONS: Peter, Alexis, Jonah, Macarius, Philip, Hermogenes, Philaret, Innocent, and Tikhon of Moscow; Charitina of Amisus; Gregory the Archimandrite of Chandzoe, in Klarjeti, Georgia; Methodia of Kimolos; Damian the Healer, and Jeremiah and Matthew of the Kiev Caves; Kosmas in Bithynia; Charitina, Princess of Lithuania; John, Metropolitan of Euchaita; Mamelta of Persia; Varlaam of Chikoysk; Sabbas of Vatopedi; Hermogenes of Samos; Seraphim Amelin of Glinsk Hermitage; Gabriel Igoshkin of Melekess (Saratov); Daniel and Mishael of Turnu; Uncovering of the relics of Basil, Bishop of Kineshma; Uncovering of the relics of St. Evdokimos the Unknown, of Vatopedi, Mt. Athos.

FRIDAY

OCTOBER 6

Holy Apostle Thomas
Abstain from meat and
dairy products, and fish.
1 Corinthians 4:9-16; John 20:19-31

If we wish to acquire humility, we must ask God to send us someone who will offend us.

St. Dorotheos of Gaza

HOLY APOSTLE THOMAS. Thomas founded the Christian Church in India. There was a merchant named Abbanes, who King Gundafor had commanded to find a carpenter to build him a palace. Jesus appeared to Abbanes and sold him His slave Thomas for three pounds of silver. King Gundafor marveled at Thomas' drawings and gave him much gold, promising to return to live in the palace in three years. But Thomas gave the gold to the poor and spent two years teaching, converting, and working miracles. Upon his return, the king learned about the deception and imprisoned Thomas, but Thomas told him that he had built him a mansion in heaven. The next day, Gundafor's brother, Gad, died. An angel of the Lord took the soul of Gad to heaven and showed him his brother's mansion that was built with the gold given to Thomas. The angel returned Gad's soul to his body, and he quickly told his brother about his mansion. Immediately, the king sent his servants to the prison to bring forth Thomas. Shortly after this, Thomas baptized Gundafor and Gad. While Thomas was in India, the Dormition of the Mother of God took place. All the Apostles from the various lands were caught up by clouds and taken to Her in Gethsemane. Thomas did not arrive until the third day after the burial. He was also caught up in a cloud, and he beheld Her body ascending to heaven. She removed her belt and gave it to him, saying, "Receive this, my friend." When Thomas arrived at Her tomb, he asked the others to open it, and they found that She had vanished. In the city of Melipur, Apostle Thomas converted the wife and son of the governor. For this, he was imprisoned, tortured, and finally pierced with five spears, giving up his soul. Some of his holy relics are in India, Hungary, and Mount Athos.

COMMEMORATIONS: Apostle Thomas; Virgin Martyr Eroteis; Macarius of St. Anne's Skete; Cindeos of Cyprus; Faith and companions at Agen; Peter and 39 others; Glorification of St. Innocent, Missionary to Alaska; *Hawaiian Iveron* and *O All-Hymned Mother* Icons of the Mother of God.

OCTOBER 7

1 Corinthians 15:39-45; Luke 5:27-32

*𝒟*o your prayer rule with great care.

St. Pachomios of Chios

ST. JOHN TRIANTAPHYLLIDES, THE NEW CHRYSOSTOM AND MERCIFUL. John was born to pious parents in the region of Trebizond, Turkey, in 1836. There was no school, but someone quickly taught him to read because he was very intelligent. John became fatherless at the age of fourteen, so he was forced to find winter and summer work. At seventeen, he married a humble and revered girl named Helen. One summer, while traveling by foot, John and Helen met three angels of God in the form of people. They spoke to Helen, foretelling that John would become the village priest and serve there thirty years, then they would venerate in the Holy Land, and after John's death, he would be numbered among the saints. As they had foretold, this all took place. John served the liturgy in village churches and was taught the services and the priesthood by the monks of the local monastery. When he spoke with anyone, they felt joy, and his words exuded sweetness and grace, which is why he is called "The New Chrysostom." He was a great preacher and merciful in almsgiving. He fed the hungry, clothed the poor and orphans, gave hospitality to strangers, helped the poor pay their taxes, and worked on the village roads and bridges. During a war, he asked rich friends for money to keep the poor from starving. John also had the gift of reconciling conflicts between enemies. One time, John's grandchild was beaten by a teacher and later died. Though hurt, John forgave him and had him released from jail. After St. John's death, many miracles occurred and continue today.

COMMEMORATIONS: Sergius and Bacchus; Polychronius of Gamphanitus; Julian, Caesarius, Eusebius, and Felix, at Terracina; Leontius the Proconsul; John the Hermit and 99 Fathers of Crete; Sergius of Nurma Monastery; Joseph the Elder of Khevi; Sergius the Obedient of the Kiev Caves; Abdon of Persia; Olympiades of Persia; Osyth, Princess of Chich; Dubtach of Armagh; Valentine of Moscow; Uncovering of the relics of St. John Triantaphyllides of Chaldia in Asia Minor; Uncovering of the relics of St. Martinian of White Lake.

OCTOBER 8

If the sorrows seem to us great, it means that we have not surrendered to the will of God.

St. Silouan the Athonite

ST. TAISIA OF EGYPT. Taisia was a harlot and the daughter of a harlot. She was so beautiful that men were brought to poverty to be with her, and they fought over her, leaving the doorsteps to her house bloodstained. When the monk Paphnutios heard it, he dressed as a layman and went to see her in Egypt. He gave her some gold and pretended that he wanted to lay with her. Paphnutios asked her if there was a more private place, and she answered that he could not hide from God. The monk asked if she knew God, why did she ruin so many souls? He said that fire and torment awaited her for her sins and for those she defiled. She threw herself at his feet, asking for penance. Taisia burned all her wealth, worth forty pounds of gold, and followed Paphnutios to a convent. He sealed her door shut, leaving her only a tiny window so food could pass through. He told her that she was not worthy to speak the Lord's name but gave her a short prayer, "You who made me, have mercy on me." Once each day, she ate a little bread and water. After three years, Paphnutios told her that her sins had been forgiven. But she said, "my sins have always been before my eyes as a burden; they have never been out of my sight and I have always wept to see them." Fifteen days later, Taisia died peacefully. During all-night prayer, St. Paul the Simple had a vision of St. Taisia in heaven with the angels.

COMMEMORATIONS: Taisia (Thais) of Egypt; Pelagia the Penitent of the Mount of Olives; Virgin Martyr Pelagia of Antioch; Tryphon of Vyatka; Dositheus, abbot of Verkneostrov (Pskov); Anthony, Archbishop of Novgorod; Ignatius of Bulgaria and Mt. Athos; Jonah Lazarev of Nevel (Pskov); Demetrius Dobroserdov of Mozhaisk, Ambrose Astakhov of Aksinyino, Pachomius Turkevich of Moscow, John Khrenov, and Barlaam, Tatiana, Nicholas, Maria, and Nadezhda; Iwi of Lindisfarne; Triduana of Restalrig; Keyne of Cornwall; Philip of Gortyna (Church of Crete); Synaxis of the Saints of Vyatka.

MONDAY

OCTOBER 9

Holy Apostle James
Fast-free
1 Corinthians 4:9-16
Matthew 9:36-10:8

If a person wants to get an idea about the pyramids of Egypt, he must either trust those who have been in immediate proximity to the pyramids, or he must get next to them himself. There is no third option. In the same way a person can get an impression of God: He must either trust those who have stood and stand in immediate proximity to God, or he must take pains to come into such proximity himself.

St. Nicholas of Serbia

RIGHTEOUS ABRAHAM AND LOT HIS NEPHEW. In the year 2000 BC, ten generations after Noah, when the knowledge of God had perished from among men, the patriarch Abraham was born a pagan. He was called out of his country, modern-day Mesopotamia, to the land of Canaan. Through his willingness to sacrifice his son Isaac, Abraham portrayed the love of God, Who sacrificed His only-begotten Son. Abraham became the beginning of God's dispensation for the universal renewal and salvation of man. He received the promise that all the nations of the earth would be blessed through his seed. The trials that Abraham and his righteous nephew Lot underwent are outlined in the Book of Genesis of the Old Testament.

COMMEMORATIONS: Holy Apostle James, son of Alphaeus; Andronikos and Athanasia of Egypt; Forefather Abraham and his nephew Righteous Lot; Demetrius, Bishop of Alexandria; Publia the Confessor of Antioch; Peter of Galatia; Maximos of Persia; Stephen the Blind, King of Serbia; Stephen Lazarevic, King of Serbia; Dionysius (Denis) of Paris; Uncovering of the relics of St. Sebastian (Fomin) of Optina and Karaganda; *Korsun* (Kherson) Icon of the Mother of God.

OCTOBER 10

Philippians 1:8-14; Luke 8:1-3

It ... sometimes happens that we seek things entirely related to salvation without our eager petitions and devoted actions, and yet we do not immediately obtain what we ask. The result of our petition is postponed to some future time, as when we daily ask the Father on bended knees, saying, 'Thy kingdom come,' and nevertheless we are not going to receive the kingdom as soon as our prayer is finished, but at the proper time. It is a fact that this is often done with benevolent foresight by our Maker, so that the desires [inspired by] our devotion may increase by deferment. When they have advanced more and more by daily growth, at length they embrace perfectly the joys we are seeking.

St. Bede the Venerable

ST. BASSIAN OF CONSTANTINOPLE. Bassian was from Syria, and he lived during the fifth-century reign of Emperor Marcian. He came to Constantinople and founded a monastery. Bassian was filled with virtues, and his prayers worked countless miracles, so the emperor built a church dedicated to him. St. Matrona was one of his three hundred disciples. By his example and words, Bassian converted many to Christianity and helped them along the path to salvation. He lived into great old age and died peacefully. He was buried in the church that Marcian had built for him.

COMMEMORATIONS: Eulampius and Eulampia at Nicomedia and 200 Martyrs; Bassian of Constantinople; Theotecnus of Antioch; Pinytus of Knossos on Crete; Theophilus the Confessor of Bulgaria; Innocent of Penza; Andrew of Totma, Fool-for-Christ; Paulinus of York; Ambrose of Optina; 26 Martyrs of Zographou Monastery on Mt. Athos by the Latins; Theodore Pozdeyevsky of Volokolamsk; Synaxis of the Saints of Volhynia: Job of Pochaev, Macarius of Kanev, Yaropolk-Peter of Vladimir, Theodore, Prince of Ostrog, Stephen and Amphilochius of Vladimir, and Juliana Olshanskaya; Of the Akathist Zographou Icon of the Mother of God.

OCTOBER 11

Acts 8:26-39; Luke 8:22-25

*W*hoever prays carelessly, prays sinfully.

† *Elder Efstratios of Glinsk*

ST. SAVVAS OF VATOPEDI, THE FOOL FOR CHRIST. Savvas secretly left home at the age of eighteen to live as a monastic in obedience to a strict elder at a cell of Vatopedi Monastery on Mount Athos. He patiently endured chastity, hunger, thirst, vigils, standing, and unceasing prayer. Out of great humility, he refused the priesthood and even hid on the day of his ordination. Because of enemy raids on Athos, Savvas settled in Ephesus of Asia Minor. He left for Cyprus, and after fervent prayer, he decided to take on the difficult path of foolishness for Christ. He wandered naked, homeless, silent, hungry, eating wild greens only once a week, and exposed to the elements. Some disdained and beat him; others respected and honored him, considering him a saint. Honor bothered Savvas, as dishonor would bother an ordinary person, so Savvas moved often to avoid praise. Angels and Christ appeared to him, giving him great consolation. He worked many miracles; even lions obeyed him. Savvas once came across a woman carrying her dead child. Through his prayers, he raised the child from the dead. Later, Savvas returned to Vatopedi Monastery, where he broke his years of silence. He became a chanter, a reader, a server in the dining room, and a nurse, and he had many divine manifestations. During great civil strife in Constantinople, the emperor and Church leaders attempted to persuade Savvas to become Patriarch, but he also eluded this honor. He died peacefully in Constantinople in the year 1349. About 500 years after his death, the relics of St. Savvas were found fragrant.

COMMEMORATIONS: Apostle Philip of the Seventy; Nectarius, Arsakios, and Sisinios, Archbishops of Constantinople; Theophanes Graptus the Confessor; Zenais and Philonilla of Tarsus; Kenneth of Aghaboe (Ireland); Savvas of Vatopedi; Theophanes the Faster of the Kiev Caves; Leonid of Optina; Philotheos of Mt. Athos; Jonah of Pergamos; Germanos the Hagiorite; Ethelburga of Barking; Cainnech (Kenneth) of Aghaboe; Gommar of Lier; Transfer of the relics of St. Melaine of Rennes; Synaxis of the Venerable Elders of Optina.

OCTOBER 12

Philippians 1:20-27; Luke 9:7-11

*W*ho will be so presumptuous and so blind as to think that he can preserve his own without daily help from the Lord? This is how it is, especially in view of what the Lord Himself says: *'As a branch cannot bear fruit all by itself but must remain part of the vine, neither can you unless you remain in Me'* (Jn. 15:4). *'You can do nothing without Me'* (Jn. 15:5). Since He says this, since He asserts that nobody can show forth the fruits of the Spirit unless he has been inspired by God and has worked with God, it would be foolish, indeed sacrilegious, to attribute any good actions of ours to our own effort rather than to the divine grace.

St. John Cassian

MARTYR DOMNINA OF ANAZARBUS. Domnina was a third-century victim of the Christian persecutions of Diocletian. When she was arrested and made to stand before the governor, she confessed her faith in Jesus Christ. For this, she was beaten with bullwhips and rods, her feet burned with heated irons, her bones broken, and her joints dislocated. Yet she lived to be imprisoned, and she gave up her soul there.

COMMEMORATIONS: Martin, Bishop of Tours; Symeon the New Theologian; Domnina of Anazarbus and Anastasia of Rome; Probus, Tarachus, and Andronicus at Tarsus; Maximilian of Noricum; Theodotus of Ephesus; Jason of Damascus; Juventinus and Maximinus of Antioch; Euphrosyne the Faster of Siberia; Amphilochius, Macarius, Tarasius, and Theodosius of Glushitsa Monastery; Theosevios the God-bearer of Arsinoe; Martyrs Andromachos and Diodoros; Arsenius of Svyatogorsk; Juvenal of Ryazan; Lawrence Levchenko of Optina; Martyrs Malfethos and Anthea; 70 Martyrs beheaded; Nicholas Mogilevsky of Alma-Ata; Edwin of Northumbria; Wilfrid of York; Mobhi of Ireland; Synaxis of All Saints of Athens; Translation of the relics of St. Sabbas the Sanctified from Rome to Jerusalem; Transfer of a part of the Life-creating Cross of the Lord from Malta to Gatchina; *Jerusalem, Rudensk,* and *Kaluga* Icons of the Mother of God.

OCTOBER 13

Philippians 1:27-2:4; Luke 9:12-18

C leanse your mind from anger, remembrance of evil, and shameful
thoughts, and then you will find out how Christ dwells in you.

St. Maximos the Confessor

ST. GERALD OF AURILLAC. Gerald suffered an illness as a child and
may have been disfigured by acne. Later in life, he suffered blindness. He
was born into Gallo-Roman nobility in the late ninth century and was in
feudal service to the king in Paris. Gerald considered joining a religious
order but was persuaded by the Bishop of Rodez that he could do more
good by remaining a layman. However, he was secretly tonsured, and he
consecrated his life in service to God. He gave away his possessions, took a
vow of chastity, and prayed each day. Gerald founded a church and monastery on his estate in Aurillac, where he was later buried in the year 909.
He is considered a great example of a celibate Christian aristocrat and is
the patron saint of counts and bachelors. Because he suffered from poor
health and blindness during his life, St. Gerald is also the patron saint of
the disabled, handicapped, and physically challenged.

COMMEMORATIONS: Karpos, Papylos, Agathodoros, and Agathon-
ike at Pergamus; Zlata (Chryse) of Meglin; Dioscoros of Egypt; Nicetas
the Confessor; Florentius of Thessalonica; Benjamin of Persia; Venantius
of Tours; Benjamin of the Kiev Caves; Jacob of Hamatoura; Anthony of
Chkondidi and James the Elder; Martyr Antingonus; Luke of Demena;
Cogman of Lochaish; Gerald of Aurillac (Gaul); Bosiljka of Pasjane; Translation of the relics of St. Savvas the Sanctified from Venice to Jerusalem;
Uncovering of the relics of St. Thaddeus Uspensky, Archbishop of Tver;
Translation into Moscow of the *Iveron* Icon of the Mother of God.

OCTOBER 14

1 Corinthians 15:58-16:3
Luke 6:1-10

*P*erfect love for one's neighbor is contained in love for God —which has no limit of perfection, which is eternal. Growth in God's love is eternal, because love is eternal God (1 John 4:16). Love for one's neighbor is the foundation of all other love. Beloved Brother! Seek to reveal in yourself true spiritual love for your neighbor. Having acquired it, you will acquire love for God, and you will enter the gates of resurrection—the gates of the heavenly Kingdom.

St. Ignatius Brianchaninov

YAKHROMSK ICON OF THE MOTHER OF GOD. In 1482, as a young man, St. Kosmas of Yakhromsk served a neighbor landowner by traveling with him to seek healing for his illness. They stopped not far from the Yakhrom River, and the sick landowner fell asleep. Kosmas saw a bright light coming from a tree, and there the holy icon appeared, and he heard a voice from it, saying, "Attend and understand the words of life. Live a God-pleasing life and seek the joy of the righteous, and then you will delight in eternal blessings." Many years later, an angel told Kosmas to return the icon to the place where he had found it, and the place filled with light again. He built a monastery in honor of the Mother of God and placed the icon within it. The icon was placed in the Tsar's Church of the Annunciation in Moscow in the seventeenth century.

COMMEMORATIONS: Cosmas the Hymnographer, Bishop of Maiuma; Silvanus of Gaza and with him 40 Martyrs of Egypt and Palestine; Nazarius, Gervasius, Protasius, and Celsius of Milan; Ignatius, Metropolitan of Mithymna; Cosmas, abbot of Yakhromsk; Peter Apselamus of Eleutheropolis in Palestine; Nikola Sviatosha, Prince of Chernigov; Ignatios, Metropolitan of Mithymna; Parasceva (Petka) the New of the Balkans, whose relics are in Iasi, Romania; Pachomios of Chios; Protasius of Milan; Manacca, abbess of Cornwall; Burchard, first bishop of Wurzburg; Commemoration of the Miracle of St. Paraskevi on the island of Chios; *Yakhromsk* Icon of the Mother of God.

Sunday of the Seventh Ecumenical Council
Fast-free

OCTOBER 15

Titus 3:8-15; Luke 8:5-15

If the evening is difficult for you, be silent and endure, knowing that Christ was crucified in the evening, and in the morning He resurrected.

St. Seraphim Sobolev

PROSPERESS OF LOAVES ICON OF THE MOTHER OF GOD. The name of this icon means "Helper for people in their labours for the acquiring of their daily bread." It was written at the blessing of the great Russian ascetic of the nineteenth century, Elder Ambrose of the Optina wilderness monastery. Ambrose had a childlike faith in the Mother of God. He revered all her feast days and doubled his prayer on these days. Not far from his monastery, he founded a women's monastery in honor of the Kazan Icon of the Mother of God. In the "Prosperess of Loaves" Icon, the Mother of God is shown sitting upon the clouds, and her hands are extended in blessing. Beneath her is a field of grass, flowers, and sheaves of rye. Ambrose chose the date of October 15 to celebrate this icon, which is also the day he was buried. Before he died, he ordered many photo replicas and had them sent to his spiritual children. The first miracle witnessed from this icon was in 1890, when there was a famine throughout Russia due to crop failure. But in the area of the monastery, grain was produced. A year later, there was a drought at the women's monastery, and a copy of the icon was sent. Soon after a Molieben was celebrated before the holy icon, it rained, and the drought ended.

COMMEMORATIONS: Sabinus, Bishop of Catania; Barses the Confessor, Bishop of Edessa; Lucian, presbyter of Greater Antioch; Lucian, presbyter of the Kiev Caves; John, Bishop of Suzdal; Dionysius, Archbishop of Suzdal; Euthymios the New of Thessalonica; Aurelia of Strasburg; Thecla, abbess of Ochsenfurt (Germany); Valerian Novitsky of Telyadovich; Athanasius, Bishop of Kovrov; Synaxis of the New Hieromartyrs of Belorussia; *Prosperess of Loaves* (Multiplier of Wheat) Icon of the Mother of God.

MONDAY

OCTOBER 16

St. Longinus the Centurion
Fast-free
Philippians 2:12-15
Matthew 27:33-54

top entirely talkativeness and joking, because, as we have said, where there is talkativeness (outspokenness) the fear of God departs.

St. Daniel of Katounakia

MARTYR LONGINUS THE CENTURION. Longinus served at Christ's Crucifixion and was a guard at His sealed tomb. When he saw the daylight sky turn dark and witnessed the earthquake, he said, "Truly this was the Son of God" (Matthew 27:54). Longinus was soon baptized. The Jewish elders bribed the guards at the tomb to falsely say that the followers of Jesus had taken the body, but Longinus would not accept the bribe. Because of this, soldiers were sent to his home to return with his head. He was found there in fasting and prayer, converting many pagans to the faith. Having foreknowledge of their arrival, he went out to meet them and showed them hospitality, but they did not recognize him. They ate and slept in his home while Longinus spent the night praying. He told his family what would soon happen. In the morning, he presented himself to the soldiers, and though they were embarrassed by his kindness, he persuaded them to carry out their orders. Pilate threw the head of Longinus into a dung heap outside the city. After many years, a blind woman had her son take her to the holy places in Jerusalem, but he died there. Longinus appeared to her in her distraught state and said if she uncovered his head, he would restore her sight and show her her son in heaven. She made her way to the largest dung-heap outside the city and groping she came upon a skull, and immediately she received her sight. She took the head of St. Longinus, cleaned it, and gave it burial in Cappadocia.

COMMEMORATIONS: Longinus the Centurion, who stood at the Cross of the Lord; Isaurus and Aphrodisius, who suffered with St. Longinus; Longinus the Gatekeeper of the Kiev Caves; Martyrs Dometius, Leontios, Terence, and Domninus; Malus the Hermit; John and Longinus of Yaranga, monks of Solovki; Eupraxia of Pskov; Gall, Enlightener of Switzerland; Longinus of Koryazhemka; Domna, Fool-for-Christ of Tomsk; John of Tourkoleka.

OCTOBER 17

*H*umility is the only thing that no devil can't imitate.
St. John Climacus

IN GIVING BIRTH, YOU PRESERVED YOUR VIRGINITY ICON OF THE MOTHER OF GOD. This icon was transferred to the Nikolaev Peshkov Monastery of the Moscow diocese by a merchant named Alexis around the year 1780. Giving his wealth to the abbot, Alexis became a monk there, and the icon remained in his cell. The icon was painted in oil on canvas instead of the traditional egg tempera on wood. When Alexis died, the abbot placed the icon over a chapel's exit door on a street near the monastery. In 1827 a captain named Platon was passing by the chapel at night, and he saw an extraordinary light emanating from the icon. Another time during some difficult circumstances, in a dream, he saw the radiant icon of the Mother of God in the clouds above the chapel, and he heard a voice saying, "If you wish to be delivered from temptation, pray before this icon." The icon was then taken to the monastery and put in an ornamental case. In 1848, during a cholera outbreak, the people prayed before it and were healed. On the day of the icon's feast in 1888, the royal family was miraculously saved in a train crash. Emperor Alexander III ordered all churches in Russia to offer a thanksgiving service to the In Giving Birth, You Preserved Your Virginity Icon of the Mother of God, and copies were made for many churches. In the 1920s, the original icon was lost. In modern times, a new copy of the icon was created and placed in the St. Nicholas Cathedral, and it also became famous for miracles. On Sunday, March 17, 2019, during the Divine Liturgy, an abundant myrrh-streaming of the icon took place.

COMMEMORATIONS: Hosea the Prophet; Unmercenaries Cosmas and Damian of Arabia, and Leontios, Anthimos, and Euprepios; Alexander of Semipalatinsk; Anthony of Novgorod; Jacinthus and Callistus of Verkhoturye; Shushanik (Susanna) of Georgia; Andrew of Crete; Joseph of Georgia; Ethelred and Ethelbert of Kent; Bartholomew, Fool-for-Christ; Translation of the relics of St. Lazarus (of the Four Days in the tomb).

Holy Apostle and Evangelist Luke
Strict Fast
Colossians 4:5-11, 14-18
Luke 10:16-21

*W*hen you hear someone being accused, even though it may be true, never add more accusations, but always say something positive and be sorry for the person.

St. George Karslides

VENERABLE SYMEON AND THEODORE, FOUNDERS OF THE HOLY MONASTERY OF MEGA SPELAION. Symeon and Theodore were brothers, and they lived on Mount Athos under the guidance of Venerable Euthymios the New. They were ordained to the priesthood and were seen as wise teachers, distinguished for their asceticism. They later went to venerate the sacred places in the Holy Land, visited Mount Sinai, and defended the icons in Thessalonica and Thessaly. After a vision, they went to the Great Cave (Mega Spelaion) in the Peloponnese, where they met with St. Euphrosyne. That is where they found a miraculous icon of the Theotokos and they built a monastery. They traveled all over the Peloponnese with their fervent preaching, supporting the faithful in the Orthodox doctrines, and instructing their disciples. Having received foreknowledge of the end of their lives, they died peacefully, and their relics became a source of healing. Their biographers describe them as the first famous ascetics of Mount Athos, organizers of monasticism, defenders of the icons, builders of churches, missionaries, and miraculous saints.

COMMEMORATIONS: Apostle and Evangelist Luke; Marinos the Elder at Anazarbus; Mnason, Bishop of Cyprus; Julian the Hermit of Mesopotamia; Gabriel and Cirmidol of Egypt; David of Serpukhov; Symeon, Theodore, and Euphrosyne, who found the icon of the Mother of God in the Great Cave of the Peloponnese; Peter of Cetinje, Metropolitan of Montenegro; James the Deacon; Isidore, Irene, and George of Crete; 40 Children Martyrs; Gwen and Selevan, Welsh missionaries, in Brittany; Uncovering of the relics of St. Joseph of Volokolamsk.

OCTOBER 19

Acts 2:14-21; Luke 9:49-56

He who restrains his mouth from speech guards his heart from passions.

St. Isaac the Syrian

NEW MONK MARTYR NICHOLAS DVALI OF JERUSALEM. Nicholas' parents directed him toward the spiritual life. At twelve years of age, he was tonsured a monk and settled in Jerusalem at the Holy Cross Monastery. While there, he developed a burning desire to die a martyr. He publicly confessed his faith to some Godless men, and he was arrested and tormented, but Christians rescued him. Then he relocated to a Georgian monastery in Cyprus, and still, he implored the Lord to make him worthy of the crown of martyrdom. One day while praying before the icon of St. John the Baptist, he heard a voice telling him to go back to Jerusalem. The Theotokos and St. John the Baptist appeared to Nicholas' abbot, announcing that it was the Lord's will for Nicholas to travel to Damascus. There Nicholas entered a mosque and confessed Christ. He was beaten and imprisoned, and again Christians procured his release. But he immediately resumed denouncing their ungodly ways. Again, he was beaten and lashed 500 times and then imprisoned. St. John the Baptist miraculously healed him, and Nicholas was released. As he was preparing to go to Jerusalem, he was recognized and sent to the head judge. When Nicholas defended his faith again, he was sentenced to death. Before they beheaded him, Nicholas thanked God, having been accounted worthy to die for His name's sake. After his head was severed, he cried out seven times, saying, "Glory to Thee, O Christ our God." The Persians burned his body, and for three days, a pillar of light shone on his relics. Shortly after, Nicholas' spiritual father had a vision of Nicholas with Great Martyr George and a host of saints. Nicholas said, "Behold me and the place where I am, and from this day cease your sorrowing for me."

COMMEMORATIONS: John of Kronstadt; Prophet Joel; Varus and 7 others with him; Sadoc (Sadoth) of Persia, and 128 Martyrs; Leontius the Philosopher; Gabriel of St. Elias Skete; Demetrius of Moscow; Alexis of Petrograd; Anthony of the Kiev Caves; Cleopatra and John in Egypt.

OCTOBER 20
2 Timothy 2:1-10; Luke 10:1-15

*W*e sin against God in so many ways when we are cruel, unforgiving and so forth. The servant who receives forgiveness of his Master and who then refuses to forgive, not only sinned against the other servant, he sinned against his Master…If we fail to forgive our brother, our neighbor, then we are sinning against God.

St. John Chrysostom

ST. ACCA, BISHOP OF HEXHAM. As a young man, Acca joined the household of Bosa, Bishop of York. He later became a disciple of St. Wilfrid, the Bishop of York and later of Hexham (England). Acca accompanied him on his journeys through England and the continent. When Wilfrid died, Acca became his successor. St. Bede called Acca "the dearest and best-loved of all bishops on this earth." Acca completed and adorned the churches that Wilfred had left. He also invited an excellent singer named Maban to teach church harmony to him and the people, even though he was already a great chanter. After twenty-three years, Acca became the Bishop of Whithorn in southern Scotland. He died eight years later in 740. One hundred ninety years later, a priest at Hexham had a divine revelation to transfer the relics of Acca to a place in the church that was more fitting. St. Acca's vestments were found in pristine condition and were displayed for veneration, and many miracles occurred. Anyone attempting to infringe upon the sanctuary was driven away in a terrible manner. Once, a priest's younger brother was charged with keeping an eye on some of St. Acca's relics. The youth thought the relics would greatly enrich another church. So two times, he attempted to remove them, and both times a fierce heat drove him back.

COMMEMORATIONS: Artemios at Antioch; Aborsam and Senoe of Persia; Zebinas of Caesarea, and Germanos, Nicephorus, Anthony, and Manatho; Gerasimos the New of Cephalonia; Matrona of Chios; Nicholas of Yaroslavl; Artemius of Verkola; Herman of Alatyr; Theodosius of Svyatogorsk; Acca of Hexham; Basil of Trebizond; Andronikos of Crete; Uncovering of the relics of St. Nikodim Kononov, Bishop of Belgorod.

OCTOBER 21

2 Corinthians 9:6-11
Luke 7:1-10

*L*aziness throws us down even from Heaven, while discouragement hurls us down even to the very abyss of wickedness. Indeed, we can quickly return from there if we do not become discouraged.
St. John Chrysostom

NEW MARTYR AND CONFESSOR BESSARION OF ROMANIA.
Bessarion was a Serb born in Bosnia in 1714. He longed for the monastic life, and at the age of eighteen, he went on pilgrimage to the Holy Land. He was tonsured a monk at the Monastery of St. Savvas at the age of twenty-four. At the Monastery of Pakrou in Slavonia, he served as a deacon for seven years, then was ordained to the priesthood. About this time, the Romanian Orthodox Church had been forced into union with Rome. The Patriarch heard of Bessarion's holy life and reputation as a preacher. He sent him to defend the Orthodox faith in the Carpathian Mountains and rescue the Orthodox people from Uniatism. Bessarion encouraged them not to abandon the faith their fathers had passed down to them. He would set up a wooden cross in the middle of each village, and people would gather to hear him speak. However, he was arrested by the Austrian army and taken to Vienna. He was placed on trial and imprisoned by the order of Empress Maria Theresa. St. Bessarion suffered much for his confession of Orthodoxy. After about a year in chains and torture, he gave up his soul to God.

COMMEMORATIONS: Hilarion the Great of Gaza; Dasios, Gaios, and Zotikos at Nicomedia; Hilarion, Metropolitan of Kiev; Hilarion of Pskov; Hilarion of Meglin; Hilarion of the Kiev Caves; Philotheos of Mt. Athos; Socrates and Theodote of Ancyra; John of Monemvasia; Theophilus and James of Omutch; Martyrs Azes, Eucratus, Zachariah, Andrew, Stephen, Paul, and Peter; Baruch, monk; Ursula of Cologne and companions; Condedus of Fontenelle; Fintan Munnu; Malathgeny of Cluain-Edneach; Paulinus of Mogilev; Alexis of Voronezh; Damian of Kursk; Neophytus of Moscow; 63 Martyrs of Jerusalem; New Martyrs and Confessors of Romania: Bessarion, Sophronius, Opera, Moses, and John.

SUNDAY

OCTOBER 22

Sixth Sunday of Luke
Fast-free
Galatians 1:11-19; Luke 8:26-39

*R*ejoice at every opportunity of showing kindness to your neighbor as a true Christian who strives to store up as many good works as possible, especially the treasures of love. Do not rejoice when others show you kindness and love—consider yourself unworthy of it; but rejoice when an occasion presents itself for you to show love. Show love simply, without any deviation into cunning thoughts, without any trivial, worldly, covetous calculations, remembering that love is God Himself. Remember that He sees all your ways, sees all the thoughts and movements of your heart.

St. John of Kronstadt

VENERABLE LOT OF EGYPT. Lot was a fifth-century Egyptian ascetic from a monastery close to the town of Arsinoe. He once spoke with his abbot, Elder Joseph, about his spiritual life. Lot said that he fasted as much as he could, prayed constantly, spoke little, often thought on the ways of the Lord, and worked at abstaining from evil thoughts. Lot asked, "What shall I do to be saved?" Abbot Joseph stretched his hands toward heaven, and his fingers became ten flames. He said, "If you desire it, you can become entirely as a fire." Lot was an inspiration to many, setting them on the path to salvation.

COMMEMORATIONS: Lot of Egypt; Seven Youths (Seven Sleepers) of Ephesus: Maximilian, Jamblichus, Martinian, Dionysius, Antoninus, Constantine, and John; Abercius, Bishop of Hierapolis; Alexander, Heraclius, Anna, Elizabeth, Theodota, and Glyceria, at Adrianople; Paul and Theodore of Rostov; Rufus of *The Paradise*; Martyr Zachariah; Theodoret at Antioch; Alexander of Cherkassy; Mellon of Rouen; James of Luga and Omutch, disciple of Theophilus of Omutch; Eulalios of Lambousa; Seraphim, Archbishop of Uglich, Menas Shelaev and Herman Polyansky, archimandrites, and Alexander Lebedev, Vladimir Sobolev, Basil Bogoyavlensky, and Alexander Andreyev, priests; *Kazan* Icon of the Mother of God commemorating the deliverance of Moscow from the Poles and Lithuanians; *Andronicus* Icon of the Mother of God.

*T*he one thing that can help a married couple is for each spouse not to justify himself or herself. If spouses justify themselves, they receive no benefit—no matter how many spiritual books they read. If they have a good disposition, if they have a Spiritual Father and obey him, they will not have problems. But it cannot be done without a spiritual referee.

St. Paisios the Athonite

VENERABLE NIKEPHOROS OF CHARSIANOS, CONSTANTI-NOPLE. In the year 1001, Nikephoros was a monk at Esphigmenou Monastery on Mount Athos. He was sent to Charsianos, a province and Byzantine fortress in Constantinople, which Emperor Basil II annexed. For thirty-six years, Nikephoros worked there to contribute to the expansion of Christianity. He also established a monastery. As a reward, his retirement was provided for, and he resettled on Mount Athos. He had the privilege of feasting at the table of Protos Theoktistos, who had authority over the monasteries on Mount Athos. When the Protos died, St. Nikephoros was bequeathed an estate. He died in peace.

COMMEMORATIONS: Apostle James, the brother of the Lord; Ignatius, Patriarch of Constantinople; Petronius of Egypt, disciple of St. Pachomius the Great; Nicephoros of Constantinople; Makarios the Roman of Mesopotamia; Elisha of Lavrishevo, Belorussia; Eusebius Rozhdestvensky, Archbishop of Shadrinsk, and Vladimir Ambartsumov of Moscow; Oda of Scotland; Ethelfleda of Romsey; Translation of the relics of St. James of Borovichi, Wonderworker of Novgorod.

OCTOBER 24

Colossians 1:1-3, 7-11
Luke 11:1-10

*K*eep careful watch, to ensure that the enemy does not make off with any who are off guard or remiss; and that no heretic may pervert part of what you have been given. Accepting the faith is like putting into the bank the money we have given you; God will ask you for an account of this deposit.

St. Cyril of Jerusalem

THE JOY OF ALL WHO SORROW ICON OF THE MOTHER OF GOD, OF MOSCOW. There are many versions of the Joy of All Who Sorrow Icon, and many of them are miraculous. According to Russian chronicles, the icon was written in 1683 by the royal artist Bezmin. It became widespread after a copy of the icon from the Church of the Transfiguration on Ordynka Street in Moscow miraculously healed Euphemia, the sister of Patriarch Joachim, from a wound on her side and an illness that the doctors failed to treat. Euphemia prayed with tears to the Mother of God. She heard a voice telling her to go to the Church of the Transfiguration and have the priest serve a moleben and sanctification of the waters before the icon, and she would receive healing. Euphemia did so and was immediately healed. It is believed that the original icon was lost. Some versions of the icon portray groups of sufferers standing on either side of the Mother of God, and She is seen standing on the clouds, with saints and angels surrounding her.

COMMEMORATIONS: Arethas of Omir and with him 4,299 Martyrs; Syncletica and her 2 daughters; Elesbaan, King of Ethiopia; Theophilus, Arethas, and Sisoes, hermits of the Kiev Caves; Sebastiana at Heraclea, disciple of Apostle Paul; Acacius of Armenia; John, recluse of the Pskov Caves; Zosimas, elder of Siberia; Athanasius, Patriarch of Constantinople; Laurence, Bishop of Balakhna, Alexis Porfiriev, and Alexis Neidhardt; Senoch, abbot of Tours; Martyrs Mark, Soterichus, and Valentine; Martyr Nerdon; Arethas Mitrenin, hieromonk of Valaam; Abramius and Abraham in Najran of Arabia Felix; Maglorius, Bishop of Dol; *Joy of All Who Sorrow* Icon of the Mother of God, of Moscow (1688).

OCTOBER 25

Colossians 1:18-23; Luke 11:9-13

*D*on't disregard your salvation. Don't let this temporal life deprive you from the eternal one.

St. Anthony the Great

NEW CONFESSOR MATRONA VLASOVA OF DIVEYEVO. Matrona was born in 1889 into a family of peasants from the village of Puzo, Novgorod province of Russia. She was orphaned at the age of six and placed in the care of the Seraphim-Diveyevo monastery. She had an early talent for drawing, and she became a nun there. At the age of 38, in 1927, the monastery was closed. Matrona and three other sisters moved to a village where they led a peaceful life, making embroidery for a living. After five years, the sisters were arrested for anti-Soviet propaganda, and Matrona was sentenced to three years in a camp. When this ended, she worked as a cantor, guard, and sacristan at a village church. But a year later, she was arrested again as a contra-revolutionary religious fascist and sentenced to ten years where she worked as a janitor. After her release, she worked for the church. Two years later, she was arrested again and exiled. In the last years of her life, she returned to her native village of Puzo. Locals remember her as meek and quiet, and she spent most of her day in prayer. She died peacefully in 1963. In 2001 the Holy Synod Council of the Russian Orthodox Church added her to the Synaxis of New Martyrs and Confessors of Russia.

COMMEMORATIONS: Tabitha (Dorcas) of Joppa; Anastasius the Fuller at Salona; George of Amastris; Marcian and Martyrius the Notaries; Macarius of Paphos on Cyprus; Crispinus and Crispinianus, martyred under Diocletian; 2 Martyrs of Thrace; Martyrius the Deacon and Martyrius the Recluse of the Kiev Caves; Matrona the Confessor of Diveyevo; Martyrs Vallerios and Chrysaphus; Martyr Savinos; Philadelphus and Polycarp; Martyrs Nikephoros and Stephen; Martyrs Faustus, Basil, and Silouan, at Darion; Martyrs Papias, Diodorus, and Claudius, of Pamphylia; Varus of Egypt; Martyr Vallerinos; Front of Perigueux; Miniatus of Florence; Commemoration of the Great Miracle of Panagia Prousiotissa.

St. Demetrios the Great Martyr
Fast-free

2 Timothy 2:1-10; John 15:17-16:2

*L*eave the past to the mercy of God, the present to His love, and the future to His Providence.

St. Hesychius of Jerusalem

GREAT MARTYR AND WONDERWORKER DEMETRIOS THE MYRRHGUSHER. Demetrios was baptized a Christian by his parents. His father was the Roman proconsul of Thessalonica during the early fourth-century reign of Emperor Maximian. When he died, Maximian appointed Demetrios to succeed his father. Maximian charged Demetrios with exterminating Christianity. Instead, Demetrios immediately began to preach the Christian faith and root out pagan customs. When Maximian learned that Demetrios was a Christian, he summoned him. Knowing his fate, he had his servant Lupus give away his earthly possessions to the poor, and he fasted and prayed in preparation for martyrdom. Standing before the emperor, Demetrios confessed his faith in Christ and his disgust for the idols. Maximian had him put in prison, where an angel appeared, saying, "Peace be with thee, thou sufferer for Christ; be brave and strong!" At dawn, soldiers entered his cell and killed him with spears. His body was cast out to be devoured by wild dogs, but Christians secretly took him for burial. A small church was built over his relics. One hundred years later, when a much larger church was being built on the same spot, the incorrupt relics of St. Demetrios were uncovered. Since the seventh century, fragrant myrrh has flowed beneath the saint's crypt. When Emperor Justinian attempted to move the saint's relics to Constantinople, flames shot out of the tomb, and a voice commanded him, "Leave them there, and don't touch!" St. Demetrios is the defender and protector of Thessalonica.

COMMEMORATIONS: Demetrios the Myrrhgusher and Lupus; Athanasios of Medikion; Anthony of Vologda; Theophilus of the Kiev Caves; Demetrius of Basarabov; Demetrios of Misti-Konakli; Alexander of Guria; Glykon, Leptina, Artemiodorus, and Basil; Joasaph of Mt. Athos; Cedd of Lastingham; Eata of Hexham; Luian and Marcian; Boris of Nevrokop; Translation of the relics of St. George of Ioannina.

OCTOBER 27

Colossians 2:1-7; Luke 11:23-26

A man in this world must solve a problem: to be with Christ, or to be against Him. And every man decides this, whether he wants to or not. He will either be a lover of Christ or a fighter of Christ. There is no third option.

St. Justin Popovich

MARTYRS CAPITOLINA AND EROTEIS OF CAPPADOCIA. Capitolina was a wealthy noblewoman from Cappadocia, and her handmaiden was Eroteis. During the third-century persecutions of the emperor Diocletian, Capitolina was brought to trial as a Christian. Before the governor Zilikinthus, she confessed Jesus Christ as the true God. When she resisted all threats and persuasions to renounce her faith, she was sentenced to beheading and put in prison. Eroteis went to the prison and begged Capitolina to pray that she may also be found worthy of martyrdom. Capitolina told Eroetis to go home and sell all her possessions and give the money to the poor. When Capitolina was brought before the judge the next day, Eroteis hurled stones and abuses at him. After they beheaded St. Capitolina, they tortured Eroteis, and miraculously her wounds were healed. When she was cast into a furnace, she emerged unharmed. Finally, St. Eroteis was beheaded.

COMMEMORATIONS: Alexander, Bishop of Guria and Samegrelo; Nestor of Thessalonica; Mark of the isle of Thasos; Procla, wife of Pontius Pilate; Kyriakos I, Patriarch of Constantinople; Capitolina and Eroteis of Cappadocia; Nestor the Chronicler of the Kiev Caves; Demetrius of Basarabov in Bulgaria (Bulgarian Calendar); Sergius Chernukhin of Danilov Monastery; Ia, virgin of Cornwall; Uncovering of the relics of St. Andrew, Prince of Smolensk.

SATURDAY

OCTOBER 28

Holy Protection of the Theotokos
Fast-free
Hebrews 9:1-7
Luke 10:38-42, 11:27-28

*K*now that we must serve not the times but God.

St. Athanasius the Great

ST. ATHANASIUS I, PATRIARCH OF CONSTANTINOPLE. As a young man, Athanasius became a monk in Thessalonica. He settled on Mount Athos and lived in a cave near Iveron Monastery before joining Esphigmenou Monastery. Because of his ascetic struggles, he gained the gift of tears. To avoid praise, he went to live as an ascetic hermit. Then he went to Mount Galesion to the Monastery of Saint Lazarus, where he was in charge of the sacred relics and vessels. Here he heard the voice of the Lord from a crucifix telling him to go into pastoral service. Soon many people went to him for spiritual guidance, so he organized a women's monastery. When the Church needed a Patriarch, Athanasius was unanimously chosen. In this capacity, he worked diligently to strengthen the Church. However, due to his strictness and reforms, a group of influential clergy forced his resignation. For the next ten years, Athanasius again lived in solitude until he was asked to return to the throne, where he remained for another seven years until discord arose and he returned to his monastery. Towards the end of his life, Christ spoke to Athanasius, reproaching him for not fulfilling his pastoral duties. Athanasius repented, and Christ forgave him and bestowed him the gift of working miracles. St. Athanasius died peacefully around 1310.

COMMEMORATIONS: Protection of the Most Holy Theotokos (Greek Calendar); Parasceva of Iconium; Kyriakos of Jerusalem, and his mother Anna; Athanasius I, Patriarch of Constantinople; Terence, Africanus, Maximus, Pompeius, and 36 others; Stephen the Hymnographer; Terence and Neonilla of Syria, and others; Febronia, daughter of Emperor Heraclius; Arsenius I of Srem; Firmilian of Caesarea, and Malchion; Neophytus of Urbnisi; Parasceva of Pirimin; Angelis, Manuel, George, and Nicholas of Crete; Job of Pochaev; Michael Lektorsky of Kuban; Arsenius of Cappadocia; Constantine Dyakov of Kiev; Demetrius of Rostov; Nestor of the Kiev Caves; Feofil, Fool-for-Christ; Hyacinth of Vicina (Romania).

OCTOBER 29

𝒪nly prayer, silence and love are effective... It is better to turn to the heart of other people through secret prayer than to their ears.

St. Porphyrios of Kavsokalyvia

ST. ERMELINDIS, ANCHORESS IN MELDAERT. Ermelindis was from a very illustrious family in modern-day Belgium in the late sixth century. She was given an upbringing befitting her birth, but she thirsted for nothing but seclusion, prayer, and the word of God from a young age. To prevent any marriage proposals, she made a vow of virginity and cut off her hair. She left her parents and hid in the little town of Bevec, where she would go to church barefoot and pass her days and nights in prayer. An angel warned Ermelindis that two young squires were setting traps for her virtue, so she moved to Meldaert. She passed the rest of her days eating only wild herbs and living the austere life like the desert ascetics of old, overcoming the flesh and the devil in many combats. When she died in the seventh century, it is said that angels buried her and chanted hymns for her funeral. Forty-eight years later, the miracles her relics worked were made known, and she was moved to a convent. Icons of St. Ermelindis portray her surrounded by angels presiding over her funeral. Her relics have been moved several times and even hidden during conflicts. Now they are enclosed in a magnificent reliquary of gilded bronze.

COMMEMORATIONS: Anastasia of Rome; Abramius the Recluse and his niece Mary, of Mesopotamia; Anna (Ephemianos) of Mt. Olympus in Bithynia; Melitena of Marcianopolis; Athanasius of Sparta; Timothy of Esphigmenou Monastery; Abramius, archimandrite of Rostov; Sabbas the Commander; Serapion of Zarzma, Georgia; Martyrs Cyril, Menas, and Menaeus; Abramius, recluse of the Near Caves in Kiev; Ermelindis, hermitess in Meldaert (Belgium); Colman of Kilmacduagh (Ireland); Eberigisil, Bishop of Cologne; Glorification of St. Rostislav, Prince of Greater Moravia; (Last Sunday of October: Commemoration of the Miracle of St. Nicholas the New in 1943).

OCTOBER 30

Colossians 2:13-20; Luke 11:29-33

*O*nly if you see yourself as ZERO, being full of passions, can you see
God. If you cannot see that you are nothing, then you cannot see
God. God lives only in the humble person.

† *Gerontissa Makrina of Portaria*

VENERABLE THERAPON THE ASCETIC AND WONDER-WORKER OF LYTHRODONTAS. Three hundred refugees escaped from
Palestine to Cyprus during the seventh-century persecutions by the Arabs.
Therapon had lived in the Palestinian desert, where he learned monasticism,
prayer, vigils, humility, and abstinence. In Cyprus, he found a desolate site
with water close by, near the town of Lythrodontas. After many spiritual
struggles, he was granted the gift of performing miracles. The faithful would
go to him to be cured and receive proper Christian teachings. He died
peacefully and was buried at the place of his ascetic struggles. After many
centuries, his holy relics were miraculously found. A light appeared over
a bush on three separate nights, so the residents decided to cut the bush,
where they discovered the tomb with St. Therapon's relics, and a church
was built. Later, a larger church was built that houses a part of the relics,
and they are carried in a procession once a year on the saint's feast day. The
relics have performed many miracles for pilgrims who arrive with faith,
so he was given the name "Wonderworker." A scroll on one of his newer
icons reads, "Temperance of tongue and belly is the greatest philosophy."

COMMEMORATIONS: Tertius, Mark, Justus, Artemas, and Cleopas, of
the Seventy; Zenobios and Zenobia of Aegae; Alexander, Cronion, Julian,
Macarios, and 30 companions; Eutropia of Alexandria; Asterius, Claudius,
Neon, and Neonilla of Cilicia; Asterius of Amasea; Joseph I Galesiotes;
Marcian of Syracuse; Dometius of Phrygia; Martyr Manuel; Stephen Milu-
tin, King of Serbia, and Dragutin and Helen; Therapon of Lythrodontas;
9 martyred by fire; Jotham Zedghinidze of Georgia; Varnava of Hvosno
(Old Calendar); Finding of the relics of St. Stephen-Urosh III of Decani,
Serbia; Uncovering of the relics of St. Eutropia of Kherson; *Ozeryansk* Icon
of the Mother of God.

OCTOBER 31

Romans 16:1-16; Luke 11:34-41

It is necessary for a disciple and follower of Christ to take up his cross. The cross means the various difficulties and sorrows associated with a Christian life. Crosses may be external as well as internal. To take up your cross means to tolerate everything without complaining, regardless of how unpleasant things might become. For example, if someone has insulted you or laughed at you or provoked you, bear it all without anger or resentment. Similarly, if you helped someone and he, instead of showing gratitude, made up deceitful tales about you or if you wanted to do something good but were unable to accomplish it, bear it without despondency. Did some misfortune befall you? Did someone in your family become ill, or despite all your efforts and tireless labor did you repeatedly suffer failure? Has some other thing or person oppressed you? Bear all with patience in the name of Jesus Christ.

St. Innocent of Alaska

MARTYRS GORDIANOS AND EPIMACHOS. Gordianos and Epimachos were from third-century Rome during the Christian persecutions of Emperor Decius. They confessed to being Christians and were arrested. The governor urged them to deny Christ by sacrificing to idols, but they refused. After various torments, they were beheaded. Their bodies were laid side by side in a crypt on the Via Latina close to Rome, in a cemetery that bears their name. It is now part of an archeological park and can be visited.

SAINTS COMMEMORATED: Apostles Stachys, Apelles, Amplias, Urbanus, Aristovoulos, and Narcissus; Spyridon and Nicodemus the Prosphora-bakers; Maura of Constantinople; Epimachus of Pelusium; James of Mygdonia; Epimachos the Roman and Gordianos; Anatolius of the Kiev Caves; Nicholas of Chios; Foillan of Burgh Castle; John of Chicago; Seleucius and Stratonica his wife; Martyr Pais; Leonid of Vologda, Euphrosynus of Kazan, Anatole of Tver, and Innocent of Volokolamsk; Stephen, Barnabas, Trophimus and others; 3 Martyrs of Melitene; 12 Virgin Martyrs; Martyr Abramius; Quentin of Rome; 100,000 Martyrs of Tbilisi.

As I have come to understand, some people resemble the honeybee, and some resemble the fly. Those who resemble the fly seek to find evil in every circumstance and are preoccupied with it; they see no good anywhere. But those who resemble the honeybee only see the good in everything they see. The stupid person thinks stupidly and takes everything in the wrong way, whereas the person who has good thoughts, no matter what he sees, no matter what you tell him, maintains a positive and good thought.

St. Paisios the Athonite

WEDNESDAY

NOVEMBER I

St. Cosmas and St. Damian
the Holy Unmercenaries
**Abstain from meat and
dairy products, and fish.**
1 Corinthians 12:27-13:8
Matthew 10:1, 5-8

*O*ur salvation consists of faith and hope in the mercy of God.
St. Macarius of Optina

NEW MARTYR JAMES OF KASTORIA, AND HIS DISCIPLES DEACON JAMES AND MONK DIONYSIOS. James fled to Constantinople when his jealous brother falsely reported to the Turkish authorities that he had found a treasure. James became wealthy as a sheep merchant to the sultan's palace. One day while a guest in the home of a Hagarene official, James would not eat meat since it was the fast of the Holy Apostles. He proceeded to relate the following miracle. He said that his wife became possessed, and he spent much money to cure her, but to no avail. A friend told him to take her to the patriarch of the Christians, and He works miracles. As soon as the patriarch opened the Gospel over his wife, the roof of the church suddenly opened and a heavenly light filled the whole church, and his wife was made well. When James heard this, he was filled with zeal. He distributed his wealth to the poor and went to Mount Athos, eventually settling at Iveron Monastery. He lived in solitude, prayer, fasting, and all-night vigils, and he guided many disciples. Later, however, St. James was tortured and martyred by the Hagarenes, together with his disciples James and Dionysios. Many miracles have taken place through his wonderworking relics which lie in the Monastery of St. Anastasia Pharmakolytria, near Thessalonica.

COMMEMORATIONS: Holy Unmercenaries Cosmas and Damian of Mesopotamia, and their mother Theodota; Cyrenia and Juliana in Cilicia; Helen of Sinope; David of Evia; John and James, in Persia; Caesarius, Dacius, Sabbas, Sabinian, Agrippa, Adrian, and Thomas at Damascus; Hermeningilda the Goth; James of Mt. Athos, and James and Dionysius; David the Great Komnenos, with Basil, George, Manuel, and Alexios; Martyrs Cyprian and Juliana.

NOVEMBER 2

Colossians 4:2-9; Luke 11:47-12:1

*P*rayer is forgetting earthly things, an ascent to Heaven. Through prayer we flee to God.

St. Nektarios of Pentapolis

ST. ANTHONY THE CONFESSOR, ARCHBISHOP OF THESSA-LONICA. A short biography of St. Anthony was written by a presbyter of Thessalonica. Because of the Arabic raids on Aegina, Anthony fled to Thessalonica, as did his relative St. Theodora. Anthony was highly educated, and at a young age, he embraced the monastic life. He was elected Metropolitan of Dyrrachium because of his virtuous manner of life. During this time, the second period of Iconoclasm began under Emperor Leo V. Anthony stood before Leo and delivered a defense of the holy icons. In response, Leo had Anthony tortured. He endured incurable wounds that shook his health. He was exiled but was recalled when Emperor Michael II took the throne. Two decades later, Anthony was elected Archbishop of Thessalonica, but this was short-lived, as he died a few months after the holy icons were restored in 844. Anthony was buried in the Church of St. Demetrios. Forty-six years later, his relics were uncovered and found incorrupt. St. Anthony is numbered among the saints of Thessalonica but not in the synaxaria of the Orthodox Church. His only icon can be seen in the Church of St. Gregory Palamas in Thessalonica.

COMMEMORATIONS: Acindynus, Pegasius, Anempodistus, Elpith-ephorus, Aphthonius, and those with them, of Persia; Anthony the Confessor, Archbishop of Thessalonica; Attikos, Eudoxios, Agapios, Karterios, Eustratios, Pactobios (Tobias), Nikopolitianos, Styrax, and companions, at Sebaste; Marcian of Cyrrhus in Syria; Martyrs Domna, Domnina, and Cyriaca; Cyprian of Storozhev, former outlaw; Bishop Victorin and Basil Luzgin, of Glazomicha; Erc, Bishop of Slane, Ireland; Gabriel Urgebadze of Georgia; Justus of Trieste; Lambros, Theodore, and one who is anonymous, in Vrachori; Martyrs of senatorial rank beheaded under Marcus Aurelius; *Shuisk-Smolensk* Icon of the Mother of God.

NOVEMBER 3

Colossians 4:10-18; Luke 12:2-12

*B*etter is he who edifies his soul than he who edifies the whole world.
St. Isaac the Syrian

ST. ANNA VSEVOLODNA, PRINCESS. Anna was the daughter of Great Prince Vsevolod Yaroslavich of Kiev, and her mother was the daughter of Roman Emperor Constantine Monomachos. Anna became engaged but decided not to marry. Instead, she took monastic tonsure at the monastery her father had built for her in Kiev in the year 1086. During a trip to Constantinople to select a new Metropolitan of Russia, Anna was impressed by the scholarly learning in Byzantium, which then was the center of culture and education. When she returned home, she introduced an innovation of learning for women. Anna started a school for girls at her monastery, which was the first school for girls in Russia. She selected the teachers, requirements and curriculum, including rhetoric, writing, singing, and practical crafts. She also introduced the Roman tradition of education for upper-class women in Kiev. Later, during the twelfth and thirteenth centuries, convent schools became common in Kiev. These were founded by princesses, noblewomen, and abbesses. Many aristocratic and clerical women became literate and educated in Greek, Latin, mathematics, and philosophy, and some became noted writers. St. Anna died peacefully in 1112 and was buried at her monastery, which was destroyed later under the Tatar invasion.

COMMEMORATIONS: Achaemonides (Hormisdas) of Persia; Theodore of Ancyra; Snandulia of Persia; Pimen of Zographou; Akepsimas, Joseph, and Aeithalas of Persia; Elias of Egypt; Hubert of Liege; George the Younger of Neapolis; Nicholas, Radiant Star of Georgia; Acepsimas of Cyrrhus; Pirminius of Germany; Anna, Princess of Kiev; 9 Martyrs slain by the sword; 28 Martyrs slain by fire; Martyrs Dasius, Severus, Andronas, Theodotus, and Theodota; Winifred of Wales; Rumwold of Buckingham; Translation of the relics of St. Apostolos the New; The Meeting of St. Sava and St. Symeon the Myrrhgusher of Serbia at Vatopedi; Dedication of the Church of Great Martyr St. George in Lydda.

NOVEMBER 4

2 Corinthians 5:1-10; Luke 9:1-6

*W*ell, if you seek to find Him only through the prayer, do not let a single breath pass without it. Just be careful not to accept any fantasies. For the Divine is formless, unimaginable, and colorless; He is supremely perfect, not subject to syllogisms. He acts like a subtle breeze in our minds.

St. Joseph the Hesychast

MARTYRS AGRICOLA AND VITALIS OF BOLOGNA. Agricola taught the Christian faith to his slave Vitalis during a time of Christian persecutions under Emperor Diocletian in the year 304. They both were arrested and tortured. Vitalis did not cease praising God. Every part of his body was covered with wounds and blood, and he prayed that Christ would receive his soul. As soon as his prayer ended, he gave up his soul. The persecutors thought that seeing the torture of Vitalis would change Agricola's zeal, but instead, he became encouraged. Infuriated, they hung him on a cross and pierced his body with many huge nails, and he died. St. Ambrose discovered their relics about ninety years later in Bologna. He took some of the blood from the bottom of the tomb and the cross and nails and gave them to a devout widow in Florence who had built a church in that city. It is said that a church in Bologna dedicated to Vitalis and Agricola was built over the remains of the Roman amphitheater where their martyrdoms took place. Over time those who have requested assistance from Saints Vitalis and Agricola have received help.

COMMEMORATIONS: Ioannicios the Great of Bithynia; Nicander, Bishop of Myra, and Hermas the priest; Sylvia, mother of Gregory the Dialogist; Porphyrios the Mime of Ephesus; Mercurius the Faster of the Far Caves in Kiev; Luke, Bishop of Novgorod; Nicander, founder of Gorodnoezersk Monastery, Novgorod; Paul, Metropolitan of Tobolsk; Simon of Yurievets and Zharki, Fool-for-Christ; John III Doukas Vatatzes the Merciful, Emperor of Nicaea; George Karslides of Drama, and his sister Virgin Anna; John, Stephen, and Isaiah the Georgians; Clether of Cornwall; Birnstan of Winchester; Agricola and Vitalis of Bologna.

SUNDAY

NOVEMBER 5

Fifth Sunday of Luke
Fast-free

Galatians 6:11-18; Luke 16:19-31

The soul is in the world, since it is born; but mind is above the world, since it is not born. A soul, which understands what the world is and wishes to be saved, has a rigid rule—to think every hour within itself 'Here comes the trial (of death), and the inquisition (of deeds), where you will not be able to endure (the glance of) the Judge, and the soul is about to perish.' Thinking thus, it preserves itself from worthless and shameful pleasures.

St. Anthony the Great

COMMEMORATION OF THE MIRACLE OF ST. SPYRIDON IN 1673. A plague struck the island of Corfu in the seventeenth century. It was first seen in one of the suburbs and soon spread, and the people were terrified. For three nights, they saw a light on the bell tower of the Church of St. Spyridon and the figure of St. Spyridon, who had died in the year 348. He was carrying a cross in one hand, appearing to be driving the pestilence away. At the request of the people, the governor of the island decreed that every year, on the first Sunday of November, a procession with the saint's relics would be held in honor of this miraculous event.

COMMEMORATIONS: Galacteon and his wife Epistimia, at Emesa; Apostles Hermas, Patrobus, Linus, Gaius, and Philologus of the Seventy; Gregory, Pope of Alexandria; Domninus, Timothy, Theotimos, Theophilus, Dorotheus, Carterius, Eupsychius, and Pamphilus, of Palestine, and the 3 virgins of Palestine; Jonah, Archbishop of Novgorod; Hilarion, recluse of Troekurovo; Silvanus, Bishop of Gaza; Odrada, virgin of Balen; Martyr Kastor and Agathangelos; Gregory of Cassano, Calabria; Cybi, abbot in Cornwall and Wales; Kea, Bishop of Devon and Cornwall; Dositheus of Glinsk Hermitage; Commemoration of the Consecration of the Church of St. Theodore the Tyro in the Sphorakion; Commemoration of the Miracle of St. Spyridon in 1673.

NOVEMBER 6

*P*ride is…the utter poverty of the soul, disguised as riches, imaginary light where in fact there is darkness.

St. John Climacus

HIEROMARTYR PAUL THE CONFESSOR, ARCHBISHOP OF CONSTANTINOPLE. Paul was from fourth-century Thessalonica. He became the secretary to Patriarch Alexander of Constantinople and then was ordained to the priesthood. As the Patriarch lay on his deathbed, he chose Paul, who was in his early thirties, to succeed him. Emperor Constantius and the other Arians railed at this, so Paul was deposed, and the Arian Eusebius of Nicomedia was made Patriarch. Paul went to Rome, where he found St. Athanasius the Great, also in exile. With letters from Pope Julius, Paul returned to Constantinople, and after the death of Eusebius, Paul ascended the throne again. However, when Constantius heard this, he once again exiled Paul. The emperor's brother, Constans, who was Emperor of the West, told Constantius that if Paul and Athanasius were not allowed to return to their sees, he would come with troops to restore them himself. But after Constans' death, Paul was secretly expelled to avoid a riot by the people. He was chained and taken to Cucusus, Cappadocia, where he was left in a small house to starve to death. After six days, the Arians found him still alive. They set upon him as he was celebrating Divine Liturgy and strangled him with his omophorion. In the thirteenth century, St. Paul's holy relics were transferred to the Church of San Lorenzo in Venice, Italy, where they still reside.

COMMEMORATIONS: Paul the Confessor; Herman of Kazan; Gregory the Cross-bearer of Russia; Luke of Taormina; Winnoc of Flanders; Luke of the Kiev Caves; Demetrianos of Cytheria; Barlaam of Keret; Barlaam of Khutyn; Paul of Corinth; Martyr Nicander; Nicetas of Orekhovo-Zuevsk; Barlaam of Andreyevskoe; Gabriel of St. Michael Skovorodsky; Gabriel (Gur) of Lytkarino; Illtyd of Wales; Leonard of Noblac; Agapios the Presbyter; Cowey of Portaferry; Elias of Paris; Translation of the relics of St. Melaine of Rennes; Synaxis of the New Martyrs of Sarov; Commemoration of the falling of ash from the sky in 472.

NOVEMBER 7

1 Thessalonians 1:6-10
Luke 12:42-48

*F*or as long as a man lives there are many changes in his life....
There have been many righteous men who have fallen from their
righteousness, and many sinners who have climbed up and taken
their place.

St. Isaac the Syrian

**VENERABLE LAZARUS THE STYLITE AND WONDERWORKER
OF MOUNT GALESION.** Lazarus was a well-educated young man from
tenth-century Magnesia. He loved God and became a monk in Palestine
at the Monastery of St. Savvas in Jerusalem. Lazarus lived ten years in
ascetic struggles, winning the love and respect of his peers. The patriarch of
Jerusalem ordained him to the priesthood, and he went to live on Mount
Galesion, near Ephesus. He saw a vision of a fiery pillar that rose to the
sky, with angels around it singing, "Let God arise and His enemies be scattered." On this spot, Lazarus built a church dedicated to the Resurrection
of Christ, and he began to live on a pillar. God granted him the gift of
insight and prophecy. Monks gravitated to him to be nourished spiritually.
Lazarus foretold the date of his death, but his disciples prayed to God to
permit him to live longer, and God granted him another fifteen years. St.
Lazarus died peacefully in 1054 and was buried near his pillar, where many
miracles occurred.

COMMEMORATIONS: 33 Martyrs of Melitene; Auctus, Taurion, and
Thessalonica, at Amphipolis in Macedonia; Cassina and Melasippus, their
son Antoninus, and 40 children converted and martyred, at Ancyra; Theodotus of Ancyra; Alexander of Thessalonica; Athenodoros, brother of St.
Gregory the Wonderworker; Herculanus of Perugia; Lazarus of Mt. Galesion
near Ephesus; Zosimas of the Annunciation Monastery at Lake Vorbozoma;
Willibrord of Utrecht; Cyril Smirnov of Kazan; Michael Gusev of Diveyevo;
Joseph Petrovykh of Petrograd; Translation of the relics of St. Cyril, founder
of Novozersk Monastery; *The Joyful* Icon of the Mother of God.

Synaxis of the Archangels
Abstain from meat and
dairy products, and fish.
Hebrews 2:2-10; Luke 10:16-21

*P*rove your faith with works of love toward your neighbor.

St. Paisios the Athonite

SYNAXIS OF THE ARCHANGELS MICHAEL AND GABRIEL, AND ALL THE HEAVENLY BODILESS ANGELIC POWERS. In the fourth century, Pope Sylvester and Patriarch Alexander established this day to celebrate the nine orders of angels. According to a Church Canon of the fourth-century Council of Laodicea, angels are not to be worshipped. Each angel has its particular service, but all are equal in honor. The hierarchy of the nine orders is six-winged seraphim, many-eyed cherubim, godly thrones, dominions, virtues, powers, principalities, archangels, and angels. Archangel Michael is the leader of the angelic army. His name means, "Who is like God." When Lucifer and his followers were cast from heaven, Archangel Michael said, "Let us give heed! Let us stand aright! Let us stand with fear!" Archangel Michael defends the Garden of Eden, he told Abraham not to sacrifice Isaac, he told Lot to flee Sodom, he protected Jacob from Esau, he took the soul of Moses from the devil, and he changed the course of a river in Asia Minor to protect a holy spring in a church. In Orthodox churches, the image of Archangel Michael is situated on the left side of the icon screen, and Archangel Gabriel on the right. The name Gabriel means "the power of God." Archangel Gabriel announces the mysteries of God.

COMMEMORATIONS: Synaxis of the Archangels Michael, Gabriel, Raphael, Uriel, Salaphiel, Jegudiel, Barachiel, and Jeremiel and the other Bodiless Powers; Maria (Martha), Princess of Pskov; Michael the Blessed of Chernigov; Willihad, Bishop of Bremen (Germany); Tysilio, abbot of Meifod; 70 Monk Martyrs on the Island of Flowers; Commemoration of the fallen heroes of the Arkadi Monastery, Crete.

St. Nektarios of Pentapolis
Fast-free

NOVEMBER 9

Ephesians 5:8-19
Matthew 4:25-5:12

He who is unconcerned about the salvation of his soul is at risk of twofold danger: he may either be unexpectedly snatched by death or abandoned by the grace of God.

St. Nektarios of Pentapolis

ST. NEKTARIOS THE WONDERWORKER, METROPOLITAN OF PENTAPOLIS. Nektarios was born in 1846 in Selyvria of Thrace. When he was twenty-nine years old, he became a monk on the island of Chios. Because of his virtue, he was ordained a deacon and was assistant to the Patriarch of Alexandria, who sent him to study theology in Athens. He was ordained to the priesthood and later was consecrated Metropolitan of Pentapolis. Due to jealousy and alleged improprieties, Nektarios was removed from office. He was rejected again in Athens and sent to the island of Euboea, where the people embraced him. He became the Dean of the School of Theology in Athens and published many of his theological works. He retired to the island of Aegina in 1910 and established a convent there. Ten years later, he was admitted to a hospital ward for the poor and incurable in Athens, where he gave up his spirit. When they placed the saint's sweater on the bed of a paralytic, he immediately regained his strength and walked. A beautiful fragrance filled the room for many days after the saint's death, and this room is now a chapel. St. Nektarios was buried at his convent in Aegina, where he remained whole and fragrant for years. Many miraculous healings have taken place throughout the world through the saint's prayers.

COMMEMORATIONS: Nektarios (Kephalas) of Pentapolis; Onesiphoros and Porphyrios of Ephesus; Eustolia and Sosipatra of Constantinople; John the Short of Egypt; Matrona of Constantinople; Symeon Metaphrastes of Constantinople; Onesiphorus of the Kiev Caves; Anthony of Apamea; Theoktiste of Lesvos; Claudius, Castor, Sempronian, and Nicostratus of Pannonia; Parthenius Bryansky of Ananyevsk; Alexis Zadvornov of Yaroslavl; Martyrs Christopher and Maura; Euphymios and Neophytos the Serbians of Mt. Athos; Martyrs Narses and Artemonos; Helladius, monk; Benignus of Armagh; *The Quick Hearer of Mt. Athos* Icon of the Mother of God.

NOVEMBER 10

1 Corinthians 4:9-16
Luke 13:31-35

I am about to say something that may appear strange, but do not be astonished nor startled at it. The Offering of the Eucharist is always the same, whether a common man, or Paul or Peter offer it. It is the exact same Offering which Christ gave to His disciples, and which the Priests now administer to you. This is in no way inferior to that, because it is not men that sanctify even this, but the Same who sanctified the one sanctifies the other also. For as the words which God spoke are the same which the Priest now speaks, so is the Offering the same, and the same can be said of the Baptism, that which He gave. Thus the Faith is of a single Whole.

St. John Chrysostom

VENERABLE THEOSTERIKTOS, ABBOT OF SYMBOLA MONAS-TERY. Theosteriktos was abbot of the Monastery of Symbola in Bithynia on Mount Olympus. His monastery was known for its strong stance against the iconoclasts. He died in peace, and written in his icon scroll is, "Longing for God wipes away longing for parents." His two notable disciples were St. Timothy and St. Plato, the uncle of St. Theodore the Studite. Plato later established the Sakkoudion Monastery, where St. Theodore first became a monk.

COMMEMORATIONS: Erastus, Olympas, Herodion, Sosipater, Quartus, and Tertius (Terence), of the Seventy; Arsenios of Cappadocia; Orestes of Cappadocia; Nonnus of Heliopolis; Milos (Miles), in Persia, and Aborsam and Senoe; Eucharius of Trier; Constantine-Kakhi of Kartli; Theosteriktos of Symbola; Justus of Canterbury; 10 Martyrs of Gaza; Martyrs Orion, Niros, and Calliopios; Augustine of Kaluga, and Ioannicius, Niphon, John, Alexis, Apolloius, and Michael; Procopius of Kherson, and Seraphim of Optina; Demetrianos of Antioch; Commemoration of the torture of Great Martyr George upon the wheel.

NOVEMBER 11

2 Corinthians 4:6-15
Luke 9:37-43

*T*he answer to our anxiety is not drugs, alcohol, tranquilizers, or psychiatric treatment. It will not be cured by Yoga or some new age or eastern meditation practice. The problem is that we have lost God as the center of our lives. Once we make our love of God the primary focus of our lives and allow His grace to work through us, then no matter what circumstance we encounter in life we will be comforted and embraced in His love. All anxiety disappears. This is the aim of the Orthodox way of life—to put God first and seek the Holy Spirit. The anxieties of modern life are only symptoms of our separation from God.

St. Paisios the Athonite

MARTYR DRAKONAS OF ARAURAKA IN ARMENIA. Drakonas lived during the late-third to the early fourth-century reign of Emperor Diocletian. Christians were unjustly arrested, persecuted, and slaughtered. Drakonas was not arrested, but he presented himself before the governor Decius, boldly confessed his faith in Christ, and reviled the gods of the idols. For this, he was cruelly tortured and imprisoned. When he remained steadfast in his Christian faith, he was beheaded.

COMMEMORATIONS: Menas of Egypt; Theodore the Confessor of the Studion; Stephen-Urosh III of Decani; Euthymius and Nestor of Decani; Maximus of Moscow, Fool-for-Christ; Vincent of Spain; Martyrius of Zelenets; Neophytus and Stephen Urosica of Serbia; Victor and Stephanida, at Damascus; Nicodemus the Younger of Beroea; Bartholomew the Younger of Rossano; Drakonas of Arauraka in Armenia; Milica (Eugenia), Princess of Serbia; Synaxis of the Saints of Decani; Myrrh-streaming *Montreal* Iveron Icon of the Mother of God.

NOVEMBER 12

*T*hose who have really determined to serve Christ, with the help of spiritual fathers and their own self-knowledge, will strive before all else to choose a place, and a way of life, and a habitation, and exercises suitable for them. For community life is not for all, on account of covetousness; and places of solitude are not for all, on account of anger. But each will consider what is most suited to his needs.

St. John Climacus

ST. LEONTIUS STYPPES, PATRIARCH OF CONSTANTINOPLE. During the reign of Emperor John II Komnenos, Leontius was a presbyter at Hagia Sophia. He was elevated to Patriarch in the year 1134. He was known for his severe penances upon relatives and servants of a princess in the emperor's court who employed magical practices. Leontius also presided over a synod that condemned Bogomil mystical writings. They were withdrawn from circulation and burned, but it is believed today that the writings had been misconstrued and were in fact Orthodox texts in line with the teachings of St. Symeon the New Theologian. The fear and condemnation of these texts stemmed from a movement a few decades earlier when the Bogomil leader entered Constantinople with his twelve disciples, bringing many to his faith. He was burned to death, and many Bogomil heresy trials followed this. Later, a group of preachers was organized to act as thought-police to keep the spread of heresy in check.

COMMEMORATIONS: Martin the Merciful of Tours; Prophet Achias of Silom; John the Merciful; Martin of Terracina; Nilus the Faster of Sinai; Nilus the Myrrhgusher; Leontius (Leo), Patriarch of Constantinople; Emilian of Vergegio; John "the Hairy" of Rostov; Nicholas of Marmaran; Sabbas of Nigdi; Varnava the New Confessor; Martyr Arsakius; Sinell of Cleenish; Machar of Aberdeen; Cadwaladr, king of the Welsh; New Martyrs and Confessors of Nasaud, Romania; Mark Markoulis of Kleisoura; Commemoration of the Miracle of St. Spyridon in 1718; *The Merciful* Icon of the Mother of God; (1st Sunday after 11/10: Translation of the holy relics of St. Gregory of Assos).

MONDAY

NOVEMBER 13

St. John Chrysostom
Fast-free
Hebrews 7:26-8:2
John 10:9-16

*S*ome people, if they stumble at all, or are slandered by anyone, or
   fall ill with a chronic disease, gout or headache or any such ailment,
at once begin to blaspheme. They submit to the pain of the disease
but deprive themselves of the benefit. What are you doing, man,
blaspheming your benefactor, savior, protector, and guardian? Or
do you not see that you are falling down a cliff and casting yourself
into the pit of final destruction? You do not make your suffering
lighter, do you, if you blaspheme? Indeed, you aggravate it, and
make your distress more grievous. For the devil brings a multitude
of misfortunes for this purpose, to lead you down into that pit. If he
sees you blaspheming, he will readily increase the suffering and make
it greater, so that when you are pricked you may give up once again;
but if he sees you enduring bravely, and giving thanks the more to
God, the more the suffering grows worse, he raises the siege at once,
knowing that it will be useless to besiege you anymore.

St. John Chrysostom

ST. EUGENIUS II OF TOLEDO. Eugenius became a cleric in the Cathedral of Toledo and later an archdeacon of Bishop Braulio during the seventh
century. Eugenius was chosen as his successor when the archbishop died, even
though Braulio tried to retain him. However, the office of archbishop was so
distasteful to Eugenius that he fled to lead a monastic life, but the king forced
his return. Because Eugenius was inexperienced in Church government, he
would consult with Bishop Braulio. Eugenius was small in stature and feeble
in health, but he was zealous. He reformed the ecclesiastical chant of the
Divine Office and achieved distinction as a writer. Though lacking polish, his
work was full of fire, spirit, and poetic movement. St. Eugenius also wrote a
treatise on the Holy Trinity, most likely against the Arians.

COMMEMORATIONS: John Chrysostom, Archbishop of Constantino-
ple; Zebinas, Antoninus, Germanus, Nicephorus, and Manetha, in Caesarea;
Euphrasius and Quintianus, of Clermont; Bricius of Tours; Damascene of
Constantinople; Leonardo of Vienne; Eugenius II of Toledo.

Holy Apostle Philip
Fast-free

1 Corinthians 4:9-16
John 1:43-51

*G*reat is the man who perseveres in converse with God.

St. Isaac the Syrian

NEW MARTYR CONSTANTINE OF HYDRA. Constantine was raised a Christian on the island of Hydra. When he was eighteen years old, he went to Rhodes seeking work. He was hired by the governor, Hassan Kapitan, as a groomsman. One day, Constantine got drunk, and Hassan had him circumcised and dressed in Turkish clothes and a turban. When Constantine woke up the next day and realized what had happened, he didn't know what to do. After three years, Constantine's remorse drove him to Constantinople to seek the advice of Patriarch Gregory, who dissuaded him from his quest for martyrdom. Instead, Gregory sent him to Mount Athos to live at the Iveron Monastery. Praying before the miraculous icon of the Panagia, Constantine received strength and courage and was consumed by the desire for martyrdom. He went back to Rhodes and confessed his faith to Hassan. For this, he was imprisoned, lashed, and dragged over rocks. He could barely stand from his wounds. Then he was given one thousand blows to his back and feet and became unconscious. In prison, Jesus appeared to him and completely restored him. One night, a divine light surrounded Constantine, and his chains fell off to the amazement of the other prisoners. After five months, he was brought before the Turkish commander, and again he declared his faith in Christ. By the sultan's orders, St. Constantine died by hanging in the year 1800. Three years later, Constantine's mother took his relics to Hydra, and to this day, they are kept in a silver reliquary in the Monastery of the Panagia.

COMMEMORATIONS: Apostle Philip the All-Praised; Gregory Palamas of Thessalonica; Philip of Irap Monastery; Fantinus the Younger; Alberik of Utrecht; Virgin Martyrs of Emesa (Syria); Euphemianos of Cyprus; Constantine of Hydra; Aristarchus of St. Nicholas Peshnosha Monastery; Malo (Machulus) of Brittany; Dyfrig, bishop in Hereford; Gwent of Bardsey Island; Dimitri (Benevolensky) of Tver; Repose of St. Alexander Nevsky of Novgorod.

WEDNESDAY

Nativity Fast Begins
Strict Fast

NOVEMBER 15

1 Thessalonians 4:1-12
Luke 15:1-10

*H*ow many sinful acts we have to grieve for. For without grief there is no purification, and there can be no grief in the midst of continuous distraction. Without purification of the soul there is no assurance; and without assurance the separation of soul and body is full of dangers.

St. Peter of Damascus

ST. MALO OF ALETH. Malo was one of the seven major saints of Brittany in the early sixth century. He had a particular love for animals. He was baptized by St. Brendan the Navigator and became his favorite disciple. One time, Malo fell asleep on a sandbar at low tide, where the tides rise and fall dangerously. When the tide came in, everyone believed that Malo had drowned. However, the sandbar miraculously rose with the tide, and he remained safe and dry. Another time, when it was Malo's turn to keep vigil at the monastery, some jealous monks extinguished all the lamps. Looking for some light, Malo took cold embers from the hearth and held them against his chest. The embers began to glow, and he used them for light during the whole night. Later, Malo was consecrated Bishop of Aleth. He also wrought other miracles there. One day, a peasant woman went to Malo and told him that a wolf had eaten her donkey. Malo found the wolf and made it carry firewood on its back for her. A sow once strayed into a neighbor's field to eat the grain, and the swineherd threw a stone at the sow and killed it. Malo took pity on the animal and its piglets. He laid his staff on the wound, and it came back to life with his prayers. St. Malo died peacefully. His relics rested in Brittany until the French Revolution, when most of the relics were destroyed.

COMMEMORATIONS: Gurias, Samonas, and Habibus of Edessa; Herman, Wonderworker of Alaska; Elpidios, Markellos, and Efstochios, who suffered under Julian the Apostate; Justinian the Emperor, and his wife Theodora; Kyntion, Bishop of Seleucia; Malo of Aleth; Philip, founder of Rabang Monastery (Vologda); Paisius Velichkovsky of Moldavia and Mt. Athos; Thomas the New, Patriarch of Constantinople; Demetrios of Thrace; Quinctian, Bishop of Seleucia; *Kupyatich* Icon of the Mother of God.

THURSDAY

Holy Apostle & Evangelist Matthew
Abstain from meat and dairy products.

NOVEMBER 16

Romans 10:11-11:2
Matthew 9:9-13

*B*lessed is the mind which keeps perfect silence in prayer.

St. Nilus of Sinai

HOLY APOSTLE AND EVANGELIST MATTHEW. Matthew was a publican and tax collector when Jesus called him to become one of the Twelve Apostles. After receiving the gift of the Holy Spirit, he preached in Palestine for eight years. Matthew wrote his Gospel and departed to preach in Persia, Syria, Media, and Parthia. In Ethiopia, he encountered cannibals. Jesus appeared to him as a young man and handed him His staff, and He commanded Matthew to plant the staff at the doors of the church he had built. It grew into a tree that bore fruit, and a holy spring flowed beneath it. Everyone that partook of the tree's fruit and drank the water became good and meek and accepted Baptism. But Prince Fulvian did not want his people to become Christians. He accused Matthew of sorcery and gave orders to execute him. When they tried to burn him alive, the flames extinguished. Matthew gave up his spirit, but his body remained unharmed. He was put in a lead coffin and thrown into the sea. Fulvian said he would believe if the coffin did not sink. Matthew appeared to Bishop Platon, telling him to go to the shore and retrieve his body. Prince Fulvian begged forgiveness from Apostle Matthew, received Holy Baptism, and was given the name Matthew. Within a week, he abdicated his throne and broke all the idols. Apostle Matthew appeared to the bishop again, instructing him to ordain Matthew-Fulvian to the priesthood. After Bishop Platon reposed, Bishop Matthew succeeded him, continuing the work of the Holy Apostle Matthew.

COMMEMORATIONS: Apostle and Evangelist Matthew; Fulvianus, Prince of Ethiopia (in Baptism Matthew); Sergius, abbot of Malopinega; Otmar, abbot and monastic founder in Switzerland; Eucherius, Bishop of Lyon; Panteleimon Arzhanykh, abbot of Optina Monastery; Lubuinus, missionary to Friesland.

NOVEMBER 17

1 Corinthians 12:7-11
Luke 16:15-18, 17:1-4

*T*he hand that is good to the neighbor opens the hand of the goodness of God.

St. Philaret of Moscow

**ELDER DANIEL SANDU TUDOR, NEW CONFESSOR OF ROMA-
NIA.** Daniel was from late-nineteenth-century Bucharest. Once while flying
his plane, he crashed, but God saved him from this violent death as Daniel
kept saying the Jesus Prayer. After World War II, Daniel returned home to
find that his wife had left him, so he became a monk at the Antim Monastery
in Bucharest. A group of scholars gathered around the monastery, trying to
regain their spirituality. Their readings were the Bible and the Holy Fathers
of Orthodox Christianity, and their efforts were centered on the Jesus Prayer.
This group was known as the Burning Bush. Later, Daniel was made the
abbot of the Raraou Skete. He was arrested and accused of wanting to burn
Communism with The Burning Bush. One day during the winter, they put
Daniel and a friend in a -30° refrigerated warehouse. Most prisoners died
within three days. Lying face down on the dirt floor, Daniel stretched out
his arms and told his friend to "sit on me back-to-back with open arms," and
they prayed, "Lord Jesus Christ, Son of God, have mercy on me, the sinner!"
Suddenly, the place filled with a brilliant light, and they did not know what
happened next. After eight days, the guards arrived to remove the bodies,
but they found them alive and well. Daniel was hot to the touch, and the ice
around him had melted. After four years, he died in prison in 1962.

COMMEMORATIONS: Gennadios I and Maximos III, Patriarchs; Greg-
ory the Wonderworker; Gregory, Victor, and Geminus; Basil of Hamah;
Longinus of Egypt; 150 philosophers converted by St. Catherine; Zacharias
and John at Constantinople; Gregory of Tours; Gennadios of Vatopedi;
Vulfolaic of Trier; John the Cobbler; Zachariah the Cobbler and Mary;
Nicon of Radonezh; Lazarus the Iconographer; Michael-Gobron and 133
soldiers; Sebastian, missionary in America; Repose of Elder Daniel Sandu
Tudor of Romania.

NOVEMBER 18

2 Corinthians 11:1-6
Luke 9:57-62

*T*he Grace of God comes to you during the Divine Liturgy, if you have concentration, peace of mind, and think of nothing else.
St. Amphilochios Makris of Patmos

MARTYR ROMANUS OF PALESTINE WITH THE CHILD-MAR-TYR BARULAS OF ANTIOCH. During the third-century persecutions of Emperor Maximian, the prefect Asclepios of Antioch was about to enter the pagan temple when Romanus loudly declared that the idols were not gods. For this, he was suspended, beaten, and iron claws tore his sides. St. John Chrysostom writes that Romanus did this to prevent the prefect from worshipping demons. Then Romanus asked for a child to be brought to him. When Romanus asked the child Barulas whether it was better to worship God or images that people called gods, the child answered that people should worship the God of the Christians. Thus, Romanus proved the child wiser than the prefect Asclepios. Romanus and the child were suspended from a post. They struck out Romanus' tongue, and Barulas was beaten while his mother watched. Though her son thirsted, she urged him to endure and enjoy the everlasting water of blessedness. The child continued reprimanding the prefect even though he was beaten a second time and finally beheaded. By the grace of God, St. Romanus was still able to speak clearly. Therefore, he was strangled to death in prison.

COMMEMORATIONS: Platon of Ancyra; Zacchaeus the Deacon and Alphaeus the Reader, of Caesarea; Romanus of Caesarea in Palestine, with Child Martyr Barulas of Antioch; Romanus, who suffered under Maximian at Antioch; Daniel of Corfu; Anastasios of Paramythia in Epirus; Odo of Cluny; Mabyn of Cornwall; Mawes, bishop in Cornwall and Brittany; Helen of Novodevichy Convent (Moscow); Synaxis of All Saints of Estonia; Translation of the relics of St. Kosmas the Protos of Vatopedi.

NOVEMBER 19

Ninth Sunday of Luke
Abstain from meat and dairy products.
Ephesians 2:14-22
Luke 12:16-21

The heart is the room where we meet God.
† *Elder Cleopa of Romania*

ST. PHILARET, METROPOLITAN OF MOSCOW. Philaret's father was a priest in eighteenth-century Kolomna, near Moscow. Philaret studied at the Kolomna Seminary, where courses were taught only in Latin. He then attended the Moscow Theological Academy and was tonsured a monk, and soon after, he was ordained a deacon. Next, he taught at the Theological Academy in Petersburg. To make theology understandable, he had the classes taught in Russian, not Latin. He was consecrated bishop at thirty-five and was soon elevated to the rank of archbishop and then Metropolitan of Moscow. Philaret wrote and preached on how to live a Christian life, and he based his teachings on the wisdom of the saints. In 1823, he wrote the book *Catechism*, which has been influential for almost two centuries in Russia and other countries. One day a disciple of St. Seraphim of Sarov, Father Anthony, visited Philaret and spoke about unceasing prayer, and he became Philaret's spiritual father. After this, all the critical decisions of the diocese were referred to Anthony. Philaret now made great strides in his spiritual life, and God granted him the gifts of healing, clairvoyance, and unceasing prayer. He became a force in the spiritual revival of nineteenth-century Russia. Once, when Philaret was having problems with Tsar Nicholas, St. Sergius of Radonezh appeared to him, saying, "Don't worry, it will all pass." In a dream, St. Philaret received a forewarning of his death. Two months later, he died peacefully.

COMMEMORATIONS: Obadiah the Prophet; Azes of Isauria and 150 soldiers; Heliodorus, in Pamphylia; Barlaam and Joasaph of India, and Abenner the King; Patroclus of Bourges; Barlaam of Caesarea; Simon of Calabria; Barlaam of the Kiev Caves; Philaret of Moscow; Agapius of Gaza; 12 soldiers beheaded; Hilarion of Georgia; Martyrs Anthimus, Thalalaeus, Christopher, Euphemia and her children, and Pancharios; Egbert of York; Porphyrius of Simferopol, with Joasaph, Gregory, and Gerasim; Joasaph and Peter of Guslitsky; Alexis of Khust; Ioannicius of Glinsk.

NOVEMBER 20

2 Thessalonians 1:1-10
Luke 17:20-25

*A*t the appearance of thoughts that arouse you to judge your neighbor for some offense that he has done to you, when the storm of thoughts is blown to gale force and rushes for revenge, then compare your state of sorrow with the former state of sorrow of the Savior of the world. He, the Angel of Great Counsel, the Son of God, who was without sin, magnanimously endured the very greatest sorrows. How much more so, then, must we endure grievous circumstances, we who are sinful people and deserving of chastisement.

St. Leonid of Optina

HIEROMARTYR NERSES, BISHOP OF SHAHRQART, HIS DISCIPLE JOSEPH, JOHN, SEVERIUS, ISAAC, AND MANY OTHER MARTYRS WITH THEM. During the seventy-year reign of King Shapur II of Persia in the fourth century, many Christians were martyred. The Bishops of Persia, including Nerses, Joseph, John, Severius, and Isaac, were martyred. Some were beheaded, and others killed with the spear because they refused to worship the sun and fire, things that were created instead of their Creator. Bishops John, Severius, and Isaac of Persia were stripped naked, beaten, and whipped, then taken outside the city and stoned to death.

COMMEMORATIONS: Gregory Decapolites; Proclus of Constantinople; Dasius of Dorostolum; Azades the Eunuch; Sozomonos of Cyprus; Eustathios, Thespesios, and Anatolios of Nicaea; Diodorus of Yuriev; Nerses of Shahrqart, and others, in Persia; Isaac of Armenia; Theoktistos the Confessor; Edmund of East Anglia.

Entrance of the Theotokos into the Temple
Abstain from meat and dairy products.

NOVEMBER 21

Hebrews 9:1-7
Luke 10:38-42, 11:27-28

*S*hare tears with your neighbor to ease his grief. Share the joy in order to strengthen the joy, to strengthen love, and to benefit from it yourself later, because through crying you will become merciful, and through joy you will be cleansed of envy and hostility.

St. John Chrysostom

PANAGIA EIKONISTRIA ICON OF THE MOTHER OF GOD. One summer night in 1655, the ascetic Elder Simeon saw a light in the distance so bright that it illuminated the forest, but as he approached, it would move further away. This happened for many nights. One day a distant soft voice told him not to be discouraged in searching. The next night, praying and slowly walking, he happened upon the icon of the Panagia swinging high up in a pine tree with the bright light shining on it. The following day, he returned with all his fellow monastics, and in procession, they prayerfully took the icon back to their monastery. They named it Panagia Eikonistria, meaning "the swinging one." Its feast day is the same day as the Entrance of the Panagia into the Temple. This miracleworking icon is enshrined in the Church of the Three Hierarchs in the main port town of Skiathos, Greece.

COMMEMORATIONS: Entrance of the Theotokos into the Temple; Columbanus of Bobbio (Gaul); Alexander Khotovitsky of New York; Repose of St. Philaret the New Confessor of New York; *Everlasting Hope* and *Eikonistria* (Swinging one) Icons of the Mother of God.

NOVEMBER 22

Philemon 1:1-25
Luke 18:15-17, 26-30

*P*eople mostly pray as if there were no God with them, or as if He did not heed their prayers. Let us ascribe to the Lord at least the same amount of attention that good parents show to the requests of their children, at least that provident and attentive love which good parents have for their children.

St. John of Kronstadt

MARTYR PROKOPIOS OF PALESTINE. In the year 303, Prokopios was the first of all the martyrs in Palestine. Even as a young boy, he had pure habits and strict morals. His sustenance was bread and water, and then only every second or third day, or often he went a whole week without food. He was modest and edified others with his meekness and piety. He was a Reader in the Church and translated works into Aramaic. One day, he was sent from his city of Scythopolis to Caesarea. The moment he passed the gates of the city, he was taken to the governor and told that he must sacrifice to the gods. In a loud voice, Prokopios said, "There is no God but one only, the Maker and Creator of all things." The governor changed his tactic and commanded Prokopios to sacrifice to their four emperors. Prokopios laughed and quoted the words of the greatest of Greek poets, saying, "the rule of many is not good; let there be one ruler and one sovereign." Because St. Prokopios insulted the emperors, he was beheaded.

COMMEMORATIONS: Apostles of the Seventy Archippos, Philemon, Onesimus, and Apphia; Menignos the Fuller; Cecilia, Valerian, Tiburtius, and Maximus, at Rome; Procopius the Reader at Caesarea; Stephen, Mark, and Mark at Antioch; Callistus II, Patriarch of Constantinople; Agabbas of Syria; Agapion of Greece, with Sisinius and Agapius; Germanus of Eikoiphinissa; Martyrs Thaddeus, Christopher, Euphemia, Thallelaius and Anthimus; Anthony of Izeru Skete; Yaropolk-Peter of Vladimir; Michael, Great Prince of Tver; Clement of Ochrid; Michael the Soldier; Joasaph of Mogilev, Gerasim of Smolensk, Alexis of Tver, and Elijah of Tver; Eutychius Didenko, Abner Sinitsyn, Sava Suslov, and Mark Makhrov of Optina, with Boris Kozlov; Iakovos (Tsalikis) of Evia.

NOVEMBER 23

*D*o you desire that others be better off than yourself? May the Lord help us love others like that, especially those who wish us harm or treat us harshly. When the peace of Christ enters the soul, then she is glad to sit like Job among the ashes and behold others in glory; then does the soul rejoice that she is worse than everyone else. This Christ-like humility is a great mystery, impossible to unfold. From love, the soul wishes every human being more good than she wishes for herself, and delights when she sees others happier, and grieves to see them suffering.

St. Silouan the Athonite

ST. DIONYSIOS I THE WISE, PATRIARCH OF CONSTANTINO-PLE. Dionysios studied at the School of Philosophou Monastery in the fifteenth century. He became a monk in Constantinople under the supervision of his spiritual father, St. Mark Eugenikos, Metropolitan of Ephesus. He also ordained Dionysios to the priesthood. Later, he was elevated to the rank of Metropolitan and ascended to the Ecumenical Throne of Constantinople with the protection of Madam-Mara, one of the wives of Sultan Murad II. At that time, the Patriarchal Throne was contested with candidates from two competing factions. Dionysios was maliciously scandalized and deposed. He departed for the Monastery of Eikosifinissa in Drama, where he is considered its second founder. He was recalled as Ecumenical Patriarch but served only a short time due to his old age. He reposed peacefully at his monastery in Drama.

COMMEMORATIONS: Gregory, Bishop of Agrigentum; Sisinios the Confessor, Bishop of Cyzicus; Amphilochius, Bishop of Iconium; Ischyrion, bishop in Egypt; Metrophanes, Bishop of Voronezh; Trudo of Zirkingen; Dionysius I, Patriarch of Constantinople; Amphilochius of the Kiev Caves; Gregory Peradze of Georgia; Elenos of Tarsus; Anthony of Iezeru-Vilcea (Romania); Seraphim Tievar of Moscow; Boris Voskoboinikov of Ivanovo; Eleazar Spyridonov of Eupatoria, Crimea; Alexander, in Perm; Columban of Luxeuil Abbey; Burial of St. Alexander Nevsky, Great Prince of Novgorod.

If we turn our attention to our mind, we'll see a torrent of successive thoughts and ideas. This torrent is unrelenting; it tumbles quickly in every direction and at every moment—at home, in church, at work, when we're reading, when we're talking. Saint Theophan the Recluse writes that we usually call it "thought," but in reality, it's a turbulence within the mind, a scattering, a lack of concentration and attention.

St. John Maximovitch

ST. PROTASIUS, BISHOP OF MILAN. Protasius was elected Bishop of Milan in 328, and he served for fifteen years. He was with St. Athanasius of Alexandria when they spoke to the Roman Emperor Constantius II to convene a Synod against the Arians who denied Christ's divinity. The Arians claimed the Son of God was created by the Father and was therefore neither co-eternal with the Father nor consubstantial. Protasius attended the Synod of Sardica and signed its decrees, standing up against the Arians and supporting the faith of the First Synod of Nicaea in 325. He died peacefully and was buried in Milan, in the Church of San Vittore al Corpo, where he is still venerated.

COMMEMORATIONS: Hermogenes, Bishop of Agrigentum; Clement, Pope of Rome; Peter, Archbishop of Alexandria; Gregory, founder of the monastery of the Golden Rock in Pontus; Alexander at Corinth; Theodore of Antioch; Mastridia of Alexandria; Mercurius of Smolensk; Mercurius of the Kiev Caves; Mercurius the Faster of the Far Caves; Luke, steward of the Kiev Caves; Simon, founder of Soiga Monastery (Vologda); Chrysogonos at Aquileia; Mark of Trigleia; Malchus of Chalcis in Syria; Martyrs Philoumenos, Christopher, Eugene, Procopius, and Christopher; Righteous Carion; Nikodemos the Younger of Philokalos Monastery in Thessalonica; Protasius of Auvergne (Gaul); Romanus of Bordeaux; Portianus of Arthone (Gaul).

St. Katherine the Great Martyr
Abstain from meat and dairy products.

NOVEMBER 25

Galatians 3:23-4:5; Mark 5:24-34

The soul cannot know peace unless she prays for her enemies. The soul that has learned of God's grace to pray, feels love and compassion for every created thing, and in particular for mankind, for whom the Lord suffered on the Cross, and His soul was heavy for every one of us.

St. Silouan the Athonite

HIEROMARTYR PETER, ARCHBISHOP OF ALEXANDRIA. Peter served the Church during the third to fourth centuries. He became a Church reader, deacon, and then priest. He was highly educated and became head of the school of Alexandria. He was chosen as bishop during a ten-year period of Christian persecutions under the emperor Diocletian. Forced into exile, he traveled through many lands, encouraging his flock by letter. After returning to Alexandria, he secretly visited the imprisoned, assisted widows and orphans, and conducted clandestine services. According to one account, Peter was imprisoned with Bishop Meletius of Lycopolis. They would argue over the treatment of Christians who had either offered sacrifices to pagan gods or surrendered scriptures to the authorities to save their own lives during persecution. Peter urged leniency while Meletius said that they needed to be rebaptized. Peter finally became frustrated and hung a curtain between them. Diocletian gave orders to behead Peter, but a large number of Christians gathered at the prison, offering to die for their Patriarch. Fearing for the life of his people, Peter devised a way for the soldiers to smuggle him out of prison secretly so that the sentence could be carried out. St. Peter was beheaded.

COMMEMORATIONS: Mercurius of Caesarea; Katherine of Alexandria, with 50 rhetoricians, Augusta, Porphyrius, and 200 soldiers; Moses of Rome; Peter of Alexandria; Peter the Silent; Seraphim of Smolensk; 670 Martyrs beheaded; Clement of Ochrid, Bishop of Greater Macedonia.

Thirteenth Sunday of Luke
Abstain from meat and dairy products.

NOVEMBER 26

Ephesians 4:1-7
Luke 18:18-27

It is not the power of man which makes what is put before us the Body and Blood of Christ, but the power of Christ Himself who was crucified for us. The priest standing there in the place of Christ says these words, but their power and grace are from God. 'This is My Body,' he says, and these words transform what lies before him.

St. John Chrysostom

VENERABLE ALYPIOS THE STYLITE OF ADRIANOPOLIS. Alypios was a poor and uneducated young Christian man in sixth-century Adrianopolis. When he was three, his father died, and his mother placed him in the care of Bishop Theodore and in the service of the Church. When he came of age, Alypios was made a deacon. But he desired the ascetic life, so he retreated to a cemetery inhabited by demons and feared by the people. He built a church there dedicated to St. Euphemia. He also made a column upon which he would live for the next five decades. Alypios not only battled the elements but also the demons. When the demons could not intimidate him with fierce illusions, they stoned him. The weapons Alypios used were his prayers and the Sign of the Cross. When he finally prevailed, the demons fled, and the people began coming to Alypios for prayers and healing. Two monasteries were built on either side of his column, one for men and one for women. St. Alypios died in 640, at the age of 118. His sacred head is located on Mount Athos at the Monastery of Koutloumusiou.

COMMEMORATIONS: Innocent, first bishop of Irkutsk; James the Solitary of Syria; Stylianos of Paphlagonia; Alypios the Stylite of Adrianople; Peter, Patriarch of Jerusalem; Silas of Persidos; Acacius of Mt. Latros, who is mentioned in *The Ladder*; George of Chios; Sophianos of Dryinoupolis; Athanasius and Theodosius of Cherepovets Monastery (Vologda); Nikon Metanoeite of Armenia; Tikhon Buzov of Donskoy Monastery (Moscow); Consecration of the Church of St. George in Kyparission; (Last Sunday in November: Synaxis of the Achaean Saints; Synaxis of the Saints of Agia).

Abstain from meat and dairy products.

NOVEMBER 27

1 Timothy 1:1-7
Luke 19:37-44

A place does not save you. There is no place where you can flee from yourself.

St. Nikon of Optina

VENERABLE PINUPHRIUS OF EGYPT. Pinuphrius led a huge Coenobium in Egypt. He was highly esteemed for his humility, virtues, and miracle-working. But he feared the praise of men, so he fled into the far reaches of the Thebaid dressed in secular clothing to conceal his identity. He went to the Coenobium of Tabenna, which was the strictest of all. Kneeling at the entrance door for a long time, he sought the prayers of the fathers. At last, with much scorn, they admitted him. They thought he wanted to live there because he was old and lacked food. Pinuphrius remained there as a novice, and his obedience was the keeper of the gardens while under the watchful eye of a younger monk. But he completed many projects secretly during the night for the benefit of the monastery. For three years, the monks at his former monastery never ceased searching for him. When they found him and called out his name, everyone was astonished. He was taken back against his will, and he grieved because he enjoyed that state of subjection. Pinuphrius departed from there again, this time to a monastery in Bethlehem. He served as a novice, but some monks from his monastery again discovered him. St. Pinuphrius returned to his monastery for the last time and died peacefully.

COMMEMORATIONS: Pinuphrius of Egypt; James the Persian; James of Rostov; 17 Monk-Martyrs in India; Theodosius of Turnovo; Diodorus of George Hill; Palladius of Thessalonica; Palladius of Elenopolis; Nathaniel of Nitria; Akakios, Damaskinos, and Rendini; Maurice of Rome, and his 6 sons; Andrew Ogorodnikov; Nicholas of Vladimir; Nikon of the Staro-Golutvin; Joasaph of Nikolskoye; Nicholas of Peshnosha; Apollos of Moscow; Cronides, Seraphim, and Xenophont of St. Sergius; Virgil of Salzburg; Congar of Somerset; Fergus of Glamis; Maximus of Riez; Synaxis of the New Martyrs and Confessors of Radonezh; Weeping Icon *Of the Sign* at Novgorod; *Kursk-Root, Of Abalak, Of Tsarskoe Selo,* and *Of Seraphimo-Ponetaev* Icons of the Mother of God.

TUESDAY   **Abstain from meat and dairy products.**

NOVEMBER 28
1 Timothy 1:8-14
Luke 19:45-48

I must always be ready for death; I should live as if it were the last
day of my life.

St. Pachomios of Chios

**MARTYRS TIMOTHY, THEODORE, COMASIUS, EUSEBIUS, ETY-
MASIUS, PETER, JOHN, SERGIUS, THEODORE, NICEPHORUS,
BASIL, THOMAS, HIEROTHEUS, DANIEL, CHARITON, AND
SOCRATES, AT TIBERIOPOLIS.** In the fourth century, Julian the Apostate began his Christian persecutions because his sorcerers taught him that
by uttering the name of Christ, which has great power, his evil deeds would
be thwarted. Many suffered and died, and others fled to the city of Tiberiopolis, north of Thessalonica. Among them were Etymasius, Timothy and
Theodore, who later became bishops, and Comasius and Eusebius, who
became monks. They were joined later by priests, deacons, and monks,
and they assembled to study the word of God. They enlightened others
and healed them. When the rulers of Thessalonica heard this, they had the
saints seized and reprimanded, but they attacked the vanity of idols. They
declared that God had delivered them from the slavery of demons, and they
would never sacrifice to them. They were sentenced to death by the sword,
which filled them with joy. One of these sixteen martyrs, Peter, was beaten
with rods when he asked why pagans shed the blood of righteous people.
His hands were severed, and then he was beheaded. One of his hands fell
near a blind woman, and when she picked it up, her sight was restored.
The relics of all the saints were gathered and interred separately. Numerous miracles occurred there that caused many idol-worshippers to believe.

COMMEMORATIONS: Stephen the New and with him: Basil, Stephen,
Gregory, Gregory, John, Andrew, Peter, Anna; Irenarchos and 7 Women-
Martyrs; Timothy and Theodore, Peter, John, Sergius, Theodore, Nicephorus,
Basil, Thomas, Hierotheus, Daniel, Chariton, Socrates, Comasius, Eusebius,
and Etymasius, at Tiberiopolis; Christos of Constantinople; Anna, Martyr for
the Holy Icons; Oda of Brabant; Theodore of Rostov; Juthwara of Cornwall;
Seraphim of St. Petersburg; Raphael of Zlatoustov; Vincent of Optina.

NOVEMBER 29

1 Timothy 1:18-20, 2:8-15
Luke 20:1-8

So there is one great truth: that just as our heart is disposed towards our brother, in the same way the heart of God will be disposed towards us. Do you want God to forgive your errors? Do you want Him to love you with all His heart? Then you too should love and forgive with all your heart.

† *Elder Ephraim of Arizona*

ST. DIONYSIUS, BISHOP OF CORINTH. Dionysius was Bishop of Corinth during the second-century reign of Marcus Aurelius. He was an ecclesiastical writer and wrote epistles to the people of his own city and those in other provinces and cities. He urged peace and unity within the Church and admonished the people of Athens for taking the faith too lightly, almost to the point of being apostates. He gave advice about marriage and chastity and recommended that the yoke of celibacy not be placed too heavily on his brethren and to consider the weakness most of them have. He also recommended charitable treatment to those who had fallen into sin and heresy, to do good to all the brethren, and send alms to many churches in different cities. St. Dionysius was killed by the sword for his faith.

COMMEMORATIONS: Nicholas, Archbishop of Thessalonica; Philoumenos of Ancyra, with Valerian and Phaedrus; Philoumenos of Jacob's Well; Dionysius of Corinth; Tiridates of Armenia; Abibus of Nekresi in Georgia; Paramon and 370 Martyrs, at Bithynia; John of Persia; Urban of Macedonia; Saturninus of Toulouse; Pitirim of Egypt; Radboud of Utrecht; Nectarius the Obedient of the Kiev Caves; Brendan of Birr; Mardarije Uskokovic, missionary and first Serbian bishop in America (Serbian Calendar); Pankosmios the Ascetic; 6 Martyrs who entered a rock which wondrously opened and received them.

Holy Apostle Andrew the First-Called
Abstain from meat and dairy products.

1 Corinthians 4:9-16
John 1:35-51

In the end times a man will be saved by love, humbleness and kindness. Kindness will open the gates of Heaven; humbleness will lead him into Heaven; a man, whose heart is filled with love, will see God.

St. Gabriel Urgebadze

HOLY APOSTLE ANDREW, THE FIRST-CALLED. Andrew was the brother of Apostle Peter. At first, he was a disciple of St. John the Baptist. After Pentecost, Andrew taught in Byzantium, Thrace, Scythia, Epiros, and Peloponnesus. In Amisos, he converted the Jews in the temple, baptized them, healed their sick, built a church, and left a priest for them. And in Bithynia, Andrew preached, healed the sick, and drove away wild beasts. In Sinope, he prayed for the imprisoned Apostle Matthias, and his chains fell away and the cell door opened for him. The people beat Andrew, breaking his teeth and cutting his fingers, leaving him for dead in a dung heap. Jesus appeared to him and healed him, and when the people saw him the next day, they were amazed and believed. In Patras, Andrew healed a paralytic, lepers, and every disease. When the proconsul Aegeates heard all of this, he arrested Andrew and tried to compel him through beatings to sacrifice to the idols and restore idolatry to his country. When Andrew refused, he was tied to a cross upside down so that he would live longer and suffer more. Twenty thousand of the faithful stood by and mourned. From the cross, Andrew continued teaching and urging them to endure temporary sufferings for the kingdom of heaven. Suddenly, a heavenly light illumined Andrew for about half an hour, and then he gave up his spirit. Aegeates fell from a high place and was crushed to death.

COMMEMORATIONS: Apostle Andrew the First-Called; Alexander, Bishop of Methymna; Frumentios of Abyssinia; Peter I and Samuel I, Catholicoses of Georgia; Vakhtang Gorgasali of Georgia; Tudwal of Treguier; Andrew of Transylvania; Simeon of Belgrade; Elias of Valaam.

DECEMBER I

1 Timothy 4:4-8
Luke 20:19-26

*P*ray and then speak. That's what to do with your children. If you are constantly lecturing them, you'll become tiresome and when they grow up, they'll feel a kind of oppression. Prefer prayer and speak to them through prayer. Speak to God and God will speak to their hearts. That is, you shouldn't give guidance to your children with a voice that they hear with their ears. You may do this too, but above all you should speak to God about your children. Say, "Lord Jesus Christ, give Your light to my children. I entrust them to You. You gave them to me, but I am weak and unable to guide them, so, please, illuminate them." And God will speak to them, and they will say to themselves, "Oh dear, I shouldn't have upset mommy by doing that!" And with the grace of God this will come from their heart.

St. Porphyrios of Kavsokalyvia

PROPHET NAHUM THE ELKOSHITE. Prophet Nahum was from Elkosh and the tribe of Symeon. He was one of the Twelve Lesser Prophets and lived in the seventh century BC. After the death of Prophet Jonah, Nahum prophesied the doom of the city of Nineveh because of their iniquity. When Jonah had prophesied Nineveh's destruction, the king and all the people dressed in sackcloth and ashes, and the town was saved. But they did not heed Nahum's prophecy, so they experienced such floods, fires, and earthquakes that the city could no longer be found. Prophet Nahum died at the age of forty-five. His book of prophecies can be found in the Old Testament.

COMMEMORATIONS: Prophet Nahum; Onesimus of Ephesus; Ananias and Solochonus of Ephesus; Philaretos the Merciful of Amnea; Anthony the New of Kios; Ananias of Persia; Theokletos, Archbishop of Lacedaemon; Eligius of Noyon; Tudwal of Lan Pabu; Innocent Letyaev of Kharkov and Akhtyra; Leontius, Bishop of Fréjus; Translation of the relics of St. Botolph of Ikanhoe, England.

DECEMBER 2

Galatians 3:8-12
Luke 12:32-40

*S*trive not to pray against someone in your prayer, lest you destroy what you are building, by making your prayer an abomination (before God).

St. Nilus of Sinai

ST. ABBAKUM OF FTERIKOUDI, THE WONDERWORKER. There was a time when 300 refugees fled from Palestine to Cyprus during the Arab persecutions when they had conquered Palestine and Syria. The ascetic monk Abbakum took refuge in a cave on Mount Kalamithia near the village of Fterikoudi. While enduring the cold of winter, he entered the spiritual struggles of fasting, nakedness, and humility. He spent most of his time praying and was able to cleanse himself of his passions, and God granted him the gift of miracles for physical illnesses and those of the soul. He especially healed the deaf but worked many other miracles until his peaceful death in old age. A church was built in his honor, and miracles continued for those who fled to him, especially the deaf. St. Abbakum's memory is celebrated on the same day as the Old Testament Prophet Habakkuk, from which comes the Greek name Abbakum.

COMMEMORATIONS: Prophet Habakkuk (Abbacum); John, Heracleon, Andrew, and Theophilus, of Egypt; Solomon of Ephesus; Cyril of Philea; Stephen-Urosh V, King of Serbia and his mother Helen; Jesse of Tsilkani in Georgia; Athanasius "the Resurrected," recluse of the Kiev Caves; Athanasius, recluse of the Kiev Caves; Myrope of Chios; Habibus the New of Edessa; Abbakum of Cyprus; Joannicius of Devic (Serbia); Viviana of Rome; Chromatius, Bishop of Aquileia; Danax Kalashnikov of Arkhangelskoye and Cosmas Magda of Milyatino (Moscow); Porphyrios of Kavsokalyvia and Kallisa; *Gerontissa* Icon of the Mother of God.

DECEMBER 3

Fourteenth Sunday of Luke
Abstain from meat and dairy products.
Ephesians 5:8-19
Luke 18:35-43

If you want to rest, go to nature.

St. John Chrysostom

NEW MARTYR ANGELOS AT CHIOS. Angelos was a physician in nineteenth-century Argos in the Peloponnesus. While he was talking about his Orthodox Christian faith, a Frenchman began to poke fun at him, and Angelos responded to each of these attacks. He said that he could prove the holiness of his faith not only with words but also with works. He challenged the Frenchman to a public duel and told him to arm himself any way he wished while Angelos would be armed with a piece of wood. And he said, "I will slay you with the power of my faith." Angelos spent the night in prayer, and in the morning, he received Holy Communion. But the Frenchman backed out of the duel, and Angelos was saddened that he would not be defending his faith. He gave up his medical practice and decided that he wanted to become a martyr for Christ. One day, he dressed as a Muslim, went to their judge, and asked to be accepted into their religion. They thought his behavior was bizarre, so they refused him. Then Angelos pulled out a gun and threatened a Muslim, thinking they might reconsider. Now they thought Angelos was crazy, so he was exiled to Chios. He continued his strange behavior there in a manner akin to a Fool-for-Christ. Still dressed as a Muslim, he would pray in church with copious tears and hand out alms to those in need. The Orthodox Christians also thought that Angelos was strange. He began to tell Muslims that he would be a Christian martyr, and this angered a certain Muslim who hit Angelos with a gun. Because of this, Angelos announced to a pasha that he was returning to Orthodoxy. He was beaten, flattered, and offered rewards. When he refused their offers, St. Angelos was beheaded.

COMMEMORATIONS: Prophet Zephaniah; John the Silent; Theodore, Patriarch of Alexandria; Theodoulos of Constantinople; Theodoulos of Cyprus; Angelos of Chios; Cosmas of St. Anne's; Martyrs Mamas, Seleucus, and Agapius; Gabriel II, Patriarch of Constantinople; Sabbas of Zvenigorod; Gregory of Cherniksk; Nicetius of Lyons; George of Cernica; Birinus of Dorchester; Sola, missionary; Lucius of Britain; Hilarion of Krutitsa.

MONDAY

DECEMBER 4

St. Barbara the Great Martyr
Abstain from meat and dairy products.
Galatians 3:23-4:5
Mark 5:24-34

ood is invisible, as things in heaven are invisible. But evil is visible, as things on earth are visible.

St. Anthony the Great

NEW HIEROMARTYR SERAPHIM, ARCHBISHOP OF PHANARION AND NEOCHORION.

Seraphim was born to a pious family in the village of Pezoula, Agrapha region of Greece. He had a well-ordered mind and eschewed worldly pleasures as a young man. He went to the Holy Monastery of the Cold Spring, where he imitated the most virtuous brethren and was soon elevated to the priesthood. After the death of the Metropolitan of Phanarion and Neochorion, the humble Seraphim was elected. He taught by word and deed and hoped to be worthy of martyrdom for Christ one day. When Greece was under Ottoman rule at the turn of the seventeenth century, Metropolitan Dionysius of Larissa organized an insurrection. Many died, and Dionysius was captured and killed. Seraphim was falsely accused of conspiring with Dionysius, who he had avoided. The judge told Seraphim that he would be freed and honored if he renounced Christianity, but Seraphim proclaimed that he would never abandon Jesus Christ. He was imprisoned, disfigured, and left to starve. His disfiguration brought him joy, as he had now suffered for Christ. The agha ordered more vicious tortures, and still Seraphim's countenance was radiant. A shameless woman hurled insults and abuses at him on the way to his execution. Seraphim looked at her, and a power emanated from him that disfigured her face. Seraphim was suspended by his ankles and impaled. After giving up his spirit, his body was left in the elements for days, yet it was fragrant and appeared as though alive. St. Seraphim's relics were returned to his monastery, and innumerable miracles continue to occur.

COMMEMORATIONS: Great Martyr Barbara and Juliana, at Heliopolis; John Damascene of St. Sabbas; Gennadius of Novgorod; Seraphim of Phanarion and Neochorion; John of Polybotos; Damascene of Glukhov, and his father Nicholas; Martyrs Christodulus and Christodula.

DECEMBER 5

Galatians 5:22-6:2
Matthew 11:27-30

*W*hen we, with our laudations, create this 'superego' in the child, we inflate its egotism and we do it great harm. We make the child more susceptible to demonic influence. And so, as we bring it up, we steadily distance it from the values of life. Don't you believe that this is the reason why children go astray and people rebel? It is the egotism that their parents have implanted in them from an early age. The devil is the great egotist, the great Lucifer. In other words, we live with Lucifer inside us, with the devil. We don't live with humility. Humility is from God; it is something essential for the human soul. It is something organic. And if it is missing, it is as if the heart were missing from the human organism. The heart gives life to the body and humility gives life to the soul. With egotism a person is given over to the part of the evil spirit, that is, he develops with the evil spirit and not with the good spirit.

St. Porphyrios of Kavsokalyvia

VENERABLE PHILOTHEOS OF KARYES. Philotheos lived in Karyes on Mount Athos, where he was the abbot of the Cell of the Archangels of Dionysios lagaris that belonged to the Monastery of Great Lavra. He lived a life of virtue and asceticism and led others along the same path, including St. Nektarios the Athonite. Philotheos was granted the gifts of clairvoyance and foresight. He reposed peacefully in deep old age and was buried at his cell.

COMMEMORATIONS: Savvas the Sanctified; Nicetius, Bishop of Trier; Gurias of Kazan; Kosmas the Protos of Vatopedi and the monks of Karyes; Philotheos and Nektarios of Bitol, of Karyes; Martyrs Gratos, Diogenes, Abercius, Nonnos, and Crispina; Martyr Anastasias; Carion and Zachariah of Egypt; Justinian of Ramsey Island (Wales); Elias Chetverukhin of Moscow and Gennadius Petlyuk of Yaroslavl; Sergius Pravdolyubov of Ryazan.

St. Nicholas the Wonderworker
Strict Fast

DECEMBER 6

Hebrews 13:17-21; Luke 6:17-23

"*Therefore* brethren, stand fast and hold on to the traditions which you have been taught, whether by word, or by our letter ..." From this it is clear that the early believers did not hand down everything by letter, but that there was much which was not written. Like that which was written, the unwritten too is worthy of our belief. So let us regard the tradition of the Church also as worthy of belief. Is it a tradition? Seek no further.

St. John Chrysostom

ST. GERTRUDE, ABBESS OF HAMAGE. Gertrude was the daughter of a nobleman of France, and she also married a nobleman. Widowed at an early age, she devoted herself to her three sons' education, one of whom would one day be venerated as a martyr and saint, Adalbald. Her other son, Sigebert, married a future saint, Bertha. When Gertrude's sons moved on, she went to live at an oratory, a place for divine worship, and she devoted herself to religious exercises and acts of charity. She was joined there by her granddaughter, Eusebia. Gertrude later learned that her son Adalbald had been assassinated. She founded a convent at Hamage and became its abbess. Before her death in 649, St. Gertrude trained her granddaughter in religious life, and she later governed that convent.

COMMEMORATIONS: Nicholas the Wonderworker, Archbishop of Myra in Lycia; Theophilus of Antioch; Maximus, Metropolitan of Kiev; Nicholas of Patara; Nicholas of Tobolsk; Nicholas, missionary of Moscow; Dionysia, Dativa, Emilianus, Boniface, Leontia, Tertius, and Majoricus, in Africa; Nicholas of Novo-Nikolskaya; Nicholas Karamanos of Smyrna; Gertrude of Hamage; Commemoration of the divine warning of an impending earthquake in Constantinople in 1090; *Seafaring* Icon of the Mother of God.

DECEMBER 7

1 Timothy 6:17-21
Luke 21:28-33

'*God is greater than our heart and knows all things*' (1 Jn. 3:20). Through our spiritual vision we see and know the smallest movements of the heart, all our thoughts, desires and intentions in general, almost everything that is in our soul. But God is greater than our heart. He is within us and around us and everywhere, in every place, as the Single, All-seeing, Spiritual Eye, of which our own spiritual vision is but a small specimen, and, therefore, He knows all that is in us a thousand times better and more clearly than we ourselves; at the same time He knows everything that is in every man, in every angel, and in all the heavenly powers, in every animate and inanimate creature; sees as upon the palm of His hand all that is within us and every creature, being inherent in each one of them, and maintaining each one of them in its existence and functions, as the All-Provident Creator.

St. John of Kronstadt

ST. DIUMA, BISHOP OF MERCIA. Diuma was of Irish descent. He was one of four priests sent by St. Finan, Bishop of Lindisfarne, to evangelize Mercia, now known as the Midlands of England. They were granted permission to evangelize after the baptism of King Penda of Mercia. Diuma was consecrated bishop of the Mercians and Middle Anglians. The apostolic mission of these four priests was successful.

COMMEMORATIONS: Ambrose of Milan; Athenodoros of Mesopotamia; 62 priests and 300 laymen martyred by the Arians; Philothea of Turnovo; Paul the Obedient; John the Faster; Ignatius, near Blachernae; Nilus of Stolben; Ammoun of Nitria; Anthony of Siya; Female Martyr of Old Rome; Bassa of Jerusalem; Acepsimas, Isidore, and Leo; Gaius and Gainus; Gerasimos of Euripos; John of St. Sabbas; Gregory the Silent; Ambrose of Cyprus; Neophytus, Dometius, Priscus, Martin, and Nicholas; Sergius and Andronicus of Tambov; Ambrose of Kamenets-Podol; Gurias of Optina and Galacteon of Valaam; Diuma of Mercia; Repose of Elder Ephraim of Arizona (2019); *Vladimir* Icon of the Mother of God of Seliger.

DECEMBER 8

2 Timothy 1:1-2, 8-18
Luke 21:37-22:8

*H*ow can you find out if you are living within the will of God? Here is the sign: If you are troubled about anything, this means that you have not completely given yourself over to the will of God. A person who lives in the will of God is not concerned over anything. And if he needs anything, he gives both it and himself over to God. And if he does not receive the necessary thing, he remains calm nevertheless, as if he had it. The soul which has been given over to the will of God is afraid of nothing, not of thunder nor of thieves—nothing. But whatever happens, she says, "Thus it pleases God." If she is sick, she thinks: this means that I need to be sick, or else God would not have given it to me. Thus peace is preserved in both soul and body.

St. Silouan the Athonite

ST. SOPHRONIUS I, BISHOP OF CYPRUS. Sophronius was a sixth-century native of Cyprus and the son of pious Christian parents. He possessed a genius disposition, and for many years he read and meditated on the Holy Scriptures day and night. He applied himself to observe all the commandments of God with exactness and was made worthy to receive great spiritual gifts and the power to work miracles. When the Archbishop of Cyprus died, the Christians chose Sophronius to lead them. He immediately became the nourisher of the hungry, provider of the poor, helper of orphans, protector of widows, coverer of the naked, and deliverer of the afflicted. St. Sophronius died in peace.

COMMEMORATIONS: Apostles of the Seventy: Sosthenes, Apollos, Cephas, Tychicus, Epaphroditus, Caesarius, and Onesiphorus; Patapios of Thebes; Anthusa, at Rome; Cyril, founder of Chelmogorsk Monastery (Karelia); Sophronius I, Bishop of Cyprus; Parthenios of Chios; Budock, Bishop of Dol; Valerius, Bishop of Trier.

SATURDAY

DECEMBER 9

**Conception by St. Anna of
the Most Holy Mother of God**
**Abstain from meat
and dairy products.**
Galatians 4:22-27; Luke 8:16-21

*W*hat words, O Mother of God and Virgin, can describe your
divinely radiant beauty? Your qualities cannot be circumscribed by
thoughts or words, for they transcend our minds and speech. But
it is possible to sing your praises if you—in your charity—so
permit. In you, all graces are to be found. You are the perfection
of nobility in all its forms—the living portrait of every virtue and
kindness.

St. Gregory Palamas

VIRGIN-MARTYR LEOCADIA. During the Diocletian persecution,
Leocadia suffered for Christ in early fourth-century Toledo, Spain. Recent
works relate that she was filled with a desire for martyrdom because of
the story of the martyrdom of St. Eulalia. It was written that the governor Decianus was a furious persecutor of Christians in Spain. He seized
Leocadia and cruelly tortured her in an attempt to force her into apostasy,
but she remained steadfast. She was returned to prison, where she died
from her wounds. A contemporary witness wrote that when they visited
the cell where Leocadia was imprisoned, there still existed the sign of the
cross impressed into the stone because she constantly made the sign of the
cross with her fingers. Leocadia was buried in the local cemetery, and soon
a cult sprang up around her grave. In very early times, there was a church
in Toledo dedicated to St. Leocadia. Her relics were moved several times
before they were finally returned to Toledo.

COMMEMORATIONS: Conception by St. Anna of the Most Holy
Theotokos; Prophetess Anna (Hannah), mother of the Prophet Samuel;
Stephen "the New Light" of Constantinople; Narses of Persia; New Martyr
Priest Sergius Mechev of Moscow; Sositheus of Persia; Valeria of Aquitaine;
Anthimus, the Fool-for-Christ of Sofia, Bulgaria; Leocadia of Toledo, Spain;
Commemoration of the Founding of the Church of the Resurrection at
Jerusalem; *Unexpected Joy* Icon of the Mother of God.

Tenth Sunday of Luke
Abstain from meat and dairy products.

DECEMBER 10

Ephesians 6:10-17
Luke 13:10-17

*S*how great obedience, trust and acceptance towards your spiritual father, always telling him the truth.

St. Daniel of Katounakia

ST. JOASAPH, BISHOP OF BELGOROD. At the age of seven, Joasaph was enrolled in the Kiev Spiritual Academy, and it was there that he kindled a desire to become a monk. Later, when he told his parents, they implored him not to take that direction. However, at the age of twenty, he secretly became a novice. Two years later, he received monastic tonsure. Archbishop Raphael of Kiev noticed Joasaph's abilities and appointed him to the office of examiner of the diocese. He worked to correct the clergy's moral deficiencies, examined the clergy's needs, and studied the areas where the diocese might improve. He became an excellent administrator. He wrote "The Conflict of the Seven Venerable Virtues with the Seven Deadly Sins." Later he was made the abbot of the Transfiguration Mgarsk Monastery, where the relics of St Athanasius, Patriarch of Constantinople, were kept. On several occasions, St. Athanasius appeared to Joasaph as a sign of his protection of the monastery. Raphael elevated Joasaph to archimandrite and brought him to Moscow as vicar of yet another monastery. At the age of forty-three, he was made Bishop of Belgorod. In this capacity, he concerned himself with the moral condition of his flock, the piety and state of the churches, and the proper celebration of the Divine services. St. Joasaph died peacefully at the age of forty-eight.

COMMEMORATIONS: Menas the Melodius, Hermogenes, and Eugraphus, of Alexandria; Hieromartyr Theoteknos; John, King of Serbia, and his parents Stephen the Blind and Angelina Brancovich; Gemellos of Paphlagonia; Martyrs Marianos and Eugenios; Athanasios of Methoni; Thomas Dephourkinos of Mt. Kyminas; Joasaph of Belgorod; Sergius and Anna of Sreznevo.

DECEMBER 11

2 Timothy 2:20-26; Mark 8:11-21

*R*efrain from heated discussions on religious matters; there is no good in them.

St. Macarius of Optina

VENERABLE NICON THE DRY OF THE KIEV CAVES MONASTERY. Nicon became a monk at the Kiev Caves Monastery in the early eleventh century. He was a visionary and miracleworker and was called "the withered" because of his great fasting. He was once taken captive by the Tartars and was tortured and chained for three years. A relative tried to ransom him, but Nicon refused, saying that God would not have allowed him to be captured if He wanted him to be free. When his master became terminally ill, he ordered his sons to crucify Nicon on his grave after his death. Having the gift of discernment, Nicon saw that his master would be baptized, so he prayed for his recovery. The Tartar recovered, and Nicon was saved from physical death and his master from spiritual death. One day, he told his master that the Lord would free him in three days. The master cut the tendons in Nicon's legs and set a guard. On the third day, Nicon was invisibly carried to Kiev. A long time passed, and the old master happened upon Nicon at the Kiev Caves Monastery. He repented and received Holy Baptism and became a disciple of the saint. St. Nicon's incorrupt relics are buried in the Near Caves.

COMMEMORATIONS: Daniel the Stylite of Constantinople; Mirax of Egypt; Barsabas of Ishtar, and 10 companions in Persia; Aeithalas and Acepsius at Arbela; Nicon "the Dry" of the Kiev Caves; Theophanes Ilminsky of Perm and Solikamsk, and 2 priests and 5 laymen; Nomon of Cyprus; Martyrs Terence, Vincent, Emilian, and Bebaia; Leontios of Monemvasia; Luke the New Stylite of Chalcedon; Nikephoros Phokas, Emperor of the Romans; Synaxis of All Saints of Georgia; Repose of St. Kuksha of Odessa.

TUESDAY

DECEMBER 12

St. Spyridon the Wonderworker
**Abstain from meat and
dairy products, and fish.**
Ephesians 5:8-19; John 10:9-16

The goal of reading is the application, in our lives, of what we read. Not to learn it by heart, but to take it to heart. Not to practice using our tongues, but to be able to receive the tongues of fire and to live the mysteries of God. If one studies a great deal in order to acquire knowledge and to teach others, without living the things he teaches, he does no more than fill his head with hot air. At most he will manage to ascend to the moon using machines. The goal of the Christian is to rise to God without machines.

St. Paisios the Athonite

HIEROMARTYR ALEXANDER, ARCHBISHOP OF JERUSALEM.
Alexander was an aide to the Archbishop of Jerusalem in the third century. He created an ecclesiastical library in Jerusalem by collecting the growing works of noted writers. When his predecessor was martyred, Alexander was elected to fill his position. Emperor Decius began persecuting Christians, and Alexander was brought in chains before the prefect in Caesarea. He was ordered to sacrifice to idols, but he said idols were demons and a clear deception. And with a loud and clear voice, he proclaimed Christ as God and Creator of the world. He was tortured and later thrown naked into an arena with many wild beasts. He prayed, "Lord, if it is your will that I die now, may it be done according to Your will." Some beasts licked his wounds, some returned to their dens, and others rolled on the ground. St. Alexander thanked God and gave up his spirit.

COMMEMORATIONS: Spyridon the Wonderworker, Bishop of Trimythus; Alexander, Archbishop of Jerusalem; John, Metropolitan of Zichne; Therapon, abbot of Monza Monastery; John of Zedazeni Monastery, Georgia; Anthus of Palestine and Amonathas of Pelusium; Abra of Poitiers; Synetus of Rome; Finian of Clonard and Skellig Michael, teacher of Ireland; Corentin, Bishop of Quimper; Colman of Glendalough; Mardarije Uskokovic of Libertyville (New Calendar); Synaxis of the First Martyrs of the American land: Juvenal the Protomartyr, Peter the Aleut, Seraphim of Uglich; John Kochurov of Chicago, Alexander Khotovitsky of New York.

DECEMBER 13

2 Timothy 4:9-22
Mark 8:30-34

*D*o not let evil thoughts rule over you, drive them out immediately with the prayer. Oh, this prayer—what miracles it performs! Cry out the prayer, and your guardian angel will send you spiritual fragrance! The angels greatly rejoice when a person prays with the prayer of our sweetest Jesus. May Jesus be the delight of your soul.

† *Elder Ephraim of Arizona*

ST. DOSITHEUS, METROPOLITAN OF MOLDAVIA. Dositheus was born in early seventeenth-century Suceava, today's Romania. He went to the best schools of his time and to the monastery school of the Orthodox Brotherhood in Poland. He knew many languages, including Greek, Latin, Polish, Ukrainian, and Church Slavonic. From his youth, he was familiar with prayer and obedience, and he was talented in the translation of the Scriptures and the writings of the Church Fathers. He was tonsured a monk, and because of his virtues and prestige as a scholar, he was named bishop of Husi and then Metropolitan of Moldova. Yet, he remained gentle and humble with everyone. He understood the Psalms very deeply and put them into verse in Romanian, and he revised the Romanian translation of the Old Testament. Some time later, the Poles robbed Moldova and took Dositheus hostage. Still, he continued translating from Greek the works of St. John Chrysostom, St. Ephraim the Syrian, and others. When the Polish authorities pressured Dositheus, he refused Uniatism and remained an Orthodox bishop.

COMMEMORATIONS: Lucia (Lucy) of Syracuse; Eustratius, Auxentius, Eugene, Mardarius, and Orestes, at Sebaste; Arsenios of Mt. Latros; Abba Ares, monk; Auberius, bishop; Columba on Lough Derg (Ireland); Odilia of Alsace (Gaul); Innocent of Kherson; Mardarius of the Kiev Caves; Gabriel, Patriarch of Serbia; Arcadius of Vyazma and Novy Torg; Dositheus, Metropolitan of Moldavia; Neophytos, Ignatios, Prokopios, and Neilos, founders of Machairas Monastery; Repose of St. Herman, Wonderworker of Alaska; Commemoration of the miracle by the Holy Five Martyrs.

THURSDAY   **Strict Fast**

DECEMBER 14

Titus 1:5-14
Mark 9:10-15

$\mathcal{B}$odily fasting alone is not enough to bring about perfect self-restraint and true purity; it must be accompanied by contrition of heart, intense prayer to God, frequent meditation on the Scripture, toil and manual labor. These are able to check the restless impulses of the soul and to recall it from its shameful fantasies. Humility of soul helps more than everything else, however, and without it no one can overcome unchastity or any other sin.

St. John Cassian

ST. NICAISE, BISHOP OF RHEIMS. Several sources credit Nicaise with prophesying the invasion of France by the Vandals, a German people inhabiting what is now southern France. He told the people to prepare themselves and said he was ready to give himself up for his people. When the Vandals were at the city's gates, Nicaise attempted to slow them down so more of his people could escape. He was killed along with his deacon, lector, and his sister. It was said that after these killings, the Vandals were frightened away from the area, even leaving behind the treasure they had stolen. Accounts of the saint's martyrdom credit him with being among the cephalophores (head carriers), like St. Denis of Paris. St. Nicaise was reciting Psalm 119:5 when he was decapitated and continued repeating it even after his head had fallen to the ground.

COMMEMORATIONS: Philemon, Apollonius, Arianus, Theoctychus, and 4 guards converted by St. Arianus, martyred at Alexandria; Thyrsos, Leukios, Kallinikos, with others, in Bithynia; Folciunus, Bishop of Tervas; Hilarion, Metropolitan of Suzdal and Yuriev; Nicaise of Rheims; Venantius Fortunatus, Bishop of Poitiers; Hygbald, abbot in Lincolnshire; Bassian Pyatnitsky, Archbishop of Tambov; Commemoration of the Great Earthquake of Constantinople in 557.

DECEMBER 15

He who refuses to give into his passions does the same as he who refuses to bow down and worship idols.

St. Theophan the Recluse

VENERABLE PAUL THE NEW ON MOUNT LATROS. Paul lived at the Karia Monastery on Mount Latros and strove to emulate his holy abbot, Peter. At night, he would tie two large stones with a rope and carry them on his back throughout the monastery to rid himself of the passions. He would sleep standing against a tree or a rock, and he never said an idle or obscene word. During prayer, he was seen surrounded in flames with arms raised that appeared as candles. Later, Paul searched for a cave to live as a hermit, but when he found one to his liking, it was bereft of food and water. A holy elder named Matthew lived nearby, and he began to supply Paul with provisions. When Matthew prayed over the bread, it would multiply. The devil would harass Paul with fantasies, an earthquake, and would even roll boulders downhill towards him. He later went to live in a small cave atop a very high rock formation and again waited on the providence of God to sustain him, sometimes almost starving to death. But there were always those who would provide for his needs. In the guise of a giant snake, the devil once moved about Paul's cave for three years, yet he remained unharmed. He prayed for water, and excellent water came forth that never diminished. So many came to live near him that he reestablished three monasteries. He blessed a small amount of wine that he kept for guests, and it continued to multiply. For a time, he went to the island of Samos, and monasteries flourished under his guidance. He could foresee the future, and it would come to pass. St. Paul died peacefully in 956.

COMMEMORATIONS: Susanna the Deaconess of Palestine; Eleutherios of Illyricum, and Anthia, Corivus the Eparch, and 2 executioners; Paul the New; Eleutherius of Byzantium; Pardus of Palestine; Stephen the Confessor; Joseph of Petrograd; Bacchus the New; Hilarion of Vereya.

SATURDAY

DECEMBER 16

Abstain from meat and dairy products, and fish.

Ephesians 1:16-23
Luke 14:1-11

*G*od allows you to fall into temptation so that you may persistently knock on the door of His mercy and so that, from fear of afflictions, the memory of God may be implanted in your mind, and you may approach Him through prayers, in which case your heart will be sanctified by ceaseless recollection of the name of God. When you supplicate Him with faith, He will hear you, and you will learn that it is God who rescued you. Then you will understand that your Creator strengthens you and guards you.

St. Isaac the Syrian

ST. MEMNON, ARCHBISHOP OF EPHESUS. Memnon and St. Cyril of Alexandria were allies and opponents of the heresy of Nestorius at the fifth-century Ecumenical Synod of Ephesus. There were 100 Asiatic bishops, of whom Memnon was one, and forty Syrian bishops led by John of Antioch. Memnon organized a torchlight procession through the streets of Ephesus in honor of the Most Holy Mother of God. In Ephesus, he closed down heretical churches that followed Nestorius. The second session of this council met in a different location, which caused John of Antioch and the forty Syrian bishops to be two days late. When they arrived, they found that Bishop Cyril had already finished the proceedings to condemn Nestorius, and they disapproved. They arranged another council in which they deposed Bishops Cyril and Memnon, and they were arrested. However, after Cyril and John of Antioch reconciled, St. Memnon was reinstated to his see.

COMMEMORATIONS: Prophet Haggai (Aggaeus); Modestos, Archbishop of Jerusalem; Theophano, wife of Byzantine Emperor Leo the Wise; Memnon, Archbishop of Ephesus; Sophia (Solomonia), nun, wife of Grand Duke Basil III of Moscow; Nicholas Chrysovergis, Patriarch of Constantinople; Martyrs Promus and Hilarion; Marinos of Rome; Vladimir Alexeyev of Okhansk; Parasceva Rodimtseva, abbess of Toplovsky Convent (Simferopol); Arcadius Ostalsky, Bishop of Bezhetsk.

December 17

Eleventh Sunday of Luke
Sunday of the Holy Forefathers
Abstain from meat and
dairy products, and fish.

Colossians 3:4-11
Luke 14:16-24

*F*asting reveals all the weaknesses of our soul, all its soft spots, flaws, sins and passions. Like muddy, stagnant water shows its creatures and debris before being purified.

St. John of Kronstadt

ST. STURMIUS, FOUNDER OF FULDA MONASTERY. Sturmius was from a German Christian family in modern-day Austria, and he was a disciple of St. Boniface. He was trained at the monastery of St. Wigbert and spent several years as a missionary priest. Sturmius lived nine years as a hermit and became known for his miraculous healings and insightful teaching of the Gospel. He learned the best from the monasteries in Italy, especially St. Benedict's monastery in Monte Cassino, and from a two-year stay at a monastery in France. Finally, he founded Fulda Monastery, and under his wise direction and example, it became firmly established and well known throughout the land of the Franks. The monastery attracted many monks. St. Boniface would visit there for retreats, and he also chose to be buried there. St. Sturmius died peacefully in old age, and his relics now lie near those of St. Boniface.

COMMEMORATIONS: Holy Prophet Daniel and Three Holy Youths: Ananias, Azarias, and Misael; Dionysius the New of Zakynthos; Daniel (Stephen) the Confessor of Spain; Patermuthius, Coprius, and Alexander the Soldier, of Egypt; Athanasius, Nicholas, and Anthony, founders of Vatopedi Monastery; Nicetas of Nyssa; Iacchus of Triglia; Paisius of Turnovo, Cacak, and Avakum the Deacon, at Belgrade; Misael of Abalak Monastery (Irkutsk); Sturmius, abbot and founder of Fulda Monastery (Germany); Sergius Florinsky of Rakvere, Estonia; Begga of Landen; (Second Sunday before Christmas: Adam, Eve, Abel, Seth, Enoch, Noah, Abraham, Isaac, Sarah, Rebecca, Jacob, Joseph, Job, Moses, Samuel, Joshua, Barak, Gideon, Judith, Esther, David, Manasseh, Elijah, Elisha, and others).

DECEMBER 18

Hebrews 3:5-11, 17-19
Mark 9:42-10:1

*I*f God sees us accepting our present distress with gratitude, He'll either remove the causes or He'll reward us with the great crowns of patience.

St. Basil the Great

MARTYR ZOE AT ROME. Zoe was the wife of the Roman prison guard Nicostratus, and for six years, she was unable to speak. She threw herself at the feet of St. Sebastian and implored him with gestures to heal her. He made the Sign of the Cross over her, and Zoe began to speak and glorify Christ. She said that she had seen an angel that recorded everything in a book that the saint had said, and all those who saw this miracle believed. When Zoe and Nicostratus received Baptism, Sebastian told him to gather all the prisoners who wanted to be baptized. Nicostratus sent his clerk Claudius to bring the prisoners, and he also brought his sons who were sick. That evening, the priest Polycarp baptized all of them and many others, totaling sixty-four people. Some of the newly-baptized Christians left Rome, while others would gather for divine services. The Romans arrested Zoe while she was in prayer at the grave of St. Peter the Apostle, and she bravely confessed her faith in Christ. They suspended her by the hair over a foul-smelling dung fire, and she gave up her spirit. St. Zoe later appeared to St. Sebastian to tell him about her death.

COMMEMORATIONS: Sebastian at Rome; Zoe at Rome; Modestus I of Jerusalem; Zacchaeus the Deacon and Alphaeus the Reader; Florus of Amisus; Daniel the Hesychast; Phocas and Hermylus; Michael the Confessor; Living-Martyr Eubotios; Gatianus of Tours; Symeon of Verkhoturye; Sophia the Wonderworker; Synaxis of the family of St. Gregory Palamas; Consecration of the Church of the Mother of God in Chalkoprateia.

DECEMBER 19

*I*f you allow God to become the master in your house, the house becomes Paradise.

† *Metropolitan Anthony of Sourozh*

ST. SERAPHIM ROMANTSOV OF GLINSK. Seraphim was born in 1885 to a peasant family in the Kursk province of Russia. After graduation from the parish school, his parents died, and he entered the Glinsk Monastery. He was a soldier in the First World War, where he was wounded and hospitalized. There was a hypnotist in the hospital who could hypnotize almost all the other patients but Seraphim because he always recited the Jesus Prayer, "Lord Jesus Christ, have mercy on me." After that time, Seraphim took monastic vows at Glinsk and was ordained hierodeacon. When Glinsk Monastery closed, he relocated to Sukhumi. However, Seraphim was arrested in 1931 and was sent to the White Sea Canal construction. Afterward, he was hidden by a pious family for twelve years and was a confessor at the Cathedral. At last, he returned to Glinsk after it reopened and was appointed their spiritual father, wanting most to bring his spiritual children to humility. Seraphim wrote, "Everything that you need for salvation is a true humility, inner conviction that you are the worst of sinners; this is the greatest gift of God." He also said that a proud mind could not unite with the name of Jesus Christ. When Seraphim was about to die, he said, "What I have prayed all my life and what I was searching for, it is opened now in my heart, my soul is filled with grace, so that I cannot even hold it." St. Seraphim died peacefully.

COMMEMORATIONS: Boniface at Tarsus, and Aglais of Rome; Boniface the Merciful of Ferentino; Gregory (Gregentius) of Omirits; Anastasius I, Pope of Rome; Elias, Ares, and Probus, in Cilicia; Polyeuctus at Caesarea and Timothy the Deacon; Martyr Tryphon; George the Scribe and Sava of Khakhuli Monastery; Amphilochius of Pochaev; Eutyches and Thessalonica, with 200 men and 70 women; Capito of Kherson; Elias of Murom; Martyr Tryphon; Seraphim Romantsov of Glinsk Monastery.

WEDNESDAY

DECEMBER 20

St. Ignatius the God-Bearer
Abstain from meat and
dairy products, and fish.
Hebrews 10:32-38; Mark 9:33-41

*W*ith the sign of the living cross, seal all your doings, my son. Go not forth from the door of your house till you have signed the cross. Whether in eating or in drinking, whether in sleeping or in waking, whether in your house or on the road, or again in the season of leisure, neglect not this sign; for there is no guardian like it. It shall be unto you as a wall, in the forefront of all your doings. And teach this to your children, that heedfully they be conformed to it.

St. Ephraim the Syrian

VENERABLE IGNATIUS, ARCHIMANDRITE OF THE KIEV CAVES LAVRA. An inscription on the tombstone of St. Ignatius says that from his holy life, he gained the gift of miracles from God and healed many sick people with his prayers. In the general service to the Kiev Caves Saints, it says of him, "Ignatius, the monastic shepherd and healer of the sick, in our infirmities you help us by your reverence, therefore let us offer song of praise unto your memory." St. Ignatius was buried in the Far (Theodosiev) Caves. A recent biochemical examination of his relics showed that he died at approximately sixty years of age.

COMMEMORATIONS: Ignatius the God-bearer, Bishop of Antioch; Philogonios, Patriarch of Antioch; Daniel II, Archbishop of Serbia; Ignatius, archimandrite of the Kiev Caves; John of the isle of Thasos, at Constantinople; Anthony, Archbishop of Voronezh; Nikolai Chernishev, archpriest, and his daughter Barbara; Repose of St. John of Kronstadt; *Rescuer of the Drowning* Icon of the Mother of God.

DECEMBER 21

Hebrews 7:1-6
Mark 10:17-27

*N*ever lie, but always tell the truth. For all falsehood and deceit is the most harmful of all vices, and the customary work only for the devil.

St. Theophan the Recluse

MARTYR THEMISTOCLES OF MYRA. Themistocles was a shepherd from third-century Myra in Asia Minor during the persecutions of Emperor Decius. The governor Asclepius intensely sought a certain Christian named Dioscorides, who was hiding in the home of Themistocles. Soldiers happened upon Themistocles watching over his sheep, and they asked if he had seen Dioscorides. He said that he had not and asked the soldiers to let the man live since he was also a Christian and that he would replace him. When the soldiers demanded to know the fugitive's whereabouts, they said they would take him instead. They arrested Themistocles and brought him before the governor, and he openly confessed Christ. He was beaten until his organs were exposed. As they were about to tie him to a wooden post for more torments, Themistocles told the governor that it was through the wooden Cross that Christians are saved and that through Jesus Christ, God had reconciled all things. Themistocles rejoiced that he was suffering like Christ on the Cross. He was tortured on the post and then dragged over iron spikes until he died. St. Themistocles was given a Christian burial. His shepherd's staff was planted near his grave, and it took root and grew into an almond tree, and the almonds healed the faithful who traveled there.

COMMEMORATIONS: Juliana of Nicomedia, and with her 500 men and 130 women; Themistocles of Myra in Lycia; Macarius the Faster, abbot of the Khakhuli Monastery; Juliana, Princess of Vyazma; Procopius of Vyatka, Fool-for-Christ; Philaret (Theodosius), Metropolitan of Kiev; Nicetas Pribytkov, Bishop of Belev; Beornwald (Bernwald) of Bampton; Repose of St. Peter, Metropolitan of Kiev; Finding of the relics of New Monk-Martyr St. Ephraim of Nea Makri.

DECEMBER 22

Hebrews 7:18-25
Mark 10:24-32

If you are constantly angry and complaining, it is indicative of a proud soul. Humble yourself, reproach yourself, and the Lord is powerful to give you comfort and a helping hand.

St. Anatoly of Optina

ST. BORIS TALANTOV OF KOSTROMA. Boris said that he and his close relatives suffered greatly from the lawlessness and arbitrary rules of the state security agencies during the Stalin reign. His father, a priest, was condemned in 1937 by a troika, who sentenced their victims without hearing or appeal. Boris' twenty-two-year-old brother was also arrested without cause, and he died in a concentration camp. Boris wrote many letters to newspapers and magazines, refuting religious propaganda and exposing the mass destruction of monuments and churches, and this was in 1963. He wrote a letter to Patriarch Alexy, exposing the actions of the local Bishop John and asking for his removal because he was attempting to set church life in disarray. He pointed out that local authorities, between 1960 and 1964, forcibly closed 40 churches in the Kirov area. They buried the icons, plundered the church's valuables, and completely destroyed some churches. The BBC radio released the contents of this letter, and the KGB asked Boris to repudiate it, which he refused. In London, Metropolitan Nikodim declared the letter not worthy of credibility, which greatly distressed Boris. Again, he pushed back and sent a letter to Patriarch Alexy refuting the metropolitan. In 1969, St. Boris was arrested for having written anti-Soviet letters and similar texts. He died in a prison hospital in 1971, at the age of 68.

COMMEMORATIONS: Anastasia of Rome, the Deliverer from Bonds, and her teacher Chrysogonus, and with them: Theodota, Evodos, Eutychianus, Zoilos, and others, who suffered under Diocletian; Flavian, former Prefect of Rome; Boris Talantov of Kostroma; Amaswinthus of Malaga in Spain.

DECEMBER 23

**Saturday before the Nativity
Abstain from meat and
dairy products, and fish.**

Galatians 3:8-12
Luke 13:19-29

*G*od does not force, prevail over, overwhelm [or] violate human free will. God respects it absolutely, since He Himself has granted this exceptional gift of free will to man. The acceptance of the divine will by man is indicative of his cooperation and participation. The service offered by the All-Holy Virgin Mary is indeed sublime and of the highest quality, for she is offering herself in the service of God for the salvation of the world. She has thus become a co-worker in the saving work of God for the world.

† *Elder Moses the Athonite*

ST. EGBERT OF RATHMELSIGI. At first, Egbert of Northumbria went to Ireland on pilgrimage, but he vowed never to return home after an illness there. He became abbot of the Monastery of Rathmelsigi, and under his leadership, it became a training college for many missionaries in the seventh and eighth centuries. Egbert decided to take the Gospel to the Frisians, who were the Germanic peoples. He planned to "rescue the Germans from the clutches of Satan" and liberate them from their pagan customs. Through his efforts, and not the popes or other church leaders, St. Egbert initiated the proclamation of the gospel in Frisia.

COMMEMORATIONS: Paul, Bishop of Neo-Caesarea; Theoctistus, Archbishop of Novgorod; Niphon, Bishop of Constantia on Cyprus; Holy 10 Martyrs of Crete: Theodulus, Saturninus, Euporus, Gelasius, Eunician, Zoticus, Pompeius, Agathopus, Basilides, and Evaristus; Nahum of Ochrid, Enlightener of the Bulgarians; David of Echmiadzin in Armenia; Egbert of Rathmelsigi; Martyr Schinon; Paul Kratirov, Bishop of Starobelsk; Macarius Mironov of Zavidovskaya Gorka (Tver); John Smirnov of Bolshoye Mikhailovskoye (Tver); Commemoration of the Consecration of the Church of Holy Wisdom in Constantinople.

DECEMBER 24

**Sunday before the Nativity
Genealogy Sunday
Abstain from meat and
dairy products, and fish.**
Hebrews 11:9-10, 32-40
Matthew 1:1-25

*T*his night gave peace to the whole world, and so, let no one threaten. This is the night of the Most Meek One; let no one be cruel!

St. Ephraim the Syrian

NEW HIEROMARTYR SERGIUS MECHEV OF MOSCOW. Thousands mourned the death of Sergius' father, Alexey Mechev, the popular and clairvoyant lay-elder of Moscow. Sergius received a secular education, while his religious training was at home and in church. He entered the medical faculty at Moscow University and worked as a nurse at the front when the war came. He met his future wife there, and they married in 1918. Sergius remained active in the Church, in a student theological circle, and avidly studied the early Christian writers' lives, writings, and doctrines. He would often be in contact with Patriarch Tikhon, who urged him to become a priest. He was ordained to the priesthood in 1919. Ten years later, Sergius and many other clergymen were arrested because they disagreed with the Church being brought under government control. Sergius was charged with heading a counter-revolutionary underground church and was sentenced to three years in exile. This was followed by a second arrest with a five-year sentence. Afterward, he spent some years in hiding and wandering before being arrested again. He was executed for his uncompromising stand in ecclesial matters. Sergius said that his task as a priest was to create a parish family guided towards the same goal of sanctity and deification as the monastics.

COMMEMORATIONS: Eugenia of Rome, and Philip, Protus, Hyacinth, Basilla, and Claudia; Aphrodisios and Antiochus; Betimius of Scetis; Achmed the Calligrapher; Nicholas of Bulgaria; Martyr Achaikos; Innocent of Voronezh; Sergius of Moscow; Agapios of Dimitsana; (Sunday before Christmas: Holy Forefathers of Christ according to the flesh, including: Adam, Abel, first Martyr in the history of mankind, Abraham, Isaac and Jacob, Moses, Joshua, David the King, and others).

MONDAY

The Nativity of Jesus Christ
Fast-free period until January 5

Galatians 4:4-7; Matthew 2:1-12

DECEMBER 25

*K*neel at the holy feet of our Jesus and shed tears of love, follow Him with loyal dedication till death, and if the waves rise up to heaven and descend to the abyss, so be it. Our Christ, the true God, with a dreadful, divine nod will calm all the waves, as long as we have faith. Believe truly and steadfastly in Him Who said, "*I am with you always, even to the end of the age*" (Mt. 28:20). Jesus is with us; do not lose heart. He will fight for us, through the intercessions of the invincible Theotokos, and grant us the victory.

† *Elder Ephraim of Arizona*

COMMEMORATION OF THE SHEPHERDS IN BETHLEHEM WHO WERE WATCHING THEIR FLOCKS AND CAME TO SEE THE LORD. The angel said to the shepherds, "*And this shall be a sign to you: Ye will find the newborn Babe wrapped in swaddling clothes lying in the manger*" (Lk. 2:12). And they said, "*Let us now pass through as far as Bethlehem and see this thing which is spoken of as having coming to pass, which the Lord made known to us*" (Lk. 2:15). Shepherds were chosen to hear the first announcement of the Nativity, as they are symbols of Christ the Good Shepherd (Jn. 10:11). The shepherds were without guile and had simple faith. The message of the first angel is confirmed by the multitude, fulfilling the Law in which "*by the mouth of two or three witnesses the matter shall be established*" (Dt. 19:15). The shepherds are also images of the bishops and presbyters of the Church, who proclaim Christ to the world (Lk. 2:17-20). St. Ambrose writes that the news from the shepherds strengthened Mary's own faith, and he asks, "If Mary herself learns from the shepherds, why do so many refuse to learn from the presbyters of the Church?"

COMMEMORATIONS: The Adoration of the Magi: Melchior, Caspar, and Balthazar; Commemoration of the shepherds in Bethlehem who were watching their flocks; Massacre of St. Jonah, with 50 monks and 65 laymen, at St. Tryphon of Pechenga Monastery.

Synaxis of the Holy Mother of God
Fast-free

DECEMBER 26

Hebrews 2:11-18
Matthew 2:13-23

*A*s soon as we cry out to her, she rushes to our help. You don't even finish saying, 'All-holy Theotokos, help me' and at once, like lightning, she shines through the nous and fills the heart with illumination.

St. Joseph the Hesychast

MERCIFUL ICON OF THE MOTHER OF GOD. According to tradition, the Merciful Icon was written by the Apostle Luke the Evangelist. It received the name "Kykkiotisa" from Mount Kykkos, on the island of Cyprus, and was located in the Monastery of the Mother of God the Merciful. The icon has a long history. First, it was situated in one of the earliest Christian communities in Egypt. Then in the eleventh and twelfth centuries, it remained in Constantinople during the reign of Alexios Komnenos. During this time, it was revealed to the hermit Isaiah, through a miraculous sign, that the icon would go to Cyprus by his efforts. Isaiah worked hard to accomplish this, and when the icon arrived in Cyprus, it performed many miracles. To the present day, those afflicted by every sort of sickness throng to the holy icon and receive healing through faith. Even those of other religions go to it in misfortune and sickness. A half shroud covers the icon from the upper left corner to the lower right corner so that the faces of the Mother of God and the Divine Infant are not visible.

COMMEMORATIONS: Synaxis of the Most Holy Theotokos; Commemoration of the flight into Egypt; Euthymius of Sardis; Zeno of Maiuma in Palestine; Nicodemus of Tismana, Romania; Andrew of Ufa and Valentina of Russia; Archelaus of Haran in northern Mesopotamia; Constantine of Synnada; Constantius the Russian of Constantinople; Evarestus of the Studion Monastery; Tathai of Llantathan; Jarlath, first bishop of Tuam (Ireland); Leonid of Mariisk, Isaac II of Optina Monastery, Basil, hieromonk, and Augusta, schema nun; *Bethlehem, The Blessed Womb, Merciful, The Three Joys,* and *Vilensk-Ostrobramsk* Icons of the Mother of God.

St. Stephen the First Martyr
Fast-free
Acts 6:8-7:5, 47-60
Matthew 21:33-42

*B*eloved Christians! Nothing is more pleasant, lovelier, and sweeter to us sinners than the Gospel. More welcome than bread to the hungry, drink to the thirsty, freedom to captives and those in prison, is the Gospel to sinners who understand their misfortune.

St. Tikhon of Zadonsk

ST. BONIFACE, FOUNDER OF ST. PANTELEIMON MONASTERY IN KIEV. Boniface was from the late eighteenth-century Cherson province in Ukraine. He was taken into military service and participated in the battles of 1812 and those of later years. When he left the military, he and his wife ran their rural property, but he soon gave half the property to his wife, the other half to the Church and the poor, and went to Kiev, hoping to join a monastery. He was tonsured a monk at the age of 69. He was then ordained a hierodeacon. At 76, he was appointed to build the Feofania Skete, now the St. Panteleimon Monastery, which is attached to the Monastery of St. Michael. He gathered significant funds for the renewal of the church in his native land and built a new church and guesthouse at the Monastery of St. Michael. He also restored the church and built other structures at his Skete. At the age of 83, Boniface was raised to the rank of abbot. He died peacefully three years later. St. Boniface was known for his ascetic life and spiritual counsel.

COMMEMORATIONS: Apostle and Archdeacon Stephen the Protomartyr; Theodore Graptus "the Branded" of Palestine, brother of St. Theophanes the Confessor; Maximus of Alexandria; Theodore, Patriarch of Constantinople; Barlaam of Tobolsk and All Siberia; Maurice and Photinos, with 70 soldiers, of Apamea; Luke of Tryglia; Fabiola of Rome; Boniface, founder of Panteleimon Monastery (Kiev); Tikhon, Archbishop of Voronezh, and with him 160 martyred priests; Fabiola of Rome; Uncovering of the relics of St. Therapont of Belozersk and Mozhaisk.

THURSDAY

DECEMBER 28

20,000 Martyrs of Nicomedia
Fast-free
Hebrews 10:35-11:7
Luke 14:25-35

*G*ood and blessed is that simplicity which some have by nature, but better is that which has been goaded out of wickedness by hard work. The former is protected from much complexity and the passions, while the latter is the gateway to the greatest humility and meekness. There is not much reward for the one and no end of reward for the other. If you wish to draw the Lord to you, approach Him as disciples to a master, in all simplicity, openly, honestly, without duplicity, without idle curiosity. He is simple and uncompounded. And He wants the souls that come *to Him to be simple and pure. Indeed, you will never see simplicity separated from humility.*

St. John Climacus

ST. SECUNDUS THE MARTYR. It is believed that Secundus lived in the second century and was a young man of noble lineage, probably a soldier. He was not a Christian but would visit the jails in the province of Asti, Italy. He was converted to Christianity by Calocerus, who had been imprisoned by Sapricius, the city's prefect who persecuted Christians. Secundus and Sapricius were friends. They traveled together to the city of Tortona in Alessandria, where Secundus met the city's first bishop, Marcian, who was imprisoned there and later martyred under Emperor Hadrian. When Sapricius attempted to persuade Secundus to abandon his newfound faith, he refused and was tortured and beheaded.

COMMEMORATIONS: 20,000 Martyrs of Nicomedia, including: Glycerius, Zeno, Theophilus, Dorotheus, Mardonius, Migdonius, Index, Gorgonius, Peter, Euthymius, and the virgins Agape, Domna, Theophila, and others; Apostle Nicanor the Deacon, of the Seventy; Simon the Myrrhgusher, founder of Simonopetra Monastery, Mt. Athos; Babylas of Tarsus; Ignatius, founder of Lomsk and Yaroslavl; Cornelius of Krypetsk Monastery (Pskov); Nikodim Kononov, Bishop of Belgorod, and Arcadius Reshetnikov, deacon; Martyr Secundus; Wunibald of Heidenheim (Germany); Nephon the New Cenobiarch; Repose of St. Hilarion Troitsky, Archbishop of Verey.

If you struggle with zeal, if you are not slothful and fainthearted, you will know victory. The first ascetic (the Lord) is observing you. Laurel wreaths, glory, honor and blessings are waiting for you. The choir of the Saints is waiting to receive you forever in the kingdom of heaven.

St. Efstratios of Glinsk

THE HOLY 14,000 CHILDREN SLAIN BY HEROD AT BETHLE-HEM. After the Magi venerated the Infant Jesus, they were warned by an angel of God to return home another way so as not to reveal His whereabouts. The holy family then left Jerusalem after Jesus' Presentation in the Temple, forty days after His birth. Herod's high priest, Hyrcanus, and the Sanhedrin plotted with Herod how to find and kill the Holy Child. They had also foretold the birth of a new Jewish king. Herod suspected that John the Baptist might be the Messiah since the angel had appeared in the Temple to his father, Zacharias. Herod gave orders to kill John, and all the children in Bethlehem and the surrounding area, two years of age and under, which happened about one year after the birth of Jesus. These innocent children were beheaded, dashed against the rocks, or drowned. John the Baptist was never found. Herod grew angrier and killed the elders, the high priest, his wife and sons, and even the Jews in prison. Finally, Herod's body began to rot with an unbearable stench, and he died.

COMMEMORATIONS: 14,000 Infants (Holy Innocents) slain by Herod at Bethlehem; Mark the Grave-digger of the Kiev Caves; Thaddeus of the Studion; Athenodoros the Leper; George of Nicomedia; Benjamin of Nitria; Marcellus of the Monastery of the Unsleeping Ones; Lawrence of Chernigov; Basiliscus of Turinsk (Siberia); Theophilus and John of the Kiev Caves; Trophimus, first Bishop of Arles; Theophilus of Luga; Evroult of Ouche; Job Knyaginitsky of Manyava; Commemoration of all Orthodox Christians who have died from hunger, thirst, the sword, and freezing; Consecration of the Church of the Holy Forty Martyrs near the Bronze Tetrapylon.

DECEMBER 30

'*The* cup of blessing which we bless, is it not communion of the Blood of Christ?' Very trustworthily and awesomely does he say it. For what he is saying is this: 'What is in the cup is that which flowed from His side, and we partake of it.' He called it a cup of blessing because when we hold it in our hands that is how we praise Him in song, wondering and astonished at His indescribable Gift, blessing Him because of His having poured out this very Gift so that we might not remain in error, and not only for His having poured It out, but also for His sharing It with all of us.

St. John Chrysostom

VENERABLE MARTYR ANYSIA OF THESSALONICA. Anysia was a Christian maiden in late-third-century Thessalonica. When her wealthy parents died, she sold her inheritance and distributed it to the poor. She fasted and prayed with tears in solitude and in church. She regretted the length of life as this kept her from heaven. She slept little, remembering that the demons did not sleep at all. On her way to church, as was her daily custom, a Greek pagan soldier arrested her. Emperor Maximian had decreed that it was permissible for anyone to kill a Christian for any reason. The soldier tried to force her to sacrifice to idols, but she spat in his face. Immediately, he killed her with his sword. Christians buried St. Anysia, and a chapel was built at her grave site.

COMMEMORATIONS: Anysia of Thessalonica; Theodora, nun of Caesarea in Cappadocia; Philoterus of Nicomedia, and with him, 6 soldiers and 1 count; Magistrianus, Paulinus, Umbrius, Verus, Severus, Callistratus, Florentius, Arianus, Anthimus, Ubricius, Isidore, Euculus, Sampson, Studius, and Thespesius, under Julian the Apostate; Apostle Timon the Deacon, of the Seventy; Macarius, Metropolitan of Moscow; Tryphon, Bishop of Rostov; Leo the Archimandrite; Gideon of Karakallou Monastery, Mt. Athos; Anysios, Bishop of Thessalonica; Egwin, Bishop of Worcester; Uncovering of the relics of St. Daniel of Pereyaslavl.

Sunday before Holy Theophany
Fast-free
2 Timothy 4:5-8
Mark 1:1-8

DECEMBER 31

*G*od is everywhere. There is no place God is not…You cry out to Him, 'Where art Thou, my God?' And He answers, "I am present, my child! I am always beside you.' Both inside and outside, above and below, wherever you turn, everything shouts, 'God!' In Him we live and move. We breathe God, we eat God, we clothe ourselves with God. Everything praises and blesses God. All of creation shouts His praise. Everything animate and inanimate speaks wondrously and glorifies the Creator. Let every breath praise the Lord!

St. Joseph the Hesychast

ST. SABIANA, ABBESS OF THE SAMTSKHE MONASTERY. The nuns of Georgian monasteries have been outstanding with the special duties of ceaseless prayer, fasting, needlework, and the raising of orphans. Nuns have been regarded as vessels of sanctity and wisdom. Even royalty would kneel before them. Many Georgian noblemen would send their children to nuns to be raised in the Christian faith. The parents of St. George of the Holy Mountain sent their daughter Thecla to the pious and holy Sabiana, who was the abbess of the Samtskhe Monastery in southern Georgia. Sabiana raised Thecla as though she were her own daughter. Her seven-year-old brother George was also sent there, and Sabiana spent three years educating and instructing him.

COMMEMORATIONS: Theophylact, Archbishop of Ochrid; Gelasius, monk of Palestine; Dositheus, Metropolitan of Zagreb; 10 Virgins of Nicomedia; Zoticus the Priest of Constantinople, feeder of orphans; Melania the Younger of Rome; Peter Mogila, Metropolitan of Kiev; Gaius, monk; Sabiana, abbess of Samtskhe Convent; Anysius, Bishop of Thessalonica; Cyriacus of Bisericani Monastery (Romania); Cyriacus of Tazlau Monastery (Romania); Gaius, monk; Martyr Olympiodora; Martyrs Busiris, Gaudentius, and Nemi; George (Macheromenos) the Wonderworker; (Sunday after Christmas: Joseph the Betrothed, James the Brother of the Lord, and David the Prophet).

2024

Daily Lives, Miracles, and Wisdom of the Saints & Fasting Calendar

Place your order at
www.LivesoftheSaintsCalendar.com

Orthodox Calendar Company
OrthodoxCalendarCompany@gmail.com
Tel. 412-736-7840